Valley of the
Shadow

Valley of the Shadow

An Account of American POWs of the Japanese

By Colonel Nicoll F. Galbraith, GSC, U.S. Army

The views expressed in this work are solely those of the author and do not necessarily reflect the views of the publisher, and the publisher hereby disclaims any responsibility for them.

Any people depicted in stock imagery provided by Getty Images are models, and such images are being used for illustrative purposes only.
Certain stock imagery © Getty Images.

Print information available on the last page.

Rev. date: 07/20/2018

To order additional copies of this book, contact:
Xlibris
1-888-795-4274
www.Xlibris.com
Orders@Xlibris.com
773617

Psalm 23 King James Version

The Lord is my shepherd; I shall not want.
He maketh me to lie down in green pastures: he leadeth me beside
the still waters.
He restoreth my soul: he leadeth me in the paths of righteousness
for his name's sake.
Yea, though I walk through the valley of the shadow of death,
I will fear no evil: for thou art with me; thy rod and thy staff
they comfort me.
Thou preparest a table before me in the presence of mine enemies:
thou anointest my head with oil; my cup runneth over.
Surely goodness and mercy shall follow me all the days of my life:
and I will dwell in the house of the Lord forever.

King James Version (KJV)

Dedicated to Col. Nicoll F. Galbraith, Jr.,
Medical Corps, U.S. Army Reserve.
Elder son of "Nick" Galbraith and family
champion of our father's experience.

(NFG, Jr. with pastor)

Dedicated May 6th 1999.
Major Contributors:
ASSOCIATION OF GRADUATES OF THE
UNITED STATES MILITARY ACADEMY.
BATTLING BASTARDS OF BATAAN
Major Richard Gordon Adjutant
PLATOON SERGEANT ANDY N. CAMPBELL USMC
4th Marines, Corregidor
The Family of
COLONEL NICOLL F. GALBRAITH G.S.C. U.S.A.
The Family of
MAJOR GENERAL EDWARD P. KING, JR.
and Friends
PHILIPPINE SCOUTS HERITAGE SOCIETY
National
GOLDEN GATE BAY AREA CHAPTER
Philipine Scouts Heritage Society
CORPORAL EVERETT D. REAMER 80th C.A.U.S.A.
ROBERT F. REYNOLDS
Valor Tours Ltd.
The Family of
PETER S. WAINWRIGHT
LIEUTENANT COLONEL CHARLES H. WYATT
MAJOR VALDEMOR O. ZIALCITA M.C.P.A.
The Family of
MAJOR DAMON J. GAUSE U.S.A.A.C.
COLONEL SAMUEL C. GRASHIO U.S.A.F. (ret)
21st Pursuit Squadron - U.S.A.A.C.
LIEUTENANT COLONEL JUANITA REDMOND HIPPS
United States Air Corps (ret)
Angel of Bataan
BRIGADIER GENERAL WILLIAM G. HIPPS U.S.A.F.(ret)
JONATHAN MAYHEW WAINWRIGHT XII
DANIEL S. WAINWRIGHT
THE ANGELS OF BATAAN AND CORREGIDOR

(Corregidor Memorial)

(NFG, Jr., at Death
March marker)

FOREWORD

This volume is the true rendition of the never before published manuscript originally titled *Valley of the Shadow* written by my father, Colonel Nicoll F. Galbraith, GSC, United States Army, in the 1950s in Colorado Springs following his retirement. The manuscript, written in longhand on 1,100 flimsies, is "Nick" Galbraith's historical narrative describing his three-and-a-half years as a prisoner of the Japanese, from the surrender of Corregidor in May, 1942, until August, 1945, when he and his fellow prisoners were rescued/released from Camp Hoten, in Mukden, Manchuria, at the hands of a six-man OSS team and Russia's Red Army, which had just entered the Asian war. It is written in the third person, using pseudonyms for the characters. The principle five men he personifies represent a composite of his associates while on the staff (G-4, Logistics) of General Jonathan M. Wainwright, commander of United States Forces In the Philippines (USFIP) and his various "roommates" during their years of captivity. Colonel "Nick" Galbraith replaced Brig. Gen. Lewis Beebe in the G-4 position following Beebe's promotion to Wainwright's chief-of-staff in March, 1942. Other than the pseudonyms, there is very little in this story that is fiction. The narrative reflects in detail his personal memory reinforced by his extensive diary collection that he was able to maintain during his years of incarceration.

With rare embellishments, every episode, conversation, characterization and soliloquy reflects a true account of the experiences of "Nick" Galbraith and of his fellow POWs and their Japanese captors.

Many of the passages are direct quotes from his real time, first person diary entries. As such, it is an accurate and intense portrayal of the lives of senior American officers captured during the Fall of the Philippines in 1942, following the defensive campaigns on Bataan and Corregidor.

Valley of the Shadow reflects a "stream of consciousness," even a catharsis of "Nick" Galbraith's "soul" during and after his years of severe degradation of his very existence and that of his prison mates. He believed that a narrative format, rather than a first-person chronology, allowed him to impart the often disturbing emotions that drove POW mentality and behavior. Perhaps a primary audience for *Valley of the Shadow* would include members of the psychological and sociological professions, as it delves deeply, and with a good deal of cynicism, into the psychologic and moral responses of senior American officers, generals and colonels, in times of extreme deprivation at various prison camps. The account refers occasionally to Allied officers, British, Australian and Dutch, captured elsewhere in Asia.

"Nick" Galbraith devotes entire sections in his diaries to such as "Failures in Personnel," "Discipline," "Camp Rosters," "Literature," "Diet, "Religion" and "Orders of Battle" and offers a more interpretive account of POW life than the more chronological, first-person diary accounts of his fellow POWs listed in the bibliography. These authors, together with "Nick" Galbraith, cross-reference each other extensively. While often appearing as the camp scold, "Nick" Galbraith's was a more reticent, analytic and fastidious persona, causing him to usually hold his reflexive fire in front of his often self-centered associates. To a modern audience, his accounts of personal behaviors and attitudes of his fellow officers often reflect the adolescent and ridiculous behavior of television's *MASH* characters! His diplomatic constraints were energetically abandoned in August 1945 as revealed in Appendix 11.

A controlling factor in this psychological morass is the insistence by the Japanese that no ranks or normal military hierarchy among the captive Americans could be acknowledged, thus obviating any coordination, command or internal organization among the POWs themselves. Thus, each prisoner survived as best he could as a lone actor, not subject to normal social or professional conventions. The resulting selfishness of the prisoners was a dominant theme of "Nick" Galbraith and a disappointing one to him, as his attempts and that of other POWs to remain "civilized" under uncivil circumstances were difficult at best, often not being reciprocated among their fellows.

The ability of the POWs to obtain the food and hygiene items and to retain their labels (Appendix 9) is due to the fact that the various POW camps were located near towns that had normal civilian items for sale and were paid for by the prisoners with their weekly allowances in Japanese currency, the yen.

Of particular interest to me has been my welcome association in recent years with Mr. Harold "Hal" Leith and his wife Helen, who, decades after the war, I found residing in Golden, Colorado, a 90-minute, highly expectant drive from my home in Colorado Springs. On August 16 1945 Sergeant "Hal" Leith was one of the six parachutists that "Nick" Galbraith refers to in the closing pages of the narrative. Hal Leith then was a 25-year old member of the OSS team ordered into Camp Hoten, Mukden, Manchuria, as part of Cardinal Mission ordered by General Wedemeyer from Chungking, China, to find General Jonathan M. Wainwright and other senior American officers thought to be in that camp. Hal's own account, *POWs of Japanese: RESCUED* (2003), reflects the parallel minute-by-minute account of the mission described in his diaries by "Nick" Galbraith himself. It was "Hal" Leith who was personally responsible for General Wainwright's ability to join the Japanese surrender on the quarterdeck of the USS Missouri in Tokyo Bay. The Leith family has graciously allowed me to include Hal Leith's personal photographs which he took during Cardinal Mission.

Valley of the Shadow begins arbitrarily with look back remembrances of combat episodes in early 1942 when American forces were defending the Bataan peninsula and subsequently, the fortified island of Corregidor. It then jumps ahead to a description of several of the characters while imprisoned at Karenko, Taiwan. It then sequences through other prison camps, including Shirakawa on Taiwan, Beppu, Japan, and ultimately to Chengchiatung and Mukden, Manchuria. In one telling section, "Nick" Galbraith describes time spent on the prison ship Oryoku Maru, weeks before that vessel, containing a later batch of American POWs, was sunk by American aircraft.

The Flags: omitted from the narrative is an essential historic episode when Japanese General Masaharu Homma, in May of 1942, refused to accept General Wainwright's offer of surrender on Corregidor, obligating the latter to send American officers into the field to locate remaining, but, isolated, American forces. "Nick" Galbraith was one of three selected, whose mission in northern Luzon, described in Appendix 2, with supporting documents in Appendices 3 - 5, was a final effort to avoid the immediate annihilation of the remaining 14,000 Americans on Corregidor. The "dime store" flags were provided by the Japanese to help secure that mission, enabling him to traverse areas of uncertain control in rural Luzon. The success of that mission to find a local American commander, Col. John Horan, contributed to several of "Nick" Galbraith's combat awards, including the Distinguished Service Medal. The American flag would be seen again at Camp Hoten, Mukden, in August, 1945! That brief moment, one of intense personal reflection, is captured in Appendix 11 which also includes the original diary entries describing the OSS Cardinal Mission and, three days later, the arrival of the Red Army, which had just entered the war against Japan.

Whitney H. Galbraith
Younger son of Col. Nicoll F. "Nick" Galbraith, GSA, U.S. Army, 2018

VALLEY OF THE SHADOW

It was only a matter of minutes, but they were interminable minutes, before Blake reached the high ground safely. His load was growing heavy at each step, but to Blake it would not become too heavy until he had deposited it in gentle hands back to the rear. He had no sooner reached the high and flat projection of land than he was challenged. The call came in dialect, and while Blake did not understand the words, he knew the meaning.

"This is your regimental commander," Blake called back in a loud whisper, speaking slowly and with deliberate enunciation. He wanted to make certain that the soldier clearly understood and that he took no adverse action. This was no moment to be dropped by one of his on men.

"Pass, sir," came the reply, but Blake knew that the danger was over. He doubted if he had been recognized, but at least his voice and tone had brought the results he needed. Tomorrow, he would look into further training for his soldiers when on outpost duty.

As soon as he encountered a squad of his forward troops, he gave them hasty and sharp directions. "Here, Sergeant, get a litter and have this man carried back to the dressing station. Hurry! He is bad hit. Needs a doctor quick. Be gentle."

Blake then hastened to the nearest field telephone. "Get me through to regiment, quick." He held the field phone to his ear a moment until he heard, "Canary," from the other end of the line. That was the regimental switchboard.

"Cactus, hurry!"

1

"Number, sir?" came the reply, and Blake immediately realized that he was in the meshes of a most difficult situation. Here was the only real problem he had ever encountered in his training of the native soldiers. If one ever shouted excitedly into a telephone to a native operator, that soldier would forget everything he should do and his training would appear to leave him completely. Only another native speaking in dialect can restore the man to his senses.

The moment was too serious for Blake to permit delay. It was only his fundamental knowledge of the situation and not keen mentality that put him on the correct tack. "Line test," he called over the wire.

"Sir?" came back in the receiver.

"Damn it to hell," Blake mumbled to himself, and then quickly bringing himself under control, he repeated slowly and calmly, "Line test. Line test." Surely the use of terms familiar and in the language of a telephone man would settle the operator down to normal.

"Oh, yes, sir. Canary, sir. She is working fine, sir."

A sigh came from Blake. The relief to feel that the operator was in full command of his faculties again was a pleasant sensation. "Operator," Blake began in a quiet and slow voice. He was not going to make the mistake again of exciting the man on the switchboard. "Operator, get me Cactus."

This time, there was not hitch, and Blake soon had the division commander on the phone. After identifying himself, he reported, "General, this is the night! The Japs are getting ready."

"But, the reports from your sector say that all is quiet. What brought about the sudden change?"

The general was cautious. Too many rumors had misled him in the past for him to get excited over a report of this nature until he had been fully assured.

"I was down in the ravine myself, Blake explained, "The sound of the firing was different, and I didn't like it, so I took a patrol and went down there to find out. They sure are getting ready. I could hear a lot of moving around and whispered orders. Never before have they had more than an occasional scout moving about down in the ravine."

"Well, good job, Colonel. You didn't have any damn business doing that yourself, but I suppose that is the most certain way of getting firsthand information."

Blake knew that he had violated orders about exposing himself unnecessarily when there were others trained to carry on such duties. It was not a regimental commander's function to make patrols in the middle of the night. There were too few of those senior officers, and their job was to command large bodies of soldiers, not a squad.

"If this is the time," the general continued, "it is well that we have our plans all set. Move your troops into the gaps as planned. You will have to use your own judgment when to open fire. We can't coordinate it in this pitch-blackness. But don't let a single one get through. I'll alert the adjacent regiments and the artillery to be prepared to fire on their emergency barrage lines. This is going to be a lot of fun." The general was enjoying the advantage he had over the enemy by knowing his future actions and being able to make his own dispositions to meet the threat. "I'll see that you are properly rewarded for that courageous act." Then, suddenly bristling over the phone, he bellowed, "No. I'll be damned if I will. You violated my orders by going down there and nearly lost me a regimental commander."

Blake smiled as he replaced the receiver. Generals weakened even though they had to give the appearance of rigid discipline. His smile also meant that he too was going to enjoy the fun. "Like shooting fish in a bathtub," he commented to himself as he moved toward his own command post to issue the necessary instructions to his subordinates.

Ashley continued to stare off into space, while some of the others discussed their present and future under the Japanese conqueror. As they sat in the little room at Karenko that was to be their home for an uncertain period, Ashley was apparently listening to the conversation of his companions in a half-interested fashion; but he was not inclined to enter into it. The few remarks that he contributed had the sting of sarcasm and pessimism. Something more than the present condition of affairs seemed to bother him. He actually was brooding; but, if he were asked where his thoughts were, he could probably not give a rational answer. Those thoughts were too confused yet to identify and classify.

When they arranged themselves into a recollection of the past several months, though, he was enthralled with the spectacular events in which he had had a principal role.

It was January. The defenses of Bataan had but recently been set up, and now everyone was engaged in bringing them to the highest possible state of perfection with the limited resources at hand. Ashley had command of a small detachment down on the southwest tip of the peninsula, with the mission of observing the sea to the west. Should any enemy vessels be so foolhardy as to come within the range of the guns of Corregidor, he was to send the alarm and conduct the fire. Nothing of that sort appeared likely, but his time was spent in perfecting the means of observation and conduct of fire, just in case.

His little kingdom was a jut of land that consisted wholly of a peak, jungle covered, interspersed with boulders. The spot was a nasty place, as everyone agreed. It was difficult to move over, and it exhausted each of the troops when they had to travel from their campsite at the base of the rugged hill to the top where the observation station had been set up. But each one did his duty well and efficiently. After all it was quiet there, quite different from the Abucay line up to the north, where history was being written in blood and fire. Better not complain about this location; although each one would, deep down in his soul, admit that he would be happier if he were ordered up there where the big show was going on.

Early one morning, Ashley and two of his soldiers started up the hill, as was customary. They were to be the first relief gazing seaward that day, watching the enemy ships that would slide past on their way to and from Subic Bay to the north. But the enemy was most clever, damn them—always careful to keep out of range of Corregidor's guns. By some diabolical means, they seemed to know just how far that was. They would come close to a kill zone but never quite close enough.

Ashley was in the lead as the small group laboriously picked its way up the narrow trail to the top. Before the group had quite reached the summit, Ashley heard a gasp from one of the men behind him. It was so unexpected that he halted in his climb and turned around.

"What's the matter, Sergeant?" he asked.

"Japs, Captain," the soldier replied in a horror-stricken tone.

"Where?" Ashley queried, looking in the direction that the sergeant was pointing but unable to see anything unusual.

"On the little ridge, just below us. Lots of them."

"Oh, yes, I see them now," he replied as he carefully dropped down behind a large boulder so he would not be seen. "They are working fast on something. Probably digging in."

"No, sir, Captain. From this angle, I can see better. They are bringing things up over that cliff."

"But they can't climb up that steep and rocky surface," Ashley said, trying to convince the sergeant.

"Maybe not, but they sure are doing it. Look at them now. More of them are coming over the edge, and look at those loads they are carrying."

"Gosh, you are right. Why, those are artillery guns. Look like 75s, and they are putting the parts together. They must have a breakdown model. This is real news!"

"Yes, and our quiet little sector has suddenly turned into a battleground."

"It soon will be; that is certain." Then, when the real truth of the situation was evident to Ashley, he cried aloud, "Holy smoke! They are going to cut the West Road!"

That was most ominous information. A single road ran around the perimeter of the Bataan peninsula, like a horseshoe. Each forward end stopped in the rear of the two defensive forces into which the army was divided. That was the supply and evacuation route, and the only one. All else was mountainous jungle of the most difficult sort. Now the enemy had landed a force right in the middle of the curved part of the horseshoe. If the road were cut, the left force, the I Corps, would be isolated. This was a development of the greatest moment. And each man in the little detachment needed no one to explain that dangerous situation to him.

"Sergeant," Ashley began to give his orders. He was calm and precise. All the qualities of a great soldier were present, even though he was but a youth. "Sergeant, two things. Hurry down the trail to our camp and send every man up here to me. Put Hendricks in command and tell him that not a single man is to expose himself where the Naps can see him. As soon as you have done that, call up headquarters and tell them that the enemy, at least a company, is now on Longoskawayan Point. I will take my detachment around this hill on the far side, under cover, and drive them back over the cliff. Do you fully understand?"

"Yes, sir," the sergeant replied and repeated back to Ashley the instructions that he had received. Then he added, "But, Captain, don't you start anything until I get back. I may miss it if you do."

"Have no fear there, sergeant. You will be back in plenty of time to do your share. This is not going to be any simple matter. But I cannot afford to delay, because they are getting stronger every minute. Shake it up!"

While Ashley waited until his men came up, he surveyed the situation. It never occurred to him to wait until he could gather together greater strength than his small numbers or to await instructions from his commander. Here was a job to be done, at once! He might fail to clear the hill of the enemy, but at any rate, he could delay the enemy's preparations by immediate and aggressive action.

The sergeant must have tossed a bomb into the soldiers at the camp at the base of the hill. Excitement and duty spurred them on when they received the news. Up they came, in no formation, each one rushing forward as fast as he could under the difficult conditions. Each one was out of breath and clad in what he happened to have been wearing at the moment. But no one forgot his rifle. There was a small group of seamen from one of the vessels that had been destroyed in the bay, a squad of marines that had been attached earlier to assist in guarding equipment, and a group of casuals from the Philippine Army that had been attached to Ashley's command for rations until they could be sent back to their own command.

Sergeant Hendricks was in the lead; the others trailed on behind. At a signal from Ashley, he halted and dropped down undercover. He passed the instructions on to those in rear.

"Move off to your right flank," Ashley called softly, "and halt at that big tree with the broken limb."

Ashley moved in the same direction. When he met the sergeant, he gave his instructions. "Look, Hendricks. We have a nasty job ahead. There is at least a company of Japs on that ridge off to the left. They somehow or other have climbed up that steep cliff and dragged their weapons, including artillery, up with them. Our job is to stop them in their tracks before they can get organized. If we are too late, they will cut the West Road, and half of our force will be out of action in a matter of days."

"Let's get the little devils. We'll kill every one of them." Hendricks was excited, and he let his emotions take control.

"Now take it easy, Sergeant," Ashley said, trying to calm him. "This is not going to be very simple. They are in a fine spot to hold out in spite of our effort. We must be very cautious and try to close in on them without being seen. It is impossible to get above them, so we must fight them going up hill. Let us move around the side of this peak, with every man keeping under cover. That is especially important because half of them are in white undershirts and blue denim, which makes them easily seen."

"But that makes no difference. We'll mop them up in a hurry. Them damn Japs are no good. They can't fight."

"Sergeant." Ashley spoke with some heat to impress the sergeant with the difficulties that confronted them. "I want you to get that foolishness out of your mind right now. This is a real scrap. And the damn Japs can fight! They are in a favorable position and will make every effort to do what they have come for. And another thing—there is not a soldier in our detachment who has ever fired a rifle at a man before. On top of that, they are dressed in clothes that will give away their presence a mile off. Now get this." Ashley spoke his words slowly as he pointed his finger at Hendricks. "Every man here is anxious to do the right thing, and they are all itching to go. But we must use every caution. Lots of these men are going to get hurt in spite of our best efforts, and we have to keep that down to a minimum. However, regardless of that, we have to get this job done. Come on!"

Ashley carefully moved around the side of the peak, keeping behind trees and brush. Those behind took their cue from him and did likewise. When he came within vision of the enemy, he dropped down and crawled from boulder to boulder, slowly moving toward the enemy position and looking for the most advantageous spot to open the attack.

He had no sooner satisfied himself as to the best position and had disposed his detachment than he saw one of the enemy faces look in his direction and point an arm toward the place where he was. It was too far to hear what the Japanese said, but it was evident that he had sighted Ashley and his soldiers and was informing the other enemy troops. Ashley immediately opened fire, which was the signal for the others to follow suit. The enemy dropped down out of sight. In a few seconds, their rifle bullets were pinging back.

"Hendricks, you keep firing on their position so they will be kept well occupied. I am going to take five or six men and crawl through the ravine and up on the ridge where they are and hit them on the flank.

"But, Captain, can't I go along with you? That will be so much more fun."

Ashley paid him no attention. He gathered up a few soldiers near him, gave them some instructions, and slipped down into the intervening ravine. The sergeant called words of encouragement to those left behind and moved back and forth among them, pointing out targets.

Meanwhile, Ashley crawled on forward, apparently unobserved, as no missiles were sent in his direction. He made his way cautiously down the slope, checked his men, issued further instructions, and began the hazardous trip up the next ridge. He kept well off to the flank and was amazed that the enemy did not observe him. He thought to himself that Hendricks was doing a fine job in keeping them occupied. After all, they had been caught unprepared and were fighting from behind trees and boulders without proper defensive positions.

He finally achieved the location he wanted and smiled to himself that it had been so simple. Each of those who had accompanied him was placed in favorable spots, and at his signal, they opened fire. Ashley's smile broadened into a grin as he witnessed the consternation that he caused by his wholly unexpected flank attack. Caught unawares, many of the enemy fell at the first burst of fire; others, sensing their precarious situation, had to squirm about to find protection from two fronts.

Ashley's success was not to endure. There were too many objects for the enemy troops to hide behind for protection. But he had, for the time being, put a stop to their reinforcing their positions. A showdown was due. Ashley had either to rush the position before his opponent had time to prepare a thrust against him or stand to defend himself when the attack came. To take the initiative under such circumstances would merely mean destruction without accomplishing the mission he was obligated to fulfill. To try to defend his present advantage with a half dozen men was equally silly. And, he told himself, it might be hours before any kind of a respectable force scraped together to come to his assistance.

Still, a man of ingenuity can often think himself out of a tight squeeze. And when conditions are at the very lowest ebb, that person frequently discovers that, if he can hold on a little longer and fight a little harder, the dark clouds will begin to dissipate and the light, leak through. So, while Ashley pondered, knowing that very soon he would receive an attack, an idea of great value came to him; and he promptly proceeded to execute it.

He signaled to his troops. After getting their attention, one by one, he directed them to crawl back down the ridge into the ravine, taking advantage of every boulder and tree. *The tactics book says that a daylight withdrawal cannot be successful*, he humorously chided himself. *But when we get out of this, the authorities will have to change that statement. It will not be the first principle that this most unorthodox campaign has upset.*

In spite of the fact that enemy bullets were chipping off bits of the large rock in front of Ashley, he felt it imperative that he continue to fire as rapidly as possible until his own men had reached a safer position. He kept firing and loading and firing. It was impossible to aim, and he was forced to direct his missiles in the general direction of the enemy. But he obtained the effect he was after. As soon as he felt his soldiers had reached the bottom of the ravine, he gave thought to his retirement. He turned his head and shoulders to see what lay behind him to which he could move and still keep under cover. But the instant he made that maneuver, a *ping* coming in his direction seared across his face. He had inadvertently brought up his head from behind his guardian boulder and had to pay the penalty. *Strike one on you, my young friend*, he said to himself. *That was mighty clumsy and careless.* He raised his hand to his face to inspect the damage and discovered that the burning sensation came from a nasty swath running from the bridge of his nose down to the lobe of his ear.

Exercising the utmost caution he, crawled, wormlike, backward, keeping the boulder constantly between him and the enemy. After several yards of that maneuvering, his feet suddenly lost contact with the ground. He could not risk turning around to observe. *Now what?* he queried inwardly. *It feels like a drop-off. But it surely cannot be a very deep drop, or I would have noticed it when we came up this way.* "Well, here goes," he whispered and pushed backward.

The drop was not more than two feet, but for an instant, the uncertainty made it appear bottomless. When he settled down into the protecting embrace of nature's foxhole, he took a few seconds to collect his emotions and daub his face with his handkerchief. The opportunity was now afforded to have a look to the rear to get his direction and to learn what sort of cover was available. The ground was too well filled with rough terrain objects to disturb a man of his self-reliance, and he quickly took the advantage of sliding down the incline unmolested.

When he was able to size up the situation that confronted the remainder of his detachment, he sent one of the men who had been on the ridge crawling over to Sergeant Hendricks with instructions for him to bring his men back as carefully as possible. Then Ashley proceeded to carry out the plan that he had developed. When conditions were favorable, he stood up and made as much haste as possible around the side of the peak and then up to the top, where his observation station was set up. Once there, he began to crank the generator of the radio transmitter. When it was well under way, Ashley continued the operation with one hand, while with the other he pounded out the call letters for the Corregidor control station. It was but a few seconds until he had made contact and began to explain what he wanted.

"Fourteen-inch mortar available," came over the receiver.

"Fire with data given. Will observe," he tapped back.

Seconds delay; they dragged like hours. "What is your location?" sounded in the receiver.

A noise at the rear forced him to jump involuntarily. He knew that one of the enemy had reached him! It was Hendricks.

"All the men except one—he won't go back—are down the hill at the camp," the sergeant reported.

"Well, get the hell down there yourself. Damn quick. We're sitting on the target," the captain ordered.

"Shove over," Hendricks insubordinately ordered as he gave Ashley a push that shoved him off the radio generator seat. He then calmly sat down himself and began to crank, whistling a popular tune and completely ignoring Ashley. The officer glared at him for a fraction of a second and then with a smothered oath about undisciplined soldiers and the Articles of War, he went back to the transmitter. "Present location Mt. Naqtunq," Ashley lied over the ticker. "Can observe."

"Wait," was the instruction, he received.

Shortly came the information that he had so badly wanted to hear. "Ready to fire."

"Fire!" Ashley was so excited he could hardly keep his hand steady enough to tap out the letters.

When he had finished, he raised up one hand with a jerk and crossed two fingers, an obvious indication that he hoped the first round would miss his extremely dangerous position.

A distant *boom* came from over the channel, a heavy and dull sound that carried on and on. Ashley froze in place, watching and hoping. Hendricks stared with open mouth, completely immobile. His hands were raised in the position of cranking, but he never realized that he did not have hold of the crank handles. Twenty seconds, forty seconds, sixty seconds—hours, days, weeks! Will the damn thing ever hit?

Then as both of the men waiting impatiently began to gain control over their suspense, they realized that it would take time, lots of time. The "Thing" had to go far, far up and come far, far down. In the midst of their contemplation, an amazing thing happened! The earth at the bottom of the ravine between them and the enemy slowly raised upward in a tremendous cloud. Trees and rocks and shell fragments mingled with the black smoke and were thrust upward and outward in all direction. The two men never heard the detonation, it was lost in the excitement, but the blast knocked them both to the ground.

Ashley shook himself quickly back to normal, except that he was momentarily deafened. He glanced at Hendricks, whose face was a terrible mass of lacerations and saw the injured sergeant regain his seat and start cranking.

But there was business ahead. And if Hendricks could crank, Ashley could pound the key.

"Five hundred yards right. Elevation correct," he commanded.

Ashley focused his eyes on the enemy position, and waited—waited.

Then the Thing came! The devastation was repeated, but this time it was exactly in the middle of the Japanese position. Until the smoke cleared, Ashley could not tell what the result was. Then gradually the scene began to unfold. The debris settled down. A tremendous hole had been torn in the earth. Firing had ceased, when he witnessed an incredible sight! The Japanese, crazed by the Thing, were running madly to the edge of the cliff and leaping over!

In time, Ashley recovered. He felt a tremendous sense of satisfaction. Now, he must make a report to his superior of what he had accomplished. Oh, yes, Hendricks, he remembered, was in bad shape. Ashley turned, expecting to give what aid he could. He saw the sergeant crumpled up on the ground and realized that he had turned the crank for the last time.

While his companions lolled about the mail room that was to be their quarters at Karenko, Sykes held himself aloof, both in thoughts and action. It was not that he considered himself different, for he was not normally of that bent. He would have resented it if anyone had considered him an introvert. But just now he was not inclined to join the others in the discussion of matters that were uppermost in their minds. The things that he contemplated were of a different nature.

He recalled that he'd had had many difficult moments during the recent campaign. There were other times, too, when he could have gotten into tight places if he had not been cautious and conservative. While he had sacrificed none of the requirements of the position he held, he had not seen fit to plunge boldly into dangerous situations without weighing the factors of security against the demands of duty. Since the termination of the campaign, he had been impressed with many other reasons why he should continue his careful manner of living; after all, he had no military obligations now, he thought. It was his own life only that he had to consider, and he intended to conserve that regardless of anything else. He was clever enough, so he convinced himself, to play that sort of a game without his colleagues finding out. Surely the reputation he had made for himself would carry him through this interlude of imprisonment.

Sykes recalled the orders he had received not so long ago: "Headquarters moves to Corregidor tonight. A small detachment of the staff remains in Manila as a rear echelon to evacuate the remaining troops and complete necessary destruction before the enemy enters the city. You will be one of those few."

Those instructions were simple and brief. They left a great deal to the initiative of those who composed the small group that was to remain. *Somebody has to do that job,* Sykes had told himself at the time. *And why should I not be one of them? It is a compliment to be selected,* he had consoled himself, *for I know any number of others in whom the command has less confidence and who could have been chosen if the task was to be a simple one.*

Yet, a conflicting thought disturbed him. There was Gary. *Now why was he given the chance to slip over to Corregidor while I have to do this nasty job? Of course, he is more intimate with the—*

Gosh, is it possible that I lost out because that fellow is a good "handshaker," a sycophant?

Early the first morning after the shift of headquarters, the sirens in the city sounded. Off to the north, the first one took up a wail, weird and uncanny. The tone came softly through the air, low-pitched at first, and then ascended in a graceful curve to a high shrill tone and faultlessly dropped back to the tone of origin. As it died down, it gave the impression that it would cease. But before that instant came it was away again, to repeat the cycle. In a few seconds, a reproduction of the first wail pierced the air, this time in a higher pitch and closer, louder.

More imitations, one after another, coming nearer constantly, until the entire city seemed enmeshed in these predictions of disaster. A terrible series of sounds, they were inclined to make brave men cringe and run for shelter. It was uncertainty more then fear that disturbed the emotions, for after greater experience had been gained, one strove to see what hovered overhead, and distances and angles soon became the factors that decided whether one should wince or stand his ground and shake a fist at the sky. Only a city under the merciless and unparried attack from the heavens can understand such conditions.

A different tone soon reached the ears of those standing at headquarters. This one had no variation in pitch; it was deep and steady and smooth. It could not be distant thunder. The day was too perfect. Nor did anyone think that it was caused by natural conditions. It was obvious, even to those staring in hopes of getting a glimpse of the cause, that they had never witnessed what they now anticipated. The beauty of the smooth rhythm allayed fears. Aesthetic delights had a soothing influence. Suddenly, and amplifying the joy of a beautiful sound, those below witnessed the bewitching sight of sleek and shimmering aircraft plunging out of a bank of fluffy clouds. Such a sight for the first time made even otherwise hardened soldiers gasp at the magnificence of what they saw approaching. Planes floated along in groups of three, which in turn were formed into a pattern of triplets, and then that formation was further enlarged by two others of identical size. A short distance behind a duplication of that array chased its forerunner. To complete the picture of splendor and magnitude, an additional formation, alike in style and sweep to the others, brought up the rear of the imposing procession.

"I don't believe it."

"But there they are."

"I wonder where the Japs got them all?"

"Never knew they had anything like that."

"Where are they going?"

"I hope not this way. But watch them."

As they watched, groups of small puffs of clouds appeared far below the formation. They were regular in combination, and as a unit, they shifted position laterally as the sleek assembly in the heavens moved forward.

"What are those things?" They were too regular to be a natural phenomenon.

"Why, that's antiaircraft."

"Oh!"

"Get them up higher!"

"What a target! Never know that anything like that could exist."

"A gunner's dream!"

"But they are shooting thousands of feet low. Why don't they get them up?"

"Uh-oh. What an opportunity. Why don't they do something about it?"

"I don't know, but there must be some good reason. No one would be so dumb to keep firing that far short."

"Time fuses—antiquated. They can't reach any farther," explained a knowing one.

The attention of the watchers was suddenly brought to conditions closer to them. Rifle and machine-gun fire began all around them. The first thought of each one was self-protection. They looked for places of safety, not knowing from where the firing came. A quick survey showed that it was the small body of troops that had been left behind to police the area around headquarters that was responsible.

From a position of detachment, one could get a different perspective than the soldiers holding rifles or crouching behind machine guns who witnessed such an amazing sight for the first time.

"What the hell are they shooting for? Cripes! Those planes are thousands of feet up. How do they expect to hit anything?"

"Hey, hey! Stop the shooting, you dummies."

"They have gone nuts."

"First time they ever saw anything like that."

"That's no excuse. Any soldier should know that you can't hit a target like that with small arms."

"They're not soldiers—yet."

Sykes, who had had his part in the conversation, impetuously cried, "Look! Look!"

"What? Where? What are you talking about?" the officer at his side quickly questioned.

"There!" replied Sykes, this time pointing off across Manila Bay.

All eyes turned in that direction. They beheld a sight of magnificence. Tremendous masses of clouds were rising from a point of land across the water. They were followed by others, which seemed to grow out of their forerunners to renew and enlarge the picture. Then two of the three steel vertical structures that pointed high into the heavens suddenly disappeared.

"God Almighty!" exclaimed Sykes.

The others were too emotionally disturbed and appalled at what they saw to utter a sound.

When one finally collected himself, he announced, "They've knocked out Cavite."

"And that place was still occupied, I'm sure," Sykes said.

"What a mess. The whole place is pulverized."

"And this show has just started," Sykes thoughtfully stated.

"We didn't have a plane in the sky. Why, just one or two P-40s could have had a picnic. They could have knocked them off one at a time from the rear. It would have been simple," the other declared.

"What P-40s?" Sykes asked pathetically.

Sometime later, Sykes was seated at his desk in the old building, which formed a part of the ancient wall around Intramuros, the original city of Manila. Headquarters had been housed here, but now the offices were nearly deserted. The atmosphere was eerie. Uncertainty and a feeling of insecurity predominated. All around were the signs of hasty departure. Papers that were not worth the time for destruction were lying about. Desks and chairs stood disarray. Improvised black curtains covered the windows.

The phone rang. It was ringing perpetually. That seemed to be the one activity that no problems of the outer world could possibly stop. Someone was wanting something constantly. An endless stream of requests and demands for help persisted. There was no help, but the phone continued to ring, bringing in the same requests from the same sources. They needed ammunition, gasoline, and trucks. And they had to have helmets and rifles and machine guns. They called for shoes, motorcars, and airplanes. They wanted food and artillery and encouragement.

"Yes?" Sykes called into the transmitter, too tired to give a respectable reply. "Your trucks never arrived? And you must move? God, man, I wish I could do something for you. We've shuttled those few trucks back and forth so much now that they have fallen by the wayside. You say the situation is critical? You will lose all your troops if you can't get them there by dawn? Well, take it easy. There is not a soul here but me. I'll do all I can. Somehow I'll find a solution for you."

He hung up the receiver, but before he could remove his hand, the bell jingled again. This time, he paid no attention, or perhaps he could no longer hear bells. Out of the door he stumbled, down to the street, and over several blocks to the main thoroughfare. Somehow he located a member of the constabulary, some few of which had been left behind to assist the city police.

"Say, Chief," Sykes addressed the uniformed man. "Gotta have some trucks, and quick."

"Sir, I haven't seen any sort of a truck or car for hours. The army has taken every one."

"I still have to have some trucks, and quick." Sykes spoke with heat and authority.

"Yes, sir," the officer replied. "Maybe we had better go over to the next street. The drivers have learned not to come down this main highway, because they will only lose their vehicles if they do."

A block over, the two stood and waited, not too prominently, but rather, sheltered close against a building. They knew, if they were seen first, a driver might swing around in the middle of the street and tear off in the opposite direction. Confiscation of motor transportation was something an owner had learned to avoid. He had little knowledge of what the excitement was about. But he knew that, when the truck was taken away from him, he lost his possession, something he needed to earn his living; and all he received in exchange was a piece of paper with a hasty scrawl that said something about the United States Government ... will pay ... pesos ... on demand.

Five minutes, ten minutes passed. Then the policeman nudged Sykes and said, "Here comes one."

Sykes should have been able to hear it. The noise it made was terrific. But he was not in full possession of his faculties. He was on the point of exhaustion from days and nights of most strenuous duty, with little sleep and practically no food. There had been too much to do and too little time to accomplish it. He looked up. Sure enough, rumbling down the street came a dilapidated truck of considerable antiquity. It bounced along and sputtered and made a terrific roar. Indeed, it was not much, but it was a truck. And there were not many left.

The policeman ran out in front of the vehicle. The driver brought his charge to a slow and uncertain stop.

"The military needs your truck," said the policeman.

"No good, no good," replied the driver.

"Never mind. It will do."

"But I do not own the truck, and I must take it back to my boss," argued the man.

"He will be paid for it," reasoned the policeman.

"Yet, I cannot do it," the driver continued.

"Come, come, man," Sykes burst forth. "Don't you know the law?" He was not too certain of it himself, but he had a hazy knowledge that it was legal to confiscate motor transportation in the event of war. Anyhow, the emergency was too great to stand back on precise formalities. He had a war to help win, and after it was won, somehow he would be protected and the owner paid. Of course, if the war were lost, well, in that event, no one would own anything.

"Ah, but my boss know law, too. He very smart. Keep all his trucks back in woods."

The policeman and Sykes looked at each other, amazed at the innocent betrayal of the owner and content in the knowledge that several more vehicles had so readily become available for the campaign.

"All right, man, you take your truck back to the boss. I'll ride along with you so that no other policeman will hold you up," the Filipino officer told the driver. Then, turning to Sykes, he spoke in a low voice. "I'll locate them all and have them in your hands in no time."

"Have them sent to our motor pool."

"I'll bring them in myself," he called as he braced himself for the sudden lurch that the truck took as it moved away. Stumbling back to his headquarters, Sykes felt a certain satisfaction. He could have sat back at his desk and bluntly announced with finality that no more trucks existed. But he had bestirred his tired mind and body, and with a little good fortune, he had once more been able to give value and aid to a distressed commander.

The next day, Sykes received an amazing order from the high command. In brief, that direction said that all the troops on Luzon would retire to Bataan. "Impossible," Sykes mumbled. No army in the world, even with the latest equipment and the finest training could execute such an impossible maneuver under these circumstances. *How could the general ever have arrived at that decision?* he asked himself.

Man alive, he argued, *the place to fight it out as a last stand is across the island of Luzon at some of the good defensive spots that would make it mighty difficult for the attacker.*

We could hold out for a couple of weeks, and that is the best that could be expected.

Of course, he continued to analyze for himself, *if our forces could get into Bataan, they would be able to tie things up for a couple of months. I wonder if the general is taking a terrific gamble to save those additional weeks? It looks to me that he is throwing away a sure thing for the slimmest of chances to save time.*

Sykes had to play a large part in carrying out these new instructions, and he knew that the success of the undertaking would depend entirely on the fortunes of war, those intangible things that no average man can foresee and analyze. He walked over to the wall where a large map of Luzon hung. As he stared at the printed sheet, its markings grew into reality as he visualized the actual ground with which he was so familiar. The island in general was long and narrow. Up north, in the Lingayen Gulf area, the enemy had landed first in force. The courageous order to "fight it out on the beaches" had been given. It was to be an offensive campaign, and the psychology was channeled in that direction. But the enemy's superiority in numbers, machines, and training had dictated the action. Why disintegration instead of an orderly retirement had not taken place there, neither Sykes nor anyone else could quite explain.

Somehow, commanders had kept their troops reasonably well intact and were now conducting a withdrawal along successive defensive lines. But they were being pushed back rapidly, toward the center of the island. From the south, at Batangas Bay and from Antimonan across the mountain ridge to the east, a similar retirement had been forced, again toward the same center of the island. Those two forces were backing up against each other and soon would collide at San Fernando, where they would have to integrate and sideslip westward along a single road into a rugged mountain jungle that, like a thumb, projected from the side of Luzon. That was Bataan. What bothered Sykes was how two forces in the confusion of hasty retirement toward each other, one coming up from the tips of the fingers of a hand and the other coming down the forearm, could meet in the hollow of the hand and successfully, in a single column, move out into the thumb. The hollow of the hand was the junction point, San Fernando, and what confusion there would be there! *The enemy will have us then, right in the hollow of his hand*, he meditated. There would be a tremendous mass of confusion in a single, small area. Not a friendly airplane would be in the sky to give warning or to protect. Enemy artillery, almost unrestricted, could pound the milling mass into shreds. The campaign would abruptly terminate in horrendous disaster. The American outpost would be trapped in a box, attacked from front, rear, and overhead.

Nevertheless, Sykes kept constantly recalling to himself that the commander could not have gone completely insane. There must be some intelligent reasoning behind his order. It could not be that he had closed his eyes to all reality and blindly plunged into crushing calamity. *But just what has he counted on*, Sykes asked himself, *that does not appear to me at the moment?*

In any event, it is my task to further his commands with all my strength and ability. If it turns out to be a catastrophe, he will have to answer to history. I confess that it looks bad to me, but if the general has the courage to issue such an order, I can learn something from a man with his back to the wall. He deserves everything that can be given him.

The excitement and activities of the moment soon made Sykes forget his uncertainty about the situation, to be recalled only years later, when, after gaining a more complete knowledge of the Japanese psychology, he and others were able to understand more fully a condition that now was beyond their comprehension.

From Corregidor, a proclamation was issued. Manila was declared an "open city." It had to be, Sykes convinced himself. Even though it might not be according to the modern concepts of warfare, the rights of humanity demanded it. *But what an additional handicap that will place on our effort to get these troops safely into Bataan,* Sykes brooded. *We have guaranteed not to defend the city nor to conduct any military engagements within its borders and assume that the enemy will conduct himself likewise.*

Time lost all its meaning for Sykes. The pressure and rapidity of events forced him to live from hour to hour. It was a great sense of relief when a limited number of lights were again permitted at night and the population attempted to return to its normal activity without molestation, hoping but not quite fully assured.

It was not long before they found out. The sirens took up their mournful wailing, and the roar of motors shook the air. From high over Manila Bay, an enemy air force moved on the city. Only a few citizens retained their faith that the enemy would respect the terms of the proclamation then.

"How high do you think they are?" someone asked.

"I would say they are at about twenty thousand," Sykes replied.

The first flight of three reached the waters' edge of the city. At the same instant, tremendous splashes of water, accompanied by the loud cracks of detonations, came from the mouth of the Pasig River. A few seconds behind, a similar flight performed the same mission. Then came a third and a fourth. Bombs missed the water and were sprayed over the adjacent waterfront. Manila received the brunt, turning it into a bombed city.

No antiaircraft bursts came from below. The little artillery that had been there earlier had been moved out in keeping with the honor of the proclamation. The enemy apparently had tested out the situation, for the next run of bombers came in at a lower level.

"They have dropped down to fifteen thousand feet," Sykes cried.

"What does that mean?" asked a colleague.

"Don't ask me," was the reply.

More devastation and destruction. Vessels in the harbor and river were hit; bombs sprayed over the city. Then a third run was made, still lower.

"They are getting wise to our having no AA against them."

"I'm afraid they knew it all the time," Sykes commented.

"They dropped down to where they couldn't miss."

"And the next run will be still lower," Sykes prophesied.

True enough, the succeeding planes floated in at minimum bombing elevation. Helpless men huddled wherever they could for protection against the merciless onslaught. Ships sank; walls collapsed; fires raged.

"Mighty brutal, I'd say," commented a soldier.

"They certainly are having everything all their way," grumbled Sykes.

"Wonder how long they will keep this up," mumbled his companion from his place of hoped-for safety close against a building.

"Either until they get tired or run out of ammunition," Sykes called back in a pessimistic tone. "They have not the least obstacle to worry about."

"They are having a real holiday. You can just hear them all laughing over it."

"Let the bastards laugh now. Two can play this same sort of a game."

"In the meantime, these poor devils down on the round are taking an awful beating."

"Its really bad," Sykes admitted, "but it will be a lot worse the other way around some day."

With the coming of darkness, the foray was brought to an end. The relief was great. Families rallied and counted their losses. Merchants and seamen tallied their losses. Firefighters and volunteers took up the task of combating conflagration. Manila tried courageously to take up its normal life while it waited for the next attack.

From up north came the urgent message to the military force in the south, "Haste, make haste! If the enemy overruns San Fernando, you will never get through. We will do all we can to hold until you pass by, but the situation is desperate."

In spite of being deprived of strength and energy, Sykes could not let the plan go unheeded without some effort on his part. He realized that every man and every piece of equipment would be sorely needed on Bataan. And if the southern force were cut off, about half of the defense would be lost.

So he goaded himself into action. It would be so much more restful, he told himself, if he could just curl up here on the floor and not worry about matters that he could not control. He was too tired. *Why care?* he asked.

Then across his weary mind flashed a picture of that man "with his back to the wall." *Hell*, he declared inwardly, *I can still move. Let's go try something.*

He jammed his helmet on his head; buckled on his pistol belt; and, with faltering step, hurried unsteadily outside. His car was there, but there was no sign of his driver. Sykes peered inside and noticed that the keys had been removed. A hurried look about the vicinity failed to locate the man he wanted. "Where the devil has that young fellow gone to?" he called aloud. "Hells bells." The youngster had been frightened out of his wits and had probably taken off for home, too frightened to even leave the keys in the car.

Convinced that the driver was not nearby, Sykes climbed in the front seat and fumbled with the ignition wires. Fortunately, the car was old enough not to have such security to deter him from finally pulling the wires from their sockets and splicing them together. It was a quick and inexpert operation, but the motor soon commenced to hum, and Sykes was off to the south.

His work had required him to keep a rather accurate check on the movement and location of troops and installations, and his knowledge of the Luzon road network expedited his operations. He had worked out a quick plan of action, which was to commandeer every supply truck he could get his hands on and dispatch them forward to expedite the movement of the dismounted troops. There was no enemy pressure on those troops at the moment, but stumbling along the road afoot, they were making slow progress.

He drove directly to a supply bivouac, where he knew there would be an assembly of vehicles between their trips back and forth. It was a matter of minutes only until he located the officer in command.

"Major," Sykes commenced, "I have been sent down from GHQ with orders for you to unload every truck here and send them to Muntinlupa. They will move the troops there to the north."

"Yes, sir," the major replied. "But my general has already ordered me not to release a single truck without his personal orders."

"I am sorry, but my orders to you come from higher headquarters." Sykes spoke vehemently.

"Sir, have you that in writing?" the major countered.

"Writing, hell! This is no time for writing. This is an emergency. Do what you have been ordered to by the commanding general and do it at once. I will give you my personal written instructions so that you may feel protected. We have no time to get in touch with your commander."

"Very well, sir, but you will have to take the full responsibility."

"Be assured of that. I assume complete responsibility," Sykes replied.

He felt greatly relieved when he saw immediate action being taken to get the vehicles on the road. Now he must get down to Muntinlupa as quickly as possible, he told himself, and make arrangements to load those troops and get them back to the rear. En route, he could stop at the command post of the local commander and explain to him what action he had taken in the name of the commanding general. *I hope,* he said to himself, *that I have not tied something up, but the imperative thing is to take quick action to get all these troops back to San Fernando before it is too late.*

Several other similar situations occurred, but when Sykes made contact with the local commander and explained the urgency, that commander, because of unreliable communications that denied him full information, was only too glad of the action taken. He, too, was most anxious to save his command and reach the San Fernando intersection before it was too late.

It was the eve of the New Year, and Sykes gave but a passing thought to all that the date implied. *This is going to be a year, this 1942, that the nation will wish had never occurred,* Sykes commented to himself. *What a mess we are in, and a long, long drag ahead. And Christmas, a week ago, slipped by and no one here was even conscious of it. Christ! Good will to men! Peace on earth! What a travesty. Men slaughtered, for what?*

The last of the troops had been moved to the north of Manila. Not a soldier had been left behind. Sykes had been too deeply engaged and was too weary to appreciate the part he had had in that phenomenal movement. Orders had been given for the destruction of all the bridges as the last of the troops passed across. Engineer dynamite squads had already commenced the sequence of demolition. No longer was there any chance to leave Manila by road. Sykes and his small group of companions still remained in the city. Their task was to expedite and complete the movement to the north. They had done their job.

Thousands of tons of ammunition and other supplies had rolled northward, shuttling their loads into Bataan. Other tons had been carried by water across the bay. It was all done in haste. Any vehicles that were too decrepit to make the final run lay alongside the road, where they had sputtered their last. The bay was thick with vessels and barges that had tried to get through the enemy bombing but that now lay partly visible or completely submerged.

The "Corregidor" had attempted to run the gauntlet to one of the southern islands with a heavy overload of evacuees, but it had met with a mysterious disaster. One of our own mines, reported the defenders. Sunk by one of our infallible submarines, bragged the enemy. Only a handful of her passengers survived the treacherous waters in which the natives had long ago learned it was impossible to swim. A vessel had been promised Sykes and his party from "the Rock" in which they would be evacuated.

Darkness came, but no sign of the ship. Sykes telephoned Corregidor and received the assurance that the vessel had left. An hour passed, and he was again given the message that the vessel had departed but had not returned there. One more hour passed with no sign of their transportation that would carry them to safety.

Sykes began to ponder other means of getting to Bataan or Corregidor. There was nothing afloat that could be put into use. All vessels had either made their final run to Corregidor or had been destroyed with all other property that could not be moved in order to prevent capture and use by the enemy. The roads were useless now that the bridges had been blasted. Many rivers would have to be swum. Capture was more than possible at this late hour. There were few ways to turn for safety.

But toward midnight, a signal light flashed toward the army pier, and soon a hazy mass came out of the darkness. There she was, finally. She slipped up to the pier. The last of some odds and ends of equipment that had been hastily gathered together were quickly tossed aboard. Yet even with that speed, the operation was slower than need be because the few remaining soldiers were busy watching a spectacular fire just beyond the pier. A large warehouse had been set ablaze to deny its use to the enemy. Between that structure and the pier where the vessel was resting stood the block-long office building that had formerly housed all the administrative activities of the neighborhood. It was unoccupied now, as the workers had long since fled from the bombings that raked the pier and waterfront. It was a beautiful sight to look through the windows of the nearer building and watch the play of flames beyond as they gamboled about, creating strange patterns and colors.

Suddenly, the most amazing thing happened. The quarter-mile-long office building adjacent to the pier exploded! There was no other term for the unusual occurrence.

"What in the world happened?" Sykes, who, with the others, was watching the scene, asked of no one in particular.

"I ...I ..." an officer at his elbow tried to say.

"Don't understand that," another person spoke.

After a few thoughtful minutes, Sykes ventured, "That is the strangest phenomenon I ever saw. It must be that the office building with all its windows closed got hotter and hotter inside until the pressure was so great that the walls were blown out."

While they were looking and debating, a bell sounded from within the vessel, and without any further formalities she began to back out of the slip at full steam. A mad scramble occurred to get aboard. The captain had seen the danger to his ship from the holocaust but a short distance away and gave an emergency signal to reverse engines at full speed.

Finally, all hands aboard took a parting and final look at Manila; turned; and as the vessel finally steamed toward Corregidor, Sykes and the others who had no immediate duties flung themselves onto the deck and allowed deep slumber to quickly overtake them. They had reached the mental state where the opportunity to relax overcame any thought of the potential danger of enemy bombings.

The five officers in the little room at Karenko were not in a mood for much conversation. They were pretty much depressed. Their thoughts did not reach into the future to any extent but dwelt upon the situation at hand. Conditions did not look any too pleasant. They were enclosed within a high-walled compound, and contact with the outside world had seemed completely cut off from the very beginning of their imprisonment. They were now crowded in a small room in a large wooden barracks. What else existed inside the compound, they had not yet had time to find out.

Blake tossed his haversack on the iron cot beside the single window of the room and dropped his huge frame alongside it. "This is my bunk," he grumbled.

The thought of taking care of oneself first spread rapidly, and two others quickly assigned themselves cots that they thought were next in desirability. The manner in which they took possession left no doubt but that they would resist any effort to displace them.

Paul and Cameron exchanged glances and then the slightest smile of understanding broke across Paul's face.

Cameron had no sympathy for such unorthodox actions, and he cried out, "Paul is the senior here. I think that he should have the first choice of beds."

"There is no seniority now," Blake muttered back. "It's every man for himself."

Cameron was on the verge of an insulting remark, but Paul reached over and placed a hand on his knee as a measure of caution. Cameron glanced up, and his friend shook his head in an indication of wanting to let the matter drop.

"Well, Paul," Cameron said ironically, "there are only two places left. Which one would you like to have?"

"Don't you worry about me, Cameron. Take which ever one you would like."

"Hell, no. You rank me and are entitled to a choice."

"You better cut cards to settle the matter," Ashley ventured in an almost sarcastic tone.

Paul replied in his calm and soothing manner, trying to keep down the ill feeling that was on the verge of developing, "Now that is an excellent idea. Cameron, you and I will cut the deck to see who gets the next choice."

"There is probably not a deck of cards in the whole camp," Cameron said, his point realistic.

"All right, then. Which hand?" He had pulled a small coin out of his pocket, placed the two hands behind his back, and then presented his fists, with the coin secreted in one of them, for Cameron to make a choice.

Cameron glanced at him and refused to enter into such child's play. As he looked up into Paul's face, the latter winked at him and gave a slight nod as an inducement for Cameron to take the cue and make his selection. Something about Paul and the feeling that Cameron had for him made the younger man acquiesce. He pointed to one of Paul's closed fists, whereupon Paul opened them both. The coin lay in the palm of the other hand.

"You should have picked your bunk in the first place and saved all that trouble, Paul."

"Ah, that was not trouble, Cameron. That may be a good way to settle a lot of matters that will be coming up among us."

"Which bed do you want?"

"I'll take this one," Paul said as he pointed to the one in the corner behind the door, which was obviously the most undesirable one in the room.

Cameron started to take over that one himself as a courtesy to Paul, but the latter gave him a playful push and said, "This is a time that I will exercise my rank. I won and picked this one."

"Make up your minds," Blake called in a tone of annoyance. He was obviously satisfied with his position in the room and did not deem to appreciate the normal courtesies that Paul and Cameron were exchanging.

"We have come a long way from Tarlac," Paul commented in an effort to smooth over any difficult feeling that appeared to be building up between the five officers in the little room.

His remark sent recollections through the minds of the others. True, it was a long distance from Tarlac, not only in time and place, but also in conditions and treatment. Now that the members of the little group who had been thrown together had a moment to relax, their thoughts were easily directed back over the months that had followed Bataan.

"Tarlac was not so bad when you look at it from a distance," Ashley mentioned, influenced by Paul's statement.

"Not when you compare it to O'Donnell," grumbled Blake. He, too, was influenced to look back and remember.

"Yes, Camp O'Donnell held many sad memories," Paul continued, feeling that a resurrection of those thoughts might bring forward a more sympathetic understanding among his companions.

"I wonder why they ever sent us there," Sykes questioned, "when there were so many other places available?"

Blake had his answer. It was always the same answer for all distressing conditions. "They just wanted to kill us all off. Anybody that saw what went on during the march out of Bataan can testify to that."

No one seemed willing to continue any further discussion of that episode, so Ashley moved the conversation away from that subject. "That freight train ride from San Fernando to Capas was part of the same effort."

"Wasn't that something?" Sykes asked, continuing the line of thought. "Our jaunt in the same size boxcars was a real nightmare."

"The way the Japs packed us in," Paul remarked, somewhat humorously, in an effort to dispel some of the horror of the talk, "reminded me of the way we load horses in our army."

"How was that?" Ashley innocently inquired. He had never had any experience with mounted troops.

"Well," Paul explained, "we go on the principle that there is always room for one more. So we lead the animals up a ramp into the car until it is packed with the horses standing parallel across the car. Then we pick out an 'old-timer' that is well herd-bound and turn him loose at the bottom of the ramp. He is not going to be left behind. Consequently, he tears up the ramp and crams his way into the car between two others. He fights his way in and, with his own strength, pushes the whole crowd aside to make space for him. In that way, he makes a solid pack out of all the horses. And none can fall down."

Blake gave a slight smile as he recalled how they themselves had been packed in cars by the enemy. "They certainly did the same thing with men. Only some of our people could no longer stand and had to slip down to the floor."

"And they stayed there, too, poor devils," recalled Cameron.

"And wasn't it hot in there?" Ashley asked. "The tropical sun seemed to beat down harder than ever."

"If the damn bastards had not closed and locked the door, we might have a breath of air," Blake commented.

"That was mighty bad," Cameron said. "A little fresh air might have saved a lot of lives among those sick men."

"When I reached Capas, I couldn't walk." Ashley recalled. "That ten-kilometer march to O'Donnell was really painful."

"I recall how badly you looked when we finally arrived." Paul spoke with sympathy. "I was never sure that you would pull through."

"I guess I wouldn't have if you hadn't taken care of me."

"It was not much that I did, Ashley," Paul commented.

"I will always remember, Colonel. You begged some water from one of the officers that was already there. You made me drink it when you needed it just as badly as I did."

Paul had many good deeds to his credit, but it was embarrassing to him when anyone commented on them. So he tried to shift the conversation to another tack. "It was strange how we had hoped for better conditions when we reached the campsite, only to find ourselves as bad off as ever."

"Yes," agreed Cameron. "That camp was built for a Philippine Army division of eight thousand, and they must have squeezed at least fifty thousand troops into it."

"It was rugged," Sykes added. "Many was the time that I waited in line for twelve hours to get a canteen of water. That one little faucet they had was wholly inadequate. Usually by the time the line got down to me, the water ran out."

"Yes," Ashley said, "no wonder thirsty men would drink that filthy stuff out of the river. They had to walk miles with a can to get water to cook with and could not resist the temptation to fall down in the stream and guzzle when they had the chance."

"That was most unfortunate, too," Cameron spoke up. "That was one of the main reasons we had so much disease. They certainly died by the thousands."

"Hundreds a day," Blake recalled. "Not one day but every day. It was a problem to find enough men to carry bodies to that huge ditch where they had to take them. There was no reason the Japs couldn't have done something to help out."

"I imagine they were in bad shape themselves."

"They had plenty of chance to help us," Blake quickly countered. "I personally saw a truck of food and medicines come up to the gate with a big sign of the Philippine Red Cross on it. And what happened? The guard got very hostile and chased him away."

"There were many other instances that I know about, just like that one," Ashley contributed.

"It was a difficult time," Paul stated, "and I guess those of us who got out are very fortunate." His statement of that truism brought a response from the others in the group. They paused in their purposeless actions as though to give thought to Paul's remark.

Cameron thought that he noticed on Paul's face the faintest smile of gratification at having given his colleagues something deep in the meaning of life over which to ponder. "Tarlac was quite a change for the better," he declared in an effort to emulate Paul. "Our treatment there was toned up."

Paul quickly responded with "Yes, indeed, it was, Cameron. It made me wonder if the Japs were not trying to be reasonable."

Paul and Cameron exchanged glances. Never was an intimate friendship ever so suddenly developed between two men. They had made a common gesture for the betterment of their fellow man. Without thought or plan, they became inseparably linked in a joint endeavor that only death could destroy. A tiny surge leaped up in the souls of each, and they knew that they were bound together in mind and action. They were challenged by a great purpose in life.

"They had a reason, though," Blake grumbled. "Maybe it was a bit easier there, but don't let that fool you."

"I dare say it was all a part of a plan," Sykes ventured. "And the first step of whatever they have in mind was to bring all the senior officers together like they did."

"Perhaps that was their plan to accord us some special and reasonable treatment," Paul said in an effort to keep the conversation on a lofty plane.

"Well, I may have been one of the few who did not belong to the senior group," Ashley commented, "and do not look at it as you do. But I have a feeling that they wanted to get all the information out of you that they could. That would have been one way to do it—bring all of you together and make you feel that you were getting better treatment."

Sykes spoke up. "That has possibilities. They sure quizzed us and made us write plenty of papers on all subjects."

"You do not carry your discussion on to its proper end," declared Cameron. "Did they get a nickel's worth of information out of anyone?"

"Not out of me," rumbled Blake. "I double-talked them down."

"Me too," agreed Ashley. "Every time they asked me anything, I tied them up with a phony answer."

"Anyhow, you must admit," Paul reminded them, "that your flip answers did not get you into trouble at Tarlac like they did before that."

"Gee whiz, do I remember how they handled me on Bataan," Sykes ruminated, succumbing to Paul's subtle direction. "They insisted that I tell them how many guns were on Corregidor. I kept telling them that I did not have the least idea, and they kept batting me around. Finally, they stripped me and stood me out in the hot sun until I fell. I was out cold and never knew why they went away and left me."

Blake was roused into fury. "Those yellow bastards did the same to me. They wanted to know where the tunnel was that ran between Bataan and Corregidor. Any damn fool knew that there was no such thing, but I couldn't convince them. So, what do they do but make me hunch up in that little cage they built out of chicken wire and stay out in the hot sun. I couldn't lie down, and I couldn't stand up. If I moved out of a crouch, my bare back hit that hot wire and branded me. I'll never forgive them!"

Paul, wise in the ways of directing thought, asked, "By the way, whatever happened to Preston? I saw him in O'Donnell, and he was certainly in bad shape."

"Died," Ashley whispered.

"I know all about him," Blake admitted. "Had a couple long talks with him there. You know, he belonged to my command. He was up in the lines observing for the artillery a couple days before the end. The Japs made a breakthrough where he was and picked him up. They took him back and tried to pump him for information. A lot of the questions they asked he know nothing about; and the few that he did, he never let out a chirp. They got pretty mad because he wouldn't give them the answers they wanted and beat him a number of times. But he held out after telling them unceremoniously to, 'Go to hell!' several times. They finally couldn't take it any longer and strung him up by his wrists to a limb of a tree, with just the tips of his feet touching. They pulled off his shirt and helmet, and everyone that passed by took a swat at him with a bamboo club. He was there for two days before they cut him down."

"So, that was the trouble with his hands. When I saw him, they were black and completely useless, and his head and body were full of horrible welts."

"Yes," Blake continued, "he took an awful licking. But he is probably in good hands now."

"Do you remember the time that Rodeo tossed the rope over the black cow and saved our dinner for us?" Cameron asked in a lighter vein, as his contribution toward directing the thought away from hatred and malice.

"Boy, I will I never forget that day," the ever-hungry Blake declared. "The Japs brought that thin little heifer into the compound for a week's supply of meat for a hundred and fifty hungry soldiers and promptly proceeded to let him get away from them. We were all looking out of the windows in spite of their regulations against it. When that beef went on the loose, there were plenty of sighs of disappointment."

"And the Japs hadn't the least idea what to do."

"They just stood around and laughed. Didn't seem to care one bit if the thing got away and we had no food. About that time Rodeo came out of the kitchen. When he saw what was going on, he went into action."

"The boy from Wyoming won undying fame that day. He let out a war whoop and, Japs or no Japs, ran for the gate to keep the cow from getting out of the compound."

"His yelps brought a dozen others out. As soon as they saw the trouble, they were hot after that flying beef."

"They certainly chased it all over the place for an hour, until Rodeo got that piece of rope tied together long enough to make a lasso. One healthy twirl, and he had his meat."

"Did you ever know that the Japs pulled a funny one on the men that were chasing that cow? They stood around and gave a lot of guffaws and paid no mind to where those cowboys went. But, after it was all over, the guard raised a fine row over them having come out of the barracks and over the off-limits line."

"You can't figure them out. No use trying. Like children, they were dazzled by the excitement of the moment and forgot to enforce their regulations."

"I wonder if we didn't lose our best opportunity for a getaway there at Tarlac," Blake mused. "They didn't have much of a fence to keep us in."

"Sure, we could easily have made a break. So what?" Cameron prodded him. "You know the threat that they made every day or two—that for anyone who escaped, ten would be executed starting with the top man. Fat chance that any of us would place ten others in that spot."

"But I wonder if they would actually have done that," countered Blake. "There was only one way to find out, and no one was willing to take that responsibility. But the Japs did that very thing on two occasions that I know of, and there are plenty of our people who saw it."

Paul soothed down the conversation by saying, "What a delightful contrast it was when we made the trip from Tarlac to Manila."

The others immediately took up the new train of thought. Cameron said, "That was a happy moment when we marched out of the compound to the train. It was like getting out of jail, even if for only a short time. The expectancy of anything happening was a thrill."

"Remember how the natives watched us march past?" Ashley recalled. "They all sang 'Auld Lang Syne' and then whistled 'God Bless America.' The Japs never knew what was in their hearts. That all passed over their heads."

"What a joy our ride to Manila was," Paul continued. "At every station, we had a chance to buy fruit, eggs, and chicken with the few pesos we had."

"The Japs even tried to stop that," Blake grumbled. "But there were too many Filipinos at each depot to chase all of them all away."

"Did you see all the trucks they had piled up at Dau?" Sykes asked. "Everything that they could haul out of Stotsenburg was up there for shipment back to Japan. All the iron cots and wrecked transportation, even the metal reinforcements of the destroyed buildings and bridges."

"They were shipping all their artillery out of there, too," Cameron added. "I wondered at the time how much good American blood might be lost from that before this thing is over."

"I am sure that you all enjoyed the bread they gave you when you reached Manila," Paul added.

"Now that was something," Ashley continued. "A half loaf of good American bread and a handful of brown sugar."

"There was a fluke there," Blake observed. "We'll never have anything like that again."

The conversation rambled on, from one event that had occurred on the trip from the Philippines to Taiwan to another. There had been interesting situations, as well as distressing moments.

The freighter *Nagara Maru*, tied up at the pier in Manila, received comment as well. The men spoke of its tonnage and where it might be bound with its load of prisoners. They discussed again the strange custom that they had observed. While waiting to board the vessel, they had been suddenly rushed into the covered part of the shed and required to face away from the ship. Courageous ones had turned their heads to catch a sight and reported to the others the long line of Japanese soldiers that filed up the gangplank, each carrying by means of a cord suspended from his neck a white cuboid box. Those were the ashes of the emperor's soldiers being carried back for enshrinement. Profane eyes were not permitted to gaze on that ceremony.

"They are afraid to let us see how many we killed," Blake had said at the time.

"I had a look at their cremation once," a companion had added, "and there isn't a chance in the world of the right ashes being in the right box. It was a mass affair, the little glimpse I had of it; and it would be impossible to separate any ashes afterward."

"Well, what is the difference?" Blake reflected. "All their people back home believe anything they are told by the high command."

"The symbol is the big thing," Paul had tried to explain. "The families are more interested in the soul than whether or not the ashes are really what they have been labeled. So long as their soldier has gone to meet his ancestors honorably, any physical identification is of little importance."

On the voyage to the north, the prisoners had encountered many enemy procedures for the first time. One that was most disagreeable that would be horrifying many times in the future was the close packing in of the captives down deep in the bowels of the vessel. The allotted space for each was about the area of a reclining man with perhaps three feet of air space above. It was on this trip, too, that the men learned to drink hot water instead of cold liquid to quench the tropical thirst.

It was a calm sea all the way north, and after being required to remain below so that no sight could be had of Corregidor and Luzon in passing, the restriction was successfully violated, and the prisoners crammed the deck to enjoy fresh air and light. There were few guards, and there seemed to be little effort at regulating the acts of the passengers.

Eventually, they arrived in sight of Taiwan and steamed up past the southern tip toward the harbor of Takao. As everyone was on deck, the prisoners were in a position to view that interesting natural anchorage. The vessel moved along a breakwater and headed for a very narrow entrance. The opening into the harbor appeared to be a slash of little width made through a long low hill. Perfect protection was possible to keep out any unwanted guest, but it would be a simple matter to block the ship haven by sinking a single small vessel at its mouth.

The harbor spread out over many square miles, with sufficient space for the concentration of the greatest fleet. Little work had been done on it, however. Only in the center was the water of sufficient depth for seagoing vessels. Cargo and passengers had to be moved to the shore by lighter and small boats.

"Look!" Cameron had shouted at the time and pointed to the center of the harbor, where an obviously American ship was anchored.

"Why, that's the *Cleveland*," Paul had explained. "You can read the name even though it has been painted out."

"Yes, I recall having heard back in the Philippines that she was captured at Shanghai the first day of the war."

On the deck, 130 Americans lolled about in clusters. Why they were permitted that luxury not a single one of them knew. They took advantage of the moment to observe all things and to snatch memories of the past as choice bits of conversation. The natives, in rowboats and launches, swarmed around the larger vessel calling out their wares. Only the enemy soldiers were allowed to buy. Baskets of luscious bananas, large and golden bananas, tempted hungry men. That delicious-appearing fruit was brought up the lowered gangplank, and the little men from Japan feasted while their prisoners looked on with lustful eyes.

Cameron was standing with three others watching one of the soldiers gorge himself. When he was surfeited, he still had a handful of bananas that he could not eat. He saw the Americans observing him greedily, and in a spirit of decency, he pointed to them and then to the fruit. Each of the prisoners acknowledged his gratitude and quickly sprang forward to pick up one. The prisoner who retrieved the first one shoved it into his shirt and picked up a second. Cameron looked at him in utter amazement.

He was unable to find words for the tongue-lashing that he wanted to administer. As a gesture of disgust and in an effort to teach his colleague consideration for others, Cameron lay his banana back down. It was quickly grabbed up by one of the many others who had rushed toward the source of the food supply; but the gesture had no effect on the selfish one, who merely turned his back and sauntered off.

After some delays, several small boats chugged up to the ladder that had been let down, and the prisoners were lined up to disembark. Each was required to step on a sodden mat and receive a shower from a spray gun as he started to leave by way of the ladder.

"You are now being disinfected," Sykes had announced. "We must not contaminate the sacred soil of Japan."

"Just like everything they do," Blake ventured, "in a slipshod manner. They try to copy the white man but never know quite how to do it."

Ashley added, "It is like that glass rod they gave us yesterday," referring to an interesting event of the day previous when each man was required to stoop over in the proper state of disarray while the enemy medical personnel inserted a small glass rod, which was later examined under a microscope for evidence of disease and germs.

Each of the small boats was crammed with an overload of men. On a tiny deck at each end stood a guard with a glistening bayonet attached to his rifle, which he held in in both hands ready for immediate use. That unusual precaution amazed the prisoners, as the trip from Manila had been one of much freedom and lack of effort to guard the prisoners from escape or assault. But they were on Taiwan now, as they were soon to learn.

When the vessel was finally loaded, the engine was thrown into gear and, with a lurch that sent the packed humans suddenly rearward, moved away from the larger vessel. Those near the gunwales could, by raising up on their toes, get a sight of where they were going. The launch steamed northward past the middle of the harbor and then veered to the west, coming to rest alongside a small coastwise vessel, the *Otaru Maru*, that was lying rusting some distance out from the nearest pier. The passengers were quickly transferred, and about half were jammed down the forward hatch; the remainder was unceremoniously pushed down the aft hatch. Blake was one of the first of his group to limb down the ladder to the deck below. He looked around and sniffed and then proceeded to step off the distance of the deck space.

"Fifteen feet square," he announced to the others.

On the four sides of the square, open shelves extended backward. Each of the first arrivals worked himself into the small space available. It was so tiring that one could not sit up but had to recline at all times. The space soon filled up, and the latecomers found themselves standing on the deck with no place left for them on the shelves.

"How about moving over and letting me squeeze in here?" asked a prisoner.

"No room here. Can't you see we are jammed in now?" was the discourteous retort.

"Hell with you!" declared the first speaker angrily as he swung up onto the framework and forced his way in.

Similar episodes, an occasional voluntary effort to pack tighter in order to allow another one to slip in alongside, grumbles, growls, and threats all played their part in rearranging the bodies until the last one finally had a small bit of board on which to sleep. Later, it would be impossible for anyone to claim a fraction of the center deck because the milling crowd, once its members had identified themselves with their shelves, took possession in order to straighten out the kinks in their joints.

After a few minutes down in that pit of heat and stench and thirst, the prisoners felt the need of air and water. The man nearest the foot of the ladder was the first investigator. He cautiously mounted the rungs until his head reached the upper deck. His appearance there brought forth a wild roar and a rush of feet that were plainly evident to all those down in the well. As their colleague came sliding down the ladder in full haste, they saw the guard flushed with excitement and leaning over the edge and thrusting his bayonet in a threatening manner down the hatch. The expression on his face was inhuman, and the roars that he uttered were like those coming from a beast.

"What sort of thing is that? Can it be a man?"

"He just missed slashing Bill by an inch."

"That was a fine demonstration of real hatred."

"Or else he was frightened to death and let his fear run away with him."

"They are giving us a very cordial reception to Taiwan, I must say."

"We are in a different group of hands now. The navy that brought us up here turned us over to the army in Taiwan. It has the beginnings of a very nasty situation."

"It will get a lot worse before it gets any better."

No further attention was paid to the men below until sundown. The prisoners endured as well they could the disagreeable conditions that had been forced on them. Then the sun moved on so that its rays were no longer directed down the shaft, and the heat lessened slightly. But the thirst hung on. There were other demands on the human body that could not be ignored.

Accordingly, after sundown, another attempt was made to climb the ladder and locate someone who would heed the pleas of these below. Better fortune occurred that time.

Although the guard raised a similar commotion, it was the presence of the interpreter that permitted the transfer of the idea. He peered over the edge with the excited guard, and a hundred American voices, in no uncertain tone, blasted up at him: "Air! Water! Latrine!" Simple wants, and their granting might easily avoid greater problems later. That was obvious reasoning on the part of the interpreter.

"I will talk with the captain at once," he assured them as he ran off.

Finally, after ten minutes on deck, the joy of life began to return. It was not the attainment of great ends that made men take courage. It was the contrast that this new moment had with far worse conditions that must be endured.

The men milled about the deck, and their prying eyes took in the few sights that existed. Their vessel was anchored in a projection of the main part of the harbor. A number of similar derelicts were afloat nearby. From the air, such an array of ships should be a tempting target. The prisoners were careful not to display an unusual interest in anything they saw. Nor did they discuss any such matters at the time. They had learned long since to observe unobtrusively and talk with each other later. Comparison of notes came when they were back down in the pit, out of observation and hearing of the enemy.

"A ghost ship, to say the least."

"She will never operate. Wonder why we are aboard?"

"All the gear seemed to be removed."

"Not a sound has come from the engine room once we came aboard."

"Didn't see any crew. The only Japs appear to be the guard."

"It all looks bad to me."

Finally, someone summed up the situation that had occurred to each of the others but that no one had had the courage to mention. "I have an idea that those yellow bastards are going to keep us imprisoned on this hulk in the middle of the harbor for the duration."

That was the thought in the minds of all as they, in their greatly discouraged mood, tried to make themselves comfortable for the night. Every ear was strained during waking moments for the least indication of any sound from the ship's engines. None came.

The next day, impatience and uncertainty prevailed. A bucket of rice was lowered by ropes, and it required considerable courage on anyone's part to volunteer to distribute it. It was impossible to do that to the satisfaction of all. Accusations and arguments in heated terms were tossed about. Physical conflict was avoided by the interference of others. The guards eventually worked out a procedure for the prisoners, one at a time, to go up on deck for personal relief. It was like little schoolboys raising their hands for teacher to nod acquiescence for them to leave the room. A short period was permitted for the prisoners to stretch their legs on deck and to obtain a cup of water. Then came night again curling up on a crowded plank, and listening in the dark, listening for any encouraging sound.

Sometime during the darkness, the restless sleepers were jarred into wakefulness. The cause was not so much a sound as a sensation. Gentle at first, it was not clear enough for the awakened prisoners to identify it, but it could be only one thing. It increased in tempo. *Thump ... thump ... thump ... thump!*

Engines! The old hulk has come to life. We are on the move! each one said that to himself and then lay back in a more relaxed mood.

The run up the east coast to Karenko took more than a full day. It was good to get back on land again. The prisoners were lined up and started on a march of five kilometers to their camp. The road cut away through the forest of Orientals, who lined the sides and arrayed themselves over the banks and mounds that spotted the area. They seemed to be of all ages, all classes, and all conditions. Something new and different was crossing their life, and they did not seem able comprehend the fullness of its meaning. There was no display of emotion or animosity. Children, every one of which wore a uniform, and adults alike stared with interested eyes that appeared to be making an effort to bring to their befogged minds the realization of the situation in front of them. Was it apathy or mere composure? It could not be indifference or unconcern. They were completely cognizant of the conflict in which their nation was engaged. While they were unscarred as yet by the ravages of battle, their men had marched off to the encounter, and the news of astounding victories no doubt had been relayed to them— victories over the white man whom they were told to hate because he had always been arrogant and superior. Few of them had ever seen an

Occidental. Now, in front of them, suddenly, appeared proof of their armed prowess. They were stupefied, and their senses appeared dulled.

Many Formosans were scattered among the crowds that paralleled the route. An inexperienced eye finds it difficult to distinguish between Orientals. But the prisoners, in passing so many and so close, began to notice differences in dress and contrasts in facial appearance, unlikeness in pigmentation. Most readily identified, of course, were the hill people, the aborigines, with their rougher texture and fierceness of mien. The spectacular tattooing, a broad band of blue from ear to ear across the mouth of the women and a narrow stripe down the center of the forehead and one across the chin of the men, assured that determination.

"How much farther is this place, I wonder?" questioned one of the marching prisoners.

"I hope not much. I'm about all in from this heat and carrying this bundle," a colleague replied.

"Its only another kilometer, just beyond that ridge," a third prisoner announced. There was always some one who knew all the answers and had categorical replies for any question, which only too often proved false.

"How the hell do you know? Ever been here before?" asked a voice in disgust.

"Oh, I heard it on the boat coming up here," the erudite one announced in his defense. "These barracks where we are going were originally built as a Presbyterian mission," he added in a display of ego.

Several of his colleagues looked at him and merely grunted to announce their contradiction of the information given. To them, the statement was obviously a slipshod remark. However, others who heard gobbled up the information as sound fact. And because they had something to pass on to others, which would enhance their prestige as pundits, they would never be convinced to the contrary.

In time, the column arrived at a brick wall ten feet in height, which each one of the Americans confided to himself was similar to the enclosure around the state penitentiary back home. Large wooden double doors were swung back to make the only opening through the wall. A sentry box stood adjacent. Several armed soldiers lolled about.

The Americans shuffled through the aperture, and something psychologically was taken from them, which they could never regain. Personal freedom, contrary to their will, was exchanged for a melancholia of the mind and soul. When the gates slammed closed behind them and the four walls of the compound encompassed them, a sudden realization of the meaning of freedom struck them all. For time immemorial, men have willingly sacrificed their lives that they and others might enjoy the benefits of freedom. But those whose freedom has never been jeopardized are too prone to neglect its implications and an understanding of all that it means. They become soft and consider that condition as their right. The holiday orator who tosses about references to that state of life merely bores them.

Those men who now had that freedom of thought and action summarily denied them quickly awakened to that distressing fact. It was as though a thick black curtain had dropped between them and their liberty, which had always been taken for granted. That privilege that was no longer theirs, that endowment that permitted them a vast measure of independence became, in a moment's time, a condition of life of undreamed value. It had been rudely and unceremoniously destroyed.

Time did not permit meditation or introspection. The column was marched directly to the little parade ground and arranged in an open formation. Each prisoner was ordered to strip and lay his clothes and meager possessions in front of him. It was a cloudless mid-August afternoon; the very sun, relentless and ruthless, seemed to have joined in a conspiracy with the enemy to make life for the prisoners most unbearable.

A number of Japanese soldiers clustered around the end man of the front row, where they held a noisy powwow. When they had evidently settled the subject under discussion, they examined each of the items lying in front of the prisoner. Pockets were turned inside out; hat linings were ripped out; soles of shoes were pried open; papers were scrutinized and tossed aside; seams of clothing were examined.

While that was going on, each American watched with the greatest care in expectation of learning something of which he might take advantage. Additional information was gained as the inspectors moved from one prisoner to the next. The process was similar, although the items often differed. A cigarette holder delayed the inspection while each of the members of the guard held it up and peered through it. There was something most, in their minds, mysterious about that strange object. When a roll of toilet paper was discovered, it had to be completely unrolled to assure the little yellow men that no detrimental writing had been placed on any of the sheets. A pocket lighter was an unknown quantity and had to be demonstrated by the owner. It was, thereupon, confiscated. Finding the name of a Japanese written in a small note-book was a disturbing situation to the enemy. It developed into an episode that was beyond the jurisdiction of the enlisted inspectors, and an officer had to be summoned.

A multitude of questions were fired at the prisoner and then asked over again. It only stopped when the officer became exhausted from his effort to discover something sinister behind that simple entry in the notebook. The document was confiscated and taken to headquarters for further study.

During the time that the inspectors were processing the prisoners, one after another, the nude men stood in the hot sun, waiting for the completion of the activity. Objects in pitifully small numbers were found that were objectionable to the Japanese and were confiscated—matches, lighters, flashlights, pocketknives. As the guards proceeded, they became more careless and overlooked or forgot to confiscate the same items that they earlier had felt obligated to take up.

Finally, each pair of shoes was tied together, and all were tossed on a pile. Wooden clogs appeared, and each of the prisoners was ordered to pick up a pair for his own use. The exhausted men were then permitted to dress. After the completion of this task, the hapless and thoroughly disgusted Americans were required to line up in military formation to listen and give heed to the first harangue of the camp commander.

Blake pulled a cigarette from his pocket. It was long and dark and called a "lavendera" in the Philippines because it was the favorite of the cigarette smoking washerwomen. He reached in his pocket for a match and then remembered the search a short time ago. Looking around, he noticed an electric lighter attached to a socket in the wall.

"How do you like that? They take our matches but are considerate enough to provide lighters." He walked over to the attachment and inspected it. "It sure is a cheap piece of junk, all right. Probably won't last long," he grumbled. In spite of his efforts, he could not make the lighter operate. After several attempts he tossed it aside and complained, "Busted already."

"All right, all right, have a match," Cameron called to him after he'd observed Blake's effort and his disgust.

"Where the hell did you get them? I thought the Japs had taken them all up," Blake said as he accepted the small box of matches and lit his cigarette.

"One of those things. They looked but didn't find them," Cameron replied, as he pocketed the matches. He then turned to his cot and began to inspect the bedding preparatory to making it up for use later.

"Looks like we'll have to find some straw," Ashley announced when he noticed Cameron holding up a bed sack to contemplate it.

"I guess so," he returned. "But what do you make of this?" he asked, spreading an unbleached muslin sheet over the cot for the others to see. A large number of small sections had been sewed together in order to make a sheet of proper dimensions.

"They must be hard up for cloth," Sykes commented. "It seems that they used all the scrap ends from the mill to make sheets."

Paul had been mildly amused at the conversation and the display of the sheet. In a spirit of levity he said, "I shall be very interested tonight to observe the six-foot Blake keep his feet curled up under a five-foot sheet."

All the prisoners were enjoying a light laugh at Blake's expense when, suddenly, the door was roughly thrown open by an armed sentry, who stomped into the room, followed closely by the interpreter.

The two looked about and sniffed. "Who smoke?" bellowed Pussy.

Since Blake still held the lighted cigarette stub in his hand, it was difficult for him not to admit that it was he. After all, there had been no rule issued against smoking, and there was the lighter that he'd used, even though it may have been out of order at the moment.

So, somewhat sheepishly, Blake held up his hand to show that he had the cigarette and mumbled, "I'm smoking."

"Where get light?" questioned the interpreter.

Blake started to point to the electric lighter. But before he could say anything, Pussy cried out, "No light, no electricity. Must have match. Where get?

Now Blake was in an embarrassing situation. The chagrin on his face told of the mortification he was suffering. He did not have a sufficiently agile mind to quickly speak up in his defense. Paul realized that the matter was probably not of a serious nature, so he reloaded a broad grin that Blake could not fail to see.

As no words came from the culprit, Cameron felt honor bound to assume the guilt. "I found a match on the windowsill and lit his cigarette with it," he replied to the interpreter's query. He felt that would be a more satisfactory defense than to admit that the inspectors had failed to discover his matches when they'd searched him, and it might save him the box of matches he had. Undoubtedly he would find many uses for them in the future.

Pussy sputtered and eventually announced, "Captives must not have matches. It will be punished. Maybe burn down house, and that very bad." Having covered the situation without embarrassment to himself, he took a hurried look around the room and departed, followed by the guard.

Ashley was restless. He sauntered over to the window, leaned on the sill, and stared out. "Not much space to move around," he commented.

"Not going to have much joy out of this," Blake contributed from his cot as he turned and looked out the window.

"This close confinement depresses me," confided Ashley.

Paul spoke up. "We have a great problem on our hands, not only to maintain our own morale, but also to help others that will need all the aid we can give them."

"I'm going to have all I can do to get myself through this mess. The others are no worse off than I am," Blake announced.

"Hey, look!" Ashley called, pointing out the window. "There is a pile of rice straw over in the far corner, and some of the POWs are getting their bed sacks filled. Come on, let's go!"

Each of the prisoners had long ago learned the creed of "get mine." Many thoughtful ones resented the necessity of rushing after anything that was being distributed, but they eventually had to follow the example of the majority out of self-defense. Too often, the early arrivals had taken double portions, and the stragglers were left without any. So, when Ashley gave his warning cry, all the others sprang up, grabbed their empty bed sacks, and started for the straw pile. That is, all except Paul.

Nevertheless, he did not tarry longer than necessary but merely allowed the others to precede him, and then he hastened along so as not to be squeezed out. When he reached the porch, which ran around the barracks, he showed that he had not completely lost his altruistic spirit; he called to his colleagues still in the building to come and get straw for their beds.

Shortly thereafter, the five men were again back in their tiny room arranging their cots for the coming night's slumber. A certain amount of rearranging of the long strands of rice straw inside the sacks was necessary in order to prepare the mattress as even and smoothly as possible. That operation was not a new one to those soldiers, who had lived under field conditions many, many times. So they laid the sacks on the cots and quietly manipulated the straw inside until the smoothness desired had been obtained. But Blake chose a different method. With complete lack of thoughtfulness for the others, he violently and noisily beat and shook his mattress to attain from the dry straw the results that he was after. The billowing dust from the dry straw that was given off in the room made the others choke and sputter and left a light deposit of dirt on everything.

"Hey, hey! Take it easy, Blake," cried out Sykes. "You are making an awful mess of everything."

Cameron scowled. There were several things toward which he was most unsympathetic. One was the lack of respect for the rights of others. Another was the display of inefficiency below the capabilities of the offender. Consequently, the neat little temper that he possessed and could display on appropriate, though seldom occasions was about to flare up. Fortunately, he was seated on his cot facing toward Paul and away from Blake. As the expression on his face became more indicative of the rising passion within him, Paul, wise to the ways of men, looked Cameron straight in the eyes, smiled, and shook his head as a request for Cameron to do and say nothing.

"Something should be done about supper soon," Ashley said. "It's getting along about that time."

"They're not going to feed us," grumbled Blake, "unless they give us a bowl of those rice sweepings again."

"Some of our meals on the ship up from Manila were rather respectable," Paul reminded the others, endeavoring to give a more optimistic thought to the discussion. "It may be that they have had a change of heart for the better."

"Not these Japs," Blake countered. "We were in the hands of the navy then, but we are back with the army now."

"There's no doubt that the navy is a lot more decent than the army," Sykes broke in. "They seem to have more of the white man's point of view."

"There is no doubt about that," Paul contributed. "The navy is much more cosmopolitan. They move around all over the world, see things, and meet other people. Consequently, they have a much broader viewpoint and are more sympathetic toward Western civilization."

"The army is most provincial; I have learned from my experience," Cameron announced. "They have all the oriental ruthlessness and brutality because they have always lived in a most restricted atmosphere. They are completely endued with the old traditions and culture of Japan—"

"Medieval," offered Paul.

"And to that, they have added a tremendous superiority complex because of their successes over the Chinese," Cameron continued. "Chauvinism and ego make a mighty bad combination for any one that gets in their way."

"That's us!" Blake declared.

"From what little I know about it, I have always had the impression that the navy did not want to get tangled up with this war, at least at the present time," Paul stated. "But the army was bullheaded and had the political power to push over its viewpoint."

"Ah, business afoot," cried the alert Ashley, who had kept an eye on the window.

The others in the little group peered out and saw a train of prisoners coming from a small building across the parade ground. Each was carrying two buckets, new and clean wooden buckets, and a light mist of steam gently floated up from each.

"Rice!" exclaimed Blake. "It's about time."

Long before the bucket carriers reached the barracks, every one inside had learned of the pending event. Word of that nature travels like lightning. In a few seconds, the prisoners had lined themselves on the porch. Animals of a lower classification would have rushed toward an oncoming supply of food; should the human animal be denied that joy because of a fetish commonly known as civilized refinement? Those were moments when only the fundaments of life predominated, and food was a commanding factor. In any event, that was true in the minds of most; there were several who refused to succumb to appetite, however.

The food bearers, who had been arbitrarily selected by the Japanese authorities from the prisoners at one end of the barracks and hurried over to the kitchen, strained at their task of carrying a heavy bucket in each hand. Nevertheless, in their impatience, they made as much haste as their strength and their legs permitted. A tremendous urge for speed possessed them. Placing the loads in jeopardy, each ran or dogtrotted or lengthened his stride in what appeared to be a mad effort to outdo his colleagues or to conserve a few seconds of time. Several watchers sprang forward from the porch and seized some of the pails in an impetuous desire to curtail any delay.

Exhausted and puffing, the carriers set the cargo down in the halls and, between efforts to catch their breath, transmitted the instructions given them at the kitchen: "Divide up. Twenty-five men to a bucket."

The noise and confusion that followed were amazing! Bare feet pounded on the wooden floor; clogs clanked on the boards; porcelain bowls and aluminum spoons were rattled and dropped; calls and shouts reverberated through the dark corridors; angry threats and violent gestures were commonplace. Frenzy of a delirious sort had seized and given impetus to the excitement. Above the din were heard the overtones of some few attempting to establish a semblance of order: "Line up! Only twenty five to a bucket! Move over to the next line."

The precious time that had been saved in the haste to reach the barracks was dissipated and cast aside many times over. To agree on who was to serve the food to each group was a matter of magnitude. Many declined, on that popular basis, "Let George do it!"

Others felt that a personal advantage might be gained, so they quickly grabbed the flimsy little ladles for the liquid and the small wooden paddles for the rice. With those implements they stood guard over the buckets until lessening clamor indicated their services were acceptable or until they were rudely displaced. The final decisions rested on leadership, the trust that the group had in the server, or on strong-arm procedure.

The intensity with which nearly every pair of eyes observed minutely the distribution of the food bespoke of distrust and a fear that another might gain an advantage, insignificant that it may be. But if one suspected that a few grains of rice or a spoonful of liquid more than a neighbor received fell in his bowls, there was no thought of altruistically returning the surplus. The favored one quickly rushed to his room like a dog with a bone and huddled in the corner with his back to the others until he could consume his portion without the gaze and comment of his fellows. Hazards and uncertainty had restricted man's thoughts to self, and an unspoken philosophy seized him: *All for me, and none for you.*

Paul and Cameron had sauntered from their room together and discovered themselves rushed by the confused crowd into a position in the middle of one of the groups. They stood quietly in the columns of hungry men, observing with concern the actions of the other prisoners. One of the men near the front, urged on by those near him, picked up the rice paddle and prepared to serve. No objection was raised. He was accepted as satisfactory. Another prisoner casually picked up the soup ladle with all the gesture of one trying to be helpful. No sooner had he done so than another of somewhat greater stature rushed to him and violently jerked the ladle out oft his hand. After filling his own bowl, he stood ready to serve the others as they came along. It was obvious that, if he were to be supplanted, it would require physical effort, and no one seemed inclined at the moment to dispute his authority.

Cameron frowned and muttered something under his breath, but Paul diverted him with a nudge and a nod of his head, which was, in effect, a request for him to look where Paul indicated. Farther down the hall, another soup server seemed to be struggling with the contents of his pail. Each time he raised the dipper a longish bare bone persisted in being a part of the contents, and each time the server poured the filled ladle back into the pail. Without chagrin or embarrassment, he showed an intensity of purpose not to let the bone get away from him and into the bowl of one of his colleagues. Paul smiled, and Cameron emitted a snort of disgust. Such persistence had its reward, however, for when they were back in their own room a few minutes later, they saw that same person pass by in the hall with the odd-shaped and completely meatless bone protruding from the top of his bowl.

"The cat caught the canary, see." Paul chuckled.

"And he lost my respect over a small, useless bone," replied Cameron.

"It goes to show the whole thing is mental," Paul stated.

"To think that it is only the beginning, and so much lies ahead."

Shortly thereafter, a wild bellowing from outside brought the prisoners to a state of alertness. They looked out of the doors and windows and observed a Japanese guard, a bayoneted rifle resting on his shoulder, who was calling and beckoning all those in his vision to come out.

The several Americans who were already strolling about were called to him, they lined up in formation. What was wanted became obvious to all the others as they sauntered. The few that passed near received a push or a kick to hurry them along. The urge to hasten suddenly ran through the crowd, and in the course of several minutes, the guard had, by gesticulations and growls, accomplished his purpose of lining the prisoners up in a double rank.

Five minutes later Pussy strolled down from the headquarters building and stationed himself in front of the formation.

"What a man!"

"A fine example of who should not wear a uniform."

"A ribbon clerk gone soldier."

"Imagine a pimp like that having the upper hand over us."

"God knows how long it may last, too."

Pussy threw back his head. His horn-rimmed glasses were the predominate feature of his face. He cried in a nervous voice, "The captives will now come to the attention."

Nothing happened; there was no response.

Pussy cleared his throat and called out some words in Japanese in his high-toned voice. The man with the shimmering steel blade brought about action where a mere voice was powerless. The guard tore down to the front rank and thrust his fist into the face of the nearest prisoner. His rifle butt was slammed down on the foot of the adjacent American. With his bayonet he made a thrust at another hapless prisoner, staying his action at the last instant. As he administered his violent punishment he shrieked the command, "*Kiotsuke! Kiotsuke! Kiotsuke!*"

The loud screaming brought additional sentries from the guardhouse, but by the time they arrived, the men in ranks were standing quietly at attention.

"The captives will pay the strictest heed," Pussy admonished his listeners. "They will form by letters, starting with 'A' at the right. Rearrange yourself!"

While the Americans shuffled about to take their places in alphabetical order, Pussy moved over to the right flank and began to check the ranks accurately from a roster that he carried with him. Without interested cooperation from the prisoners, Pussy's task required a much longer time than it should have. Most of the disgusted men refused to give any more aid in expediting the formation than the minimum required by the bayonets that mingled among them.

After Pussy was satisfied with his efforts, he again took his position as a commander. "Now we form skuds," he called.

"What the hell is a skud?" asked many of the men who stood in font of him.

"I believe that he means squad," came an intelligent answer from the midst of the ranks.

"Count twenty-five. That will be skud one."

The counting went awry, time and again. There was no direction. The men in the front rank counted the full number of twenty-five; those in the rear did the same. Some stepped forward and counted down to their position by pointing their finger and saying a number for their own benefit as they carried the countdown themselves. Some added to the confusion by telling others what to do or what their number should be. It was usually resented by the one being instructed. Obviously, nothing would be accomplished because of perversity, lack of interest, and stupidity. So Pussy had to adjust the matter in person; he went to the scene of commotion and counted thirteen in the front rank and twelve in the rear.

"Skud one. *Dai ichi ban*, it will be spoke of," he announced.

Laboriously, but never wavering, the interpreter arranged one squad after another. When the Japanese soldiers caught on to the procedure, they rendered considerable rough-handed assistance; and promptly taking the cue, the prisoners showed more interest in getting the matter at hand accomplished so that they might be dismissed.

"Again, pay the heed!" Pussy directed the prisoners when he had finally finished with the arrangement of the squads. "*Tenko* will you call to reveille, and the retreat will occur here like this. When time comes, all will hurry and make formation. Very serious. The officer will come for tenko. Each prisoner in front at right will be skud leader. He will bow to officer and say number of skud and how many. Soon, you must learn commands in Japanese, so no English will be spoke. Tomorrow, more instruction. Dismiss."

The Americans hurried off to their rooms, relieving their emotions by cursing and laughing and discussing with their colleagues the recent proceedings. It was a tremendous relief for many to be able to flop down on their cots and stretch out in quiet rest. Emaciated bodies tire easily, and one never knows when he may be called on to exert himself. Consequently, relaxation, as it might be permitted, became a prime consideration.

"They could at least give us a pillow," Blake complained.

"We all have pillows. Haven't you got one?" asked Ashley.

Blake raised up from his prone position and looked at the other cots and the four prone bodies.

"There's yours on the floor," Sykes said as he pointed to the spot where Blake's pillow had fallen behind the head of his cot.

"That's no pillow," Blake said as he retrieved the object. "Nobody could sleep on a thing like that. It's harder than a rock."

"It sure is a rock all right," Sykes agreed. "I wonder what it could be filled with."

"Rice husks," answered Cameron. "Take your fist and punch a hollow in it to lay on."

"That will help," Paul stated. "But at best it will put your head and neck to sleep by cutting off the circulation in a short time. The safest thing to do is to tear it open and take about half of the hulls out. It will still be hard, but it will be more flexible."

Suddenly, the harsh tones of a bugle just outside the windows jarred the prisoners from the actions and meditations in which they were engaged. Its notes were as disagreeable to the ears of those who heard it as were the rasping sounds of the enemy soldiers voices.

"Now what in Christ's name are the monkeys up to?" Blake angrily asked of no one in particular.

"Tenko. Remember, Pussy warned us," answered Paul quietly.

"We had better go. They want us to line up fast," Sykes announced as he leaped off his cot, hurriedly picked up his cap, and almost trotted out the door.

"What's he in such a big hurry about?" Blake asked, but no one replied.

The first tenko formation was a stormy one. Scurvy was the officer in attendance. While he had been present at the opening ceremonies, he had remained in the background. He had all the appearance of a mean, untrustworthy rascal, and the sores on his face were so repulsive to the Americans that he was immediately dubbed with names just as abhorrent as his looks. He was indeed fortunate to get off so lightly as to be called Scurvy.

He strutted down from headquarters and was preceded at a considerable distance by an armed guard, while in his train came the sergeant major, the sergeant of the guard, and two other guards. The purpose of the leading soldier was to assure the officer that all the prisoners would be standing at attention properly when the representative of the emperor should arrive.

Consequently, the first arrival began to bellow, "Kiotsuke! Kiotsuke!" long before he reached the formation. His commands were complied with after a fashion by the Americans, but their general disinterest brought a roar of disapproval from the guard. He was on a mission of vital importance and had only a very short time to accomplish it. He therefore took the quickest means available to obtain results, which was to hasten down the front rank, shrieking unintelligible commands and pushing and slapping. Such treatment was apparently quite orthodox and agreeable to the lieutenant, for he anticipated it as a matter of course.

The officer took his post in front of the first squad and took up a conversation with the sergeant major. At the completion of the discussion the subordinate saluted stiffly and cried his reply of understanding, "Hai! Hai!" He turned and faced the other squads and commanded, "*Yasumi!*"

Receiving no response—and that was to be the only time that the prisoners did not respond with alacrity at that command—he proceeded to demonstrate what the word meant. He called out the word *kiotsuke* and took the position of "attention" and then the word *yasumi* and stood "at ease." After he had repeated the instruction twice, there was no further wonderment on the part of the Americans.

Upon the completion of the instructions, the officer spoke to the leader of the first squad in English. "Report!"

The commander rendered a courtesy salute and replied, "First squad, sir. Twenty-five prisoners. All present."

There was no reply or movement on the part of the lieutenant. The seconds moved on, and his face changed slowly to a hardened and dangerous-looking appearance. Then he spoke to the sergeant of the guard and moved on to the second squad. The sergeant and the two privates that accompanied him knew no English, but their instructions had been, evidently, to teach the prisoners in quick fashion the Japanese method of making a report. The ugly tone of the noncommissioned officer's instructions in the vernacular was not conducive of the best results. He bellowed and demonstrated the Japanese bow. He shrieked and illustrated a hand salute. He yelled and uttered commands. Confusion in the ranks grew pronounced. Those farthest away from potential danger grumbled and cursed under their breath, while those within reach of the sergeant quivered and awaited the blow. The angry man raised his hand and slapped the first three prisoners with violent cuffs. One of the privates felt called upon to administer like treatment to several others farther down the line. It must have been that the sergeant felt his inadequacy to cope with the situation, for after he relieved his irritated feelings by physical contact, he seemed to calm down. With a face-saving gesture he moved away from the squad, eyeing them intently with angry mien as he muttered some words that only he understood.

The sergeant followed the lieutenant, one squad in rear, and at each group he proceed to handle several of the prisoners roughly while he barked out his instructions. Toward the end of the line, his efforts at severe treatment tapered off, partly because he was becoming exhausted and partly because the Americans were rapidly reaching the broad conclusion as to what was desired.

Finally, the hectic period of indoctrination drew to a close. The officer took a position in front of the formation. The sergeant major stood midway between the two. There was anger in the hearts and hatred in the souls of the helpless men as they stared at the symbols of the enemy power and meditated over the character of the inhuman treatment that had been administered. Men accustomed to sportsmanship and fair and honest dealing were, once again, completely amazed at the depraved advantage taken of an unequal situation.

During the short time the foe stood before them in arrogance, the Americans sized them up. What they saw was the accumulated racial hatred of generations and the exalted ego that had resulted from their sudden release from suppression under what they thought was the white man's insolence and presumption; then with the saving grace that often rescues the Occidental from peril, they laughed! It was a silent and invisible laugh that shook their souls like the ague. They laughed at the smirks on the faces of the enemy; at the knowledge that someday the situation would be reversed; at the squatty, little, unimposing figures in front of them; at the untidy and ill-fitting uniforms and the odd-fitting caps with short stripes of the same material that dangled down in back like fly deflectors; and at the officer-of-the-day's shoulder sash of wide red and white stripes and the sergeant's brassard of narrow strips of the same colors.

The noncommissioned officer barked the command of attention. The prisoners, only too happy for an early termination of the ceremony, smartly complied. Then the sergeant faced the officer and saluted.

He again turned toward the formation and sounded off the command that would always gladden prisoners, for it meant the termination of all things prisoner. "Yasumi!"

Most of the prisoners quickly repaired to the barracks because they wanted to get out of sight of the detested enemy. Some few, however, feeling the need of fresh air and limited exercise, remained outside to walk about the tiny parade ground.

As the sun began to slide down behind the high mountains some miles off to the west and the shadows started to finger their way along the ground, the guards felt that it would be safer to have all their charges inside. Consequently, they took their own peculiar method to put that thought into effect. At a signal from the corporal in command at the time, the sentries went on a rampage. They rushed at the men who were strolling around the compound with menacing gestures from the bayoneted rifles they carried, shouting weird commands at the same time. Whether the Americans understood what was meant or whether they felt greater safety lay within the shelter of the barracks was not quite clear to their colleagues who were observing through the windows.

Nevertheless, the strollers made rapid progress toward the building and, with good fortune, were able, without mishap, to reach that protection from the gathering storm.

Cameron and his roommates were busily engaged in preparing their beds for what they expected to be a comfortable night's rest.

They had had a hard day and were physically and mentally exhausted. Early as it was, no one resisted the temptation to give up the day's activity and to crawl into his beds of straw.

While he was tying up his mosquito net, Cameron glanced over to Paul and noticed that the older man did not possess that article of comfort. He turned in the other direction and saw that each of the others in the room were equipped with one.

"Say, Paul," he called out in a voice sufficiently loud for all to hear, "haven't you got a mosquito bar?"

"No, Cam, I have not," Paul replied almost in a whisper as though he were embarrassed for the others to hear him.

"But, you got one at Tarlac when we had that row with the Japs to get them for us, didn't you?" Cameron inquired, raising his voice louder.

Paul looked at him in amazement because of the unnecessary loudness with which his friend spoke and, in a very quiet tone, said, "Yes, I had one, but somebody evidently wanted it worse than I did. So they took it out of my bag on the boat ride up here from the Philippines."

"Well, Paul, since you have none," Cameron continued to say loudly, "you must take mine. I am much more able to stand up under mosquito bites than you."

"Not a chance, Cam. I am tougher than you think. Thank you just the same, though."

In a few seconds Paul sidled over to Cameron and whispered in his ear, "Why were you shouting in such a loud tone? It was so out of keeping with the need that you must have some good reason."

Cameron smiled back at him as he replied, "You bet! I sure did have a good reason."

Before the two friends could have further discussion on the subject, the rasping tones of a bugle sounded in the compound. "That must be Tattoo," announced Sykes.

"It's something to annoy us with," complained Blake.

Before the final tones of the bugle call had cleared the air, the Japanese guards came stomping into the barracks with a loud clatter of hobnail boots on the wooden floor and the bellowing of commands. They entered the end room, and from the intensity of the sounds that came through the thin partition, it was clear that the prisoners were being pushed around and their faces slapped.

Observant, Sykes, who had been casually looking out the window, saw the light next door that was shining out on the porch suddenly disappear. He sprang up and shouted, "Hey. They want the lights turned off. That's what they are after." Forthwith, he leaped toward the single drop cord that hung from the ceiling with a small bulb giving a dull yellow glow at its end and hastily switched off the light.

The others dove for their cots, and when the guards reached their door, all was quiet. Breathing hard from their exertions in the adjoining room, the guards looked in; snarled; and, finding little to complain about, moved on to the room farther down the hall, where they created additional commotion similar to that which had occurred earlier.

"Sons of bitches!" growled Blake.

When the lights throughout the building had been extinguished, the noise had subsided and the emotions that had occurred during it had come to rest. Cameron let his thoughts run over the events that had occurred since his arrival at Karenko. A feeling of restriction had engulfed him as soon as he had stepped inside the walled compound. A quick glance showed him the limited space in which he would have to live for some time to come. He was not possessed of any foolish optimism; he was too realistic to believe that he would be free the next day or the next or the next. The outside world was closed to him, and he felt the loss tremendously. Now, only that which was contained in the little square bordered by the high brick fence would be his to draw on for existence. To know that he was helpless and unable to improve his position by any effort on his part was only one step removed from despair and hopelessness.

But Cameron was not the sort that would ever give up. He would accept conditions from day to day and from hour to hour, meeting them with courage and trying to soften their impact. At that early stage, he was untried and undeveloped; yet there existed no reason to believe that he could not draw upon hidden resources, like any other normal man, to find sustenance that would carry him through his time of trial. If he were asked for his plan of thought and action, doubtless he would flounder in an effort to produce one. It required a trial by fire to develop latent qualities that every man should have but only a very few are able to exhibit by maintaining their dignity and respectability. The casualties under those adverse circumstances could be great, unless each one produced within himself an intense desire to strengthen himself for the purpose of assisting those who were weaker. Nothing else in the lives of beaten men was of value!

Paul, too, was pondering over the new life, which permitted no initiative on his part and which resisted and buffeted him whenever he strove to maintain his position. There was no opportunity to advance; it was a real battle not to slip too rapidly. There was no physical succor or mental stimulation. A man would have to stand or fall on an intangible thing that he had in his soul. That and that alone could save him and, through his example, rescue those who were lacking in strength and power.

"It has been an interesting day," Paul whispered over to Cameron, who lay restless on the next cot but a few handbreadths away.

"These Japs are putting us in our position mighty fast," his friend softly replied. "They have got us down, and now they are going to stomp on us."

"That is not purely an oriental characteristic. However, I do agree with you that we will be suppressed if they can have their way."

"I am afraid that many will be unable to stand up under the continuous rough treatment that we can expect," Cameron said thoughtfully.

"Do you put yourself in that group?" Paul tossed at him.

"Never!" replied Cameron with determination. "It will be a tough life, but I'll be damned if I'll let them get me down."

"Quiet!" shouted Blake from the other side of the room, where he had been disturbed by the whispered consultation.

On the following morning, a short time after the breakfast rice had been distributed, the interpreter timidly came through the barracks, calling, "Everybody outside for attention to orders. The officer will speak."

"No use waiting to get bopped. We better get out there soon," Sykes declared and hurried out to his position in the formation.

"That fellow sure gets excited." Blake spoke from his cot, without disarranging his comfortable positions.

The others smiled but said nothing. They all watched out the window; and when most of the prisoners had formed ranks, they strolled leisurely out to their positions.

Several guards, with their bayoneted rifles held in their hands prepared for any emergency, paced slowly around but took no part. They were there just in case.

Ten minutes passed and then twenty minutes without any Japanese officer appearing.

"This must be some kind of a joke," one prisoner stated.

"They just want to let us cool our heels," someone else replied.

"Well, I'm getting fed up with just standing. We all should go back and let them yell for us again."

"He ought to be here any minute," said his colleague, tying to comfort him.

It was some considerable time later that the waiting Americans saw a waddling form come out from the headquarters building that stood on a small knoll beyond the fence about a hundred yards in front of them.

"It's Buddha," ran through the ranks.

"He is starting off on the wrong tack if he thinks he can pull this waiting stuff on me."

"So what! What are you going to do about it?" scoffed the man at the speaker's elbow.

"Kiotsuke!" The cry of attention came from a weak, high-pitched voice from the rear of the ranks. Pussy, somehow or other, had came up from the rear and, upon the approach of the lieutenant, had ordered the prisoners to assume a more respectful position.

Following a conference between the two Japanese in front of the formation, the interpreter spoke to the group. "The officer will now instruct you. Yesterday, everything very bad. Captives do not learn quick like Japanese soldiers. Must learn or very bad for you."

When he completed those opening remarks, Pussy turned and talked with his senior in the vernacular. At a nod from Buddha, he bowed and again faced the prisoners. "The officer say all captives must salute every time they see Japanese. If no hat on, will bow. If wear hat, then salute with hand. Other thing, must hurry learn Japanese commands. No English!"

That duty done, the interpreter turned toward the officer to listen to another set of instructions. Upon receipt of them, he once more addressed the formation. "The officer also say that, if more than one when Japanese come by, then first man call, 'Keirei.' All then will bow. Understand? The officer order, very important.

"Each morning when tenko come, captives will face Imperial Palace—like this." He took several steps over to a post that had been erected in the ground. It was painted white, stood about three feet high, and Japanese characters were inscribed on the side. "This is Imperial Palace direction. So all will face. When face this way, then new command, 'Sai-keirei,' will be given. Most respectful bow then." He illustrated by bending slowly from the waist until his torso was parallel to the ground, while his arms and fingers were extended stiffly along his sides. After holding the position for many seconds, he slowly and with attempted dignity raised to upright posture.

During that demonstration and issuance of instructions by the interpreter, the Americans' mass thought changed from contempt and ridicule to humor. The intensity with which the enemy endeavored to impress upon their prisoners a different and strange way of life could excite only merriment in those who were observing and listening.

"What are they trying to do, make Japanese soldiers out of us?" asked one.

"Rah, rah, rah, for the dear old emp!" whispered another.

"Damn if I am going to bow to an old hitching post," declared a prisoner.

"You better, or they will drill you with one of those bayonets."

"This is a serious matter with these Japs," a colleague cautioned.

"Why the hell bow to a post of the guy?"

"Well, the emperor may be out for a walk, and they couldn't know it and bow in a different direction each time. So they standardize it and always bow in the direction of the palace. That can't move."

"It's still a lot of baloney to me."

When the formation was dismissed, Paul said to Cameron, "Let us take a swing around the compound and see what there is."

"Sure. Come on. It's about time we were getting acquainted with our new home."

The space in front of the barracks was limited. It was only one hundred yards in one direction and two hundred in the other, or thereabouts. In a very short time, each prisoner would know by heart the exact yardage from one tree to another or from the end of the building to the stone steps that led to headquarters or from a certain mark on the ground to any other similar point of identification. Physical restriction brings about a mental restriction, and the most insignificant things to a man who has the world to caper over become items of great magnitude when he is confined to a few acres.

A small area adjacent to the building had been denuded of grass by the shuffling of many feet over a long period of time. Beyond, and extending to the walls of the compound, the grass had grown without interference. That plot was cut through to the headquarters building. Another path ran off to the flank and ended at the separate kitchen shack.

A number of trees studded the area—the dwarf benihi, hinoki, and the camphor laurel. They did not belong there; a higher altitude was needed for their fuller development. Yet they were thriving, doing the best they could on the fringe of their favored environment. Shrubbery, too, had been planted around the barracks and in appropriate spots by former occupants, long since departed. This makeshift garden was scrawny from lack of care but making a gallant effort at survival. There were hibiscus, hydrangeas, elephant ears, and stunted palms. Such a sight might have been a pleasant one under more favorable circumstances.

Now the trees and shrubs were just so many obstructions that had to be avoided in the walk around the compound. The ground, too, was none too even, and many stones lay about that had to be maneuvered around. Each one would eventually have a name and could be so identified by the prisoners as they discussed the results of their exercise with each other in the barracks later.

Paul and Cameron walked toward the end wall, the one through which they had marched when they first arrived. "I wonder how many guards they keep here?" Paul asked, and they both glanced toward the small guardhouse that had been constructed recently in the corner of the compound.

"Probably a great many, judging from the number that seems to be in our way all the time," Cameron replied.

"I suggest that we turn to the left here before we come too close to the guardhouse," Paul proposed.

"A good idea. The farther away from these people we keep, the better I like it," responded his companion.

They turned and moved parallel to the wall, but before they had taken many steps in the new direction, they heard a mighty howl from the enemy at the gate. They quickly stopped and turned to see the reason for the eruption. Some of the other prisoners who were strolling about had ventured close to the post of the sentry on duty at the gate. He was bellowing at two of them and motioned for them to approach him.

"Trouble ahead," announced Cameron.

"It looks like they walked toward the guard and didn't salute him," Paul analyzed.

"But they seem to have been plenty far away," Cameron reasoned. "I'm afraid that no distance is too far away to salute these people. It's a matter of whether they see you, not whether you see them."

As they spoke, the Japanese grew more violent in his tirade, and the two Americans who stood before him were evidently trying to offer an explanation. With that, the sentry, who had been holding his weapon at the "ready" position, thrust his bayonet forward as if he intended to stab one of the prisoners The man drew back to avoid the impact, which infuriated the guard—whereupon, he reversed his rifle and, with the butt, dealt his captive a severe blow on the chest. Then, walking up closer to the other prisoner, he swung his arm and struck him hard in the face. Not content with the punishment he'd administered, he marched the two inside the small building, where nothing further could be seen. But the howls of rage from the enemy were easily heard.

Vexed over their inability to render any assistance to their colleagues, Cameron and Paul resumed their stroll.

"They are going to be difficult to get along with," stated Paul.

"Yes. They have shown us more than once in the short time that we have been here that they intend to make our lot as hard as possible," returned Cameron.

"Of course, our initial reaction to everything they do will be one of hatred and a feeling that they are intentionally trying to beat us down," Paul thought aloud.

"Well, don't you believe that is true?" queried Cameron. "All their acts so far seem to point in that direction."

"Possibly true, Cam. But I was more or less talking to myself, trying to force myself away from the emotional upheavals of the moment and to make an effort to understand these people from their viewpoint. They not only fear us, but want to start us off with rough treatment to keep us in hand."

"You are a better man than I am, Paul, to even want to look into their viewpoint. Personally, I am pretty bitter after all that I have seen and experienced," Cameron proclaimed.

"You should be; we all should be. There is no dispute there," continued Paul. "At the same time, we may not be quite honest with ourselves if we do not admit that they could have a sincere desire to handle us right according to their standards, which of course we will have to learn before we can pass that judgment."

"Far be it from me to dispute what you say. It takes a lot of courage on your part to even want to try to understand them. Most of us are willing to put them down as animals with a mad hatred in their hearts for all white men," Cameron declared vehemently.

"I, too, believe that they have that feeling toward us. But I still want to find out their side and try to reason out why they have decided to treat us in this abominable fashion."

"Well," drawled Cameron, "I sort of would like to look into that also."

"Suppose we make a real effort to do that. At least it will give us same mental stimulation, and heaven knows we will need all of that we can get."

"Okay," agreed Cameron, "but on condition that we guard against working up any sympathy for them. None of this brotherly love stuff."

"Far from it," Paul agreed. "We will put it on the basis of an intellectual approach. "We can maintain our war-induced hatred for them and exercise every opportunity to follow our mission of doing harm."

Cameron shifted his eyes toward Paul at this apparently incongruous statement. Paul returned a blank stare, but each felt that he understood fully the attitude of the other.

"So, this is the kitchen," Cameron declared as the two drew up to the corner of the compound where that building was located.

"I doubt if it is safe to peer in," Paul said cautiously.

"Far be it from me to look for trouble," declared Cameron. "We will have plenty of time to learn all about the place."

"I understand that the Japanese have put some of our people in to learn how to cook rice and that we will have to take over the operation soon."

"There is probably no question about that," returned Cameron. "It's a cinch the Japs are not going to do any work for us. I am surprised that they even started us off with that so-called instruction."

"Undoubtedly they have their own methods that they want us to follow," Paul surmised. "And of course they will have to impress on us the most economical use of fuel."

"I think their primary mission is to show us how to make a kilo of rice expand into a huge cauldron full," Cameron said sarcastically.

"Well, here we are," Paul announced a few minutes later, "back where we started from. Shall we swing around again?"

"I would like to, but perhaps we had better not get too close to that guardhouse while the Japs are on a rampage."

"I agree. It will be much safer to keep as far away as possible. I see that all the others are carefully keeping out of the sight of the sentries there."

The two Americans went inside and stretched out on their cots. It was a pleasant relaxation to lie full length. Their bodies were weak and tired easily. They accepted that action of relaxation as a normal situation. They enjoyed its present tenure. There was no reason to consider whether or not it be a permanent privilege. The thought did not arise in their minds.

Paul dozed off in a light sleep after a little conversation between him and Cameron. His companion lay stretched out in a partial condition of comfort, idly turning over in his mind the conditions of the life to which he was now subjected. The tread, heavy though it was, that only grew louder as it came down the porch outside the window was completely lost to Cameron. The latter was too far away in his thoughts to hear that sound. It would not be long until he would develop an uncanny caution, awake or asleep.

"Grrrr!" A horrible growl came through the open window.

Without realizing it, Cameron impetuously sprang to his feet and faced the surly tones. A Japanese guard leaned partway in the window with a bayonet thrust forward in front of him. He grumbled loudly and gesticulated forcibly. Cameron stood unmoved, waiting for the tirade to subside. There was nothing he could do. He could not even understand all the dialectic expressions the guard used. However, there was no difficulty in grasping the meaning. The sentry was berating him roundly for lying on his cot—that was a certainty. The monologue grew more violent, and when the guard had worked himself into a frenzy, he leaped through the window and brought his rifle butt down hard on Cameron's foot. The American winced involuntarily from the shock, and he tightened up his muscles as though for some measure of retaliation.

Meanwhile, Paul had risen from his cot and stood quietly behind Cameron. When the blow came, Paul seemed to sense the intense desire of Cameron to strike back. So he reached with his hand where the guard could not see the motion and grasped the sleeve of Cameron's shirt. It was not with the intention of forcibly stopping him from any precipitous action, but more as a warning to Cameron to be on his guard and to control himself. The Japanese finally sputtered out his anger and, with a few mumbled expressions, left through the door and stomped down the hall.

"God! How I wanted to kill that little rat! I should have driven my fist right through his ugly yellow face."

"That would have given you personal satisfaction," Paul cautioned him, "but only for a few minutes. He would have cut you to pieces without further thought."

"There is no doubt about that," Cameron admitted." "And we must not overlook the fact that they are intentionally goading us in an effort to make us raise a hand against them. That would be an excuse to bayonet us."

"Yes, and one such disagreeable incident would reverberate all over the camp. All the others would be put in greater peril. So it behooves each of us to exercise the greatest care individually so that others will not be placed in greater jeopardy because of our actions."

"I'm surprised he didn't work you over, too, Paul, when he discovered you on your bed."

"One of those times when a man is lucky, I guess," Paul explained. "He was so busy with you that he saw nothing else."

"That is probably true. They are certainly one-track minded."

"We'll have quite a thrilling tale to relate to the others when they get back to the room," Paul commented, "even though it may at your expense."

Cameron grinned and nodded his head as he sat on his cot examining his instep where the blow had hit.

"How does it look?" Paul asked.

"He knocked a nice chunk of skin off," Cameron replied. "But I don't believe any bones are broken, although it is plenty painful."

"Let's walk down the hall to Doc's room and have him take a look at it."

"There is nothing he can do. He has no equipment—nothing."

"But he has a lot of experience and knowledge and perhaps the magic touch. He might be able to say whether or not a bone is fractured."

"Then what?" Cameron asked in a resigned tone.

"You never can tell. He might be able to influence the Japs to give it some attention."

A little later, after Doc had made an examination, he announced, "Cam, I doubt if there is a fracture. But one can not be certain without taking X-rays."

"That's so encouraging!" Paul commented. "But, Doc, what do you think we can do about medical attention for our people here?"

"It has worried me a great deal since we arrived," Doc admitted. "I have given considerable thought to it and have tried to discuss the matter with the Japanese through our interpreter. Each time, they have merely brushed us aside in a rather ugly manner and refused to talk about it."

"We are going to have a great need for attention with everyone is such bad shape," continued Paul.

"You may feel certain that I will push the matter with all my ability," Doc stated. "At the same time, I must avoid being too insistent, which would only build up their resistance."

"These are hard nuts to crack," Cameron said in a knowing manner. "They will resent any suggestions coming from us. The only way to put over anything we want is to drop a delicate hint and gave them the impression it was their idea originally."

"That is valuable advice, Cam," Doc admitted, "and I will make use of it. Somehow or other, we will swing them around to the side of at least some humane treatment."

"I am sure that has possibilities," Paul sagely announced. "The very fact that they have allowed us to live and have brought us up here and established us in a camp of some apparently permanent nature would indicate they intend to give us some livable treatment, although it amounts to only the barest essentials."

Cameron's humor had to exert itself, and he remarked, "You remember the admonitions that we have received a score of times from almost every Jap who made a speech to us—guard your health."

The others had to laugh at the recollection.

"Yes," Paul said, picking up the opportunity to enliven the conversation. "That remark about 'guarding our health' came from so many different sources it must indicate some little interest in our condition."

"Unless they want to fatten us up for a later, spectacular kill," Cameron tossed to the others with a good guffaw.

"I have been told that is a common expression among the Japanese," the serious-minded doctor declared, "just like some of our expressions, such as 'so long' or 'I'll be seeing you.'"

That night, after the lights had been turned out, Blake and Sykes and Ashley were enlightened and regaled with the events of the day. They, too, had certain contributions to make concerning their experiences.

Their whispered consultation must have disturbed others who were in no mood to be sympathetic toward conversations at that time of night. From the room across the hall came a loud "Quiet, please!" It was echoed by one of the occupants of an adjacent room, and then again down the hall: "Quiet!" "Quiet!"

From then on, the command became a standard part of the prisoners' vocabulary. It was called in meanness and sometimes in politeness. On occasion it possessed a jocund tone. But it was used constantly, in one or another of its delicate shades of meaning.

Sometime during the night, Blake was forced by personal necessity to get up. He had fidgeted for a long time, trying to overcome the requirement by sheer mental domination. But it would not work. Accordingly, he crawled out from under his mosquito bar with grunts and grumbles because his sleep was disturbed, slipped his feet into his wooden clogs, and thumped down the hall with little regard for the comfort of others.

Halfway down the passage, which ran the length of the barracks, a cross hall intersected. At that vantage point, the authorities had established what was known as the *benjo* guard. It consisted of two prisoners, a table and chair provided by the Japanese, and a scrap of paper and a stub of a pencil furnished by the Americans. The function of the guard was to record the name and number of each prisoner—it was so in any penitentiary and why not here?—who was bound for the benjo. The prisoners were obligated by instructions to pass that way and not to take the shortest route, and it was required of the guard to record each trip and scratch off the entry when the prisoner returned. The time was also jotted down, and if it grew unduly long, an investigation had to be made to assure that that all was well and no captive had escaped. The line of men to be recorded was long, and the urgency in any single instance had to be subordinated to the cumbersome checking method. The reaction from a rice and water diet required an abnormal number of trips to the benjo; the unsanitary conditions of the sort of life imposed on the prisoners made necessary additional excursions of an equally urgent but more distasteful nature.

The benjo at Karenko was a separate building close to the barracks and reached by half a dozen steps downward and a path of several yards. Heavy shrubbery spotted the restricted area between the two buildings; and a single dull yellow bulb gave sufficient light when negotiating the steps. Beyond that, one had to prowl in the dark and feel the way.

On that particular night, Blake made his way sleepily down the several steps and proceeded to his destination. Halfway, he was suddenly startled by growling. "*Kura!*" A guard stepped from the shadow of the shrubbery. His bayonet was extended in front of him. Blake had no knowledge of the words he used, but it was evident that the guard was bent on making trouble. More mean and guttural sounds pierced the night air.

Blake decided that the disturbance was being created because he had failed to salute the guard who had hidden behind the foliage— whereupon he bowed in the accepted manner, or so he thought.

The guard was not to be denied his opportunity, which was evidently self-made, to harass the prisoner. Blake's bow was unacceptable. It was not sufficiently stiff or formal; the arms were not properly arranged; the fingers were not straightened; his head was not correctly aligned.

Each of those criticisms was clearly impressed on Blake by the growls and motions of the Japanese soldier. In spite of Blake's need for haste, he had to remain there and listen to the guard's tirade.

Those already in the benjo remained in the security of the darkness. Those who were following Blake formed a line, fearful of passing him and the guard at that precarious moment.

After many minutes of uncertainty, the guard required Blake to stand off to the side at rigid attention. The next prisoner in line made a bow with the utmost precision. The guard paid no attention to him, and he passed on. In sequence, the others made a precise halt and bow in a very meticulous manner. The congestion was broken and the guard moved on back into the shadows.

Blake was left standing alone, a forlorn figure, with no knowledge of how long he might have to remain in that position. The word spread rapidly throughout the barracks. Most of the prisoners had been awakened by the screams of the sentry, and the tale of Blake's trouble was related by the returning men.

Sykes heard the story in the hall as he was moving along to the desk in order to check out. In his mind, he had already decided to exercise the greatest caution to comply with all the regulations he could recall. So when he passed along the walk between the two buildings and at the spot where Blake was still standing, he drew himself up very formally and executed his best bow. No sooner had he recovered than wild shrieks came from the shrubbery at his rear. The guard had moved over to the other side of the wall and had tricked Sykes into bowing in the wrong direction. The situation was so ludicrous that every one who had witnessed it was regaled with laughter, except Sykes, who had tried diligently to conform but had been caught in the meshes of the guard's artifice.

After breakfast the following morning, Cameron and Blake were alone in their room. It was a moment that Cameron had been hoping for over since his first night at Karenko. He wanted to do someone a favor, and he wished to penetrate the thoughts of Blake to better understand some of his actions.

"Say, Blake, what are you going to do with that extra mosquito bar you have?" Cameron casually inquired.

"Oh, I got a use for it," replied Blake in a mumbled voice.

"I thought perhaps I could talk you out of it," Cameron said.

"Well, I use it for a pillow. You have one already. I don't see that you need another," grumbled Blake.

"It's not for me, of course. I wanted to get it for—"

"I'll have to hang on to it," Blake interrupted. "It'll be just the thing to patch up mine if I should get some rips in it."

"You know that Paul has none. It is sort of tough on him to take the risk of malaria at his age," pleaded Cameron. "Maybe we can make some dicker. You have the only spare one in camp."

"But I would never be able to get another one. If something happened to the one I am using, I'd have no spare," Blake hedged.

"All right, all right, Blake," Cameron said as his ire rose. "What is the deal? What do you want for it?"

"I guess it is worth twenty bowls of rice," argued Blake.

"Let's see. Three bowls a day, seven days a week. That would be just about one week's rations that I would have to do without. Sounds pretty severe to me for something that you do not need and have two of anyway."

"Well, you asked what deal I would make. I need the rice to keep from starving," replied Blake.

"And somebody would have to actually starve to meet your terms. It wouldn't be of much use to him then," Cameron stated.

Blake shrugged his shoulders and said nothing.

"Okay! If you change your mind, Blake, let me know."

"You have the first option on it," the owner returned. As far as he was concerned, the subject was closed.

But not so with Cameron. He was not to be frustrated that easily. When he set about a definite purpose, he pursued it diligently until he had achieved his aim. Willing though he was to admit temporary defeat in his attempt to obtain Blake's possession, he realized that by persistence and shrewd trading, he could eventually achieve his purpose.

Dropping further consideration of the matter for the time being, he turned his thoughts to Blake's selfishness. How, Cameron asked himself, could one man refuse to help another under such circumstances? The normal thing would have been for Blake to give his extra net to Paul as soon as he discovered that Paul did not have one. That refusal was not like Blake. What had come over him? Why should he wish to hoard his possessions, limited though they were, when he had no need for them, and yet someone vitally required them for his very health? Had life under stringent conditions completely reversed the more important values of life? Had Blake succumbed to the baser instincts of human nature and thrown away the standards of respectability? How could he possibly respond to the requirements of a colleague in such a selfish manner? *If that is the criterion to be set here, in this close confinement, then we are in for very difficult times,* Cameron surmised, *times when men will snarl at each other and refuse to exhibit the attributes and qualities of decency.* It was difficult enough to contend with the enemy without having to battle each other for existence.

Some weeks later, Ashley was sitting on his cot examining a strange condition in his ankles and lower legs. "Say," he spoke to the room in general, "look at those ankles. They are puffed up double size."

"You have it, too, have you?" Sykes asked. "I've noticed it in my legs for the past couple days." He exhibited his feet to others in the room. They were badly swollen.

"What do you make of that?" Blake queried, as he glanced down to his own ankles.

"It is diet," announced Paul. "Probably a form of beriberi from eating polished rice and nothing else."

"Well, I haven't had enough rice to cause anything like that," declared Blake.

"Its running all through camp," stated Cameron. "I don't know what they call it, but Pete has it up to his hips. They are as large as elephants' legs. As a matter of fact, he is in the hospital now." Cameron referred to a room that the doctor had finally been able to persuade the Japanese to allot him for use by prisoners who were in such condition that they should be confined to bed. There were no other facilities, only beds in a separate room. The doctor was able to look after the patients, but he had no means for treating them.

"They took George there this morning," Paul reported. "He has something of the same sort, only it has worked up into the upper part of his body. To listen to him breathe sounds as though his lungs were full of water."

"Good God. What will be the outcome of that?"

"He will probably drown in his own fluid."

"You fellows are mighty cheerful," Ashley stated.

"I think you should go down and see Doc soon," Paul advised. "He might be able to tell you what to do."

Ashley did as Paul suggested.

The doctor took one look and said, "Edema. It is getting quite prevalent all over camp."

"But what makes the swelling?" Ashley asked.

"It's an abnormal accumulation of liquid," the doctor replied. He pressed his thumb into spongy flesh above the ankle. The imprint remained there for some time, a condition akin to that a sculptor would achieve by pressing a thumb into his moist clay.

"What can be done for it?" Ashley further inquired.

"About the only help I can give you is to tell you to lie in bed with you feet up. Your kidneys will take care of a lot of it."

"Gee, Doc, I have to go out to work with the others. Anyhow, the Japs would raise an awful row if they caught me on my cot."

The doctor smiled. He knew the problem, but this time he had a solution. "We had a conference with the authorities just this morning. Because of the prevalence of edema and other ailments, we convinced them that they were losing a lot of labor by not getting the patients well as soon as possible. So they agreed to remit lying on cots if I guaranteed it was essential. They gave me a batch of red tickets so each authorized person could have one pinned on him and the guard would not bother him. Here is one for you."

"Thanks, Doc. But I was wondering, do the guards know about this?" Ashley fearfully asked.

"Probably not, and the first ones will likely get worked over by them, although the lieutenant told me he would instruct the guards."

"It doesn't sound like a sure thing to me, but I will take a chance with the others."

At tenko the following morning, the Japanese corporal who had been placed in dictatorial control over the prisoners' embryonic medical facilities called out of ranks the worst of the walking edema cases. Through the interpreter, he issued to the doctor certain instructions, which were conveyed in too quiet a tone to be heard by the curious prisoners. However, they observed with the utmost intensity that strange procedure. Their serious mien at the expectation of learning about a cure for the ailment that was bothering most of them was suddenly transferred to suppressed mirth. The patients who had been called out of ranks slipped off their clogs, rolled up their trouser legs, and in bare feet marched around in the morning dew that covered the parade ground turf. The Imperial Japanese Army had discovered the cure for edema!

The camp commander's initial speech given to the prisoners on the day of their arrival at the Karenko camp contained many statements that gave grave concern to his listeners. Not the least of those were the expressions "loath to labor" and "you are not allowed to lead an idle life." At the moment of their utterance, a fear swept through the souls of the Americans. Impressment into labor organizations had long been anticipated by these prisoners of war. There were many reasons for them to resist that requirement, but two stood out in their minds. One was personal. It related to the distaste for the type of work that might be expected and to the physical condition of the prisoners, none of whom was in sufficient health for manual labor. Their lives were in jeopardy. The other objection was to giving any assistance to the enemy war effort. Which of those two, if either, was the more offensive to any was completely a matter of his conscience. If the personal predominated, it could be attributed, at least in part, to sick minds, a condition to which, under the circumstances, they were entitled. In any event, serious resistance or defiance to avoid aiding the enemy would immediately become a matter of personal consideration, because then a prisoner's life would certainly be forfeited without ceremony.

There were two bent reeds on which the prisoners hoped to lean as official arguments to counteract the eventual labor requirement. International convention prohibited forced labor from prisoners of their rank and position. The clause was clearly stated, but it was vague in interpretation. The Japanese government had not signed the convention, but the premier was reported to have stated in a radio broadcast shortly after the commencement of hostilities that his government would abide by the provisions of international law.

The other argument on which the prisoners hoped to preserve their position and security was that the group was composed of all the top senior grades of the captured Philippine defensive force. There had existed in occidental thought the belief that the military profession certain moral values. They were not circumscribed by national considerations but were ethical factors to be subscribed to until an enemy took the initiative of casting them aside. They embraced moral respect for an enemy soldier and the profession he represented; rejection of debased and contemptible actions; and the recognition of the honorable status of a prisoner of war. Should the senior officers camp be successful in having the enemy accept that contention, it would not only materially benefit the members thereof, but it might also vitally influence the type of treatment to be accorded the other prisoner camps under the control of the Japanese. While the senior officers' camp had no contact with the others, nevertheless, the effort of the commanders who comprised that group to have the white man's moral and ethical views prevail was the only possible way they had of rendering assistance to their recent subordinates.

It could not be expected that that obligation would be foreseen and steadfastly adhered to by all former commanders; time and space and weaknesses of the flesh would naturally militate against it. Only leadership of a stellar quality would maintain that position unremittingly.

Within a week after the prisoners had arrived at Karenko, the anticipated blow struck. One morning a tenko formation was called, and every American, except the few who had been detailed for duty in the kitchen, was required to be present. There were grumbles and comments of dissatisfaction at the harassment in being turned out of the relative comfort of the barracks, but a feeling of curiosity also permeated the group. What was up? No one yet had the least conception of what the reasons for the formation might be.

After the prisoners were lined up, the camp administrative detachment went into action. That was an organization divorced from the guards and subordinate to them. It was composed of Taiwanese soldiers who, because of their ethnical background, were not considered acceptable as frontline combat troops. Naturally, the Japanese guards from the empire proper looked upon them as inferiors and treated than accordingly. On that particular morning, at a command from the lieutenant, the little Taiwanese soldiers came running up to the front of the formation with their arms laden with hand tools. They quickly deposited their burdens on the ground and hastily lined up for further instructions. The already reduced state of morale in each prisoner dropped to a lower level. The specter of forced labor was about to become a reality.

"Sons of bitches!" growled Blake, setting his teeth and darkening his face with a deep frown.

Cameron, standing adjacent to him, uttered a heavy sigh, which proclaimed his resentment.

Ashley uttered, "Here it comes! They are going to work us to death now."

"Well, if they want us to work, I suppose we'll have to do it," declared Sykes. The statement did not enhance his reputation among his colleagues.

Only silent contemplation came from Paul.

The tools that all the prisoners stared at were crude and few in quantity. They consisted primarily of hand sickles and a type of tool new to the Americans, a long handle with a short but wide mattock-like implement at the end. It combined the qualities of a pick and a spade.

The tools were distributed equally among the several squads, and the prisoners were marched off to a plot of ground immediately outside the compound. Grass and brush had overgrown to a considerable extent. The Americans with tools were lined up at one end of the plot and instructed in procedure. The ground was to be skinned down and the refuse carried to a small gulch and piled up the therein. Thirty minutes would be the working time, at the end of which tools would be shifted to the other group, which meanwhile was to sit at the side and observe the first working detail.

"They are not going to make me work," declared Blake, who had seated himself in the shade of a small building.

"The Japs have presented us with a nice problem," Paul thoughtfully said. "We will have to get our heads together and work out some sort of action to stop this before it gets beyond our control."

"The way to stop it is to refuse to work," Blake cried vehemently.

Cameron followed up Paul's remarks. "I suppose the appropriate thing would be to have a committee with our interpreter go see the camp commander and try to convince him that this is a violation of international convention. We will probably have better ground to stand on and will not raise his anger if we go ahead today and follow his instructions." The latter remark was directed at Blake.

Apparently the same thought had occurred to Paul. "I am inclined to agree with you."

When the minutes slipped by after the noon meal and the prisoners were not called out for work, the Americans began to relax and develop the feeling that perhaps some miracle had happened to alter the situation on their behalf. When it became assured that no labor was to be performed, Cameron and Paul again discussed the possibility of having a committee present their case to the camp commander. So they arranged for a few of the squad leaders and their own interpreter to make a trek up the hill to headquarters. That particular spot, while enclosed by the high brick wall, was not really a part of the main compound, and only by stretching the regulations imposed on the prisoners as to the bounds permitted could it be said that that area was available to them. But in those early days, prisoners were artless and unsophisticated in knowledge of Japanese procedures.

No sooner had the little group placed their feet on the steps that would take them up the hill than the guard on duty at the building above them came charging down with flashing bayonet. The American interpreter, taken aback at that sudden display of hostility, sputtered out a plea to see the camp commander. His request made little impression on the guard, who, from a close scrutiny, appeared to be possessed with fear. It required some discussion to convince him that he was not faced with rebellion but only an innocent desire to talk peacefully with the captain. Ordering the delegation to remain where it was, he turned to go back to headquarters to inform the captain.

The commotion, however, had already brought Evil Eye out from his office. After the guard's report he walked down to the group of prisoners.

The interpreter spoke up and said in the vernacular, "Sir, we would like permission to discuss with you the labor we are being required to perform."

The camp commander was placed in a predicament; it showed very clearly from his actions and hesitancy. He refused to discuss the subject that had been presented and cried, "This is against the rules. You cannot come here. I will not discuss matters with you. Only the senior officer may present suggestions. He must first see the officer of the day, who will present the matter to me." With that dictum, he hurriedly turned and rushed back to the security of his headquarters.

After tenko that evening, the Japanese officer of the day was approached in accordance with the captain's directions, and the labor situation was presented to him. He squirmed and pressed his lips tightly together and would probably have fled from the conference if he had not been intentionally hemmed in by several of the prisoners. Consequently, he had to listen to the argument presented, although it appeared that he was paying little attention.

Upon the completion of the prisoners' presentation, he acted most reticently, simply saying, "I will consider."

"That looks to me like the good old American runaround," Cameron mentioned to the others in the group when the lieutenant had disappeared.

"Yes, just another brush-off. We'll get little help there."

A discussion with one of the Japanese officers was an event of great importance to all the prisoners. In their minds, such a contact invariably had the possibility of being a source of news, and news was exceedingly scarce where men were isolated behind a brick wall with armed guards constantly in attendance. Consequently, the outcome of the conference with the lieutenant was awaited with impatience. No sooner had the little group started back to the barracks than it was besieged by their associates, who were starving for information.

"What did he say?" "Did you get it fixed up?" "Tell us, quick!" "What did you talk about?" and many similar comments came from all directions.

It was impossible to reply to them all, and the gist of the conversation was relayed a number of times to those nearest at hand, to be passed on to others and then on again until the tale had become greatly expanded or lost all its meaning.

Cameron walked through the barracks to the rear porch that ran the length of the building. Along the outer edge was the long washbasin within its many faucets above it. The construction was of sufficient extent to take care of a goodly portion of the residents at one time. Cameron proceeded to open one of the taps and wash and refresh his hands and his face. While he was in that process, Ashley walked up to an adjacent spigot.

"Mighty cold water they have here," Cameron said.

"It is very refreshing," Ashley replied.

"Too bad we could not have had this on the way out of Bataan. Think of the lives it would have saved," Cameron reflected.

"Life is a funny thing," commented Ashley. "When we needed it so very badly, we couldn't get a drop. Now there is so much that no one cares about turning it off."

"It comes from the mountains over there. Did you notice the little filtration plant high up in that notch? You can see it only in daytime, but now there is only a light visible." Cameron looked in the direction of the high and rugged mountains a few miles westward and pointed a finger for Ashley to see the towering masses that were only dark shadows in the fast departing twilight.

"Those mountains are beautiful specimens even in the dim shadows."

"One gets quite a stimulation from them," agreed Cameron." I spend lots of time each day gazing at them and wondering what is going on up there."

"Maybe some day we will find out," Ashley spoke in a reverie. After a lapse, he continued, "I could be very happy up there all alone, with my freedom and no bayonets to push me around."

"Come on, old man," Cameron mildly reproved him. "Get hold of yourself. Things are not as bad as we think they are. Let's go on into our room."

When they entered, they heard Blake complaining. "That was an awful taste in the soup tonight. Nigh made me sick."

"I think it was that new bucket in which they brought the food over," explained Paul. "It was made of balsam wood and will give off that flavor for a long time."

"Well, I hope some other squad gets that bucket in the future. I don't want to taste that again," grumbled Blake.

"What did you mean by 'soup,' Blake?" Cameron chided him, referring to his earlier remark.

"It wasn't much, I admit," Blake said. "Green water!"

"There certainly was no nourishment in it," Sykes contributed. "I doubt if there were fifty calories in a whole bucketful."

"Green leaves boiled in water," reflected Cameron. "Say, Paul, wasn't that the same weed we find in the Philippines?"

"Yes, I am sure it was." Paul laughed. "*Kangkong.* And for that reason, I have been keeping very quiet about it."

"Why?" grunted Blake.

"You will probably find out only too soon," replied Paul. Then quickly altering the line of thought, he said, "It grows wild along the streams and only the poorest persons will eat it."

The inference Paul dropped to the others in his room came true only too soon. The prisoners had just turned out their lights when the first ones felt the dire effects of the greens they had eaten for the evening meal. They leaped out of bed and ran to the outside. Haste was imperative.

The benjo guard was at no other moment under such an emergency. First in pairs and then squads and finally by the score, the harassed men hastened out into the darkness. In a weakened condition, they returned only to discover it imperative some minutes later to repeat the process. Their great salvation was that none of the Japanese guards had selected that particular time to annoy them. Any such delay or interference would have been disastrous!

The summer days sped past. The war was far removed, both in space and understanding. No one knew or could find out the happenings just outside the wall, let alone the history that, in the making, saw the world torn asunder thousands of miles afar. August, September, October! Blustery weather roared in from the Pacific. Somewhere within hearing, the surf beat its heart out as it rushed and swept up on the beach to recede in a long swish that never died out before another thunderous roar brought in the next swell of the sea. The rise of the sun was a spectacle each morning. Many who had never noticed before that magnificent appearance of the life giver now stood in awe and wonderment. Because of the continuous cloudy condition of the heavens and their changing appearance from the effect of strong breezes, patterns of shades and colors overhead changed constantly, dull and timid at first and then bright and sprightly, finally piercing and rampant as the full glory of the bursting sun leaped out in splendor. The first indication in the early morning was a reflection on the clouds high in the west from the sun still low beneath the eastern horizon. Why the coloring first showed in the west mystified the inexpert observers. Then the rays of the sun would rapidly move onward, now hidden by cloud banks, now seeping around the edges of others, breaking into smaller fingers that then would later rejoin and again separate as they were strained by the floating formations. Dull grays turned to deep purples, which unhesitatingly altered into burnished copper, only to finally transform into a brilliant white gold.

The air grew progressively chillier as it was swept in from the sea by a disagreeable and penetrating wind. Men's breech clouts gave way to cotton slacks, remnants of the campaign. Some few possessed two, and they donned them both with a feeling of luxury because of the additional possession. Odds and ends of sweaters helped several. Prisoners were not too proud to wrap around them any additional rag they could get their hands on.

Precious sheets of unbleached muslin patches issued by the enemy lost their identity and were put to essential use as garments hidden from view by a tattered uniform. Discovery of that willful destruction of Japanese property might have resulted in more serious destruction. The risk had to be taken. Men were cold.

As time rushed onward, the prisoners found it more difficult to maintain any semblance of physical comfort. Some relief could be obtained during the daytime because of the activity at their forced labor and the freedom they had in being able to swing arms and legs about. But when night came and they were required to lie on a small cot, conditions became unbearable. The sleazy blankets loaned by the enemy were just so much weight without appropriate warmth. Most of the Americans had been able to bring along an army blanket from the Philippines. It was of wool and soft in texture. Some few had salvaged two such items, and they snuggled up warm in them each night.

A few had none, and they spent the winter without any aid from their more fortunate colleagues. Some raincoats, a few shelter halves, bits of clothing tossed on top helped in a small way to retard the penetrating cold air that always sifted its way under the covering and chilled the skeletons huddled beneath.

Men hunched up in circular fashion and shivered until fitful sleep finally took possession. In a few hours an indwelling bell would ring. Benjo time! They would laboriously crawl out of their nest, not to disturb the interlaced and heterogeneous covers. Each prisoner had, by tedious experiment, learned the best manner of preparing his bed to obtain maximum warmth. There were no special preparations needed for the dash out into the darkness. All the clothing that one could muster was already in use on his emaciated frame. Once the mind was made up, it required only a quick leap, a step into a pair of clogs, and a rush down the hall.

"Gee, but I was cold last night," announced Ashley after he and his companions who occupied the same room had jumped out one morning and taken a quick wash in the cold water on the rear porch. Usually, no one spoke or paid any attention to another until after he had had an opportunity to fully wake up and attain a decent mood.

"That was the coldest night we have had, I believe," Sykes had the temerity to declare. Any statement, whether intended as fact or opinion, was subject to immediate challenge. There was always someone in hearing who would religiously take it upon himself to dispute any remark.

"Oh, no!" argued Blake. "Night before last was worse."

"In any event, last night was bad enough for me," Paul said in an effort to avoid the heated argument over trivialities that was sure to come if someone did not divert the conversation.

"It was bitter," agreed Cameron, supporting Paul. "What are we going to do when winter really comes?"

"I had everything I could get my hands on piled on my bed, and still I froze," proclaimed Blake.

"They have to give us something to keep warm with or we will all die of the cold," Ashley complained.

"The trouble is that none of us has any body heat left, and all the blankets in the world would have no effect."

"This Jap junk is just like a couple of boards piled on you," grumbled Blake. "Why don't they put a little wool in the damn things?"

"It's a cinch they are not cold all day and night like we are," Ashley said.

"I should say not," Cameron assented. "Look at that good food they carry past us every meal—abundance of rice, delicious-smelling soup, fried fish—"

"And what do we get? A couple of spoons of rice a meal," Blake stated with truth.

"I don't understand it at all. The book says that prisoners have to be fed the same rations as depot troops," Ashley reflected.

"The little bastards never read the book," proclaimed Blake.

"They've all popped out in wool uniforms this morning," announced Sykes, who was gazing out the window. "Have a look."

"Mmm," murmured Cameron. "But look at the Taiwanese soldiers. They don't get any wools. That's cotton they have on."

"It's lined for winter wear, though," asserted Ashley. "Look how it bulges out."

"And we have to go around in these khaki rags that we fought a war in," growled Blake. "Nice people, these Japs."

"I heard a grand story out in the benjo a moment ago," Paul mentioned.

All further conversation immediately stopped. Each person turned to hear the speaker, waiting with suspense. Here was one of the greatest sources of comfort in prison camp. A rumor, and from the benjo, too! That was the choice source for transmission of intelligence at the time. Any remark emanating from there was blessed with the mantle of truth, regardless of how impossible it might be if it were only analyzed. Prisoners would even stop in their hurried gobbling of their rice if any one walked in and said he had just heard in the benjo that ... And now, at a most unexpected moment, when each one was still shivering as he complained of the cold night, Paul, good old trustworthy Paul, who would never maliciously pass a rumor, startled them with a declaration of momentous importance.

"What did you hear?" Sykes inquired with impatience.

"Hurry up. Tell us," cried Ashley.

Blake was too dumbstruck at the sudden turn of events to make any comment. He merely stared at Paul with anticipation.

Cameron looked at the carrier of tidings and smiled. It was so unlike Paul to repeat anything he could not substantiate. Perhaps he was willing to have a good joke this morning, or maybe the old scoundrel really had some news to offer. It was true that he never carried the tales that came out of the benjo—that one place where men seemed to suddenly gain a great affinity for one another.

"You may take it for what it is worth," Paul prefaced his statement, "but I was told by a very reliable source"—that was the stamp of approval, *a reliable source*—"that the Japs are going to issue some cigarettes today."

An earthquake could have occurred or the heavens could have fallen, so great was the consternation at that declaration. No thought was given to any reasons for or to who might have transmitted the information. This was something too close to the hearts of all to be discounted. This was gospel truth!

"They'll probably give us about two cigarettes apiece," brooded Blake. "Just enough to tease us."

"That will be wonderful!" chirped Sykes, unmindful of what his colleague had stated.

"I could sure do with a good smoke after all these weeks without any," Ashley assured the others.

Cameron was quiet, lost in contemplation. Tobacco was a sore subject with him. Unbeknownst to himself, he had allowed the feelings of desire and hope to take possession of his reasoning. The realization that there would be no tobacco suddenly hit him when he was unprepared for it. That was a most unusual situation for him to be caught in unprepared for it. It did not occur frequently, but he had human weaknesses, even though he was very clever in conquering them.

When the prisoners were brought up from Manila, each of them had a pittance of tobacco. They had been assured that Taiwan was a great tobacco center, which it was, and that the product would be available in abundance. That belief was accepted by Cameron, and he looked forward to an additional supply as soon as his few cigarettes were gone.

On the day following the last enjoyable smoke, he realized that he was suddenly cut off from further supply. During the first twenty-four hours that he was hemmed in by the wall at Karenko, he had concluded that there was no possibility of getting any more food than the enemy wished to issue to him. Consequently, he had made up his mind that, if he could not have enough to keep alive, he would starve. And that was that! There was no remorse or anger in his soul. It was a mental condition. If there was insufficient food, there was nothing he could do about it. He would have to accept the inevitable. But he never analyzed the tobacco situation the same way. It was a matter of always looking forward to tomorrow, when surely relief would arrive. When it failed to materialize, his mental state grew worse; and his desire and craving for a cigarette grew worse. For weeks, the matter had plagued him because he continued to hope and neglected to act intelligently about the matter and make up his mind to give up tobacco.

So when Paul made his declaration, Cameron reacted as though he had been struck by a bolt of lightning. He was stunned, and he did not regain his composure until sometime during the day when Paul's "rumor" actually became a settled fact. Life was good to him again, he thought.

"Paul, this has saved my life," Cameron mused after he took the first puff.

"Just what do you mean?" inquired Paul. "A little thing like a cigarette surely is not that important when you have already given up most everything of value in life."

"For some reason or other, I have been craving tobacco ever since they cut us off."

"Now, look here, young fellow," Paul admonished him in a parental tone, "don't tell me you have a weakness such as that. I suppose next you will build up a food complex like most of the others and toss away your respectability."

"Did it strike you like that?" he asked, puffing harder than usual.

"I thought of all people you had real stamina."

Cameron looked Paul in the eye; took a deep puff, which he slowly inhaled; and then flicked the remainder of the cigarette into the corner. Paul smiled at the conquest Cameron had made over himself.

One unusually cold morning, the little group crawled out of their cots, and each one began to swing his arms about in an effort to improve the circulation. As men will under such depressive circumstances, they glared at each other and had no word of cheer to offer. That sort of attitude had always been of concern to Paul, who disliked seeing his associates slump into such a condition of antipathy toward each other.

Frequently, he had discussed the situation with Cameron, who was making a tremendous effort to reach up to Paul's influence.

"Why don't we warm each other up?" Paul asked in a cheery voice. "Let's get in a circle and pummel the fellow in front. That should be a lot of fun, and it will warm us up." He intentionally neglected to mention that he believed it might also cheer them up.

Cameron sprang to Paul's aid and called on the others to help form a ring. Only with reluctance did they do so, but after several good hard blows on each other, they began to feel warmer. Then their effort began to be fun, and they did not limit their strokes to the back but pummeled each other all over the body. In a few short minutes, each one was howling with laughter, and they continued their exertion until they were exhausted.

At the call for tenko, they rushed out to the formation in the finest of spirits, which none of their colleagues from the other rooms could quite understand. But their laughter soon began to permeate the crowd, and they, too, had enjoyed a change of spirit from deepest depression to various degrees of exhilaration.

"Wonder what they are going to have us do this morning?" Ashley asked after the prisoners had lined up for the daily labor.

"Something new, I guess," answered Cameron. "We finished that plot behind the warehouse last night. There is nothing else to do there."

"They'll find something nasty for us," muttered Blake.

After being checked off and issued tools, the column was moved out of the gate and in a direction different from the customary one. The route ran parallel to the wall of the compound and then angled off and crossed over the side of a small rise. The grade up which the prisoners had to walk was an insignificant little rise for any man in normal health. He likely would never have noticed the incline. But today the weary Americans had negotiated only a hundred yards when the weaker ones began to falter. Their tools took on tremendous weight and bore down on their shoulders, while their legs grew wobbly and could not be controlled. Their inability to continue was obvious, and the prisoner interpreter called over to the noncommissioned officer who was conducting the march and explained that some of the prisoners were so old and ill that they had to rest. The soldier was unprepared for that situation and probably had not the slightest idea what to do if some of the marchers faltered and could not continue. So he accepted the advice of the interpreter and called a halt. The prisoners remained where they were for several minutes until they were rested and then continued on their way. The entire trek was less than a mile, but the column was halted alongside an extensive area that was anything but farming land.

"What are we stopping here for?"

"The guy is lost. He doesn't know where to go."

At that moment, the soldier required the squad leaders to call the roll, an obligation that was placed on them prior to departure from the compound, again when halted for rest at the farming spot, once more when lined up to march home, and finally upon arrival at the compound before dismissal. "What do they expect to do here?"

"Some mistake has been made. You can't plant anything in that ground."

"Take a look at the trees and brush."

"It's filled with big boulders too."

The prisoners were not held in suspense long. A few sharp commands to the American interpreter started action.

"The noncommissioned officer states that we will clear this ground for planting. He wants the POWs to line up along the road and move forward with tools, taking out all the obstructions. Those without tools are to follow and carry the debris back across the road and pile it up. Sorry, boys, but that is what the young man wants."

"Hey, Mac, do we have to dig up all the weeds too?" some one asked. There were always questions from the same few who never, never understood.

The interpreter made no effort to answer him. He knew that the others understood what was to be done; and if one or two professed ignorance, they would quickly find out the answer by observation.

Forced labor, farming, was one of few major subjects of thought and conversation. At other times and at other places, the variety of important matters of concern to the prisoners would be slightly different. Now, in addition to labor, they consisted of food, which was of constant concern because of its lack of quantity and variety; the benjo because of the need for excessive indulgence; mail, none of which had yet been sent or received; tobacco, which was a great aid in forgetting the pangs of hunger; and security, a condition that always was uncertain. Freedom and the progress of the war at that stage of the prisoners' confinement were not the important matters that they would become at a future and distant time. It was true that rumors played a large part in their lives, yet they were trivial in comparison to the more significant factors pertaining to existence.

Resistance to physical labor and an effort to accomplish only minimum requirements were diligently practiced by nearly all. On occasions one might, for the sake of exercise, show an active spurt of endeavor, but his strength and the laughs and sneers of his companions would limit that effort to a few minutes of effort. Then, as might be expected, a handful of prisoners felt it to their advantage and hoped for personal gain to contribute what they thought was an honest effort to the enemy's demands.

"Those yellow bellies are going to squeeze every ounce of work they can out of us," Blake declared as he took a few feeble swipes with his *kuwa*.

"They certainly eased us into a full day's work in a smart manner," said Cameron.

"Hell, yes," Blake agreed. "We started out on a half-day schedule, working every other half hour. Now we sweat all day with only one ten minute 'yasumi' each morning and afternoon."

"They are trying to kill us off," asserted Ashley.

"The amount of work you do will never hurt anyone." Paul laughed, in a friendly effort to cheer him up. "You haven't raised your kuwa once since we started."

"Ease up there, Sykes," Blake called over to his colleague. You'll be having the Japs think we all should be doing that much."

"Sykes raised up, stretched his back, and made an attempt to smile. He was embarrassed, and for a while, he stalled as the others were doing. The guards paid little attention to what amount of effort the prisoners put in their assigned task. It was of no concern of theirs. The mission assigned to them was to guard the white men. But the administrative soldiers were the overseers. They had to meet certain requirements, and if the labor of the Americans did not produce that amount, they would have to explain to their superiors. Now and then, they would growl at one of the prisoners or push another one in their desire to produce greater activity. Yet only on certain occasions were they able to obtain results. The prisoners quickly learned and practiced devices to circumvent labor. In fact, they frequently spent more energy in avoiding that effort than the cost of the work itself.

Suddenly, the captain appeared at a bend of the road. He was strolling out to the farm to inspect and had appeared without warning. The noncommissioned officer in charge spotted him and started racing down the line of prisoners, bellowing commands and waving his arms in a great display of energy for the benefit of his commander. "Faster work or will cut rice. Quick!"

"Son of a bitch!" mumbled Blake.

As soon as the captain came abreast of the prisoners, who were now diligently at work, the overseer called, "Kiotsuke!"

Each prisoner gratefully halted in his endeavors and stood at attention while the noncommissioned officer saluted and reported to the captain. The officer nodded and directed the men to continue their work. But as soon he made his early departure, the prisoners slumped back to their role of saboteurs of time. Even the overseer appeared so relieved that he sat down under a tree and paid no further attention to his charges.

It was about that time when the Japanese authorities decided to let driblets of news enter camp. The reasons for that concession were never quite clear to the Americans. But after considerable debate over the possible intentions the enemy could have had in mind, and it was universally agreed that there was purpose behind it, the prisoners felt they had arrived at the correct conclusion. Indoctrination in the Japanese philosophy of life, mode of living, and character of thought was obviously one purpose. About half of the news received persisted along that line. The other major reason appeared to be an effort to break the morale of the prisoners, because all the information permitted

them, which was not of a propaganda variety, dwelt on the tremendous
military and economic successes of the Japanese Empire.

The ever vigilant Sykes, who frequently annoyed Blake by sitting
on Blake's cot and staring out the window, cried to his colleagues one
day, "Something big is up! Here comes Scurvy toward the barracks on
a run."

"Move over so I can sit on my own bed and have a look," ordered
Blake.

The others moved to positions of advantage so that they, too, might
be able to see the approach of the lieutenant.

Paul looked a moment and then withdrew, disinterested. He strolled
to the door and stepped out into the hall.

"Here is some more of the story," he called back to the others in the
room. "One of the guards has just brought in a blackboard at the far
end of the hall."

About that moment, another soldier bellowed the long drawn-
out call for the American interpreter, which was the Japanese way of
pronouncing the occidental name. Whenever instructions were to be
given, he was always called, and many times a day he had to run to the
end of the hall to receive from an enemy messenger orders that he was
required to transmit to the squad leaders. Yet it was not the enemy alone
who called him from his room. Almost hourly, day and night, one of his
colleagues would cry for him to come to the rescue of an unfortunate
prisoner who had run afoul of a sentry.

On this occasion, the interpreter responded as usual. After receiving
a short direction, he went down the hall, calling for all the squad leaders
to report to the Japanese lieutenant.

When they assembled, they saw the blackboard set up on a chair
and the officer scribbling figures on it with a bit of chalk. He soon
finished and then appeared so exalted over the information that he was
about to impart that he refused to use the interpreter. Instead, he spoke
to the prisoners in English.

"Big battles on sea have occurred! Brilliant Imperial Japanese forces
have annihilated United Nations. Three battles at Solomon Islands,
another at Santa Cruz, and night action at Lunga have been glorious

victories!" He paused for breath, while the prisoners waited with hearts sinking. "See here, on board. I have given figures sent out by Imperial Japanese government, who never brag or make mistake. Look! Allies lose, sunk and heavily damaged, five battleships, six carriers, thirty-six cruisers, twenty-nine destroyers, ten submarines, twenty-three transports, and many other vessels. And here in this column, you see lost eight hundred and fifty airplanes."

To receive information of those staggering losses seemed to make the listeners partially collapse in their chairs. The carnage at such an important time when American troops had evidently commenced action on a large scale was terrific. How could such losses ever be replaced? Only a negotiated peace could be the outcome.

After a dramatic silence, Scurvy continued his report on the war's progress. "Japanese very gallant fighters and destroy most of Allied fleet. But we report with regret that fifteen imperial airplanes failed to return."

The squad leaders were too stunned with this news to comment among themselves. It was not until they had reported the same information to their colleagues that any serious discussion of the terrific disaster occurred. The prisoners retired to their rooms to talk the situation over with their fellows.

"I don't believe anything they say," Blake declared, not from intelligent analysis but from his firm belief that everything their captors said was false.

"It must be true, or they wouldn't put it out," announced Sykes as he flopped down on his cot.

"Wonder where we got all those ships?" inquired Ashley, who was attempting to analyze the matter.

"We couldn't have that many, after Pearl Harbor," reasoned Blake.

But the lieutenant said that they were Allied ships, the whole fleet," Sykes asserted.

"It seems to me that we had better be cautious about accepting everything he said," reflected Cameron. "There is probably truth in there having been some naval actions."

Paul spoke up. "That is a mighty good place to commence an analysis. It is more than probable that an action has occurred. Otherwise, the Japanese would not be so enthusiastic about giving us the news."

"Even if we accept the most unusual situation where losses were 50 percent, figure it out for yourself what a tremendous navy we must have had," Cameron continued to follow up Paul's argument. "It's hardly conceivable that we could put such a force in action so soon, so far away."

"But what if the losses were 100 percent?" Sykes quickly asked.

"That could be. But can you really visualize the Japs knocking off everything?" Cameron tossed back at him.

Sykes was silent.

"The biggest weakness in the whole report is the statement of the enemy losses, fifteen airplanes," Paul persisted. "And they didn't even admit those as losses, only 'failed to return!'"

The debate went on. Once a prisoner had declared himself or made up his mind, no logic or argument would make him admit a change in his belief. That would be a display of weakness, and most everyone considered himself a man of importance. The spectacular subject of conversation that had entered the camp and the possible truth or deception in that information continued to be the main discussion for many days. It overshadowed for some time any desire to even talk about food. But it gradually tapered off with the passage of the days, and with its departure the heartaches, too, disappeared.

One day, the squad leaders brought around the information that the Japanese authorities would open the bathhouse one day a week for the prisoners. That particular accommodation had been reserved exclusively for the enemy soldiers, and the Americans had been denied the privilege of even entering that place, which was adjacent to the kitchen and utilized the cooking fires to heat the bathing water. Up to this time, the only washing facilities available to the prisoners was the cold water that ran from the taps on the rear porch of the barracks and the two large circular vats in front of the benjo. Originally, those two concrete tubs had been erected for the laundry facilities of the troops that occupied the barracks. Upon the arrival of the new occupants, they were pressed into service for all the various purposes for which men need to use water.

The center portion of the huge container was the fresh water receptacle, while around the perimeter a score or so of small individual sinks had been constructed. Between each sink was a boarded portion on which articles might be laid or clothes scrubbed. Because of the peculiar construction of the washing vats, they had been dubbed "birdbaths" by the Americans. Their use, as well as the limited amount of water, which few appreciated at the time, was restricted during daylight hours only by the whim of the individual guard on duty at the time.

As the cold weather came on, the facilities on the rear porch were used less and less; when the air temperature dropped, so did that of the water.

"'Bout time the little bastards woke up and gave us a chance to have a bath," grumbled Blake, between puffs on a small butt of a cigarette.

"I knew they would take care of us when the got around to it," Sykes declared, which caused some of his companions to glare at him.

A schedule was announced in which each squad was given a time during which it could occupy the bathhouse. The first group rushed over at the appointed hour. Four members of the contingent reached the closed door at the same instant, and instead of extending normal courtesy to one another and standing for one's colleagues to enter first, each man tried to bolt in at once. That procedure was, by this time, the accepted method among the vast majority of the prisoners. Politeness had long since been cast aside. It was "survival of the fittest" in even the minor things of life. "Get mine and to hell with the other fellow" became the accepted philosophy for most.

Pushing and shoving each other, the four burst into the bathhouse and were astounded to find several Japanese soaking in the large sunken tank in the center of the room. They immediately bellowed at the intruders and ordered them out. The remainder of the American squad collected outside the door and remained shivering there some time until the enemy soldiers finished their bathing.

The windows and doors of the barracks were filled with curious prisoners as they watched initial group go to the bathhouse and return.

Not the least insignificant thing ever happened, let alone a major event such as hot water bathing, without most of the members of the camp carefully observing and fully investigating all the aspects thereof. Never satisfied with seeing, they would ply the participants with questions and then debate the matter for days on end.

Minutes before the second group was to go in for their bath, its members began to assemble at the door. Instructions had been issued that there was to be no overlap inside the building, but that did not prevent one being on the scene early and ready to take his advantage. So most of the prisoners thought. Anyhow, the hot water may give out, or the building might disintegrate, or the Japanese could change their minds, or some similar disaster might occur. But down in the soul of each of those who felt that way lay the real reason for his peculiar action. That was his inane insistence that no one else should have anything that he could not have. No one would dare deny that philosophy, let alone to himself. It became a ruling attitude in a prisoner's relations with his colleagues.

Paul sensed the presence of that peculiar condition in an aggregated form because of the unaccustomed luxury that was about to be enjoyed. "Why don't we all go over together when our time comes? If we allow the anxious ones to go on ahead, it will be much less congested for us."

He nudged Cameron, who promptly understood and lent his support to the worthy endeavor. "Sure, let's do that. Anyhow, we have just this one tin washbasin for the whole room to use so it will be lots better to go together."

Sykes and Ashley were too timid to resist his leadership and lay back on their cots in resignation. Cameron laughed to himself as he watched their disappointment. *They are fairly drooling to rush over ahead of the others*, he said to himself. But Blake had different views. He did not speak. But giving the impression that he had not heard the comments of the others, he picked up the washbasin, hurried out of the room, and walked rapidly to the bathhouse. Paul and Cameron gave each an understanding look.

In a short time, the four others proceeded across the parade ground together. Paul kept up an idle chatter as he moved slowly along, trying to impress on his roommates that there was no need for haste.

They entered the door and stripped off their clothing, which they hung on pegs. "So, this is the way his imperial majesty's soldiers bathe," smirked Cameron.

"It looks very delightful," Sykes stated without too much care for his own true feelings.

"What's the big tub for?" Ashley inquired.

Cameron explained. "That is the Japanese method. They squat down and dip the water from the vat and splash it over themselves. Then they proceed with a good soaping—"

"Fat chance we have to soap ourselves. Haven't seen a bit of soap for months," interrupted Ashley.

"Then they toss more water over themselves to rinse off, Cameron continued. "When that is completed, they get into the vat, which is filled with water as hot as they can stand it, and soak there until they are exhausted."

"I think I will take a shower," Ashley said and moved toward one of the three attachments against the wall.

"Showers are rather unusual in a Japanese bathhouse, but I will try one," Paul said to Cameron.

Cameron watched. Ashley let out a howl as a stream of cold water rushed from the shower and suddenly struck him. He had stepped in behind another prisoner and thought it was flowing at the proper temperature. Cameron gave a mighty laugh at the younger officer's discomfiture and turned to see what was happening to Paul. He was standing under the shower turning and twisting the knobs but getting no results. Moving over to the third attachment, he tried that one, and again nothing happened.

"Fine plumbing they have here. Three showers, two won't work, and the other has only cold water," commented Cameron.

A few of the group had gotten into the large vat in the center of the room and were having a grand splash in the hot water. As the others were preparing to join their colleagues, the door of the building was thrown open, and one of the Japanese guards stomped in. He shrieked and waved his arms at the bathers in the huge tub and forced them to clamber out in rapid time. With further indications that left no doubt in the minds of the prisoners, he shuffled out and disappeared up the path toward headquarters.

"I guess you birds will keep out of the marble tub that belongs to the Imperial Army now." Cameron laughed at his companions when the threat of dire action had passed.

"How do they expect us to bathe if we don't use the big tub?" asked a dejected prisoner.

"Use a pan and dip the water from the vat and splash it over you."

"But don't get in the water," sang another.

A day or so later, the prisoners were enjoying their last few minutes in barracks before responding to the work call. The tiny pushcart that two soldiers dragged to the market each day was being pulled into the compound. "Here comes the cart," cried someone who had first observed it.

That was the signal for the occupants to swarm to the parade ground side of the barracks with hope and expectation that something of value would be on the load.

"Pretty slim today," Blake said, as he had likewise reported every day that he had seen the cart come in.

"What's on it?" inquired Ashley.

"A little of the usual," replied Blake, "a couple of handfuls of grass and a bundle of 'walking sticks.'"

Why don't they give us the same food?" cried Ashley. "Most of that on the cart goes to the Jap kitchen."

"Fifty Japs get three-fourths, and two hundred Americans get the rest," complained Blake. "But there'll be a day!"

On one occasion, Cameron and Ashley were sitting together in their room engaged in idle chatter. "Say, Ashley," Cameron said, suddenly changing the subject as a thought struck him, "how are you coming with that deck of cards you were making?"

"I finished up the last one just yesterday," he replied.

"They didn't turn out any too well."

"Let's get up a foursome and have a rubber of bridge."

"Swell idea," agreed Ashley.

He stood up to reach for the cards, which he had laboriously made during his spare moments. There was no need to look for them as the meager possessions of any prisoner were lying on the single shelf that adorned the room and were exposed to common view. Ashley tossed his accomplishment down on the bed and said, "Here, shuffle them. I think Paul is out in the banjo, and I'll run down Sykes somewhere."

Cameron picked up the stack of cards and looked at them with wonderment and merriment. *Quite an accomplishment,* he admitted to himself. *How he ever found enough bits of cardboard to make them amazes me. The destitution in this compound is appalling, and you cannot find a bit of string, a piece of paper, or even a lost button lying on the ground. What the Japs haven't carefully redeemed, these eagle-eyed prisoners have long since picked up.* While he was contemplating and shuffling the cards, the others walked in. Soon, a rubber of bridge was in being.

For a half hour, they had an enjoyable time and soon overcame the difficulties of sitting on a cot and handling small and thick bits of cardboard.

From the end of the hall, another prisoner called, "Kiotsuke!" And the card players knew that a guard had entered the barracks. They continued the game but were on the alert to jump up and bow the instant the sentry appeared at their door. When he arrived, they leaped to their feet and each gave his most presentable bow. It was always best to take the matter formally and get it over with, rather than be slipshod and arouse the ire of the soldier, who had been trained to consider such slovenliness as an insult to the representative of the emperor.

The Japanese stood in the doorway with his bayonet thrust forward in front of him. Slowly glancing around the room, he let his eyes rest on the cards lying on the bed. He raised his head to stare at the prisoners and then let out screams of anger, while the Americans stood quietly in complete dismay. The shouts and bellowings went on and on, until the guard seemed to have exhausted himself. Thereupon, he moved up to each prisoner in turn and gave each a hard blow in the face. Then he picked up a fistful of cards from the cot and tossed the pieces of cardboard into the corner. Feeling satisfied with the punishment he had inflicted, he strode out the door and down the hall.

"Evidently he did not like our playing cards," Paul stated.

"I couldn't understand everything he said because he was screaming so," Cameron explained. "But the main thing was that we were assembling unlawfully."

"That will be a new rule we will to be careful to follow," admonished Sykes.

"They are certainly difficult to keep up with," Cameron decided. "It seems that any soldier who comes tramping through whatever barracks can make any rule he cares to on the spot, whether it agrees with the regulations that the camp commander has published or not."

"I do not quite get the point he was making, Cam," admitted Paul. "Just what do you think he had in mind?"

"It was none to clear, and I do not think that he had fully thought out his orders before he gave them," Cameron asserted. "He was saying that no more than two of us were permitted to be together at a time."

"But five of us live in this same room," Sykes stated, showing a desire to more fully get the meaning of the new instructions so that he would not violate them in the future.

"That is Japanese logic that only they can explain," replied Cameron.

"Well, we better pass the word around to the others," Paul said thoughtfully, "so that they may be on their guard in the future."

Some time later, Blake was lying on his cot, scowling and mumbling to himself.

"What's the matter, Blake, having a nightmare in broad daylight?" Cameron chided him from his seat on the wooden bench alongside the deal table.

"I was just looking at our shelf," he explained and pointed an arm to the single board that ran the length of one wall and on which everything owned by the occupants of the room was kept. "Sykes's stuff is on my part."

"Hell, you don't own enough to take up the space you have." Cameron laughed. "What do you need any more for?"

"I'm entitled to my share of the shelf whether I use it or not."

"Blake, you are welcome to as much of my portion as you want," Paul offered.

"I don't want yours. I just want my one-fifth."

The point was too insignificant for a normal person to ever raise, but now another prisoner was encroaching. That was fatal at Karenko. So Blake rose up, looked about for something to use as a measuring device, and finally settled on his waist belt, that being the only thing he could find as suitable. With a great deal of effort, he measured and remeasured the length of the shelf; calculated where the divisions should be; and then, with a stub of pencil, scratched dividing lines along the edge of the board.

"Nice job. Now we all know where we stand," Cameron stated ironically. "But you have missed a much larger point in living by denying us the privilege of extending courtesy to another POW who might want to use part of our portion."

Paul made a sound to Cameron, which meant a caution not to become embroiled in an argument, while Blake made no indication of hearing and flopped back on his cot.

Unexpectedly one day, a most exciting event occurred. Members of the guard rushed back and forth between the front gate and headquarters. Occasionally an officer hurried past. Something of an emergency nature was about to happen. It could not be Allied troops coming to rescue the prisoners. That thought was too far-fetched. But every American centered his attention on the compound gate; something was about to happen there. Everything else was momentarily abandoned—food discussions, forced labor arguments, hatreds, discourtesies, jealousies.

The puffing and wheezing of a broken-down truck sounded from down the lane that led to the camp, and shortly, that vehicle rumbled through the gate. Behind it came two others in a similar state of repair. They drew up in front of the barracks, and members of the guard quickly formed between them and the prisoners, who were forced back into the barracks. White men, gaunt and tired and emaciated! It required two looks to identify them because of their haggard appearance. Then a cry of welcome in spite of orders. The Mindanao group had arrived.

For many months, the fate of those troops had been discussed, and many a strange rumor had been spread through the camp. Now, here were the senior officers of that force, looking as weak and ill as those already at Karenko, and soon everything that had occurred south of Luzon would be told.

"Good God! Look at the luggage they brought along," a voice cried.

"How did they ever save that and get the Japs to drag it up here for them?" asked another.

"They certainly got a lucky break somehow. Think how the Japs treated us coming out of Bataan. They stripped us of everything except the clothes on our back."

Further discussion tapered off because it lost its importance. Each person watching the proceedings was too much concerned with his own thoughts to care about idle speculation. One small group was counting faces. Who was missing?

But the vast majority, with rapacious eyes, stared at the baggage truck. Material possessions counted more than anything else. What could these new arrivals have in those trunks and rolls? What could they demand for barter? Would they eventually hang their garments on the clothesline, unguarded, so that they can be easily …?

That night was a gala occasion. After hours of delay, and while the authorities directed the moving of cots from a warehouse to several of the vacant rooms in the barracks and other delays because the Japanese had made no preparations for the new arrivals, the older tenants began swarming into the rooms of the new arrivals. Acquaintances were renewed; reports on losses were disseminated. Then, having prepared the way by a display of gracious fellowship, the hard bargainers began to wedge their way into the wares of the men from Mindanao.

"Did you have much to eat down there?" was the first question Blake asked one of his friends as soon as preliminaries were over.

"It was fair," came the reply. "The Japs let us run our camp pretty much by ourselves. Frequently, we had cattle available, and vegetables could be bought."

"You will find it much different here," Blake gloomily reported. "Nothing but a little rice. And they work the hell out of us."

"From the looks of you here, that must be true."

"No tobacco, either," Blake added with disgust.

"We were able to bring a little along," his friend admitted. "Here we have a pack of lavenderas." The newcomer reached into his kit and extracted a pack of Filipino native black cigarettes, which he tossed over to Blake.

"Thanks! They are worth their weight in gold." Blake opened the package; took out a cigarette, which he lit; and inhaled deep and joyfully.

"When they told us we were to leave and come north, they said that no heavy baggage would be brought along. But we got hold of the captain who was in charge of the movement and told him that, if the crowd had their luggage with them, they would be so concerned with it that no one would want to escape. We thought he would be more concerned about his own neck than overruling the colonel, who had gone on to Davao. And it worked. He didn't realize that there was not slightest chance of anyone making a break because there was a heavy guard thrown around us as soon as they decided to move us."

"Mighty lucky," agreed Blake. "I wish a chance for a break would come our way. But we are right in the middle of a hostile country and can't even speak the language. Then the bastards will execute ten for every one than gets away. Slim chance!" After a moment of additional contemplation, Blake asked, "Haven't got any extra wool clothes, have you?"

"Sure. Soon as I can get at my trunk. What do you need most?"

"Shirt, sweater, and slacks. Anything to keep warm in. These nights about have me licked. Freeze all the time."

"That's tough, Blake. I can fix you up with a light sweater. And I have a pair of heavy blue slacks that had belonged to my dress uniform. I know damn well that I'll have no need for those for a long time, and you are welcome to them for the warmth they'll give you, if you don't mind the color."

"Thanks. That will be wonderful," Blake quickly said. "Color won't mean anything around here. We got to keep from freezing."

"I might have a pair of wool socks I can help you out with too," Blake's friend added sympathetically.

"Okay. But listen. Don't give away anymore of your stuff to the others," cautioned Blake in a spirit of helpfulness, now that he had been assured of reaping a harvest. "Make them give you rice for anything else you don't want. I'll get some swaps for you. The way for some of us around here is to arrange a trade and get a little cut from each one in the trade. Sometimes we have to make a three-way swap, and that means three cuts."

Blake was unabashed, but his friend merely muttered an, "Mmm," obviously disappointed to learn that such procedure was in effect.

One night, shortly thereafter, Cameron felt a light touch on his shoulder. Between his sense of responsibility for the duty he had to perform and the cold, disagreeable weather that denied him sound sleep, it was a simple matter for him to become promptly alert.

"It's that time," whispered Paul in order not to disturb any of the other sleepers. "You are on duty in about two minutes."

"Right!" Cameron responded. "I'll be there in a jiffy."

Paul quietly slipped out of the darkened room and proceeded down the hall. Before he had passed through the doorway, Cameron had eased out of his bed and reached down for his clogs. He carried them in his hands in order to maintain a noiseless walk down the hallway. Some few of the prisoners had consideration for the slumber of their colleagues; but many others had grown careless, and their thumping along in the middle of the night could be stopped only by the growls of those whom they disturbed.

At the cross hall where the guard table sat, Cameron nodded to Paul and said, "All right. You are relieved. I hope you get some sleep."

Before Paul rose up from his chair, he reached down and pulled from his feet the ankle-high slipper that he had sewn together from some salvaged rags. "Here. Put these on," he ordered Cameron. "They may help a little to keep those dainty little feet of yours warm."

"No thanks, Paul," Cameron tried to refuse. "I'll only wear them out that much sooner for you."

"Young man, do as I say, or I'll give you the old 'one-two.'" Paul humorously raised up his arms in a pugilistic manner. "And slip into this, too," he added as he pulled off a ragged coat that some Mindanao friend had donated. "When you wake Sykes, pass them on to him. But be sure he gets them back in the morning."

"Much obliged. Now, run on to bed. It's only two hours to reveille, and you will have a hard time getting any sleep in that short time. Its too damn cold."

Cameron sat down to take over his brief hour tour as benjo guard. When that obligation had first been established by the Japanese authorities, two prisoners were required to be on duty constantly, being relieved by two others in turn at the end of the hour. Some days earlier, one of the prisoners had neglected to awaken the man who was to relieve him; as the delinquency was not detected by the Japanese during the remainder of the night, no one had seen fit to adjust the situation back to normal. The common feeling was that, if an advantage could be gained, there was no reason to intentionally penalize themselves merely because an order had once been issued by the enemy. Orders were constantly being altered at the whim of any enemy guard who came in contact with the prisoners. Anyhow, if a sentry should come through the barracks who knew that two men should be on duty, it might be possible that he would think the second benjo guard was making his rounds of the barracks, as were his orders, to inspect for fires and any unauthorized moving about by the other prisoners. Should he ask if the second man were on duty, the customary and indefinite reply would be that one of the Japanese guards sometime before had said that only one prisoner was required. Who said that? I do not know. I was not on duty. It was a long time ago. That was commonly known as the "runaround" in American slang. It seldom worked, but it invariably was attempted if an advantage might be gained.

Fists often smashed into prisoners' faces because of it—dumb Japs were frequently less dumb than rated by the prisoners—but there was always the thought each one had that, in the mass of prisoners, there was always somebody else who would get the punishment. Cameron set to his task of recording names and numbers of those who passed by the desk bound for the benjo. On their return, he ran a line through the entry. The actions of some of his colleagues who, for reasons of their own, slipped out other exits without reporting their departure to him were squinted at by Cameron. He did not feel honor bound to comply with all the rules of the enemy. The more accepted conception of obeying regulations was to comply only with those that the enemy actually enforced. There were a few, however, who, out of fear or hope for personal advantage, accepted literally each rule that any individual Japanese might make on the spur of the moment. It would have been bad enough if they obeyed such regulations at the time, but they carried on their insistence for months afterward, in spite of the fact that none of their captors ever seemed to know anything about the particular rule in question.

The paper on which Cameron was jotting down his recordings just could not accommodate any further notes. It was completely filled to capacity. The spaces and margins were gone, and where it could be visibly done, earlier records had been written over, palimpsest like. "Of all the damn silly ideas," he muttered to himself. Keeping a record like this that had no earthly value. The only possible use would be for some statistician to compile the number of gallons of fluid that a given number of people in a given time under these conditions—Oh, hell! So what? "Now, if the Japs," he debated with himself, "want to know who is out of the barracks any particular moment, that can be told in a much simpler manner. I'll fix that up first thing after tenko in the morning," he promised himself.

Cameron called Sykes a few minutes late in order to avoid joining the great fraternity of prisoners who would do just the opposite in order to gain a minute or two for their own advantage. Small stuff, Cameron told himself, when men have to cheat over such insignificant things. Anyhow, they always have a row on their hands because the fellow they wake up is just as jealous of those seconds.

Sykes came out promptly to take over his duties and was grateful for the loan of Paul's garments to keep him warm. "Who else is on duty this hour?" he asked Cameron.

"You are all alone," replied Cameron as he yawned and started back to his room. "Don't let the spooks get you."

"But there must be a second POW on duty. That is the order," Sykes cried at him.

Cameron turned and said, "The other man got lost sometime during the last couple of days, and no one thought it important enough to worry about."

"Oh, Cameron, you can't leave me like this. You must find out who should be on shift with me and get him on the job. Why, guards will come in here and blame me for it, and I'll get beat up."

"Take it easy, Sykes," Cameron cautioned him. "Just tell them that the second man was called off by one of other Jap guards some time ago."

"Oh, no! No!" Sykes cried, obviously frightened over the risk that Cameron had tossed at him.

"It will take several minutes for me to run the matter down, so sit quietly at your job until you hear form me. You will have to write on the wall because there is no more paper." With that, Cameron went directly to his room and to bed. "Let the young man worry about how he can please the yellow bastards, which he seems to want to do," he mumbled to himself.

"What are you making, Cam?" Paul inquired in the morning when he observed his friend working over several small pieces of cardboard that he had gotten from some scraps that had been left lying around.

"Just a minute, and I will show you," he replied. He put the finishing touches on one of the papers and said, "Now look, all you fellows. I have an idea that I want to sell you, and it will save us all a lot of bother. It's very simple. 'P-cards!'" He gave each of the prisoners in the room a small card on which was inscribed his POW number. "The idea is this: Instead of all this monkey business about running a bookkeeping system when you have to go to the john, just lay that card on the table when you rush by. You save time. The guard knows you are out. Nobody has to worry about rustling paper and pencil."

"But, Cameron," cried Sykes, "They have ordered us to write the names and numbers of each one on a record and—"

"Raspberries," Blake blurted out. "You go ahead and write your name anyway the goddamn bastards say. I'm using this P-card. It's a swell idea."

"Me, too," said Ashley.

Paul was too engaged in suppressing a guffaw to comment. It tickled him to witness the contrast between Blake and Sykes. Finally, when he gained control of himself, he spoke. "Now this what I call an intelligent operation, Cameron. We'll use them tonight, and I'll bet my shirt that every POW here will do the same tomorrow."

The conversation tapered off into inane subjects and was about to die out when, suddenly, Ashley spoke up in a loud voice. "Wish we had some cows here so we could get some milk."

"Well, that all depends," Blake said as he prepared to take over the discussion.

Paul and Cameron glanced at each other. They recognized the signs. Recently, Blake had developed a most objectionable quality of running away from whatever subject one of his companions might bring up. He assumed superior knowledge on any item of discussion and made an effort to explain to the others like a parent speaking to a four-year-old child.

"Now the Jersey cow," Blake went on, "gives off much less milk than the Guernsey, but it's richer in butter fat. I had three cows back in 1927, at Fort Totten, a Guernsey, a Jersey, and a Black Angus. My mess sergeant was an old farmhand and he took care—"

"Here come the chow buckets! Bowls out!" Blake was interrupted by a voice down the hall.

The mad scurrying throughout the barracks caused the old structure to rock and shake. The same group of prisoners, as always, had forgotten to place their rice bowls on the proper place on the tables ready for the servers. At the signal, "buckets on the way," they rushed with noisy haste to carry their bowls to the proper place. Many others spontaneously tore about with little purpose. The approach of the food buckets had the identical effect on the occupants of the barracks, or at least a great percentage of them, as that produced when the farmer carries his swill to the sty.

"They will have me doing the same thing next." Cameron spoke to Paul as the two were reclining on their cots.

"It is a difficult thing to overcome that rushing after food," Paul counseled.

"I don't understand it. Nobody will be left out, and each one will get his share, little as it is."

"The animal instincts in man comes forward when he refuses to use his intelligence to overcome them," Paul reflected. "Don't let us catch you doing the same thing."

"What I fear is that, if I don't get there as soon as the others, some hungry gut lover will grab up my bowl as well as his own."

"That would be a sorry situation," commented Paul.

"He would likely have a good fight on his hands, if he did," Cameron declared.

"Patience, now," cautioned Paul, smiling at Cameron.

When the bowls of rice had been brought in and before the occupants had a chance to sit down to their meager breakfast, Ashley shouted, "That fellow serving rice is not doing it fair. Just watch him sometime. Some bowls he fills by bearing down hard on the serving paddle. And others he just lightly presses. It makes a big difference."

"I saw him, too," Blake concurred. "Good thing he pushed down hard on my bowl, because if he gave me a light press, I'd have socked him. I got rights here and nobody is going to get more than I do."

"Colonel," Sykes addressed Paul, "I've heard a number of complaints about the server. Why don't you, as one of the older officers, speak to the squad leader and have him replaced?"

"I'll be very happy to tell him that a number of complaints have been registered," Paul responded, "and leave it up to him to investigate the matter."

"I think that you ought to demand that he be replaced," insisted Blake, missing the point. "He is going to take the food out of our mouths."

"You know what happens in this army. The first one that complains has the job given to him," Paul reminded the others.

"I think you would make a fine server," Ashley commented. "We all can trust you."

"You are very kind," replied Paul. "But I'm pretty wobbly at my age, and slow. Your rice would be cold before I could get it all served out."

"Nevertheless, you would stop the argument about the honesty of serving," Cameron urged. "I'll be glad to give you a hand."

Word flashed through the squad in rapid style that Paul had been approached to take over the rice server's job; and before he could speak to the squad leader, he found the rice paddle being handed to him by his predecessor, who was only too happy to relinquish that thankless task.

So at the next meal, Paul reached the bowls, two at a time, from the shelf and handed them to Cameron, who stood over the bucket of rice and scooped the grains into the bowl. Then with the paddle, he'd press down the contents and smooth off the top. *It would be a simple matter*, Cameron commented to himself, *for me to bear down a little harder on my bowl. I would get an advantage over the others that way. But I wonder exactly how much difference it would make—surely not more than a very few grains—with all those hawkeyed POWs watching every minute gesture. I could not do it unnoticed. Anyhow, I can see that the temptation would be most difficult to overcome if one were not on his guard constantly.*

On a certain day, the squad leaders were called to headquarters for a conference, a situation that set all sorts of wild and weird rumors adrift. So many prisoners always had answers for everything that occurred. In spite of being invariably proven wrong, they persisted in, categorically announcing the future outcome of any and every situation, as they alone were either clairvoyant or were familiar with all the details. Their listeners were, according to the attitude assumed by the lecturer, presumed to be immature and lacking in wisdom. Consequently, during the hour that the conference continued, many reasons were pronounced in sagacious fashion. Where two such were in conflict, a heated debate took place between their respective advocates. No one would admit the validity of any other thesis than the one he had originally fathered. POWs of that ilk took it for granted that their intelligence and wisdom was unsurpassed and undebatable.

"Now we will find out how little these brilliant forecasters know of what was going on up on the hill," Cameron said to Paul as the two sat on the porch steps watching the squad leader coming dawn from headquarters.

"They certainly have declared every possible answer in the book," returned Paul with a chuckle.

"I heard at least twenty different answers—another Allied navy sunk, Germany had sued for peace, more rice, cut in rice, no more work, winter clothes to be issued, letters may be written, no more reign of terror by the guards, and a whole hatful of other things."

"Not a one of them be right."

"What's the story?" Cameron called to the approaching group.

The reply that was shouted back was entirely foreign to any thought that had been bandied about. It caused dismay in some, joy to others, hope in a few, but derision in most.

"Gonna have a pig farm!"

It was minutes before all preconceived views could be cast aside and the value of the announcement determined. The prisoners looked and spoke to each other with a variety of emotions.

"How do you like that, Blake? Pigs!" Cameron called to his roommate through the open window.

"We'll never get a chance to eat one, I betcha," he grumbled.

Paul had been busy obtaining more details of new venture from the squad chief. "The plan is to build some pens and raise liters," he announced to Cameron.

"What's the dope on pig farm I just heard about in the benjo?" called Ashley breathlessly as he joined Blake at the window.

"That's the word from the Japs," answered Cameron. "We are going to set up some sties, get a couple old sows, and start production."

"Admirable, to say the least," Ashley commented mournfully. "Maybe in a year from now, some will be large enough to butcher, but I'll be dead by that time."

Paul turned and addressed him direct. "The scheme has possibilities. They are going to buy a number of different sizes, so that will be some available for the soup at regular intervals. And that should start soon. So cheer up, Ashley. I believe they have turned over a new leaf."

"Not that gang of yellow bastards," Blake insisted, undoing Paul's effort at raising morale.

"What I do not see is what we are going to feed the animals," Paul deliberated. "There isn't a single scrap of anything in this camp. POWs leave no swill."

"How are we going to buy these pigs?" Cameron asked, with uncertainty in his voice. "Whose money are they to use?"

"The chief said the Japs intended to collect all the yen they have paid us so far," replied Paul, "because we have no way of spending it."

"Hell, I've used mine for the benjo long since," declared Blake. "They've got a fat chance of collecting any from me."

"I always wondered why they ever paid us that stuff," Ashley said.

"No doubt it was merely a gesture to look good on the record," Cameron analyzed.

"Probably so," Paul confirmed. "I have wondered from that first day they called us in to sign the payroll. They gave us credit for the same amount of yen that they pay their officers of equivalent rank."

"And paid us 5 percent in cash and said the rest would be put in their postal savings," Cameron continued.

"To help them carry on the war with our money," declared Blake. "We'll never see any of that money."

"Don't believe it will be worth anything when this war is over," Paul prophesied.

"They never gave our enlisted men a nickel, either," Ashley stated. "Now they are going to pick up the little they gave us. They sure must be getting hard up for cash to fight on."

"They are short of everything," Cameron said. "Metal especially. Look how they are picking up every bit of scrap they can get their hands on. Even pulled down the couple of clothesline posts."

"Remember how they stripped the Philippines before we left?" Blake reminded the others.

"They sure did," Ashley recalled. "All the iron cots from Stotsenburg, every wrecked automobile from Bataan, even the reinforcements out of the destroyed concrete bridges."

Sykes woke up at that moment, complete contentment on his face. "This is the first big news we have had," he ventured.

"What?" growled Blake.

"Why, the pig farm, of course."

"Don't be no Pollyanna," cautioned Blake with disgust.

"It's wonderful! They are making an effort to get us more food, especially meat, which we haven't had since we came," Sykes enthusiastically replied.

"I hope you are right," said Cameron, still unconvinced.

"They've called for carpenters, and I have volunteered," Sykes announced.

"You are a carpenter?" inquired Paul with interest.

"No, but somebody has to do the work," Sykes replied. "And it will relieve me from farming."

"And give you a good standing with the Japs," Blake muttered with sarcasm. "Maybe they'll give you an extra bowl of rice."

"How about a hand of bridge," Cameron quickly said in order to avoid any unpleasantries. He was absorbing the influence that Paul spread for the elevation of sociable living. "We can have the kibitzer stand guard and watch for the Japs!"

The times that Cameron indulged in meditation and introspection were frequent. There were tough moments as he shuffled along in the column on the way to the farm, during which he preferred to turn matters over in his head rather than engage in idle chatter or listen to the complaints and grievances that the others thought they had. While he leisurely moved his kuwa up and down in simulated work, his mind was active in discussing with himself those affairs that were uppermost in his thoughts. Then at night, after he had curled up under the odds and ends that he was able to collect for bedclothes and as he lay shivering before comforting sleep took possession, he had his finest opportunity to analyze conditions.

It is strange, he thought, *how ideas will trickle through your mind when you are relaxed and growing drowsy. Try as you will, you cannot pin them down to a definite analysis. Then suddenly, everything blanks out. But on the morrow, the problem appears clear and simple, and you wonder why it ever disturbed you. Something happened while you were asleep; the old mind must have kept clicking unbeknownst and finally come up with the right answer.*

It was during those times that Cameron cogitated over his fellow man. So many other subjects were of more immediate concern because they vitally affected the daily and hourly lives of the prisoners. The hazards of living under those ruthless and restricted conditions were many indeed. But there was not one over which any soldier had the least control, unless it was in keeping out of the sight of the captors as much as possible. There was no possible way of exercising any control over the quantity of food made available. Many complaints had been registered against the forced labor they had to undergo, but no relief could be expected. The brutality of the treatment accorded was something that sprang out of the soul of the Japanese soldier and was aggravated and urged on by his superiors as part of the national plan. Mail? That was a joke. No one expected to receive or to send any.

Then there was the wall! Though it appeared to be constructed of brick and too high for a man unaided to clamber over, it was by no means a stationary and inanimate structure. The prisoner who glanced at it and dismissed it from his thoughts was dead—dead because the vividness and verve of life had departed from him. It was the wall, the wall alone, that was the dominating influence in every prisoner's life. Only a very few ever realized it. Because it was so closely aligned with the thoughts and actions of all within its confines, it loomed large in Cameron's efforts to penetrate and understand the reactions of his colleagues. Life was breathed into the wall the instant the Americans passed through its gate. From then on, it became a living monster that leered at every prisoner and, like a leech, sucked his substance. Daily, the four sides of that inhuman brute moved inward and compressed the inhabitants in mind and action into smaller and smaller confines until even breathing was restricted. That tiny world of the prisoners shriveled constantly as new means were devised to subject them to a condition that would squeeze out the last breath so that the record could show "death from natural causes."

After the major camp policies had been put into effect—hard labor and brutal punishment and inadequate food—and the intended results were not immediately forthcoming, greater refinements and more subtle procedures became evident to the prisoners. And as the wall flailed that lash on the bare, sweating backs of emaciated humans, it howled with mirth because it could grind its heel into the neck of the Occidental. The accumulated spleen and venom of a thousand years could now be poured with satisfaction onto a handful of representatives of the white man. *But why do those damn Americans persist in living? We should have slaughtered them long ago,* wailed the wall. *And they even dare to laugh! But wait; we can make it more painful and lingering, if they want it that way.*

Cameron was fully alert to all that the wall meant, and he was aware of the effect it was having on his fellow prisoners. It was symbolic of all the conditions they were undergoing. Once the door through the wall had been slammed shut, liberty, freedom of action, and even hope had been forced out. Those were most precious acquisitions too often taken for granted. Most any possession too often loses its value to the owner when he lives with it continuously and without fear of its loss. But let someone else try to take that possession away, and the real worth immediately becomes apparent to its owner. It was some such condition as that which Cameron began to feel had taken hold of the captives. They might not be able to explain it in their depressed condition, but it was reflected in their actions and behavior. *So many have lost all sense of respectability and decency,* Cameron meditated, *and have cast aside all the fine values of life in this scrap for existence.*

Why has not culture and refinement stood up? he asked himself. Are they as superficial as they appear to be here? Why cannot a man die, if he must, with his chin up and with dignity and not ignominiously and dragging down others with him? The basic quality in man seems to come out when the pressure is on. Some seem to bear up under severe restriction and preserve their dignity; too many others give in to inordinate selfishness. The latter are not interested in heroics; they want to maintain life at any expense.

It is so absurd, Cameron declared to his soul, *for men who occupy the station in life that we do, which is surely above the average cross section, to crumble morally the way we are doing here. I do not understand why so many persist in considering only themselves and will not raise a hand to assist another if it will cost them the least sacrifice.*

Then on the other side of the question, Cameron continued to contemplate, *how does Paul continue day after day to make sacrifices to materially and spiritually help others? What sustains him? What keeps alive his will to render assistance? Is his breeding better, or has he learned more from life than the rest of us? Or is there something else that keeps that sly old rascal on his high standard of ethical living?*

Being sorely hurt by the conduct of his colleagues, Cameron decided to talk the situation over with Paul during their saunter around the parade ground one evening. Cameron felt a strangeness in trying to discuss ethical and moral conduct. He had always been a realist, meeting the problems of life as they occurred, but not neglecting the foresight a practical man would engage in. Yet the very existence of that intelligent realism in his being caused a turmoil in Cameron's soul; something constantly tugged at him to make an effort toward straightening out the lives of the walled-in men, including his own. There was no question in his mind but that he was slipping rapidly, in spite of his desire not to. Constant observation of others and the fight he was forced to make to keep from being imposed upon could not help but lower his standards. And he resented that fact of his succumbing to these strange and difficult conditions. *I'll be damned*, he insisted to himself frequently, *if I will let these half-wits drag me down to their level.* Without fully realizing it he had taken the first step forward and upward by acknowledgment of his own weakness and having a determination to overcome it.

"Uh, say, Paul," Cameron began, hesitatingly and awkwardly, "what do you think has happened to our people here?"

"In just what way do you mean?"

Cameron had hoped that he need only ask an occasional question of Paul and that his friend would do all the talking. The younger man was ill at ease because he was entering a field of discussion foreign to him. "Well, Paul, you know …uh, uh …how many of the people here are acting. They seem to have lost everything that men in their station of life and with the culture that we always felt they should have—"

"Yes, Cam," Paul cut in, "I understand your point But let me say, before you have a chance to criticize too strongly and lower yourself, that the matter must be looked at with a sympathetic viewpoint."

Cameron felt repulsed. It had never occurred to him that his colleagues needed such charitable consideration of their problems. They were all mature men and had better than average opportunities for development. And they were failing! However, he had too much confidence in Paul to idly dismiss his remarks. Perhaps those thoughts could be tempered with his own and a sensible solution arrived at. Anyhow, Cameron concluded, Paul was one of the kindliest men he had ever met. He was a man who leaned far backward in his relationships with others—at his own expense, too, because someone was always taking advantage of him. Nevertheless, those with highest principles would admit that Paul was worthy of the name he carried. "No doubt you are right, Paul," Cameron eventually admitted.

"Life is a very peculiar situation, Cam," continued Paul. "There is little perfection. A man's culture and altruism are often advanced to the same degree that he is relieved from struggle for existence. People here have not had to worry too much in the past for their successes, and the traits we see now were held under control by comfort and luxury. So we never saw those unfortunate traits to any extent. Yet they existed as fundamental qualities in everyone. The human being is still an animal at heart. It is how well he has learned the better way of life that determines his conduct when the going is against him."

"You are doing a grand job of standing up under these severe circumstances, Paul. So why can't more of the others do the same?"

"You are very kind, Cam. Whether you are right or wrong, the fact that you are willing to concede that point and declare it proves that you have not slipped too far yourself."

"Well, I'm all tangled up at the moment. I try to be decent and respectable toward the others but get no place. They just elbow me aside and think I'm a sucker."

"Do you think you can raise standards and ethics without taking some punishment or making some sacrifices? It is the very fact that you make those sacrifices that you benefit spiritually. In its simplest terms it means that anyone can give away something for which he has no need, but the man who offers something that is vital to him has done the world a real good and has elevated his own character. The greatest joy in life is received when you give up something you need to one who requires it more than you do. That is not limited to material things. We have a tremendous opportunity here to help the less fortunate. The answer is to give of yourself, to keep giving and never be discouraged over the lack of visible results. Live the finest sort of life you can under these appalling circumstances. It will pay dividends, in time."

"But, Paul, how are some of these people ever going to hold up their heads again with any dignity, that is if they over get back home?"

"They will get back home. Start on that basis, without discouragement. Then to answer your question, I know of at least one man who would have said, 'I forgive them!'"

Cameron did a lot of thinking that night as he lay in the darkness of his room. *Paul*, he said to himself, *may take a lot of pushing around by some of these mean people who take advantage of his kindness. But, God, what a man he is! What strength! What character!*

It was still too deep for Cameron to fully realize and to decide upon his own procedure. More thinking had to be done, more analysis. The distasteful actions of many of his colleagues rankled him. *Why should they deserve help when they refuse to help themselves?* he queried of his soul. *I can get along,* he continued to meditate, *and not lose my respectability.*

Sure, you can get along, he thought he heard Paul saying to him, but what of those whom you could help if you had the courage to make some sacrifices? The only person who can assist others is the one who has conquered himself first. Your obligation is clear, so ...

One cold morning the prisoners were lolling about their rooms waiting for the call to assemble for the march to the farm, where they would have to expend their limited strength in clearing land and planting vegetables. There was no purpose in going out in the cold December air until they were forced to. Even though the temperature was the same inside as it was out, some little comfort could be gained in relaxing on cots and chairs. As was customary, all eyes were concentrated on the headquarters building from where the Taiwanese overseer would eventually emerge and stroll down the path to the barracks. When he approached close enough, he would call out in a loud voice, "Tenko! Tenko!"

It was all quite a routine by now. It never varied. One day was much like any other. But this time as the tired men watched, the usual procedure did not occur. Time slipped past the normal hour for assembly; no sign of working tools was present. The prisoners looked at one another but said nothing. Ten, fifteen, twenty minutes rolled past. This was unbelievable! Something had gone amiss! A restlessness waved through the barracks. No one could take advantage of the precious minutes by relaxing. Each person was tense, wondering why the delay.

Then, suddenly, the enemy—in the form of the interpreter—came running down the path. That was most unusual. Something different was about to happen. The little misshapen and bespectacled Japanese with his sword awkwardly dangling from his waist entered at the end door, and as he rushed down the hall called in a breathless voice, "Tenko in ten minutes. Best uniform will be worn."

"The damn rat!" mumbled Blake. "Imagine anyone having a 'best uniform.' All I got is these same rags I work in every day."

"Apparently some very special thing is going to happen," Paul stated, trying to suppress his laughter over Blake's remarks.

"He said we had to put on our best uniform. So we will have to dress up the best possible way." Sykes was a great believer in doing everything exactly as the enemy ordered. He scurried in haste to rearrange his working clothes so that his outer appearance would be improved, even if just a little. After pulling off his ragged outer coat, he removed the cotton uniform shirt that was the next layer of clothes beneath. He then slipped the coat on again and, finally, squeezed into the uniform shirt, which gave him the same warmth even though he looked like a bulging porker. A rag of blanket end, which he used for a muffler, was transformed into a tie for his shirt.

"I'll be goddamned," screamed Blake. "You are a hell of a of help to the rest of us!"

The other men in the room were inclined to agree with him.

The prisoners soon lined up, and the guards made the rounds to inspect them. The first American on the end of the line had his attention called to the absence of a couple of buttons from his tunic and paid the penalty by receiving two hard slaps in the face. A civilian coat worn by the man at his elbow called for a thrust of a rifle butt on his foot and a hard kick on the shin when he raised his foot in agony. The guards were on a rampage and evidently expected each one to appear in a well-groomed military fashion. Just when they would have ceased their summary punishment, if they had not been interrupted, would be hard to say.

But a detachment of the guard marched up at that time and took position on the right of the line as a part of whatever ceremony was about to be conducted. After they had aligned themselves, two Taiwanese came from the rear, lugging a table, which they placed at some distance in front of the formation. As soon as that had been completed, the door of the headquarters building opened and the camp commander strode forth, members of his staff in his wake. As reviewing officers, they took position on the far side of the table facing the Americans. The formation was then formally presented to the captain, who, after making his acknowledgement, climbed up on the table.

"Another speech from old Evil Eye."

"What has the old bastard got on his mind this time?"

"It must be pretty good if we have to miss work to hear it."

"And get all prettied up for the occasion."

"What is today, some Jap holiday?"

"It's the eighth."

"Eighth? Eighth of December! Christ Almighty! This is the first anniversary of Pearl Harbor. No wonder they are having all this stiff formality."

Further speculation suddenly stopped, for up on the hill at headquarters, an amazing sight took form. The administrative sergeant major made an appearance and started down the path with a slow goose-stepping leg action. He held his head high and looked into the sky. On his hands, he wore a pair of white gloves, and with arms fully extended, he carried an elongated, white cloth-covered box. There was nothing about that episode that could be taken seriously by a group of Americans. They had been too well indoctrinated on past occasions, however, to display the humor that bubbled up within them. The thin line that divided a serious moment from farce was quickly torn down by the prisoners whose sides began to shake with merriment.

The sergeant major, stiff-legged and with his arms held forward, finally reached the table on which the captain stood inflexibly. The noncommissioned officer presented the box to his commander, who reached forward, raised the cover, and removed a rolled parchment. With dramatic fervor, he unrolled the script and, holding each end in one hand, began to read.

After the first few words, he hesitated, and the interpreter called out, "Pay heed to Imperial Rescript!"

"What the hell is a rescript?"

"The guy said, 'Pay heed.' If you keep quiet, maybe both of us will find out."

Holding the parchment, the commander read out this proclamation:

> We, by the grace of heaven, Emperor of Japan, and seated on the throne of a line unbroken for ages eternal, enjoin upon thee, our loyal and brave subjects. We hereby declare war upon the United States of America and the British Empire. The men and officers of our army and our navy shall do their utmost in prosecuting the war. …
>
> To ensure the stability of East Asia and to contribute to world peace is the farsighted policy that was formulated by our great, illustrious, imperial grandsire and that we lay constantly to heart. …

More than four years have passed since China, failing to comprehend the true intentions of our empire, and recklessly courting trouble, disturbed the peace of East Asia and compelled our empire to take up arms. ...

Eager for the realization of their inordinate ambition to dominate the Orient, both America and Britain, giving support to the Chungking regime, have aggravated the disturbances in East Asia. They have obstructed by every means our peaceful commerce and finally resorted to a direct severance of economic relations, menacing gravely the existence of our empire. ...

Our adversaries, showing not the least spirit of reconciliation, have unduly delayed a settlement. ...

This trend of affairs would, if left unchecked, not only nullify our empire's efforts of many years for the sake of stabilization of East Asia but also endanger the very existence of our such nation.

The situation being as it is, our empire, for its existence and self-defense, has no other recourse but to appeal to arms and to crush every obstacle in its path.

The hallowed spirits of our imperial ancestors guarding us from above, we rely upon the loyalty and courage of our subjects in our confident expectation that the task bequeathed by our forefathers will be carried forward and that the sources of evil will be speedily eradicated and an enduring peace immutably established in East Asia, preserving thereby the glory of our empire.

Inscribed by the Imperial Sign Manual and the Imperial Seal the eighth day of the twelfth month of the sixteenth year of Showa.

All formations of the Americans were under the so-called command of a prisoner officer of the day. It was his obligation to see that the prisoners were properly lined up at the appointed time. He would take the initial roll call and make a report to the Japanese officer, who promptly rechecked the assembly for his assurance.

Scurvy was standing out in front one day. It happened that certain representations had again been recently made to the authorities about the forced labor that was imposed upon the prisoners. One of those moments existed when tension could be felt rather than seen. The Americans resented their treatment, although they wisely refused to show the least resistance, while the enemy gave the impression of being uncertain of what to expect. Scurvy issued instructions to the prisoner officer-of-the-day, who turned about and transmitted them to the Americans. It may have been from fright or uncertainty or misunderstanding or just plain stupidity—none of the prisoners were able to satisfy themselves on that point—that he expressed himself as he did.

"The Japanese officer says that some who were not sick did not go out to work yesterday. Work on the farm is entirely voluntary, but all the prisoners must go to work."

That statement struck the prisoners, as all enemy logic did, about the same as a joke coming from a comedian on a vaudeville stage. It was little wonder that a couple resounding horse laughs came forth to jar the sensibilities of the Japanese lieutenant. He immediately bristled up, feeling an insult had been rendered his position as a representative of his imperial majesty.

After a moment's deathly pause, he spoke in a low voice to the American, turned, and faced the formation.

"The Japanese officer wants to know why the laugh."

"Why the hell don't you tell him yourself," Blake mumbled to no one in particular.

"That was mighty stupid," his neighbor offered. "He could have used a little intelligence and explained something, anything to Scurvy instead of trying to get the whole crowd into a jam."

There was no motion in ranks. The remark of the officer out front was addressed to no one especially, and no one felt responsible to speak for the formation. The seconds ticked by; the lieutenant grew angrier with each breath he took; something was about to happen.

Finally Scurvy sputtered several words in his vernacular, and the armed guards that surrounded the Americans came running up to him for instructions.

Cameron's knowledge of the enemy's language served good purpose at that moment. He understood what was afoot and, at grave risk to himself, stepped out of ranks and walked up to the Japanese officer, whom he addressed in English. "Lieutenant, a mistake has been made. The POW officer-of-the-day expressed himself in very bad English, and some of the prisoners laughed because he did not know his own language."

"I did not understand it that way," replied Scurvy. "I believe they laugh because of work."

The lieutenant did not seem aggrieved and Cameron wisely thought that he might better agree with him in expectation that the matter might be dropped. "Perhaps you are right," he said.

"Inform the prisoners if they do not want to farm voluntary, it will be called off, as it causes the authorities too much trouble."

Cameron turned and addressed his colleagues as directed, trusting that the situation had taken a turn for the better. He had no more than finished when one of the POWs in the rear rank uttered another laugh that was heard by the little group up front. That was too much for Cameron to hope to defend, coming as it did at the time he was trying to placate the lieutenant, and he stood at attention fearful of the outcome.

"Why?" called Scurvy, intending to find out the reason for the laugh.

There was no reply, and Cameron was too discouraged to put forward an alibi. He watched the lieutenant and waited for the explosion. But Scurvy had more subtle means with which to deal with recalcitrant prisoners. His eyes flashed, and his teeth ground together. The muscles in the lower part of his cheeks bobbled in and out. Finally he spoke. "Tell the POWs that work is voluntary and is considered exercise. If anyone does not want to work, he may submit his name to the squad chief. But no work, no eat."

For the evening meal that night, there appeared to be a most obvious reason why the spoonful of beans each man usually received was missing. And it could not be without intention that the pittance of rice had been materially reduced.

"You made a gallant gesture this morning," Paul told Cameron at the first opportunity.

"And look what I got from my own people. I tried to save their necks, and they showed their gratitude by trying to cut my throat."

"It does seem that way, and you may be justified in thinking they are not worth the effort," agreed Paul. "But do not forget the big thing, Cam. It is trial by fire, and the way you come through will be the measure of your stature."

The following morning was Sunday. Work was not regularly scheduled for that day of the week. The reasons appeared obscure to the prisoners. That day in the Christian calendar was observed by the Japanese only in their commercial relations. Witness Pearl Harbor, the prisoners had frequently said to themselves. Sunday had no other significance for the Japanese. Other days throughout the year were recognized as holidays and for relaxation and gala occasions.

Cameron spoke to Paul. "You haven't told me what luck you had with the camp commander yesterday."

"It is all arranged. Sorry I have been too busy to inform you. I went to the interpreter, and he got permission. There is a padre down in the town, he told me, but he is not permitted to come out to the camp."

"Well, who will conduct the services then?"

"I guess I will, Cam, unless you would like to."

"Oh, no! Oh, no! That would be out of my line." Cameron laughed back at him.

Paul smiled, sagaciously. He knew that he was as subtle an operator as the Orientals. Perhaps Cameron would think differently some day.

"We got word around to the squad chiefs this morning," Paul continued, "and we will assemble under the two balsam trees in the compound."

That first religious service, without benefit of clergy, was a success. Paul read a simple service, but he was restricted by the authorities to the little prayer book that he had uncovered after a diligent search throughout the camp. No sermon was permitted, and Buddha himself had been delegated to observe. The only difficulty arose when Paul announced that they would sing the first verse of "Battle Hymn of the Republic." Buddha immediately interposed and stated that no patriotic music was permitted.

"Very well," Cameron quickly announced to the group as he stepped to the front. "Let us sing, 'Glory, Glory, Hallelujah!'"

"The twitters that slightly delayed the rendition and that resulted from Cameron's quick thinking were lost on Buddha. When the service was over, many prisoners walked up to Paul to express their gratitude for his efforts in arranging and conducting that first opportunity they had had to worship their God together. Many times, the authorities had been approached, but each time they had refused to give permission. On occasions, they had refused to even listen to the request.

While the little group was huddled around Paul, Buddha approached Sykes. A few of the others noticed and commented among themselves adversely. Sykes was too frequently talking with one of the enemy, smiling and bowing. What was he after, special treatment? They were yellow bastards and should be left alone. One could not be friendly with them without losing his self-respect. And also, sometimes during those frequent conversations, the Japs could not help but learn things that might be best kept from them. That fellow Sykes better watch his step, and he required a lot of watching himself. "He is either one of us or he isn't," they said.

Others turned and glowered at Sykes. They did not hear what Buddha had said, but there was no mistake about Sykes's attitude. He bowed several times; smiled; and, in a subservient manner said, "Very fine, very fine. Thank you, sir. Thank you."

Such servile fawning was sickening to most of those who were observing. They turned their backs and left. A few who were filled with curiosity lingered. Severe restrictions bring forward basic characteristics in a peculiar manner. There were some who had already slumped into a puerile and childlike state. To them it was great news and something of unusual interest when a prisoner conversed with one of the enemy.

Just think what may come out of it, they must have thought. Perhaps some first-class information, which they would be first to learn about—being first in anything meant so much to a weakened mind—had been gleaned. Or maybe there was trouble between the two, and those POWs who watched would be actual witnesses to a catastrophe of the first magnitude that would be news of the first magnitude for news-hungry colleagues.

This time their curiosity paid well. As soon as Buddha left, Sykes rushed to those who had lingered and breathlessly announced, "I have great news. I am the only one in camp that he told."

"What is it? What is it? Hurry up!"

The impatience of his friends could not hurry Sykes. It was essential that he first impress on them that he had been the one selected, the only person in the entire camp, to be the custodian of tremendous information. "Just think," he cried," he told me … Well, of course, we are very friendly," he continued in a more calm tone. "Naturally, he would tell me first because I probably know him better than anyone else."

The effervescence of Sykes' egotism made no impression on his listeners. They wanted the news, and his explanation was just so much palaver that delayed the receipt of what they impatiently desired to hear.

"What did he say? What's the dope?" they anxiously inquired.

"The story is this," he replied as he leaned forward with an upraised hand and finger to make his pronouncement more effective. "Packages have arrived! Red Cross packages!"

"Jesus! Red Cross packages!"

"Are you sure?"

"God Almighty! Food!"

"They have come just in time!"

Sykes had no more than uttered his words than one of his listeners took to his heels bound for the barracks. That remark that he had heard was too vital not to carry with the utmost dispatch to all the others. He, too, was stimulated by the fact that he could dispense news of magnitude. It made him hurry to be the first one to race through the building with glad tidings. What kind of packages, when they would be received, verification, and other important matters were of little concern to him. This was no rumor. Did not the lieutenant say so? The fact that it came from Sykes and might have been garbled was given no consideration. His requirement was to rush onward and get credit for spreading the tremendous new first.

"Food! Food! Red Cross packages are here. Maybe we'll get them today," he cried at the top of his lungs as he ran down the hall.

Consternation! Those who heard and could understand what he had called were astounded. It was a terrific shock to starved men to be suddenly informed that food from home, from America, was within their reach. Maybe we will live after all, they told themselves. Good God! There would probably be some canned meat; some sugar perhaps; and possibly a bit of dried pork, the fattest pork you ever saw! Some laughed as a relief; a few shed tears in their emotion; many were silent because the impact of the news dulled their senses; here and there a skeptic smirked.

Paul looked at Cameron, and Cameron looked at Paul.

"It could be," Cameron said, quietly.

"I hope so. But think what havoc has been played if it is only another rumor or garbled statement."

"It is too damn bad that these matters cannot be properly censored and investigated before some idiot runs off at the mouth and stirs up the whole crowd."

"Easy now, Cam."

"It's true. The half-baked monkeys have thrown away all their intelligence and act like a bunch of unfortunates in an insane asylum!"

"Be sympathetic, Cameron. They are unfortunates, and they are in an asylum."

"Damn it, Paul, you know they have been that way all their careers. The finest thing that was done was to send them over here and get them out of the way so they couldn't retard the progress of the war."

"Quite an indictment, Cameron. You are in a position to justify that statement?"

"Not yet, Paul. You know better than that, and I wouldn't say it to anyone but you. I've got to get it off my chest. Sorry I blow up this way, but it is better to do it with you than somebody else who would not understand. The trouble is that I cannot understand why this crowd has fallen to pieces the way they have. Of course, it has been tough going, and the ones who have come this far are hanging on by a slender thread. Why haven't they got enough guts to fight the thing through, instead of giving in to all this damn selfishness, hatred for each other, and childlike and animal actions."

"Cameron, suppose we pass up all the reasons for those things for the time being. Let us try to realize that they exist and make an effort to help where we can."

"Right, Paul. You are a great help toward settling me down. I want to do all I can to help, in spite of the fact that I am not in too good a position to be of much assistance."

"It's all in the way you look at it. Don't slip. Keep your mind alert, or as much as is possible under these circumstances. So long as you can give of yourself to help someone else, you will save yourself from destruction. Once you give up, you will be just like the others of whom you complain."

"You have me there, Paul. I'm afraid there is only one choice."

"How about this story we just heard; we have gotten away from the condition of the moment."

"We better run it down and see what truth there is in it. As soon as that fellow is through passing his news around, we might talk with him and try to settle him down."

At that moment, Sykes burst into the room. "Isn't it wonderful? Just think, food from home."

"Paul and I were just talking about it. We thought we would get that chap in a quiet corner and calm him down. Then we could find out more definitely where he heard that story and what truth there might be to it."

"Start you investigation right here with me," Sykes replied. "I was the one that the lieutenant told it to."

"Swell! Tell us, Sykes, just what he said."

"Very simple. Red Cross boxes are here."

"Just where is 'here'?" Cameron inquired. "Do you mean here at Karenko?"

"Oh, no, not at Karenko. They are down at Takao. Just unloaded from a ship."

"Mm," hummed Paul. "Are they going to be distributed to us prisoners?"

"Well, I suppose so. The lieutenant said we were to have them."

"Did he say when?"

"No-o-o, he didn't. But Takao isn't very far away."

"Depends upon how you measure distance," Cameron interposed. "You must consider mileage, transportation facilities, the desire of the Japs to get them to us. Maybe they will be bombed before we get our hands on them."

"Are you sure that they are food packages, Sykes?" asked Paul.

"Oh, I'm positive of that."

"Did Buddha say so?"

"Not in so many words. But they couldn't be anything else. That is what we want most," countered Sykes.

"That may be the reason why they are food packages—because that is what you want, most of all," Paul replied.

Sykes attempted to justify his interpretation of the lieutenant's statement, but his effort was feeble and unconvincing. The defense he prevented was quickly ripped asunder by calm and intelligent questioning.

After being satisfied in his own mind as to how much of the tale to believe, Cameron felt it would serve no purpose to embarrass Sykes any further. In consequence, he said, "We have no control over the matter, one way or another. So all we can do is to sit here and wait to see what the outcome may be."

"My advice is to drop all thought of food packages until they are delivered," Paul sagaciously announced. "You can worry yourself to death over something that may never happen. If they do show up suddenly some day, just consider it a stroke of good fortune that occurred unexpectedly."

"An act of God," Cameron called over to Paul, his eye twinkling, with a meaning that might have been less capricious than it appeared. Paul smiled in return, and his heart within him was gladdened.

As the December days dragged onward, the weather grew fouler. It was damp and cold and blustery. Ragged cotton clothing and starvation rations could do little toward building up resistance. Conditions were growing worse; sickness became more prevalent; ruthless treatment by the guards flourished under the prompting of their officers.

In spite fear of discomfiture, fear of uncertainty, and loss of hope, an occasional bright light filtered through the dark clouds of despondency. Returning from the farm one day after being pushed hard to accomplish more work than usual, the tired and dejected prisoners were suddenly buoyed up from the mire of depression in which they had sunk by the announcement that met them as they entered the gate of the compound.

"Letters! Letters! They are going to let us write letters home!"

For days and weeks and months, each prisoner had hoped and prayed that he would be permitted to write home to those who were waiting in agony to hear from him. Perhaps some day he might have the good fortune to receive a letter, but that was relatively unimportant compared with the intense desire to get a word or two back to his loved ones indicating that he was still alive and had come through the horrors so far without succumbing. As a result, the announcement was shocking in its suddenness. Questions innumerable were asked: When may we write? What about a scrap of paper and a pencil? Do we have to have stamps? How will they deliver letters when there is no contact with America? Can we say anything we want to?

There were no answers. As many different kinds of questions were advanced as there were minds to think them up. The men bustled about in mad haste, without purpose or direction. That was one of the inexplicable effects that the leering wall forced upon helpless men within its grasp. Hurry, hurry! Rush, rush! Everything must be accomplished at breakneck speed! Now and then, one of the prisoners would return to a degree of normalcy for a moment. He would then stare disdainfully at his colleagues who were rushing excitedly to accomplish the insignificant things that loomed so great in their lives. Such actions were ridiculous in the thoughts of the observer. Nevertheless, he himself would slip into the same manner in spite of his best efforts to avoid it.

While most of the prisoners were bouncing about, the squad leaders were called together by the interpreter. They were given instructions that fully covered the plan of writing home. That information was passed on down to the various rooms to be further disseminated to the rest of the prisoners.

"Here you are, fellows," Cameron remarked as he entered his room. "One prisoner, one card! Fill in the answers to the printed questions. Write nothing else on the card, or it will not be sent. On the other side write the name and address of the person to whom you are sending it. Now listen! They insist that these cards be sent to close relatives only. I have to make a record of the addressees and their relationship and turn it in to the Japs. So let your consciences guide you. Don't give me the name of a friend. Make it your grandmother if you can't do any better." Cameron felt that he had given complete instructions. All anyone would have to do would be to read the card and do what he had told them. But he had been in behind the wall too long not to know that even this simple little matter would bring forth a multitude of questions. He turned to Paul and whispered, "Now for a barrage of questions."

"Is a sister a close relation?"

"Do I have to answer all these questions?"

"This printed statement says, 'I am well.' I can't write 'yes' to that, because I want them to know the truth. I'm in a hell of a shape, and I'm entitled to say so."

"There is no place on here to tell where we are. Can't we add Karenko, Taiwan?"

"How do we tell them where to reply?"

Cameron sat on the edge of his cot with his chin held in his hands, grinning at Paul. He kept his back to the others and completely ignored their questions. If an intelligent one came forth that he had not covered in his explanation, he would endeavor to answer it.

For many days thereafter, the writing of that first card home became the chief conversational topic of the prisoners. In itself it was a small matter, but in value to the writer, it was of tremendous importance.

There had been no letters sent from the prisoners to their families since the Day of Mourning, when Bataan fell. And for those on Corregidor, none had been sent since the last submarine had silently slipped into Manila Bay and out again that final night. Now, this moment to get word about their well-being created a great stir in the drab lives of the prisoners. It was little wonder that it awakened memories of the past and thoughts of those who were patiently waiting back across the broad expanse of the Pacific. What were they doing? What were their lives like under wartime conditions? Was there a food crisis? Was production under way? Were troops being massed and trained and equipped without delay?

Only their own imagination could answer these queries. Each one harkened back to the last message that he had received. Most had heard immediately after Pearl Harbor; then the world had blanked out for them by the erection of an impenetrable barrier that time and distance and curtailed facilities had built.

From Blake's wife had come a message that was as blunt and hard-hitting as he was himself: "Sock them with everything you got! We know you can do it."

Ashley's mother, in typical loving fashion, had wired: "Our prayers are with you, dear boy. We are firm in our knowledge that you will never let your country down. Stock up on vitamins."

With humor that could not hide the tears of courage had come Cameron's last word from home: "You have been looking for this for a long time. Wish we had a hundred thousand like you over there. Count on me to carry on here with the same will to do as you have there. When you return, I will pin your stars on you in person."

And so it went. From that moment on, the world had been cut off with utter finality.

Gradually, the joy and thrill dissipated. Life grew back into the burden that it had been earlier—the sameness, the drabness, the tension. From the east, the penetrating winds of the Pacific whistled across the compound and the new farm area where the virgin land was being prepared for early planting. The wall continued to dominate all things.

Life was being gradually squeezed out of each of those unfortunates who had to suffer the whims and caprices of the wall.

The food situation had grown worse than ever. There had been no meat. Nor had there been fish. The little cart had been pushed up the hill from town by two Taiwanese soldiers almost every day. Occasionally it would be forgotten or would fail to arrive because there was nothing to be purchased. At best, it carried only enough greens to give a sickening color to the water in which they were boiled. A small teacup of rice was the standard ration for each meal. When matters were displeasing to the authorities, even that pittance was slashed. The many promises made that an increase would be given if certain tasks were completed in a given time were never fulfilled. The pig farm that had been looked forward to with such relish turned out to be just a tantalizing bit of the compound. The few animals were fed the same rations as the prisoners, plus the scraps from the enemy soldiers' kitchen—there was never anything left over from the Americans' mess—and accordingly refused to grow into the bulk that had been established as a requirement before they could be butchered. All to be gained from the pig farm was the swarm of flies that bred there and the foul odors that persisted in wafting through the barracks.

Rumors from all sources helped to sustain and encourage. News was occasionally given out by the Japanese, but it was of such a propaganda nature that it possessed small value. Hardly anyone kept abreast of the calendar. There was no need to know what day of the month it was. Everyone knew that he was cold and miserable and that the sun never broke through the dark and stormy clouds that drifted by close overhead. They knew that every day they were fortunate to see draw to a close meant they had beat the white-whiskered old man with a scythe out for another few hours of existence. The only thing to their credit was that they had sufficient stamina and intelligence remaining not to strike back at a guard when he administered torture and ruthless punishment. They still could realize that that was the goading that was expected to incite them to resist, for which extermination could be exacted.

Then, suddenly, a most unusual situation occurred! The prisoners awoke one morning to a day filled with glory. The darkness of the heavens had slipped away during the night. Overhead there was brightness in the blue of the sky, and the contrasting cumulus clouds made a setting for an artist to delineate. The weather had taken a favorable turn; it was warmer and delightful. The stormy winds had ceased to swirl and cut capers around the compound. Every man perked up, smelled the fresh air, raised his chin a little higher, and vowed he still could keep life within him. It was Christmas Day!

That amazing frame of mind that was presented to those prisoners at Karenko on that day in 1942 was a landmark that none would ever forget. Its appropriateness and unexpectedness was an omen. The very fact that its qualities lasted only for the day added impetus to the belief that it was a sign not to be disregarded. Rancor and ill feelings among the prisoners were suppressed by an invisible force. Spirits buoyed up. Courtesy and kindness were prevalent. Men's thoughts were elevated.

"What a day, Blake, what a day!" Cameron called to his colleague as the two walked out for tenko.

"Pretty neat." Blake grinned back. "I wonder if the little bastards will give us a little more to eat today," he added.

"Eat? Hell, Blake. A man doesn't want to eat on a day like this. He would be wasting the wonderful minutes that he could use to take in the fragrance of a beautiful day."

Ashley joined them. "Look at the mountains. What has happened up there?"

They turned their heads and raised their eyes to the top of the long ridge that ran from north to south a few miles away. The heavily wooded crest line, thousands of feet above them, had been hidden from sight for weeks by the ominous clouds that had hung overhead. Now it was white and rested on a purple base.

"Snow!" cried Blake. "I'll be damned if it isn't snow!"

"It surely must be," replied Cameron. "Couldn't be anything else."

"That is the first snow I have seen in ten years," Paul declared as he arrived in time to hear the other remarks.

"Good morning and a Merry Christmas!" The voice was familiar, but the joy and good fellowship were strange. The others turned and saw that Sykes had joined then.

"Merry Christmas to you, Sykes," Cameron said. "It will be difficult to discount this day. There must be a purpose in it."

"God is in His Heaven!" Paul ventured.

"Somebody, someplace is trying to tell us something," came from Cameron.

"It means to me that we are to take courage," Ashley pronounced, "and realize that matters are on the upgrade for all of us."

Paul picked up the cue. "Things like this do not just happen. There must be direction someplace. It has to have a meaning."

"I'm certain it does. And it is not hard to guess." Sykes prophesied, "It must mean glad tidings from home."

"Yes," continued Paul. "We can feel certain that everything is fine on the home front and that substantial progress is being made on the battlefront."

"They're getting along all right," chimed in Blake. "What about things right here? Are they going to give us some extra food today?"

"I heard some talk about that," Paul assured him. "We will know soon when we see what comes into the kitchen. In the meantime, we can forget the electric wires they have just finished putting around the top of the wall and the new guardhouse they just completed and the smells from the pig sty."

When the few spoonfuls of rice that constituted the morning meal for each man had been delivered, distributed to the bowls, and quickly consumed, the prisoners lay back on their cots cautiously. They had learned to exercise care not to violate that order about sitting or lolling on their beds. The minutes wore on, and there was no call for working details. The men began to take heart. *Perhaps they are going to leave us alone*, they thought. It would be the least they could do on this day.

Paul and Cameron sat together in the shadows of their side of the room. Some excitement seemed to bestir their souls. Close scrutiny of them, if anyone had thought of any good reason to exercise it, might have shown that they felt great anticipation.

Finally, Cameron could not restrain himself any more, and he spoke to Paul, "Do you think they'll do it?"

"They assured us, as you well know," Paul replied.

"At the time, I believed them," Cameron countered, "but they have had the night to sleep over it and may well have changed their mind."

"The captain himself approved. Yet they have an easy habit of forgetting promises. However, I am going to retain my confidence until he fails us."

"Anyhow, it's a good thing we told no one else. Just imagine how quickly the word would have gotten around. Then, if nothing happened, the disappointment would really have been bad."

"Let's watch the cart when it comes in. That will tell the story," Paul said.

"They'll probably unlock that small emergency gate behind the cookhouse; it will save them hauling a heavy cart so far around to the main gate."

"I wonder if they are that smart?" questioned Paul.

"If they are we won't know until mealtime, because we can't get near them to see."

Accordingly, noon came and, with it, a call for extra prisoners from each squad to report to the cookhouse to carry food. That was the first inkling the prisoners had that something unusual concerning their food was about to transpire. It was a most amazing situation, which had never occurred before! Consequently, everyone rushed to the porch of the barracks to investigate. When they witnessed their colleagues returning with more than the pails of rice, they were aghast; and in their excitement and impetuosity they rushed back and forth shouting the good news of additional food.

"Paul, we've done it!"

"Thank God! Cam, our plan has worked."

"Your plan, Paul. It was you who figured out how we could get the interpreter to speak to the captain and explain to him how this was our great religious day."

"But you were there to support me, Cam. When I was too frightened to speak, it was you who stepped up and asked for a supply of extra food to celebrate. And do not forget that, when we returned from headquarters and the other POWs questioned us, you had the presence of mind to say you were just asking for a little medical attention for me!"

Their conversation was interrupted by the howls of joy, which by that time were sounding through the barracks.

"A whole orange apiece!"

"And a banana per man!"

"Good God! Meat in the soup!"

"Sure enough. Meat! The first we've had!"

"It ain't much. Pretty slim."

"Just enough to flavor the muddy water but, I'm grateful for that!"

"Oh, boy. Shelled peanuts!"

"Swell, even though they are only raw goobers."

"How many did you get? I counted mine, and there were thirty-seven."

"I got more than that, forty-one."

"You owe me two! Come on, divide up."

"Hell with you, soldier!"

A day that never was forgotten! Good will toward men?

The spirit of the occasion did not die with the unexpected but highly acceptable increased rations for the noon meal. There were certain acts and symbols pertinent to Christmas Day, and the sudden release felt by all the prisoners brought those to mind. On the pretense of taking a short constitutional, as Paul remarked to his companions, he slipped out of his room shortly after finishing his food.

Keeping his eye alert for any of the enemy guards, he meandered to the far side of the benjo; and when he was certain that he was not being observed, he reached over and quickly detached a branch from a small, scrawny evergreen bush. He held his stolen possession close to his side as he hurried back to the barracks unobserved. From the shelf in his room, he took down a square-faced gin bottle. That had been his canteen on the march out of Bataan, and he had clung to it rapaciously ever since. A light cord fastened to the neck of the bottle for slinging it over his shoulder was easily and carefully removed. Again reaching up on his shelf, he extracted from the shadows a carefully folded bit of wax paper, which on an earlier occasion had covered a carton of Japanese cigarettes. Never was the most meager item ever discarded. A future use was always foreseen. Paul wrapped the paper around the bottle; and as he held it in place with his fingers wondering what he could use for a binder, one of his companions saw his predicament.

"Here, I have the very thing to tie it with," said Ashley, fumbling about on his portion of the shelf and retrieving a narrow piece of red paper.

"The very thing is right," Paul agreed, reaching for the colored strip that had once bound a pack of enemy toilet paper—that vitally important commodity but an almost useless one because of the thin and crumbly material from which the flat sheets were made.

The evergreen branch was thrust into the paper-wrapped bottle, and Paul's efforts were understood by the others, who had been curiously watching.

"My contribution," Cameron marked and laid on the table a small gob of cotton that he had salvaged from the packing in a bottle of pills some time in the distant past. Pulled apart into smaller bits they made a fine snowy decoration for the green branch.

"There you are, boys, a real Christmas tree!" Paul explained gleefully when his work was finished.

"Pretty neat," commented Sykes.

"Mm," muttered Blake. "But you can't eat it."

"Oh, wait a minute," cried Sykes, jumping up and searching through the pockets of his jacket, which hung on a peg. Finding what he was after, he knelt on Blake's cot and began to mark on one of the window panes.

"Where in the name of heaven did you get that?" Cameron asked when he saw Sykes scrawling on the glass with a china-marking pencil.

"One of those mysterious things that crops up," replied Sykes as he continued his artistry. He finally wound up with a recognizable sketch of a wreath with a large bow tied on it.

"That is a grand Christmas atmosphere, all right," commented Paul when be viewed the finished product.

"Well, get off my bed now," grumbled Blake.

About dusk that evening, an amazing thing transpired. The door of the room suddenly opened, and the smiling Buddha entered. "Kiotsuke!" called several of the well-indoctrinated prisoners in unison.

That word was constantly on the tip of everyone's tongue, to be rattled off in a loud tone whenever one of the enemy appeared within sight. The prisoners had long since swallowed their pride. It was preferable to pay the amenities demanded than to accept the brutality that failure was sure to bring.

Buddha waddled into the room, made a slight oriental bow, and astounded his listeners with his remark. "Merry Christmas." He grinned with a wide slash across his broad and pudgy face.

Sykes made a meticulous bow and returned the greeting. "Merry Christmas to you, sir!"

The others were too disgusted or disinterested to make any reply.

"Won't you sit down?" asked Sykes in a polite manner as he pulled the bench out from the table. He was too wise to point to the more comfortable seat on one of the cots. Those were never to be used as seats, and it would be inappropriate to ask one of the lawmakers to violate his own rules.

Buddha, however, amazed the Americans by flopping down on the nearest bunk and stretching out his huge and soft bulk its full length. "We try to get turkeys for the POWs, but no turkeys on Taiwan," he said.

Dirty liar! Everyone knew what Blake had mumbled silently to himself.

"Other camps on Taiwan most unhappy," Buddha continued. "Could not get extra food for them." He rose from his relaxed posture and stretched his muscles. His eyes came in line with Paul's tree.

Now for some trouble, Cameron spoke to himself inwardly. *He is about to get nasty over the little branch broken from the evergreen bush. What quick alibi can I think up to save Paul?* he inquired internally.

But the unpredictable Buddha merely pointed to the tiny decoration and said, "Very nice. The British room upstairs nice too. Must go now." He shuffled out of the door without further ceremony, and no one paid any attention to Sykes's punctilious, "Kiotsuke!"

"Let's go have a look at the British room," Paul proposed when Buddha's step was heard far down the hall.

"I don't want to see it," parried Blake. "What those dopes do doesn't interest me." Blake was not internationally minded.

"Come on," replied Cameron. "I'll go with you."

They climbed the stairs to the upper porch and strode down to the large room that held forty prisoners and had been dubbed the "British room" because of its occupants.

The trip was well worth their time and effort. Beautiful!" exclaimed Paul as he stood at the doorway and peered in.

"Ingenious!" countered Cameron.

From the cords and wire that ran the length of the room and that were used to hang clothes on, hung suspended white and pink and yellow paper stars. They were of varying sizes and had been cut from the different colored packages that Japanese cigarettes had come in. Bits of tinfoil had been shredded from the packages of tea that had, on rare occasions, been brought into the compound by the enemy and, as festoons, dangled form the wire. The platoon-sized mosquito net, the type of protection the Japanese Army furnished its troops against insects and one of which had been procured for that particularly large room, had been folded lengthwise along one side. Its wide blue border was left exposed, and other stars cut from tinfoil had been pinned across its face. An attractive marigold plant had been surreptitiously dug up from where it grew near the wall and now reposed in all its splendor on one of the tables.

"You have done a grand job here, Brigadier," Paul complimented the nearest Britisher.

"'Tis well done, indeed," he replied.

"Weren't you a bit timid about taking such a risk?" asked Cameron. "'Japs never take very kindly to anything we do here."

"Quite so, but we have come a long way since our arrival." He spoke with an adenoidal twang.

"Yes, I recall your arrival," replied Cameron with a smile as his thoughts raced back to that evening several months earlier.

For several hours, enemy soldiers had given an indication of a portending event. Readjustments in sleeping arrangements among the prisoners had been hastily made. Additional bunks had been moved into the barracks, and several tables were carried out in the open in front of the building. Over the tables a large electric light had been suspended temporarily. Questions were asked of the enemy soldiers to obtain information, but all those efforts were rebuffed with noncommittal shrugs of shoulders. Commotion of that degree could not be discounted. Rumors grew apace. They expanded and grew more authentic as they progressed from man to man. The prisoners were unable to relax, and they tore from room to room and from barracks to benjo to hear the latest word and to repeat it with embellishments. During the evening meal, the uproar and conflation were greater than normal. Every prisoner knew the correct analysis, so he thought, and he insisted upon being heard. It was impossible for one to agree with another; that would be a mark of weakness to have anyone know as much as someone else. Nearly every prisoner wolfed down his bit of rice and unceremoniously rushed out to the rear porch to wash out his bowl and clean his spoon. Those safely put away for the morrow, he lingered on the front porch or wandered around the path in front of the barracks. Whatever position he choose, it had to be what he thought would be the most effective one to witness all that was to transpire.

Impatience grew as the time passed and nothing transpired. It grew dark; tenko was called. Every prisoner was required to repair to his barracks; no one could be trusted out of the building after nightfall. The greatest fear was that nine o'clock would come before the event transpired. That was the moment when lights had to be extinguished and prisoners had to be in bed.

But all speculation suddenly terminated when an unusual disturbance occurred. The gates were flung open, and several sputtering army trucks drove in. That occasion produced the same effect as the muezzin raising his arms and calling the Muslim faithful to prayer. All activity and all conversation immediately stopped. Each one of the prisoners rushed to a point of vantage. The few who were caught in the benjo at the sound of the commotion had to terminate events in a distressing manner and hurry out front to see and learn hand what was going on.

Uniforms of khaki, uniforms of forest green, strange insignia were the first things to note. The next thing was that these were white men. The fact that Japanese guards accompanied them proved that they were allies. To cheer or not to cheer one's allies or other white men. *What's the use! The hell with 'em! We're better than they are, the goddamn foreigners!*

The trucks came to a jolting halt. The men aboard looked about and decided they had reached the end of their trip. They tossed off their odds and ends of luggage and leaped laboriously to the ground. Guards quickly sprang forward with an undue display of efficiency and bellowings—in the Japanese Army one's career hinged on the commotion and wild animal instincts he could display in front of his superiors—and quickly herded the newcomers into a column with the leading man at the tables. One after another, they were expected to sign one of the sheets of paper presented to them. Each of those documents had space for ten names under a heading that said something about, "On my honor ... Will not escape ... All on this sheet are responsible and will be executed."

The Americans had earlier signed similar papers, not knowing or not caring.

Unexpectedly, a spectacular incident had occurred. One of the Britishers picked up the paper and read what be was expected to sign. He tossed it back on the table with a gesture of negation. The camp commander, Evil Eye himself, who was acting as master of ceremonies, sprang up from his chair with flaying arms and horrible screams. A dozen guards rushed in from all directions with their bayonets at the thrust position toward the helpless and unarmed prisoner who had dared to utter moral defiance at the command of his imperial majesty, the emperor of Japan. A quick order from Evil Eye stayed the anxious desire of the guards, and the recalcitrant one was rushed off to the newly constructed and as yet unoccupied *eso* (guardhouse).

Blake had many supporters when he cried, "Just what you'd expect from a dumb Englishman. What difference does it make what you sign for these Japs?" Perhaps Blake was thinking of Bunker Hill, or had something more recent disturbed his intelligence?

"That takes a lot of guts, Blake," Cameron thrust at him. "It's a pretty good man who will maintain his ethics with a lot of shimmering steel pointed at his heart."

"That fancy talk hasn't got anything to do with it," Blake said, trying to make his argument convincing. "Look what they did at Singapore. Folded! They didn't even fight."

"Of course, Blake, I realize that you have all the answers to that episode." In honeyed tones, Cameron was pouring out his most vitriolic sarcasm. "Undoubtedly, after many generations of historical research, the record will prove your contention."

"Well, it's true. They folded up in a hurry. Look how long we hung on." Blake was willing to jump at conclusions in an effort to fully justify his feelings.

"Yes, Blake, we were heroes, great heroes. But don't strut with your head too high when you get back home. Calm and placid judgment may decide differently." Then, with a laugh to relieve the tension, he added, "In any event, the British and the Dutch have arrived. Hong Kong, Singapore, Java, Sumatra! We're going to get lots of news!"

"Say, what ever happened to Pittman?" Cameron asked his roommates one day as they were all seated at the table consuming their midday rice. "I saw him at Mariveles before we started to march out of Bataan."

"Orani! He got that far but was in mighty bad shape. We thought the few hours' sleep we got there would help him snap out of it. But he never woke up."

"That's tough," Cameron replied. "He did a mighty fine job at Abucay."

"How about Hal Jennings?" Paul inquired. "Anybody know about him?"

"Yeah," Blake stated. "He was up in my sector, you know. We started over the Pilar-Bagac Road together. The Japs herded a bunch of us onto a bridge-building detail for several days. He was down in the river floating logs across. I think the current was too strong for him, and he was carried downstream. All the Japs on the bank started firing at him. He disappeared."

"He was a stout soldier," Paul commented. "Just the sort to resist capture and try for a getaway."

In a faraway voice, Ashley remarked, "No doubt he is happy now. I wish I had taken the chance instead of going through all this."

Paul and Cameron exchanged understanding glances. Then Paul quickly attempted to divert Ashley's thoughts by saying, "By the way, Ashley, Jack Snyder has never shown up, has he?"

"Jack had some rough moments—" Ashley started to explain.

"I know all about him," Sykes broke in. "He took off for the hills and is probably up in the Bontoc country now."

Ashley slowly pivoted his chin, which was resting cupped in his hand as he turned his head to look directly at Sykes. After a pause, he quietly asked, "Just how do you know that?"

"Well," Sykes defended himself, raising his hands and shrugging his shoulders, "it's common knowledge. Many of our people saw him take off in the dusk, and none of the Japs even fired at him."

"That's an interesting story," remarked Ashley. "We were pretty close to each other. Classmates and came over on the same boat. I was there." Ashley hesitated, and his eyes moistened.

His companions noticed how affected he had become and sat in silence, respectful silence.

"The warehouse at Lubao. I was with the last group that left. The Japs took a dozen Filipinos out of the crowd and made them dig a ditch. Then they had to drag the boys out of the warehouse, the ones who went down during the night and got trampled on. They had to lay them in the ditch. We all watched. Some of those lying there tried to get out, but the Japs stuck their bayonets into the guts of the Filipinos and made them fill up the ditch with earth. I saw Jack there! He turned his head and moved an arm. I went mad and rushed forward! And look!" As he cried that last exclamation, he pulled up his shirt to display a long, red sear across his belly. "The damn guard made a pass at me. Too bad he didn't get it right, and he would have if some of our own men hadn't held me back." Ashley made no effort to retard the tears that slipped from his eyes. In spite of the dampness, there was the flash of a killer peering out. No one felt inclined to make any remarks for fear of rousing him to a more bitter hatred. "Don't tell me about Jack slipping up into the hills. That's just some more of your half-baked gossip. You chatter like an unintelligent monkey without the least knowledge of what you are talking about."

Ashley could speak no further. His head drooped.

After several seconds of the utmost quiet, Paul laid an affectionate hand on his shoulder.

Saturdays, by enemy direction, were designated for a general cleanup and inspection. Frequent arrivals of persons in high position also called for a complete housecleaning—the steady stream of visitors was regarded by the prisoners as a means of release of oriental curiosity by looking at the white animals in a cage. Generals, colonels, and all other ranks and ages among the prisoners were required to carry water for cleaning, to scrub floors on their knees, to wash window panes, to cut the grass with hand sickles, and to tidy up the compound without benefit of brooms or rakes. At first, some of the older prisoners with age and position attempted to complain over being subjected to such indignities, but the privates of the guard quickly dispelled any resistance by threatening to use their bayonets and actual use of the heavy clubs they carried.

Future resistance developed from a variety of moods. A small group meticulously complied with every order given by the enemy, from fear or hope for preferment or because of small mental stature that was unable to reason matters out. Others displayed filthy personal habits and just did not care about the conditions under which they lived. The largest group resisted because of their disdain and contempt for their captors, and they quickly learned how to satisfy the men with bayonets by giving minimum effort. More than one prisoner learned that, by being a laggard, the others in his group would have to carry his share of the work. Pride and his reputation among his associates were given little consideration in his desire to do little or nothing.

Sykes was flitting about his room one cleanup day, rushing from one task to another as though the burden of the entire camp rested upon him. He was not one to shirk work, but in his impetuousness, the results he obtained were none too thorough.

"Take it easy," grumbled Blake, when Sykes's rapid darting about disturbed his calm. "You got plenty of time."

"But the Japanese ordered a thorough cleaning this morning," Sykes replied without lessening his efforts.

"What do you mean? Some damn little private came through here and made a couple of remarks. You fall for it as though he was Christ himself."

"We have to be clean or take the consequences," Sykes continued to defend himself. "Anyhow, you remember what Scurvy said at the last inspection. 'White soldiers haven't learned much because they can't clean up very well.' We have to uphold our position."

"So what? You can fawn on the little yellow bastards all you want to," Blake vehemently declared. "Every time you cater to them, you put the rest of us in a bad spot, because they then think the rest of us should do the same.

Cameron looked at Paul and blinked his eyes. He was amazed that Blake could arrive at such deduction.

"What are we going to do for cleaning material?" Paul asked when he felt the conversation between Blake and Sykes had reached the point where it might better be diverted.

"Don't know how they expect us to shine up this dump when they don't even give us a rag or a piece of soap," Blake retorted.

"I've used my last piece of toilet paper on these windows, and they still aren't clean." Ashley was never hesitant to donate from his meager possessions for the benefit of the others.

"It about broke my heart to use my undershirt to scrub the floor," replied Cameron. "Those holes could have been patched up, and I could have worn it for a long time. But now look at it!" He held up the article to show its shredded condition and black color.

"I'm afraid you wouldn't have gotten much use out of it, Cam," chided Paul. "There hasn't been a piece of thread around here for weeks."

"But I solved the thread problem," Cameron replied. "Look!" He picked up the hem of his mosquito net and showed how, by careful work, he could extract threads from the woven material. "It's not very strong thread, but it does the job."

"That must be where some of these perpetual sewers get thread. Some of the POWs in the other rooms spend every waking hour sewing, sewing."

"It's a release, something to do to keep from going crazy."

"When they reach that stage, they are already nuts," Blake said. "Some of the guys were born that way. They just piddle their life away on nonsense."

"Tenko! Tenko-o-o!" a rasping Japanese voice sounded outside the barracks.

"Now what the hell is up?" queried Blake.

"That is strange," cried Sykes as he hurried to the window to have a look. "They said there would be no formation but that we would be inspected in barracks."

"Who is 'they'?" snapped Blake.

"Why, Buddha, who told me so yesterday."

"So, you have been flirting with the Japs again," growled Blake. "This just proves they give you the runaround."

"But it is very valuable to have the close contact that I have. It keeps us in touch," countered Sykes.

"Come on, boys," Paul spoke up. "We better drop our housework for the time and line up outside. The young sentry seems quite agitated."

Some minutes later, the prisoners were lined up to the satisfaction of the guard supervisors, but not until the recalcitrant and tardy ones had been slugged by the enemy soldiers for the delay. Meanwhile, the interpreter had wandered down from the headquarters building and now stood before the formation. He was so unimposing, the prisoners thought to themselves as they viewed his poor carriage, his ill-fitting uniform, the long sword that dangled from his waist and rested on the ground, and the horn-rimmed spectacles under the peak of his cap that gave him the appearance of a bullfrog with bulging eyes.

"Attention to the orders," Pussy shouted in his high-pitched, weak voice.

The guards moved around the formation to see that all the prisoners were standing at attention and showing proper respect. They could control the actions of the POWs but were not in a position to control their thoughts.

"It is the order, which all POWs will obey, that after 1943 starts, no longer will the word *Japan* be used. It will be *Nippon*! The Imperial Nipponese Empire! Because we conquer East Asia and expel the white man, the change is made. It is ordered by the emperor! Dismiss!"

As the prisoners wandered back to the barracks, each one seemed inclined to utter a pleasantry or to joke over the turn of affairs.

"So they want to be Nips now," Paul said in his quiet manner.

"Yes," Cameron replied. "It appears they are feeling their oats."

"I confess that I do not quite see the distinction."

"It's rather a fine one," explained Cameron. "The new name has broader implications and refers to Greater Japan."

"What do you suppose will be the proper name when they lose everything?" Paul asked with a touch of humor.

"Are they going to lose everything?" Cameron tossed back with a grimace.

"Now, Cam, don't change the subject. What will be the correct name for the former Nipponese Empire?"

"Honshu!"

"Will you have a look! See what the well-dressed POW is wearing this winter." Cameron was chiding Blake over the strange garb he was putting on one cold day. "How can you possibly wear British clothes when you rate those people so low?"

"Gotta keep warm," he replied, unabashed.

"Those should be mighty good slacks, Blake," Ashley said as he reached over to have a feel of the warm wool olive drab trousers Blake had crawled into. "That's what they call their battle dress, I believe. And that gray flannel shirt is what they wear in the Indian Army."

"What, no jacket to match the slacks?" Cameron asked.

"Couldn't find one big enough for me," Blake replied.

"That cuff on your slacks can be buttoned up and ought to keep a lot of cold out," Ashley continued.

"Blake, you old rascal, you must be a good trader to talk them out of wool clothes in the middle of winter," Cameron ventured.

"It was easy," the proud new owner declared. "They are lousy with clothes. The Japs brought their heavy baggage up from Singapore for them, you know. They have everything in the world."

"They probably have, all right. Considering the truckloads that came in, each man must have two wardrobe trunks, a couple of footlockers, a huge bedding roll, and a flock of suitcases."

"Some guys get all the breaks in the world."

"As a result of all the uniform trading around the camp, the appearance of the prisoners is quite a conglomerate one," Paul stated.

"That might be dubbed the 'international mix.'" Cameron laughed.

"They haven't gotten all those clothes from swapping, either," Ashley remarked. "Some thoughtful POW lifted my wool shirt and the only socks I own from the clothesline this morning."

"The hell he did!" declared Blake. "This crowd is sure getting low when they steal from somebody else who is as bad off as they are."

"I am afraid it has been going on for some time," Paul announced. "A number of instances have been known in the past several weeks. This is the first time one of us has been involved."

"That's a pretty low trick," Cameron agreed. "Looks like, if we are wise, we'll bring all our washing into the room to dry. You can't leave it out in the sun and air unless you stay right there to guard it."

"We might put all our washing together on one line and take turns watching it."

"Not to change the subject," Cameron spoke up, "but has anyone heard more about those Red Cross packages we were going to get before Christmas?"

"That was just another dirty Jap trick to tantalize us," Blake cried.

"Nip trick is right," Cameron thrust back, agreeing with him but also correcting him.

"Hell, Sykes, sit down and relax," Blake suddenly called out. "You have been rushing around and fiddling with things for the last hour and haven't accomplished anything."

"But I have so much to do," replied Sykes.

"Such as what? You aren't going any place."

Cameron whispered over to Paul. "When these minor irritations get on tough old Blake's nerves, we are really cracking up."

"It's hard to tell how those little things will hit you," Paul whispered back. "I feel them sometimes myself, and I'm mighty docile. It seems to be the continuous repetition of insignificant things that finally get on your nerves."

"With these failing minds, you certainly have to use every effort possible to keep doing and thinking things worthwhile. So few seem to realize that or they are too far gone to do anything to help themselves."

"That is where you come in, Cam. You know, like too few do, that the situation exists. Knowing that, you must keep busy to help others. It will not only be of value to them, but it will be of great value in keeping you mentally sound. I'll give you an example; watch me." Paul then spoke aloud so the others in the room could hear him, "Oh, Sykes, I've been meaning to ask you how your engraving is coming along. You were doing some fine work there. Haven't finished it up yet, have you?"

"No. I just got tired and had many other things to do."

"Let me have a look at it, will you?" Paul kept after him in order to direct Sykes's thoughts along some useful channel.

"Sure," Sykes replied, feeling proud at Paul's interest in his work. He reached down from his shelf the army canteen that he had carried since the days on Bataan. On one side there had been engraved an American spread-eagle, while on the other, a list of the major engagements of the recent campaign had been laboriously inscribed.

"I think that is very artistic, Sykes," Paul complimented him.

"You do mighty, mighty nice printing, too," Cameron chimed in. "What sort of an engraving tool did you use?"

"Just this short twig off a tree, long enough for a good handhold," he replied as he displayed the instrument. "Drive a nail in the end, and sand off the head by rubbing it on the stone steps out back."

"I never seem to be able to get a sharp enough edge on mine," Ashley said, showing interest.

"Oh, that's easy," Sykes explained. "Just draw it back and forth carefully over a stone. Here is one I picked up out in the compound just for finishing purposes. Use that on your tool whenever you want a better edge."

"Thanks, Sykes, I'd like to."

Blake had become enthused during the conversation and felt challenged to show his handiwork. So, he brought out his mess kit and lid, exclaiming, "There are a lot of hours on this. Every date of importance since Pearl Harbor is on this. I've left plenty of space to put on many others. This big space down here near the border, that is for the date we get released and will be in double-size letters."

"That's the boy, Blake," Cameron proclaimed. "The biggest date of all in the biggest letters. And it is just around the corner."

"Ouch!" cried Ashley, suddenly squirming around on his seat and clasping his hand to his hip.

"What happened to you all of a sudden, boy?" asked Paul.

"I have the sharpest pain there right below my hip," he replied, laughing in his embarrassment at having cried out. "The same sort of sharp hurt like a hot needle hit me in the arm yesterday."

"That is funny," Sykes spoke up, feeling his upper arm. "That is the same thing that I've been bothered with lately. Wonder what it could be?"

"Sounds like a nerve to me," Paul said.

"Oh, you guys are falling apart; that's all," called Blake.

"Did you bruise yourself?" Paul inquired, trying to analyze the condition.

"No," Ashley replied. "I haven't touched a thing except my bed when I lie on it."

"That sounds like the answer to me," ventured Cameron. "You probably have injured a nerve lying on that hard cot. Why don't you shake up the straw in your mattress and try to loosen the hard pack it has made. That might make it a little softer."

"I suppose we'll have many more things like that to disturb us before we get away from this malnutrition," complained Sykes.

"I know they are trying to kill us off by slow starvation," Ashley declared glumly.

Paul looked at him steadily. He had been concerned about Ashley lately and the attitude he was assuming. The wall was playing havoc with him. No longer was he the young and energetic person he had been a short while ago. That fellow needed some help. Better talk it over with Cameron and see if they could not arrive at some means of cheering Ashley up before it was too late.

About that time, Cameron sniffed the air and looked around the room. Not finding what he expected, he rose and started for the door, saying, "What under the sun do I smell?" Opening the door, he saw another prisoner walking down the hall. "Hey, Walt," he called to him. "Is that you with the garbage odor?"

"Blah to you," Walt replied in an ugly mood.

Cameron had no intention of rousing Walt's ire, so he called to him in a jocular manner, "Bring it in here, Walt, and let us in on the secret."

Walt came back to the doorway. And when he framed himself in the opening with the shadows playing on him, the others in the room looked at him and with the same thought felt that he was a typical POW just as some caricaturist might draw him. Then they sheepishly glanced at each other and discovered there was but little difference between him and them. He was gaunt and unshaven. The beard he had grown was not because it was an attractive addition but because he had no facilities to keep his face clean shaven. It was a stiff, bristly composition that grew irregularly. It was padded with gray and brown and so unsightly that it gave the impression that this was most uncomfortable to the wearer.

No hat covered Walt's uncut air. Attached on the front of his head, the hair was hardly distinguishable, as baldness was creeping up him. His clothes were the last remains of a khaki uniform that had gone through the siege of Bataan. It bulged outward from the pressure of heterogeneous items of clothes he had collected from various sources and now wore for warmth. Oh his feet, he wore the soft shoes, so called, that were required by the authorities to be worn inside of barracks.

Living under Japanese home conditions, where the floors were covered with matting, there was some sense in the minds of the prisoners for wearing footgear of a soft texture, not shoes or clogs which would rip the matting to shreds in a short time. But it never was clear to them why the heavier type of footgear was not appropriate on the plain wooden floors of the barracks and especially when the weather was cold enough to require reasonable covering for the feet. It had been presumed by the POWs that such a requirement under the conditions in which they lived was merely one more stupid harassment the enemy could inflict upon helpless prisoners. Another reason was, no doubt, the desire to deny them the use of occidental shoes, which were required to be locked up. Without them, the possibility of prisoners trying to escape was materially lessened. A white man could not get far wearing clogs.

Walt's footgear was similar to many others. It consisted of pieces of cloth that he had been able to gather up and, with the aid of a needle and thread and perhaps someone partially skilled in maidenly functions, sew them together in some form that might serve for a few weeks. Many other prisoners had to use their last pair of socks until they could no longer be held together; after that it meant going barefoot, cold or no cold.

After a glance at Walt, the matter that concerned the occupants of the room most was the pipe in his mouth. Then what was coming out of it drew attention. Several pipes were in use in camp. That was one item the Japanese were little concerned with, as very few of them had learned to enjoy that occidental luxury. But the pipe that Walt had was different from anything heretofore seen. It was obviously carved out of material at hand. Some sort of root had been scooped out for a bowl, while a stout reed of unknown origin had, by some means, been reamed out to make a stem. The thing actually worked! It was the smell of the smoke coming from it that had caused the original rumpus.

"Say, Walt," Cameron asked, "what are you smoking?"

"Tea leaves," he admitted.

"Tea leaves!" his listeners cried in unison.

"Sure. Some of the boys in my room had a little tea they brought up from the Philippines. We brewed each batch a half dozen times until there was not the slightest color left and then we tossed them out. I gathered up the remains, dried them in the sun and used them for tobacco. They smoke all right. But Christ! How they smell!"

"My dear friend," Paul spoke in a humorous vein, "in spite of your profanity, no one will disagree with you."

"Smells just like the benjo, only a different flavor," someone tossed into the conversation.

While he did not realize it fully, the wall had enmeshed Blake completely within its ruthless tentacles. In the battle between the effects of the wall and any one of the human souls within its confines, it was a matter of how well the individual realized his position subordination and how much fight he had left in him to overcome the relentless pursuit of the wall to beat him into complete submission. No one ever doubted his physical courage, his energetic drive to overcome, or his loyalty to the persons with whom he was associated. At least that was true until his freedom of thought and action was denied him. Even he, if pressed, would probably have admitted that there were more brilliant minds than his that could rapidly size up a situation, any situation, and arrive at a sound solution. They could reach that conclusion and take the necessary action, while Blake was still plodding through the maze of conditions that confronted him. Blake was reasonably well educated, but he had found that it was difficult to pursue, with any great degree of diligence, the subjects that he had selected in college. Somehow or other, he had been able to make passing grades, and he always was rankled at the restrictions imposed upon him by academic life. It was little wonder that he had felt a joyful release from that confined atmosphere when, in 1917, a war had given him the opportunity to chuck away restraints and engage in a more buoyant life.

Then, too, Blake, being a big man and an active man, had grown to be a great food consumer. It had never been necessary to restrict himself. He was healthy, and food was easily procured. Under such circumstances, eating became a habit more than a necessity. Like any habit over which it has not been necessary to exercise control, Blake's eating had become a fetish. He'd lived and loved to eat.

Because of one of those characteristics or a combination of them, Blake was easy prey for the wall. Somewhere along the line, he had not prepared himself for the difficulties he now faced. The wall was able to leer at him maliciously, laugh at him without fear of reprisals, and jostle him about at will. Of course, Blake could never understand that, not even if someone explained it to him. He felt suppressed, imposed upon. Since all things that he had learned to love and enjoy had been removed from his reach, his soul cried aloud in rebellion. He was not willing to accept the limitations imposed upon him and try to readjust his living to meet those reduced standards.

At least the thought never occurred to him to consider that new philosophy of trying to find contentment in a life of denial. Instead, he harbored resentment in spite of the fact that under no circumstances could he alter the conditions imposed upon him. The only relief he could obtain must come from a changed mental outlook. That was beyond his comprehension, however.

Nevertheless, Blake was not alone in that unintentional yielding to the machinations of the wall. Many others likewise had succumbed without realizing it, whether for similar or different reasons.

Ashley, like Blake, had demonstrated in combat that he was an alarming contestant, but with a difference. Ashley was not the slow, plugging type who would stand toe-to-toe end exchange blows. He had a greater flair for the use of intelligent maneuver. When a situation confronted him, he gave it thoughtful analysis and unhesitating decision. In him rested the makings of a great soldier, but conditions denied him his opportunity. Being an intelligent soldier, Ashley was never disturbed by that denial.

Other conditions did disturb him, though. He resented restrictions like anyone else did, but those denials hurt him particularly hard because they erected a barrier between him and one to whom he was passionately devoted. Without a thought that he could ever be torn away from the love and close fellowship of that person, he had given completely of himself and received similarly in return. Daily, hourly throughout his life he had leaned and been leaned upon. Nothing was ever said or done that was not in harmony or complete agreement between them. Each needed the other; each lived for the other. Separation was fatal.

The wall, wise to the ways of humankind, knew all those things. It was too malicious and too brutal not to take full advantage of its superiority. When a man started to deteriorate, the wall gleefully took advantage of him by striking him down and grinding him into the ground. It was unfortunate for Ashley that his background failed him and was the cause of his early submission to the unholy demands of the wall. Poor Ashley did not realize his failures anymore than did Blake. In spite of his intelligence, he never realized the predicament he was in. Nor did it occur to him that there was relief for him if only he would make the effort.

Sykes, too, was lost, but in a different manner. There was no question about his high standing as a professional soldier. Out of his years of training and varied assignments, he had built up an enviable reputation. The position he had occupied during the campaign was not the result of undirected fortune. He had been carefully selected, in the full knowledge that he would handle his position in a creditable fashion. And he had done that very thing and had received the plaudits of his superiors. Yet, down deep in his character, there lay a flaw which Sykes himself was not cognizant of. It was a subconscious response that grew with the years and, because of its delicacy, was discernible only to his close colleagues and was hidden from his superiors. In a hierarchy, position and prestige and advancement are partly influenced by the attitude and personality one shows toward those above him. Respect and loyalty are taken for granted, but diplomatic subtlety in those relationships often has a far-reaching effect. Most human beings enjoy commendation, are influenced favorably when someone agrees with them, and are apt to bristle if a subordinate irritates them.

One of the unfortunate characteristics in a man that so often shows itself in his thoughts and feelings, without premeditation on his part, is that, by virtue of occupying a superior position, he believes himself to possess greater intelligence, more ability, and surpassing wisdom. Often he is correct in that silent assumption; too often it happens that the reverse is true. Imperfections in the determination of relative position are difficult matters to foresee and overcome. Accordingly, a man by skillful management is frequently able to place himself in a position of preferment with his superiors that is beyond his worth. Such actions, whether intentional or otherwise, are frowned upon by one's colleagues and are often invisible to one's superiors because of the spirit of egotism.

Sykes could be accused of that habit of catering, even though he was unaware of it. It had paid him dividends, when on occasions, he had to resort to such procedure.

Characteristics, on occasion, were sharpened by contact with the machinations of the wall. At other times, they crumbled with that collision. Invariably, it was the good in man that was destroyed and the evil that was forced to the front. The influence that the wall exercised over lives was an astounding situation. Like nearly everyone else, Sykes was primarily concerned with his own existence. Perhaps he was fortunate in having but few opportunities to decide the great issue of self-preservation versus the rights and desires of others to live. Unlike many who would ruthlessly sacrifice their colleague for their own gain, Sykes sought preferment in a manner that affected him alone, although the results may have seeped over to a slight degree into the lives of others.

Truckling to the enemy became an obsession with him and dominated his actions. He manifested a subservience to each Japanese person with whom he came in contact, to a point where it raised the resentment of his colleagues. Each one of the enemy was scrupulously catered to. Sykes went far afield to render fastidious bows in the oriental manner. Smiles and condescendence became habits. Conversations were struck up on all occasions. Requests for favors were frequent. It was little wonder that the other prisoners who observed those things felt that he placed them in an unfortunate position. If he was so servile to the enemy, why could not the others be forced into the same position by increased ruthlessness? That question must have occurred to the authorities, Sykes's colleagues told themselves.

On the surface, Paul appeared docile and tractable. He accomplished what he was ordered to do without unduly overtaxing himself. Complaints never came from him. All things were accepted impassively and without emotion. But within himself, Paul never failed to exercise a high degree of intelligence. He was a smooth and diplomatic operator. He kept out of the limelight and never gave the enemy an opportunity to be critical of him. It was his matured judgment and understanding of human nature that rescued him from disaster on many an occasion. Yet there was something else that steadied him and gave him a great stimulus to come successfully through the ordeal of a prison camp. That was his willingness and ability to give of himself for the benefit of his fellow man. It was often a tremendous sacrifice to pursue that commitment, but the spiritual stimulation of aiding others to climb up out of the dregs was instrumental in maintaining his sanity.

It was character, likewise, that saved Cameron. It not only saved his life and his mind, but it preserved his dignity and self-respect and permitted him to return home eventually with a clear conscience, while others who had fallen by the wayside in their dealings with their brothers in arms were not able to look their colleagues honestly in the eye. Cameron was not involved in idealistic thoughts. He was a realist and never allowed flights of fancy to influence his analysis of any problem. Sound, substantial, dependable, with an enviable degree of intelligence and professional ability—that was Cameron's rating by colleagues and superiors.

Yet the wall respected neither any person nor any factor in life. The finest of characters had to joust with the insidious power that the wall spread in every direction, just as did those of lesser worth. At whatever point the least flaw or chip or weakness existed, the wall ruthlessly hammered away until the opening grew larger and larger, and the wedge it had driven in expanded and finally shattered all elements of character with which it came in contact.

But the wall's offensive could be thrown back. No average man could hope for that success, however. The few who gained that mastery proved by their numbers that only the exceptional person could weather the ordeal without serious detriment. Two tremendous factors loomed up as cumulus-covered peaks might in the path of an unwary airmen. They had to be visualized, understood, and conquered; otherwise all was lost. Realization and recognition of the implications and ramifications of the wall's subtle maneuvering were essential. If a character was weak inherently or had been temporarily beaten down by conditions, it might be expected that keen perception had flitted away and the thought of physical survival alone remained. The closing in of mental pressures, relentlessly and certain, because the character was no longer there to offer resistance, gave an erroneous restricted vision and presented an erroneous perspective.

The several who were strong enough to recognize the enmeshment in which they were contained and through which they must battle had another vast step to take. They must have or must develop the will and resolution to conduct a strenuous spiritual contest against the leering aggressor. When self was conquered, the ultimate in happiness and satisfaction was achieved by accepting the opportunities to help the others who were less fortunate.

Cameron was battered and badly bruised by the jabs and blows laid on him by the ungloved fists of the wall. Many times, he reeled under the impact; and while he might be momentarily beclouded from depression and anxiety and pommeling, his soul never let up in its constant demand that his conduct remain of the finest character.

The reign of terror was on! Both the open and the subtle violence on the part of the enemy went far beyond the intention to merely exact discipline. There were ominous implications in that procedure whenever it was put into effect. It appeared to the prisoners to stem from a military embarrassment somewhere in the southern seas or from some disagreeableness that had its origin within the compound. The severity imposed was intended as a release and demonstration of enemy ego and an effort to display assumed superiority over the white man. It further appeared to be a directed and intentional effort at human destruction because of the tantalizing procedure to force a prisoner to respond. It was that response the enemy seemed to want, a mere raising of an arm in self-defense or a blow in retaliation. The legitimate reason for the use of a bayonet or machine gun would then have been present; slaughter would have been justified; and Japanese skirts would have been clean should ever the world be called upon to judge. It further appeared to be a directed and intentional effort by the lieutenant to supervise the evening count of the prisoners.

"Here they come!" cried the hawkeyed Sykes, who constantly bounced around with the curiosity of an old woman devoted to neighborly gossip across the backyard fence. He had leaped onto Blake's cot, where he now kneeled as he leaned forward to get the best view from the window.

"Get the hell off my bunk!" demanded Blake. He was always more concerned with matters at hand than those that were brewing, despite any relative importance.

"Wonder what happened this time?" Ashley inquired.

"I don't know," confessed Sykes. "But the minute I saw Scurvy hurrying over to the guardhouse, I knew that something had gone wrong."

Ashley and Blake had, by now, joined Sykes in observing the happenings outside. The guardhouse was a small wooden structure near the main gate. It had evidently been constructed especially because of the new purpose for which the compound was now being used. A tiny porch faced outward and permitted a view not only of the entrance through the wall but also a major part of the interior. It was on that porch where constantly sat one of the guard reliefs.

The enemy military code required its guards to do duty through the turn of the clock of three-hour cycles. The first hour was spent in sitting erect and motionless on backless wooden benches like automatons and being instructed and quizzed on their military proficiency by the sergeant sitting at a table in the rear. At the approach of an officer, all the guards were required to leap quickly to their feet and call in their loudest voice, "Kiotsuke!" That first hour was intended to produce two effects. It assured the military hierarchy that officers would be adequately saluted and that the second hour, when the soldier walked his post, would be properly performed because it was a welcome relief from the severity of the preceding hour. The last hour of the cycle was intended for the guards to obtain what rest they could while they awaited the next cycle.

Sykes had seen Scurvy hurrying to the guardhouse, where he conferred quickly with the sergeant. In a few minutes, the guards on the porch, as well as those resting outside grabbed their bayoneted rifles and, like a well-drilled football team, rushed out into the compound. The group scattered in many directions, some barging into the barracks and others into the benjo, while the remainder hurried screaming toward POWs who were wandering about the compound.

When each guard approached one of the prisoners, he snarled and, with gesticulations and growls, indicated that the helpless prisoner had committed some breach. He had not bowed properly or quickly enough. There were holes in the clothing that he wore. He was not standing at attention in the required stiffness of manner. He was not freshly shaven. Those and a dozen other complaints were registered, as were many that could not be understood by the quivering POWs. Then brutality was exacted. In a frenzy, the guard would thrust his bayonet against the prisoner and then would strike him with the rifle butt or punch him in the face. Any sort of brutality might occur, with the evil expectation that a hand would be lifted in defense. That would call for a quick insertion of burnished steel. But the prisoners had witnessed that conduct in the early days, and the experience had made them extremely cautious. Another factor that mitigated a retaliatory response was that undernourishment, over a long period of time, had made them quite docile, had taken the spark of fight out of them. Consequently, the prisoner stood placidly and accepted the punishment as the lesser of two evils.

About the same time, the sentries came running from the guardhouse. Paul and Cameron burst into their room.

"They are on the way; be on your guard!" Paul breathlessly warned.

"Yes, we know. We see them coming," replied Sykes. His tone conveyed more than a mere announcement of his agreement with Paul. It had the unfortunate implication, as was only too common among prisoners, that he already knew anything and everything that anyone else tried to tell him.

"What went haywire with the little yellow bastards?" Blake asked.

Cameron spoke up. "You know that British brigadier they call Happy? He was out at the laundry tubs in the birdbath washing his clothes. Scurvy came along and said something about it not being the proper time to scrub clothes. Happy is like the rest of the Europeans that have spent most of their lives in the Orient and have kept natives in their place. He hasn't fully changed over to the new philosophy, and he gave Scurvy a grumble that this was the only time he had to wash. He got what you might expect, a lot of shrieks from Scurvy and a hard bop to the face."

"The British never learn," announced Blake. "Why did they have to be sent here to our camp?"

"Maybe they know more than we give them credit for, Blake," Cameron stated, inferring that he was coming to their defense. "There might be two ways to look at this problem of ours here. Could it be that we are taking too much lying down just to keep out of trouble? The Europeans have had many generations of experience in dealing with the Orientals and, in the long run, may be able to show us a trick or two."

"But they are awfully crude about it," countered Blake. "They aren't subtle."

Paul and Cameron smiled at each other. There was much in what Blake was trying to point out. The British, and the Dutch as well, had been deeply ingrained with the viewpoint of maintaining the white man's superiority among the natives of the Orient. Any relaxation would cause a loss of prestige. It was necessary to assume a demanding position, never to mix socially, and to maintain one's dress and conduct on the highest plane. When the Americans came to the Orient after enduring the accusations of "imperialism," they made a feeble effort to emulate such tactics. But it had fallen flat because it was not embedded deep in the democratic soul as Americans practiced that philosophy. How severely it was pursued was in direct relationship to the ego of the individual involved. It could be developed into a personal glorification, its adopter strutting like a peacock.

Sykes bustled about the room putting things in shape as he thought the enemy guards would prefer to see them. The others looked at him with a feeling that his activity was based less on fear than a desire to please.

"Take it easy, Sykes," blurted out Blake. It irked him to see anyone rushing about and disturbing his calm.

"But we have to have things in shape if the guards come in here to inspect," Sykes retorted in defense of his actions.

"It will make little difference how perfect conditions are." Cameron spoke from a stretched-out position on his cot. "The Nips are on a rampage. They are out to find something wrong, and they will not ask for alibis."

"That is right," agreed Paul. "We haven't a chance. If they want to maul us, they don't have to have a reason that is acceptable to us. They merely proceed."

"But, they have issued orders," countered Sykes, who was perspiring over the fact that the others in the room were not following his example.

"Who the hell is 'they'?" shouted Blake. "Some goddamn private comes in here with a grouch and grumbles something to show his authority, and from then on you take the thing seriously. He is the only guy who knows anything about the order he issued, and chances are that he has forgotten all about it or has been transferred in the regular turnover of guards. So you are just an overgrown sucker or maybe something else to keep insisting on obeying everything you ever heard from these monkeys."

Cameron lay on his cot with his hands clasped behind his head and chuckled at Blake's remarks. *The bird may be awful dumb in a lot of respects*, he thought to himself, *but he certainly has analyzed that situation in good fashion. The way the matter hits me is whether I would have had the courage to speak out and tell Sykes just what I thought. Or, then again, did it take moral courage or was it just plain stupidity?*

"They'll be here any minute now and start batting us around," Ashley prophesied.

It was not the fear of a beating that concerned him. Too many times had he been subjected to that to be unduly concerned over it. There was something, however, that was preying upon his mind, and that was the feeling that he was invariably singled out—that the enemy had something against him personally. So far he had not discussed that thought with any of his colleagues; it was just developing in his mind and was probably not fully realized. Matters of the mind just casually grow so often. And suddenly one is jolted with the realization that a serious situation exists, one that has quietly sneaked up without its presence being known.

"You know, Ashley, the guards cannot work over every POW. They just have not got the time or the strength or the persistence. Our room may be passed over as well as not." Paul was most considerate of the feelings of the others and never neglected an opportunity to spread a word of cheer if there was any logic to support it.

"They haven't missed us yet," Ashley contended, "on their reigns of terror. Our room seems to be in a vulnerable spot. And it's always me they seem to see first when they come barging in."

"Now, Ashley." Cameron laughed, but that laughter was not intended to pass off idly the feelings that the younger officer expressed. Cameron had recently begun to have some concern over the actions and discussions of Ashley. They were not always orthodox, but only a man with keen perception could see the strangeness of them. "You will have to admit that this welt on the top of my head and this bright scar across my cheek are a couple of Nip reminders that even you can't show."

Ashley looked at Cameron and shrugged his shoulders as he said, "We'll see. They are stomping down the hall now."

Paul had discreetly closed the door into the hall. It was an ineffectual effort. If the guards were looking for POWs, the obvious expectation would be that they would be hiding behind closed doors. That was occidental logic, but it seldom fit the Japanese mind. The enemy guard in the pursuit of his task was easily diverted by a small thing that might have an immediate appeal. A closed door in a darkened hallway could be overlooked because a noise or a light elsewhere attracted greater attention. Behind the door, the prisoners remained very quiet. Each had smoothed out the blanket on his cot to show no indication of it having been surreptitiously used. The prisoners saw to it that all their buttons were in use on their clothes, and they quietly aligned the table and benches.

The ashtray received unusual attention to give it the appearance demanded. That article was invariably a nuisance to the prisoners. Because of the Nipponese fear of fire and the belief that white men, because of carelessness or by intention, might start a conflagration, an extensive ritual had been built up concerning smoking. Matches and lighters long since had been confiscated, or so the enemy thought. Each room originally had been provided with a lighter connected with the electric outlet, but they were of such flimsy construction that the best efforts of the tinkerers among the prisoners were unavailing in the attempt to keep them in operation. The ashtray, however, was the greatest source of annoyance and grew to be a symbol of enemy harassment. The allowance was one for each room. A tin can, half-filled with water, seated in a wooden container was the item that played a large part in the lives of the smokers. Smoking regulations had to be fully complied with whether there was anything available to smoke or not. Prior to evening tenko, each tray had to be cleaned out and with the others, lined up in an inverted position in the hall. The benjo guard at night was made responsible to ensure that the correct number was accounted for and a card had been pasted on the wall indicating the correct count. After tenko in the morning, it was permissible to return the trays to the rooms. Since they had to rest on the table constantly, which was presumed to require the prisoners to sit at the table whenever they smoked, it was not particularly appetizing at meal time. Pipe smokers would forget and lay their pipes in the tray. Too late, they would discover their error and retrieve them from the mess, amid the guffaws of their companions. Anytime someone jolted the table, a minor disaster occurred.

It was little wonder that means were taken to circumvent the role that the stringent orders gave the prisoners. In time, each smoker numbered among his possessions a small tin receptacle that he could use while in a more comfortable posture than sitting at the table. The problem was not to get caught and to find a safe hiding place for the unauthorized article.

With those few adjustments made to avoid any obvious delinquency, the prisoners stood quietly in their room, awaiting the entrance of the rampaging guard. It would be soon now, for the Japanese who was prowling through that end of the barracks was already in the adjacent room. His shrieking gutturals and the havoc he was causing made such violent noise that the thin board partition was of small worth in retarding the sounds.

Apparently something very unusual had been discovered by the enemy, for his cries were of great violence. Suddenly two pairs of feet started down the hall toward the guardhouse; one padded along in soft slippers, and the other thumped in hobnails.

"Uh-oh!" proclaimed Cameron. "Someone is being taken to the eso. That's bad. No telling what might happen to him there."

Ashley was white. He gave the appearance of a man visualizing the horrors that were about to occur, feeling that he was to be called upon next to endure them. After a moment, he sat down on the bench and wiped his palm across his brow.

"It's all over, Ashley," Paul calmly announced. "That guard will not be coming back here. He has his hands full of greater excitement than he will get by coming through the rest of our rooms."

His remarks appeared to give Blake encouragement, because he promptly flopped down on his cot to relax.

One after another, the others let their tension drop, except Sykes. He remained in a standing position to be certain that he would not be violating any orders should a guard suddenly come in.

"Sure, Ashley," Blake popped off, "take it easy. Don't let the little bastards scare you."

"Subside, Blake," bellowed Cameron in wrath, "subside! This matter is over your head."

"I believe that it will be a good idea if I stroll down the hall and see if the commotion has stopped for the time being." Paul tried to stop any further comments among his friends for fear they might lead to unfortunate remarks.

Nothing further was said, and Paul continued to relax on his cot. He had had no intention of leaving in the first place.

Tenko that night was a time of tension. The prisoners, wise to Nipponese procedure, made every effort to please the Nips and give no cause for reprisal. They hurried out to the formation at the appointed time and lined up with alacrity, standing stiffly at attention whenever the guards were in their vicinity. Yet that was hardly enough, for the guards persisted in their mission of harassment and were stayed only by the early arrival of the lieutenant to supervise the evening count of the prisoners.

The usual formalities followed. The Nipponese officer, flanked by his staff, went from squad to squad, where the POW leader meticulously bowed and gave his report of the presence of the members of his squad.

Ashley stood in the front rank and, out of the corner of his eye, watched the approach of the lieutenant, who shuffled along with his samurai sword slapping at his ankles. A fearsome wave of unexplainable origin suddenly swept through Ashley's being. He had an intense desire, an uncontrollable urge, to strike the foreign officer with all the strength at his command. *Right in that pudgy face would be the ideal spot*, he brooded. *Then when he falls*, Ashley continued to speak inwardly, *I will jump on his head and crush him into the ground. I will not stand for this persecution any longer.*

As the lieutenant drew closer, Ashley's muscles grew taut, and his breath came with greater rapidity. Some sinister force had him in control. His thoughts lacked clarity. The result of his act and the recrimination that would follow never crossed his mind. It would be a release for him once he shown his mastery over that symbol of his persecutors who was coming closer toward him. *Another few steps*, Ashley analyzed, *and it will be the best moment to smash him in his ugly face. Coming from the direction that he is might be unfortunate, because I must use my left hand. But I have enough strength there to drop him in his tracks; I am sure.* Ashley weaved as he shifted his weight. His fist was tightly clenched, and his mouth opened in order to get more air, which his rapid respiration demanded. He wanted to wipe the sweat from his face, but there was no time for that.

Most unexpectedly, a blow struck him on the arm! His companion standing next to him in ranks had noticed Ashley's weaving as he prepared himself for the assault and had struck him sharply to warn him to stand stiffly at attention. The blow was effective, and the film suddenly cleared from Ashley's mind. The horror of what he had been about to do struck him like a blast of frigid air! He slumped in relaxation as he realized he had been saved from a terrible fate.

Yet the situation did not pass off lightly. The sentry, ambling along in the wake of the lieutenant and carrying a bayonet that glistened as the floodlights fell upon it, was bright-eyed and observant. The movement by the prisoners in the front rank close to him startled him into action. Rushing toward the prisoner standing next to Ashley, the guard shrieked and thrust his steel pointed rifle close to his heart.

Far down the line, Paul spoke in whispered tones to Cameron, who was standing adjacent to him. "What under the sun is that fellow shouting? Can you make it out?"

"He is screaming so loudly," Cameron replied, "that it is difficult to get his meaning. But it is something about insulting the officer and the emperor."

The wild cries of the guard echoed throughout the compound. He had worked himself up to the fullest frenzy; the sentry grasped his weapon with one hand and with the other struck the prisoner with his complete strength on the side of the head. Then shifting the rifle to the other hand, he administered several blows on the other side. The unfortunate man dropped in his tracks. Not satisfied with the punishment, the Nipponese kicked the prone and senseless man hard in the ribs with his heavy hobnailed boot.

The lieutenant walked on unconcerned, but to a man, the prisoners built up a burning wrath of hatred that only the knowledge of quick reprisal was able to control. They knew only too well that the least show of resentment would mean a bayonet thrust in their entrails. They had seen it happen before and were guided by the recollection.

The formation was dismissed, and the Nipponese officer, surrounded by his satellites and several of the guards, started to stride off toward the headquarters building.

Showing no small amount of moral courage, one of the squad leaders made his way toward the lieutenant and asked for permission to speak with him.

"What you want?" growled the officer.

"Sir, I wish to make a complaint to the camp commander about the treatment the guard gave the POW several minutes ago."

"No complaint," shouted the lieutenant. "Nipponese soldiers do not make mistakes." He turned away and hurried along the path.

Meanwhile, the guard who had so brutally assaulted the prisoner wandered back to the scene of his exploits. He stood near the fallen man with his bayoneted rifle held in both hands as though he defied anyone to dispute his actions.

The prisoners ignored him, and several, including Ashley, stooped over to pick up the injured one. They carried him carefully into the barracks and laid him on his cot. Doc came hurrying in with a pan of water he had quickly obtained from the porch in the rear of the building. Others crowded around. There was little that could be done. There were no facilities. Only the tender and affectionate touch of the man of mercy was at hand to restore the injured man to his senses.

"What started it all?" someone asked.

"It was my fault, every bit of it," Ashley admitted.

"What happened? The first thing I knew the guard came up screaming and started to work Harry over." It was more of a tone of curiosity than one of interested helpfulness.

"I think you had better all clear out of this room," Doc said in a demanding voice, which produced the results he wanted. Doc examined Harry's eyes and bathed his head with cool water. "Not so good," he whispered to Ashley, who was holding the basin of water for him.

"He took some mighty hard blows," Ashley declared.

"Undefended blows like that can cause a lot of damage. He has a concussion. Wouldn't be surprised but that he has a broken rib or two. The guard kicked him with a lot of force."

"Good God! And I am to blame!" cried Ashley in torment.

A little later, he strolled back to his room and flopped down on his cot, tossing his arm over his eyes. Paul stopped putting his bed in order for the night, walked over to Ashley, and sat down beside him. He laid an affectionate hand on the younger man's shoulder and softly spoke to him. "I don't believe I'd chastise myself like this if I were you, Ashley."

"If it hadn't been for me, it would never have happened," Ashley replied without shifting his position.

"When the guards are on a rampage, anything might occur," Paul consoled. "In fact, they do not even look for excuses, as you know. If the mood strikes them, they'll work anyone over."

"But Harry is in a hell of a shape. Doc says he has a concussion and maybe some broken ribs."

"That is most unfortunate, and all of us sympathize with him just as you do. But there is nothing we can do to help at the moment. Good old Doc is right there with him and will see that he gets all the attention that is possible. A concussion is not necessarily serious, and perhaps he will be all right in a short time."

Ashley took his arm down from his eyes and shook his head back and forth. He was obviously concerned and felt that he was responsible. "He saved me from a terrible thing. Some crazy idea hit me that made me want to pounce on that damn Nip lieutenant and crunch him into the earth. Just before I leaped, Harry poked me on the arm, and I came back to normal. The guard saw the motion and beat him up for it."

"Greater love, you know, Ashley. Why don't you let him have the credit for saving you instead of building up remorse within yourself?"

"Maybe you're right. I'll look in on him the first thing in the morning and see if I can do anything."

After the lights were turned out that night and the prisoners had crawled into their cots, Cameron raised the side of his mosquito bar and softly called across the few inches that separated his cot from Paul's.

"Paul, aren't you asleep yet?"

"No, far from it," he replied, raising his own net to get closer to Cameron. "This is the time I do my thinking, when all is quiet. It's the ideal moment for meditation. What's on your mind?"

"Ashley! We have a problem cut out for us there."

"Yes," replied Paul. "That's what I was thinking about."

"The youngster seems to be developing a complex of some sort."

"He certainly acts irrational now and then, as though something was preying on his mind," Paul conceded.

"Have you noticed how he writes letters, long letters? And there isn't a chance in the world of his ever sending them out."

"That is a release, some means that he has found to overcome or hide whatever problem is annoying him."

"It is no wonder to me that he is cracking up," Cameron declared. "The surprising thing is that all of us haven't done that long ago."

"I am not so sure that it has reached that point yet. The mental pressures here are severe, it is true. Yet Ashley is a stout lad. He did a beautiful job during the campaign, as we all know."

"That may have something to do with his present condition," Cameron stated. "He proved that he was active and energetic and capable. Now all opportunity is taken away from him, and he has to live under suppressed and depressing conditions. It is the opposite extreme."

"Unquestionably, there is much in what you say," declared Paul. "But I believe we are pushing his condition a little farther than it actually is. Perhaps that is a fault that we have because of our reduced ability to see and think clearly. He has given certain appearances of abnormality, but I doubt if there is anything seriously wrong that cannot be brought back to normalcy."

"Paul, regardless of how serious it may be now, you and I are going to have to take him in hand and make a decided effort to cheer him up."

"That we will do, and at once. At the same time, we must diplomatically find out from him just what he has on his mind."

"Right," agreed Cameron. "But he must not know that we are prying into his affairs. That might spoil all our efforts."

"I believe that we are smart enough to handle the matter with the utmost discretion. What do you think of mentioning it to Doc? He ought to have some good ideas."

"Why not hold up on that until we have learned something really definite to talk to him about," suggested Cameron. "The less discussion we have and the fewer people we tell our suspicions to, the less chance of Ashley getting wise to what we think. Once he learns how we feel, he will develop a resistance; and from then on we will not have his confidence."

"Very well then. Let's keep our eyes and ears open and talk the situation over with each other whenever one of us learns anything of importance. And, by the way, my young friend, it is a pleasure to see how you are progressing in your desire to give of yourself to help others who are less fortunate."

"Well, Ashley is a likable kid. Anybody would want to help. Some of these poor bastards around here, however, don't deserve to have a finger raised to help them."

"I prophesy that you will change your thoughts some of these days," Paul said.

"Hell no! Go on to sleep, you old duffer."

Paul chuckled audibly as he rolled over on his other side.

On the following Sunday morning, Doc strode into Cameron's room, where the occupants were lolling about in an effort to be comfortable but feeling tense for fear they might be caught by the prowling guards violating one of the many picayunish Nipponese orders. He carefully closed the door behind him, while the other prisoners carefully watched him.

"This is a big day," Doc declared. "I am one year older."

"Well, congratulations."

"Nice going, old man, but this is a hell of a way to spend a birthday."

"How many years, Doc?"

"You look ninety, but l suppose you are only seventy."

Doc raised his hand to stop the repartee. "Hold on now," he said. I've come on a goodwill mission. I hit the half-century mark today, and I have brought you a little gift to help celebrate."

"You have got the matter backward, Doc," Cameron said. "It is we who should do something for you, after all the many things you have done for all of us."

"Close you eyes and open your mouth," ordered Doc.

"Oh, no, not me," grumbled Blake.

"Come on. I will," offered Paul, willing to play whatever game Doc had in mind. Childlike, he did as Doc had asked, while Doc pulled from his pocket a tiny four-ounce bottle and a small medicine dropper.

Squeezing some of the contents from the bottle, he placed several drops on Paul's tongue.

The minute Paul tasted the fluid he opened his eyes and smiled, asking, "Where did you ever get that?"

"Who is next?" queried Doc.

"If Paul can stand your tricks, guess I can," ventured Cameron. "Come on, my life is in your hands."

Doc repeated the process with Cameron, who immediately shouted, "Bourbon! Of all things!"

"Bourbon," shouted Blake as a smile spread across his face. He got up from his cot and walked over to Doc, now willing to take a chance.

Each in turn received a sample of the liquid. They licked their lips and acted like youngsters tasting their first ice cream.

"Three drops each," said Doc. "It's all I can spare. I want to spread it as far as possible."

"How did you ever produce that miracle?" asked Blake. "Haven't tasted anything like that since the war started."

"Did you do the Nips out of that?" Ashley questioned.

"Maybe they have started to let us have some medicines," Doc said with enthusiasm. "I always thought they would." He gave the impression that Ashley's question was to be answered in the affirmative.

"No such luck," Doc replied. "I've been carrying this tiny bottle around ever since the days at Tarlac, waiting for this big opportunity. I wanted all of you to help me celebrate."

"Thank you, Doc. It was most thoughtful of you," Paul said.

"It has been a happy moment, and my sincere regards on the grand occasion." Cameron reached his hand out to shake with Doc.

"I have got to get along to the next room," Doc declared. "See you all later."

Blake flopped back own on his cot next to the window. Cameron did the same in the shadows of the far side of the room. Paul went to the benjo, while Sykes and Ashley slumped down on the bench beside the table.

"That was nice of Doc to spread a little cheer," Cameron said to no one in particular.

"Yes," replied Ashley, "It—"

"Kura!" suddenly came as an ugly and ominous shout from the porch outside of the window.

Each person in the room sprang quickly to his feet, as though shot from a cannon, and stood stiffly at attention in the approved Nipponese fashion.

God, it's Mr. Murder, Ashley said to himself. *How did he ever slip up here without same POW outside seeing him and calling, "Kiotsuke"? We are in for it now!*

Whenever a guard came into contact with a prisoner, his actions and the treatment he accorded were matters that were entirely up to his discretion. Regardless of what he did, no complaint against him by a prisoner would ever receive the slightest consideration by his commanders. It was thought by some of the POWs who tried to be honest with themselves in their study of conditions that perhaps while a guard's actions against a prisoner would always be upheld in public, undoubtedly his commanders would take appropriate action out of the sight of prisoners in order to keep that guard from violating orders and the policies of the higher command. That thought was countered by other thinking prisoners, who insisted that no action was ever taken against a guard for his actions, whether the treatment he administered to prisoners embarrassed his superiors or not. That was proven by the very fact that the guards continued to deal out the same ruthless treatment, day after day, as well as invent other procedures according to the ingenuity of the individual solder. That fact was further attested to by the close scrutiny the prisoners gave each member of the guard detachment. They were carefully observed to see if they followed during their period of duty the routine that was set up and were additionally looked over for any marks of physical violence, that being the accepted procedure for obtaining discipline in the enemy army.

Whenever a guard ran across a condition that he wanted to criticize, and especially when the frequent "reign of terror" was in effect, the brutality of a guard was prompt and certain. Mr. Murder was the outstanding exponent, the symbol of ruthlessness. The name the prisoners had attached to him was not without merit. Not only his actions but also his very appearance identified him as a man dangerous to the safety of those who could not defend themselves. Small and slender though he was, he exhibited great courage in single-handedly assaulting any number of prisoners. But that courage was superficial in nature and rested only on the bayoneted rifle he carried and the authority of the camp officials he represented. Sometime in the recent past, a strain other than pure Nipponese had entered the bloodstream of his progenitors. That condition was apparent from a close scrutiny. Most prisoners reached the conclusion that he was, in part, an aborigine headhunter from the mountains of Taiwan. A great scar across his cheek from the bridge of his nose to the lobe of his ear was identified as a bolo slash. It was very impressive in adding to his personification of cruelty.

The sudden appearance of Mr. Murder at the window shocked the sensitive soul of Ashley, and the monomania of the young officer leaped forward in his mind. It was he, Ashley, upon whom the wrath of Mr. Murder would fall. Could he control himself against the assault, or would he give in to his emotions and fight back?

The thought frightened him. He knew enough to realize that any retaliation on his part would be fatal. But what was that urge within him that stirred him up and demanded action that overruled his thinking processes? What a confusing state to be in. Did he have a second mind someplace that overrode his emotions to a degree that his normal thinking processes could not retain control?

Ashley inwardly visualized Mr. Murder with his savage sneer leap through the window and come directly at him. Angry snarls curled the guard's face into a frightening sight. He raised his arms and extended his rifle until the bayonet on the end was close to Ashley's chest. Then with all his strength, he lunged! Some force within Ashley responded reflexively. His left arm came up, and the flat of his hand struck the side of the shining instrument and deflected it. At the same instant, Ashley turned sideways and quickly grasped the muzzle end of the rifle with his two hands. He slid them down the stock until they were cupped around the forward hand of the guard. Grasping hard, Ashley thrust forward with all his weight and strength. The suddenness of the maneuver threw the enemy off balance; and as Ashley pushed the weapon up over the right shoulder of Mr. Murder, the guard was forced to relinquish his grip on his rifle or suffer a broken arm. He thumped to the ground flat on his back, while Ashley stood over him holding the bayonet close to his enemy's body. A quick thrust, and all was quiet.

But loud voices and scurrying feet suddenly broke the stillness and severely jolted Ashley into conscious reality. He glanced down at the body lying at his feet. It was Blake, slowly turning over and straightening up. Mr. Murder had struck him a hard uppercut with the butt end of his rifle and now stood leering over him, well satisfied with his accomplishment. Ashley felt faint. His illusion was rapidly dissipated by his sympathy for Blake and his hatred for the guard who took such an unnecessary advantage of a helpless person.

During the remainder of the day Ashley was nervous and shaking. He was concerned about emotions within him that he was unable to understand or control.

When tenko was finished, Ashley took down from his shelf a small bundle of papers, scraps of papers on which he had written many letters. He knew they would never be sent, but they gave him a release in writing his troubles to the one person in whom he could confide. Carefully selecting several sheets on which he had earlier written only on one side, he dropped down on the bench beside the table. The small electric bulb dangling from the ceiling above gave off a dim, yellowish glow. It was necessary to lower his head close to the paper to see what he was writing. With a stub of a pencil he set to his task:

Dearest Mother,

Again I come to you with my problems. As I have told you so often in my previous letters, I worry endlessly about you and the fears you must have for my safety.

You have leaned so completely upon me and I upon you during the many years since Father went. As I find time in this horrible place for meditation, I realize more and more how well you have taken his place in my life, without mawkish sentiment or undue influence. So it is easy for me to talk with you as man to man.

There may be one or two other prisoners here with whom I could intimately discuss my problems for my own good, and I propose to seek them out. It will be for my own good, I am certain.

But I have built up such a great resistance against the majority here that I hesitate to honor them with my confidence. They simply could not understand. Another man's problems would be beyond their comprehension. Their selfishness and ego are inconceivable. Each one lives for himself alone and would not hesitate to sacrifice another if he could gain the slightest advantage for himself. They squabble and fight, argue and harangue, are discourteous and disagreeable. I do not understand how they can cast aside all the fine things of Christian living merely because of the pressures of restricted existence. No one thinks of or cares about anyone else. The only time a person is chummy with another seems to be when he wants something the other one has. Once he obtains that, he casts the other aside.

Of course all of this is not always true. There are some who insist upon retaining their dignity and character. Probably they lived that way before they were cooped up in this place, while the others lived the same sort of life they lead now but whose ugliness went undetected because of being covered up by the superficialities of their so-called culture. Anyhow, the prisoners who are trying to lead a respectable life will come home with their heads high and unashamed.

I must stop now. The time for rest has arrived. That off-key bugle will sound soon, which means that the lights must be off and everyone in bed instantly. I send you all the devotion of your son and partner.

Paul and Cameron had observed Ashley at his letter writing, and they had cast knowing glances and nods of the head at each other.

"Come on, Paul," Cameron called, jovially, "let's take that swing around the compound."

It was the following Sunday afternoon and the first opportunity the POWs had had for a week to relax and get together.

"Now wait a minute, Cam," Paul replied with a laugh. "I'll go with you only if Ashley will come along and be on my side in any arguments."

"Okay!" Cameron agreed. "Ashley goes along to defend you."

Paul and Cameron each took one of Ashley's arms and marched out of the building. It all happened so quickly and spontaneously that the maneuver would not have been a smooth one unless it had been premeditated. The two close friends had been waiting for the right moment to get Ashley off in a quiet spot and had laid their plans well. They did not intend to be frustrated.

With light hearts, they strode twice around the little compound, talking inanely but in a very friendly manner to Ashley. Next they reached the steps at the far side of the compound that led up to the headquarters building. Paul cried, "I must stop here a bit and rest. You wild Indians who eat meat all day have too much vigor for me. Come, let's sit a while."

"I think that is a good idea," Cameron quickly agreed. "Here Ashley. There is room for three."

The three officers sat down and began to pass pleasantries about. Paul and Cameron were trying to lead the conversation toward a discussion of Ashley and his condition without frightening him away.

"This rugged life is mighty hard on some of the POWs," Cameron declared finally, looking at Paul with anticipation that he would quickly respond.

"It is a most unusual situation," Paul said. "A man without understanding help from his friends cannot be expected to maintain his equilibrium going it alone. The task is too great for a single mind to bear up under the pressures we have to endure here. Each person needs help."

"You have opened up a subject," Ashley began as he took over the conversation, much to the amazement of his friends, "that is most distressing to me. I don't mean to barge in and discuss myself first. But after we talk about your problems, I want a chance to toss mine into your laps for whatever help you can give me."

"Ours will wait, Ashley." Cameron conceded. "Paul and I have already had same opportunities to talk those over. So we better start with you and let you get off your chest the things that are annoying you."

"The trouble is that I haven't the faintest idea what is wrong with me," Ashley continued. "Nearly everyone here gets under my skin because of their selfishness. And then those damn Nips are always prowling around taking out their spite on me. If I could only—"

"Those are two big points," Paul remarked, interrupting Ashley. "The first can be overcome in part, and the other one can be completely discounted."

"That's my feeling, too, Ashley," agreed Cameron. "We have been through those matters many times, Paul and me, and we have reached the conclusion that he offers."

"Don't take it too lightly," Ashley asked. "Those are vital matters in my life."

"Indeed not, Ashley," Cameron remarked with understanding. "They are too serious to all of us to be taken lightly. Our entire mental stability, and even more, hangs on how satisfactory an answer we can give ourselves to the problems you mention."

"That's right, Ashley," asserted Paul, nodding his head thoughtfully. "The first problem, our relationship with each other, and that is not your problem only because each one of us here is confronted with it, cannot be completely solved. To solve it fully would mean readjusting everyone's thoughts and actions to agree with what we would like. That is obviously impossible. So, Cameron, how well have you learned your lesson? What is the only alternative?"

"Well, Paul," Cameron answered, "I can throw out my chest and go to the head of the class."

"Yes?" Paul prompted him as Ashley looked from one to the other with bewilderment.

"If we cannot adjust the others to our way of thinking, we must adjust ourselves to theirs."

"You two are talking riddles," declared Ashley. "Just what must I do to lick that situation where everybody annoys me?"

"You must start down in here, son," replied Paul, tapping his finger on his chest. "Deep down in your soul is where you answer has to be found. You must have a desire, an intense desire, to get along with the others regardless of how annoying they are to you. Once you can acquire that, your mind will clear up as though a fog in which you were enmeshed had suddenly disappeared."

"That is a tremendous mission you have assigned me," declared Ashley. "I don't quite see how a normal man can suddenly change his dislikes and distaste for others to a feeling of respect and consideration for them."

"Sure, it's a tough assignment," agreed Cameron. "But if I can make headway with it, I'm certain that you can. It won't come with a snap of the finger. That's too much to expect. Yet you can be successful by telling yourself that's what you want and then working at it constantly, little by little."

"But you do not tell me anything specific," Ashley pled. "Just exactly what must I do or say?"

"All right," Cameron said. "Take this for your first lesson. Go back into the barracks and pick out the guy you hate the most. Say, 'Good afternoon!' to him pleasantly and give him a smile. Offer him a cigarette."

"I know exactly what will happen," returned Ashley. "The big lug will grab the cigarette and then think that I am a sucker. Anyhow I haven't got a cigarette."

"You have missed the point entirely, Ashley," Paul asserted in his calm and soft voice. "It makes little difference what he does or thinks. You are thinking selfishly. The joy and stimulation that you will receive from that act is what counts. It is you who is the important person at the moment. You must conquer yourself first. After that has been accomplished, you will be able to swing the others over to you."

"Here is your cigarette, Ashley," Cameron said, handing one of his precious smokes over to his friend.

"Use it in your little plan."

A strange emotion swept through Ashley. There was nothing dull-witted about him, and he was affected greatly by that display of graciousness and courtesy. It was the same act that he had been urged to perform. Now he was experiencing the feeling that must come to one who received a gesture of civility and politeness. It could not be embarrassment that stirred him in such a fashion, he contemplated. The feeling was too joyful and stimulating for that.

"I understand fully, gentlemen," Ashley announced slowly. "You have spoken and acted in a way that I never dreamed of. I have been a damn fool, I guess. Don't expect me to thank you for all this. Expressing gratitude for such a tremendous gift as you have given me would be sort of silly."

The three prisoners sat quietly for several minutes. There was nothing further to be said, and each one realized that fact.

After a while, Paul broke the silence by humming a little tune. Musical accomplishment was not something of which he could boast, and his off-key effort was just the touch to make Cameron and Ashley burst into controlled chuckles.

Paul seized upon the moment to carry on the conversation. "Let's clean up that second problem before we disband this conference."

"Yes," agreed Cameron. "And that is the simple one. It almost solves itself."

"I'm willing to admit beforehand," Ashley said, "that you have the right answer. But what is it?"

"It starts off like the other one," explained Cameron. "You have a feeling down inside you that the Nips intentionally seek you out for all their brutality. Each one of us could feel that way if we were not careful."

"True! True!" cried Paul with more heat than he was accustomed to show. "We are so ridiculous on occasions, we humans. All we have to do is to look about and see that no one is immune to their ruthless treatment. That should upset our persecution complex in short order. But in our weakened condition, we are not apt to use the best of judgment."

"That is where a friend comes in," Cameron stated. "Anyone here is liable to slip a bit mentally, and I dare say most of us have. And it's mighty hard to lick that problem alone. So you have to have someone on whom you can lean to lend a bit of encouragement and sort off jolt you out of your depression. If you bottle that stuff up inside of you, you are lost."

"You hit the bell there, Cameron," Paul testified. Then looking over to Ashley, he said, "Son, listen to the sage. You have gotten yourself all wrapped up with a complex. I'll bet half of the men here in camp feel that same way. The saving grace with you is that you now realize it, and you can toss it off because you can see how silly it is. But that is not all. You have been through the fire and have come out unscorched. But you have an obligation to the others who are less fortunate. It is up to you now to forget about yourself and go out and help the others who are floundering."

Ashley was thoughtful for some time. He had built up the fullest confidence in Paul and Cameron. What they said made the greatest of sense to him. It was no simple matter to cast aside those feelings that had seriously disturbed him for a long time. Yet, in his mind, he felt that he could control and subdue them. However, down somewhere in his body, he had that tingling sensation that bespoke of the dominance of the emotions over the will.

"Thank you, both of you," Ashley eventually said. "You are most optimistic about my ability to throw this off."

Paul and Cameron glanced at each other. They knew they had stretched their argument a little, and they knew that Ashley realized the problem would mean a tremendous battle with himself if he were to overcome the feelings that controlled him. But the condition with which he suffered had been brought out in the open, and that was the healthiest factor of all.

Later that afternoon, while seated in the corner of their room, Cameron said to Paul, "You know, I've been thinking a lot about our talk with Ashley."

"Yes?" queried Paul with anticipation.

"It impressed upon me more than ever before that we who are only half crazy," he replied with a grin, "have a real responsibility to the others who are completely 'nuts.' I think that we have to take the initiative and make an active effort to do what we can to help them."

"Mm," hummed Paul. "We have been doing a few minor things of that sort, but I agree with you that we should adopt that as an inspired mission. Surely, we can lose nothing but may be able to save a lot of people."

"Why don't we make a real study of the situation and arrive at some sensible means of actions."

"Right, Cam. Suppose we start right after supper. We can tour the barracks and make a mental note of everything we see that appears to be abnormal."

"We'll do it. Probably will not run across anything really exciting, but we can no doubt find plenty of insignificant things that will point to trends."

"I am sort of excited about this investigation," Paul told Cameron as the two started on their quest after the evening rice was eaten. "There is a tingle of a thrill in this Sherlock Holmes business. There is also the stimulation of having a set objective for which we can employ our minds."

They strolled slowly down the hall from their door, but before they had gone more than a few yards, Paul nudged Cameron. Before them was one of their older colleagues for whom they had always maintained a high regard. He stood before them clad only in his underwear with one arm clutched around the wooden rice pail in which the food was brought over to the barracks from the kitchen. In his free hand, he gripped a spoon and, with hurried motions, scraped and scraped the interior of the container. The spoon would go to his mouth, and his jaws would work with intensity, while his short beard, which grew in a forward direction, bobbed up and down like the beard of a billy goat. Neither Paul nor Cameron could control their chuckles at such ridiculous antics, but at the same time, they had a feeling of compassion for a man whose hunger deluded him into believing that he could gain any nourishment out of an empty bucket. The prisoner who had served the rice from the bucket earlier, with many eyes observing him, had seen to it that every grain had been removed and distributed to the bowls of the prisoners.

Paul and Cameron sauntered down the hall to the end. As they turned the corner into a cross hall, they were suddenly confronted with a half-dozen similar food buckets setting on the floor. Rushing from one to another, with the impetuosity that indicated a fear of someone taking away his possessions, was another POW. He would peer into one, scrape his spoon around the interior of another, and pick up a third to get a closer look into it.

When they had moved on, Paul said to Cameron, "That poor devil really is in bad shape. He didn't get three grains out of the lot."

"And he went to all the trouble to bring those pails down here from the other squads. He thought he could scrape them in private, without anyone taking them away from him."

They proceeded out on the rear porch, where a long sink with many water faucets stood. Nearly all of the places were taken by prisoners who were washing their bowls and spoons after the evening meal. The man at the end spigot ran a little water in his bowl, sloshed it around in the container, and then drank it. No minuscule of food would escape him!

At a faucet nearby, another prisoner finished cleaning his bowl. To drain the surplus water from it, he raised the bowl high over his head and violently shook it. His neighbors, right and left, uttered howls of disgust at being splashed in the operation, but the bowl shaker was quite undismayed and unconcerned. He chose to dry his utensil in that manner, and to hell with the comfort of anyone else.

A newcomer rushed into an unoccupied place farther down the line. For some inexplicable reason prisoners behind the wall feel it essential to their well-being and betterment to rush madly at all times. He proceeded to brush his teeth with violent motions and a liberal use of water.

"Goddamn it!" cried his neighbor at his elbow. "Watch what you are doing!"

"I've got to brush my teeth," replied the offender. "If you don't like it, you shouldn't have come in here."

"Of all the damn crust! I was here washing my bowl when you came barging in."

The teeth brushing went on with as much vigor as before, while the angry man rinsed off his bowl and left.

"Say, listen, bub!" spoke the prisoner on the other side of the new arrival, "don't try to get by with that stuff with me. I don't give a goddamn how old you are or what your rank was. If you splash me again, I'll teach you some manners by pushing that ugly puss of yours out of shape."

"Hey! You haven't any more right here than I have."

"Just start using that brush again before I am through, and I'll show you damn quick who has the right to be here."

"Well, hurry up," cried the newcomer. He could not afford to further arouse the ugly mood in the man next to him. "I'll wait a minute till you get through."

"That will be very courteous, I must say," his neighbor sarcastically replied.

"Let's go on back to our room, Paul," suggested Cameron when the commotion had subsided. "I've seen enough for the time being."

"Come on then," conceded Paul. "It all seems so silly, but I suppose if we were not constantly on guard we would find ourselves acting the same way."

"I'm afraid that, in spite of any effort, we will slip up more here than once as the pressures and conditions grow worse."

"You may expect them to grow worse from day to day. There is no reason to anticipate any betterment. And that will be the test, my good friend. Are you a man of character or not?"

"Paul, I'm just as weak as anyone else. A man can take just so much of this constant hammering at his nerves, and then he will blow up."

"No one can dispute your privilege of blowing up once in a while." Then after a moment, he added, "If you are big enough to make proper amends afterward."

"You are well named, Paul," Cameron declared shortly thereafter when they had returned to their room.

"Oh, I have several names," Paul testified as he tried to change the subject. "My superiors in the army respectfully refer to me as Colonel, but my colleagues call me Paul. Yet my intimate friends—God bless them—call me Old Duffer."

"Paul is much more appropriate and relevant. It is packed with meaning."

Paul, with embarrassment, chuckled to himself.

"Good evening!" shouted a voice with a decidedly British accent. A head peeked in the door at the same time. "Any rumors tonight?"

"Haven't heard a thing of any importance, Brigadier," Cameron called back to the Englishman. "But come in anyway."

"Cawn't delay. Must hurry on. I'm provoked, because I've been gypped."

"Gypped?" Cameron innocently asked. "What does that mean?"

"That's one of your bloody American expressions! It means what you get when you don't get what you should get."

One day some time later, a few of the prisoners were deeply engrossed in reading newspapers. Other POWs were leaning over their shoulders to get snatches of the contents, while many others were moving about restlessly in their impatience to have their turn at the meager number of papers that had been distributed. It was a gala day when papers were brought in. *The Nippon Times*, printed in English, was the only information that the enemy ever permitted the prisoners. The edition was three or four months old whenever it arrived and was ostensibly uncensored news from official government sources, according to the statement printed on the front page. The news the paper carried was so obviously lush with propaganda even that its intent was quite apparent, even to men who had been out of touch with the world for a long period. Quotes from the American press in an effort to ridicule those statements were a real source of information. A story carried in one column would be inadvertently denied by careless editing in an adjacent column. While the papers were scoffed at by the POWs, they were always sought after because they contained the only current reading material that flowed in behind the wall. For days after their arrival, attempts would be made to analyze and piece together items that had been read, and rumors for some time thereafter were bigger and hotter than ever.

In his room, Blake was the only one who had one of the papers. The other occupants were lolling about, awaiting their turns.

A huge guffaw came from Blake, and he called out, "Here is one for you. Listen to this red-hot news: 'During the past week, furious fighting has occurred on Island X X, whose name is withheld for strategic reasons. Our ever alert airmen discovered a huge convoy of many combat ships, cruisers, and carriers steaming madly to the north. Flashing the word back to rearward bases, our aviators continued their observation. In a very short time, the Imperial Nipponese Air might, augmented by our brilliant naval forces, which had been lying in wait for such a maneuver, thunderstruck the enemy forces. The attack was made in spite of the fog of early morning. Our gallant airmen, in utter defiance of furious AA fire, conducted devastating operations. They blasted ship after ship. Those that refused to sink were body crashed and self-blasted by our aviators and sent in flames to the bottom. Our gallant naval forces then took over the action and annihilated the transports in the convoy. The government is happy to announce officially, after carefully checking the reports, that complete destruction occurred. All our planes returned safely.

"'The following day, the enemy made a pernicious encroachment upon our area with devastating attacks. They had the audacity to attack our positions by blind bombing. Later, the first waves that struck our beaches were crushed. The next wave of the persistent enemy was smashed. The few troops that had secured a footing were quickly annihilated.

"'Our gallant troops brilliantly executed a previously planned strategic advance to rearward prepared positions. Our security has been greatly strengthened, and the enemy has expended itself after horrible destruction.'"

"That sounds like the Nips took an awful licking someplace," Cameron said.

"That's right," agreed Sykes. "And you can check one more island off from their control."

"They probably felt it was necessary to make some comment on a large-scale engagement," Paul analyzed, "even though they lost the action. Now they find it difficult to choose words that would give their own people the impression that a victory was scored."

"Of course they have to announce those major changes in their fortunes," reasoned Cameron. "It would be placing the government in a difficult position with the Japanese people if the natives suddenly woke up to the fact that the next assault was to be made on their home shores. Should the high command keep all their losses secret, that is exactly what would happen unexpectedly some day."

The great interlude in the lives of the prisoners dragged along with painful slowness. Each tick of the clock checked off another moment of unaccomplishment in their careers and brought them that much closer to the end of their existence. The wall gleefully extracted its toll. Men's hair grayed; their flesh wasted away; dental deterioration increased; faces became drawn and wrinkled; weakened minds played havoc with thought and action.

Paul and Cameron were lounging on the porch one day. They could observe the guardhouse without themselves being conspicuous. The new guard had just arrived and was taking over its duties from the old. Once a month, that ceremony occurred, and prisoners were always interested in the event. Would the newcomers be brutal? Or would they treat the POWs with some degree of consideration? Perhaps one of the soldiers would be willing to make friends and maybe drop some hint as to the affairs going on in the outside world.

"All the guards are concentrated in one spot," Paul casually marked. "If we had one good machine gun, we could handle the whole batch in a jiffy."

"And the camp could clear out of the gate in no time," Cameron answered. "But after that, what? There would be no place in this Nip country to hide."

"Unfortunately, there is probably not a single friend we could count on within a hundred miles."

"What I want to see," Cameron continued, "is a big American tank come rolling up to the gate, and a rawboned, tobacco-chewing Arkansas sergeant pop his head out of the turret and yell, 'Come on, you guys! Getta hump on. Let's get out of here!' Wouldn't that be a thrill?"

"We are still a long way from that," Paul replied, "although some of the men here have optimistic viewpoints. A little action on a island a thousand miles to the south gives them the feeling that tomorrow we will be free."

"I wonder," Cameron contemplated, "if such attitudes could be classified as optimism. In some, I am certain, it is just plain ignorance. But, in others, if I am to be charitable, it is a reaction from a weakened mind that no longer can make logical deductions."

"Probably so. Just as many others take the opposite tack and sneer and scoff at everything. Their outlet is through an expression of pessimism."

"Strange thing, too; once a person has settled into one of those grooves, everything that enters his life is viewed from one of those two extremes."

"You know, Cam, a psychiatrist would have a brilliant opportunity here in camp to learn more about the fluctuations of the human mind than he would encounter in a lifetime of normal study."

"And all of that opportunity is simply going to waste. No record is being made of it; no research is being conducted; it will not even be remembered when this crowd gets home and scatters in all directions."

Paul smiled as he said, "None of those who are acting so queer now, including you and me, will care to bring the subject up. Each one will fall back quickly in that unfortunate military rut where a soldier struts with ego and feels that he is faultless."

"Why, Paul, you are not weakening and becoming critical, are you? I never heard you say anything like that before."

"Cameron, maybe the wall is beating me down too."

"I have my doubts on that score. But then you were merely stating an undeniable truth."

While they were conversing, Paul and Cameron had kept alert to observe what the guard was doing. When they saw the new members of the detachment start to carry on their duties, each turned without comment to the other and strolled back to their room. It was best not to be in the way of the sentries, if it could be avoided.

Their room was empty when Paul and Cameron entered. They looked about and tidied up several things that were misplaced. There was little point in deliberately giving the guard something to complain about.

In a few minutes, the slow shuffling of hobnailed boots along the wooden floor of the hall signified one of the guards was making his way from room to room. When he stopped at each door, the loud cry of "Kiotsuke!" came from the occupants, accompanied by the unmistakable sounds of men leaping to their feet as a mark of respect, respect that was forced and not voluntarily given.

The trod came nearer. And the unlatched door was pushed open with the end on a bayonet, which was attached to a rifle held cautiously in the hands of the new sentry. He was apparently prowling through the barracks in uncertainty and did not intend to blunder into a trap. Cameron and Paul extended the required courtesies and continued to stand while the Nipponese glared at them.

Finally, he entered and walked around the room, curiously inspecting the few items that lay on the shelves. He approached the window where the light shone on him fully. Cameron and the soldier looked at each other intently. Recognition flashed through each of them at the same instant.

"Tsuji!" Cameron spoke in a low voice.

"It is the major!" replied the soldier as he lowered his rifle and allowed the butt to rest on the floor.

"It has been a long time since we parted, Tsuji."

"Much has happened since then," replied the guard. "Perhaps it is best to forget all that went before."

Cameron was very much interested in the man who stood before him, but he did not like the attitude the soldier had assumed. In order to break down the barrier that stood between them, Cameron said in a friendly manner, "Won't you sit down?"

The Nipponese flopped down on the bench, and Cameron and Paul carefully sat on the edge of their cots. They were uncertain whether they would be denied that privilege, but each of the Americans knew that the only way to find out would be to experiment. No outburst came from the guard, so Cameron continued, "You are a very good soldier, for I see you are a superior private with three stars."

"Yes, Tsuji is a fine soldier. Tsuji does everything well."

"I always thought so, too. You did very well when you were with me."

"It was necessary then. My mission was to work for the American officer. It was there I learned much that was great help to Japan. Many others did same thing. But, I am a houseboy no more! Time has changed. Now Americans are houseboys for Japanese!" Tsuji's eyes flashed, and his jaws pressed hard together. "No more do we have to be servants. Soon we go to America and make all people there bow to the emperor. Then everything belong to Japan—gold, big factories, automobiles, women. We take!"

"When do you expect to go there, Tsuji?" Cameron inquired with curiosity.

"Very soon now," replied the guard. "Then Japanese no longer have to work hard. We will have much. Americans will be our slaves. They looked down on us for many years."

"But, Tsuji, you were born in America and know all about us—how we live, what we think, what we are like. Surely you don't hate us."

"Every Japanese hate Americans. They laugh at us and look down on us for many years. But we are patient and wait. Then they make war on us. That is too much. So Imperial Army annihilate all Allies! That is the truth! We have been told so! For long time, I hope to see you in Japanese control, you and all Americans. We work hard for that. Now we win and will soon take over your country."

With a hard thump of his fist on the table, Tsuji jumped to his feet. He had made the usual tirade that he had heard so often from his superiors, and he was filled with a fanatic zeal. Sweeping out of the room with a blustering attitude, he stomped down the ball, crying, "The Land of the Rising Sun! Banzai!"

Cameron walked to the door and peered down the darkened hall at the departing soldier. Paul moved alongside and glanced over his shoulder. Through the open door at the end of the hall, the sun was drooping over the top of the wall. Tsuji was silhouetted in strutting outline as he started dawn the steps to the ground. "Only it is a setting sun, my young friend. You and the rest of your treacherous tribe are a little slow in comprehending that."

"Cam." Paul spoke slowly after he turned back into the room. "Perhaps something to our advantage can be gained from knowing that young man. That hatred he professes is superficial and has been acquired only since he returned to Japan, or I miss my guess."

"You don't miss your guess," Cameron replied. "You are dead right. Tsuji worked for me and my family for many years. He was a perfect servant, an ideal houseboy—honest and courteous and practically a member of the family. I know him too well, even better than he knows himself. All this tripe he sputters has been pushed down his throat by everyone he serves under. He was always unusually loyal to me, and I cannot be convinced that he really is so ignorant to believe all the stuff he has heard. Too many years in America! One does not lose that spirit overnight. But as you say, knowing him can probably be turned to our advantage one of these days. We will work on it."

At that moment, Blake swept into the room. "Those damn Dutchmen!" he cried. "Always getting into trouble. Why the hell did they have to be sent to our camp, anyway?"

"Now, son," said the imperturbable Paul, "what have the Dutch done to upset you?"

"The new guard is on, and one of them caught a Dutchman coming out of the benjo with his bottle in his hand. And then the Nip went on a rampage. He has the Dutchman standing up at attention out there."

Cameron burst into laughter. "It's a tough break for the poor devil, but that damn bottle procedure is the silliest thing I've ever heard of."

"Don't see why they can't be normal like any other white man," Blake declared, "and use paper."

"It's their custom," Paul explained. "They consider it more sanitary."

"Dumb, I say," continued Blake. "Then they got to wash their hands, if they don't forget it, and refill the bottle. And the damn fools keep on doing it. In the middle of winter. What happens when the water in the bottle freezes up?"

"I suppose that is one of the tricks of the trade, to learn how to overcome that difficulty."

"For me, I'll use paper," Blake said with finality.

"If you can get it," Cameron chided. "We have been without paper of any kind for some time."

The next day, a joyful cry came from the direction of the kitchen. "Ba-nan-as! Come and get 'em!"

Blake leaped off his cot as though hit with an electric shock. "Did you hear that? Bananas! 1 didn't know any had come in."

The POWs from each squad who had been detailed to carry the rice buckets that day started toward the kitchen with receptacles in hand to bring back the fruit for distribution to the members of their squad. This was a gala occasion, which happened so seldom that it would be talked about for days to come. Usually the hawkeyed prisoners knew far in advance what was to come out of the kitchen. But once in a while, the little pushcart that brought the food from the nearby village each day would be rolled into the rear of the kitchen through an emergency gate built into the wall at that point. When that gate was used, the cart and its contents were hidden from view.

When the call from the kitchen came, Sykes, too, jumped to his feet. He picked up a washbasin and started in a rush for the door.

"Now where the hell are you going?" asked Blake.

"To get our squad's bananas," Sykes replied without delaying his departure.

"Wait a minute; wait a minute," Blake called. "You are just going to tie things up. The bucket carriers are on the job. They will handle it. Sit down and take it easy. You are always butting in."

Sykes responded in part. He turned back to the window, where he looked out to see if the designated POWs were actually on the job. Because of the fact that food was being issued, it might be expected that all responsible prisoners would have hastily completed their jobs.

As a matter of fact, a good percentage of all the men behind the wall would be present, out of curiosity and to assure themselves that no one or no group received an advantage over them. To protect one's interests required a personal presence, many thought; little faith could be placed in others to be honest with those not present.

For some time, Cameron had been developing a feeling of annoyance at Sykes and his actions. Sykes continually moved about in a nervous manner, with rapid and impetuous actions. It was disturbing to the others in the same room with him, especially so because of the very restricted space and the complete absence of any privacy. Again, prisoners felt a constant tension to keep from being surprised by a guard. If one person in a room should make a quick movement, like jumping up from his cot suddenly, even though it was only an innocent call for the benjo, the involuntary responses of the others made them simultaneously jump up. Some prisoners never seemed to learn that many of their actions were most disturbing to their colleagues; perhaps they never gave a damn, as some others thought.

That fellow Sykes is a very irritating person, Cameron meditated. *He keeps all of us in this room upset by his bouncing around and his effort to control everyone and everything. Yet there seems to be nothing malicious about him; he merely possesses an insane desire to be a great commander. I wonder how much of that attitude*, Cameron tried to reason to himself, *he had before the war or if it is an outcropping of ego that has been suppressed by this rigorous confinement. He treats us as if we were three-year-olds. Every minute detail of our lives he scrutinizes with hawk eyes and tells us how we should handle the matter. Does he not realize that we have lived forty or fifty or sixty years and have certainly learned something of the world? That nervous tendency to do everything himself makes him most difficult to live with. And so much of that effort is ill directed because it is impetuous. At least he is not lazy, as many are, and carries more than his own load of the work to be done. It seems to make little difference that someone is detailed each day to do certain things like carry rice buckets, or serve, or fetch water. He will rush in and try to do the job himself, which causes endless confusion. There is no system possible when he is around. Then if someone has a job assigned that he does not like to do, all that is necessary is to procrastinate a bit, and Sykes will jump in and do it. He must have some sort of mania, which I would never try to explain. What if he were a commander and handled his troops in that fashion? God! What devastation would result!*

In spite of it all, Sykes had a nobility of character. Never would he do or say anything that might hurt someone else. *But what can I do to change the situation?* Cameron queried himself. *Growling at him or telling him to mind his own business will not reduce his emotional instability. Neither will a calm discussion with him of what we think are weaknesses. In either event, he will be embarrassed or may not take kindly to it. Then where would I stand? I would be in the same position that he is now in, an irritating person. The only other answer is to keep my mouth shut and endure his antics the best way I can. But God! How much longer will this be? It may carry on for years more. Long before then, I'll be as crazy as anyone else. Maybe when we all reach the raving stage, and we'll never realize what the other fellow is doing.*

In short order, the bananas were brought over from the kitchen and laid out on one of the tables in each squad. The POW responsible for the distribution to the members of Cameron's squad was, at the moment, as many of his colleagues felt, not too bright. Once, he had been well-fed and portly, with a jovial disposition. But the continuous reduction of rations during the campaign and the slim rice diet behind the wall had altered all that. His flesh had been whittled down to more evenly match his small frame, having been consumed for bodily existence. Now, huge hunks of skin flopped below his jowls and hung loose around his belly. His disposition had similarly deteriorated; it was projected from his face, his watery eyes and dark areas beneath, his pallor, and his sunken cheeks. Henry had been a very affable and sociable person, once upon a time. By this time, he had grown irritable and acted constantly on the defensive. His task of equalizing the distribution of a few dozen bananas would have been a simple matter for a child under normal circumstances. Walled-in men behaved uglier than usual when anything was to be parceled out among them, especially if it was food. The more a person needed, or thought he needed, something, the less refinement he would display toward gaining his ends. Just let a competitor appear to obtain the least advantage, and the cloak of culture was cast off, and the basic instincts of a wild animal were present.

Poor Henry began to perspire as he surveyed his task. Two score eyes were focused upon him, scrutinizing every move, and many tongues made ready to criticize whatever action he took. With rare judgment, Henry lined the fruit up in a long row, the largest one at one end and tapering off according to size until the tiniest lay at the other end of the row. Then he stood back and viewed the layout. It was not quite to his liking, so he moved a few back and forth until he was satisfied with the sequence. Placing his hands on his hips, he cocked his head at an angle and gave a little sigh of accomplishment.

"That fourth one should be moved up one place," someone in the staring group whispered loud enough for Henry to hear.

Henry looked up with an unpleasant expression. Without a word, he made the change. It was simpler to accept the criticism than to be obstinate. He paused as he continued to look at the spread before him. Perhaps another suggestion might be offered to relieve him of the total responsibility. The silence in the room was deadly. When Henry counted the number of fruit, he calculated that there would be two for each man in the squad and three left over. So, he picked the three small green ones from the end of the row and set them aside.

"That will be his commission," said a snarling voice in the crowd.

"He worked so hard he needs a little graft," cried someone else sarcastically.

"Listen, you goddamn tramps, if you want to take this over, step aside." Henry finally blew up, and his temper flared.

Not a sound came in response, and Henry sensed that there was no one in the group who had the courage to stand up and say that he could do the job more efficiently. Then Henry took the largest and the smallest of the fruit and placed them together. The next largest and the next smallest he then placed in a pile. Continuing in that order, he finally had arranged a pair for each member of the squad.

"We'll cut cards," Henry announced. "High man gets first choice."

"The hell with that!" blurted out an angry voice. "We'll follow the same order that we cut the last time."

"No soap!" declared Henry. "That was a month ago and has nothing to do with this."

"Hell it hasn't! That cut of the cards was to set up the order for all future issues."

"You must be first man up," Henry cried.

"Well, so what!" the man bellowed, advancing toward Henry.

"Why, you cheap little bastard." Henry thrust at him with intense anger, moving in his direction.

The situation developed so fast that none of the others were ready for the onslaught. Henry and his antagonist began raining blows on each other and then clutched, finally falling to the floor. By that time, the others had collected their wits sufficiently to pry the two apart. Each of the participants in the rowdyism fought against the restraint imposed upon him. They lunged against the arms holding them like a pair of gamecocks in the hands of their trainers.

After snarling at each other and calling each other vile names, they gradually subsided in their efforts. In time, they gained their freedom. But no sooner had they been released than Henry grabbed a heavy bamboo stick lying in the corner of the room and rushed at his opponent. Wildly flailing, he pummeled his enemy several times before the other POWs were able to put a stop to the fray.

Cameron and Paul had wandered up when the call came to cut cards, and they arrived just as the initial stages of the row were being enacted. "Well, I'll be damned!" Cameron said with disgust.

"It's too bad," replied Paul." But do not judge. These are trying times. One never knows who may be next."

"They will never get me down that much."

Paul glanced at Cameron with a friendly look. "I certainly hope not, son."

Pussy was making an announcement at tenko. "Give the attention! Commander of Army of Taiwan will make the inspection tomorrow. It is the order that barracks will be clean. Skud chiefs will have grass cut. Everything neat. Other orders later. Dismiss!"

Cleaning up for inspection had long since become a routine. The POWs were called upon with such frequency to put things in shape for visitors that it became a standing joke. They considered themselves like monkeys in the zoo, to be viewed by every passerby. Some thought that, because of the seniority of the occupants of the camp, these many inspections were a part of the Nipponese method to stimulate their own people into a greater war effort by visible proof that the white man was not invincible.

So the prisoners pitched in to place the compound in shape for the great man. Some of them worked. Others stood idly by, unconcerned. Many merely went through motions to satisfy the guards. Each one had his own method, regardless of the fact that the prisoners, somehow, must complete the task by a given time. There would be enough men who would carry the load so that the enemy could not accuse the POWs of rebellion or refusal to work.

There was little difference between this inspection and any of the many others that had preceded it. A tenko formation was ordered, and the greatly augmented guards ran to and fro like wild animals on the loose. They gave the impression, as military subordinates do the world over, that they had a dread and fear of the great commander about to visit them. As a release from their tension, they pummeled and barked at the men standing in ranks. It seemed to weary prisoners the commotion and harassment lasted for hours.

Then suddenly came the hurried shrieks, whose difference in tone identified them as more momentous than their forerunners. The prisoners stood erect and quiet, facing to the front. The Nipponese soldiers took their position quickly, while Evil Eye, the camp commander, stiffened up and waited.

A huge man in uniform, booted and spurred, with a half dozen underlings hurrying along behind, marched to the front and took his position facing the camp commander. Salutes and bows and more salutes, with the POWs participating in some of them, followed in rapid order. There was a moment of silence, and then a most unusual thing happened!

At a growl from the captain, two of the prisoners ran forward and stood in front of the great man. They gave him a punctilious salute, which the commander of the Army of Taiwan did not choose to recognize. Obviously, the little ceremony had been planned and directed.

"Gee-zus Christ!" cried the first prisoner to recover from his astonishment.

"The little yellow bastards!" came almost in unison from a score of throats.

The prisoners stared in amazement at the commanding general of the American forces and the commanding general of the British forces, who had been required to trot side by side up to the enemy commander.

"We are honored with your presence here today, General Ando," said the commanding general of the American forces.

"We thank you for the pig you have brought us," said the commanding general of the British forces.

Having accomplished their required mission, the two soldiers, in spite of their age and position, dogtrotted back to their place in ranks.

"How do you like that?" asked a voice.

"That is about as low as Nips can sink, making those two generals trot out to the front and give a little speech."

"And the old, fat slob wasn't enough of a soldier to even return their salute."

"I wonder how they feel being made to gallop up and salute that skunk."

"Well, if the Nips ordered it, they had to go through with it or take a bayonet in the fanny."

For days thereafter, the barracks buzzed over the details of the episode. Tremendous events occurred so seldom. They could not be ignored.

"Say, there, my good friend," Cameron chided as Paul stepped up on the porch, "I've been watching you for the past twenty minutes hanging around the kitchen. You haven't developed a food complex, have you?"

"In a sense, yes, I have, Cam." Paul laughed back. "In any event, I bring you good tidings."

"What's that?" asked Blake with a sudden interest.

"Yes, Colonel, tell us," chirped Sykes.

"No more white rice," Paul announced. "They are going to issue the brown variety from now on."

"That's just like 'em," Blake wept. "They only let us have a couple spoonfuls, and now we have to have some foul sort."

"Couldn't be any worse than at Tarlac," Ashley reminded the others. "We had to eat the sweepings from the warehouse floor."

"Yes," chimed in Sykes. "We had to spread the rice out on the table and pick out the grains from the dirt."

"Nuts! What's that got to do with this new deal?" asked Blake.

"Now, boys," Paul quietly explained, "you are in for something better. Brown rice is unpolished rice."

"Sure," argued Blake, "they are pushing off the cheapest stuff they have on us."

"Don't be dumb, Blake," Cameron spoke up. "If you would come out of that chronic grouch, maybe you would learn something. White polished rice is the sort that gives us all this edema and beriberi, and there is little nourishment in it. If they leave that outside coating on the grains, it will be of great value to us."

"We don't get enough to make any difference," Blake grumbled.

"When that little is the only food you get, it makes a hell of a lot of difference," Cameron continued.

"That's right, Blake," Paul said. "Having brown rice will be of tremendous benefit."

"The change has come at a critical time," Cameron remarked. "Everybody here is at a low ebb. A little push downward, and it will be too late to recover, but the least improvement may save a lot of lives."

Paul nodded his head in agreement. Blake rolled back on his cot and considered the discussion closed. Ashley stared straight ahead in deep thought. Sykes nervously rushed out to the benjo.

"Cam, this discussion about food reminds me of something," Paul said when the room was quiet again.

Cameron looked up and asked, "What's on your mind?"

"Let's check in with Doc and see if he has had any luck with the Nips on the increased ration deal we put up to him."

"Golly!" cried Cameron. "I had forgotten all about it. Let's go!"

A few minutes later, they bounced into Doc's room, and without preliminaries, Cameron asked, "Say, my good medical friend, did you get a chance to talk to the yellow bastards about building up our ration like is discussed the other day?"

"Oh, yes!" the doctor replied. "I talked with them about the urgency of toning up our diet. Tried to explain to them that, if something is not done soon, they will lose a lot of these prisoners."

"I'll bet they were impressed over that," Cameron said with sarcasm.

"Only in a very mild sort of way," replied the doctor. "I am afraid that they are not overly disturbed when a prisoner dies. The only matter that concerns them is whether they can call it a death from natural causes. You see, since they have turned in our names to the Red Cross, they are on record. So, for the time being, the authorities no doubt want to account for everyone. They want the record to look all right in the event it is ever brought up."

"You are very kind to give them that much credit, Doc."

"Mm," hummed the doctor. "But getting back to the ration deal. I tried to explain that out diet was never over twelve hundred calories a day, and that making us work in the fields with so little food would kill all of us soon."

"What was the response to that?" Paul quelled.

"The same old story. They said there was no more food to be had but that, as soon as our farm produced, we would have plenty."

"Baloney!" cried Cameron. "They have a set system and have no intention of varying from it. Taiwan is one of the greatest producing areas in the world. There must be tons of food rotting every day because it can't be moved. So far as our farm is concerned, there will be no food coming our way from that."

"Cam," said Paul, his blue eyes and his lips stretching out into a soft smile, "you are very cynical today. But, nevertheless, I am inclined to believe that you are more than half right."

"I tried to explain to the authorities the need for a balanced diet with the proper amount of calories, proteins, fats, vitamins, and so on. It was over their heads. Then also, they had little interest. Undoubtedly,

Cameron is correct in his feeling that the high command in Tokyo had set up a standard ration—"

"Three tiny bowls of rice a day!" Cameron interrupted.

"And that the local authorities," the doctor continued, "have no desire to vary from it."

"Then, you mean," Paul asked, "they gave you no encouragement?"

"That's about it," Doc replied. "Although they did tell me they would let us buy some Wakamotos."

Paul and Cameron quickly looked up with interest. Deep in their souls, they had realized, as all other prisoners had, that the restricted quantity and quality of food allowed them would eventually be instrumental in killing them all off. But unlike most of their colleagues, they saw the danger in continually thinking and complaining about that misfortune. If we must starve to death, each of them had told himself, let it be done with dignity and self-respect. They had conquered self, their appetites, at least to a degree. Paul was more aware than Cameron of the difficulties that lay ahead to maintain an upbeat sort of philosophy.

In addition, they had taken one further step. It was still an embryonic thing, something that would need development and that would require the greatest moral courage to continue through the dark years, which they knew were ahead. They had acquired a responsibility to their fellows! Many of their colleagues, they realized, were showing signs of weakness and ugly traits because of the pressure placed upon them by the wall. Whether those traits of character were inherent and merely aggravated by the conditions under which one lived was a question that Paul and Cameron could debate indefinitely. The reasons may have been important as an academic study, but the big fact remained that a condition existed that called for whatever aid the two friends could muster and deliver.

One of the steps they had decided upon was to have Doc approach the authorities with a humanitarian appeal. Surely, there could be a thread of understanding between white and yellow, which could circumvent the international and personal hatreds that existed. As least that appeared to be a more subtle and intelligent approach than for one of the squad leaders to make a try at convincing the authorities that help for the prisoners was needed. As had been learned from past experience, those leaders had no special standing merely because they were obliged to stand in front of a squad and call the infrequent roll and perform other menial tasks for the enemy. Their infrequent efforts to have conditions improved had always been rebuffed by the authorities. If they complained to the interpreter, the matter never seemed to be carried beyond that level. When they tried to get the ear of one of the lieutenants, all they received was a promise that something would be done. To contact the high and mighty captain was an insuperable task. He was far above soiling himself by allowing a white captive to approach him.

Consequently, when Doc gave an indication that some small matter might be accomplished for the betterment of living conditions, a subject so close to the hearts of Paul and Cameron, the two friends were immediately alert for fuller information.

"Wakamotos!" cried Cameron. "What under the sun is that?"

"Yes," Paul quickly followed up, "explain that."

"Wakamotos are vitamin tablets. Just which vitamins they contain, I have not been able to find out. Wakamoto is the name of the manufacturer. Such a large percentage of Japanese drugs are of what we would call the 'patent medicine' variety. Wakamotos may be of the same uselessness or may even be dangerous. In a day or so we will have some, and then we can find out."

So, Wakamotos entered the life and diet of the prisoners. What dietary usefulness they possessed was a point that was never agreed upon. Yet they gave a mental satisfaction to anyone who used them for food. Their bartering value, like any tangible item, was great. Even the word itself brought joy by being jousted about in humor. Little things became things of magnitude behind the wall.

In a few days, a large wooden box packed with many small bottles was turned over to what the enemy called the "store." That selling agency was located in a tiny room in the barracks and kept locked most of the time. It was established, not for the convenience of POWs, but for the edification of the constant stream of Nipponese visitors that passed through the camp and for the frequent press of photographers, who snapped pictures incessantly for their propaganda sheets. A printed sign that hung on the door identified the room as the "store" and gave the days and hours when it was supposed to be open for business. Through the window, prisoners with hollow eyes and empty bellies stared at the two shelves, which held a dozen combs, several packages of tea, a small pile of children's notebooks, and some empty cartons with Japanese characters stamped on them that were placed there to fill space.

Today, the store was opened. The prisoners had long since queued up, some of them merely from curiosity, others with a mad intent to "get theirs." Some in the line had bits of paper, a printed script that was issued monthly as a token. It was used by the POWs for a variety of purposes—to take back home as souvenirs, when that day should come; to be held for the purchase of cigarettes and/or other commodities; to scratch notes on; and to serve the urgent need where a more appropriate type of paper was not available. But in general, those scraps of paper were held by desperate men, not for their intrinsic value, but because they were a possession, a gain in a life of scarcity. Each man had to make a major decision in his own mind—whether this new and untried commodity was worth the script he had to exchange for it.

"It's something to eat. I'm going to buy some."

"The bottle is what I want. I can keep something in it."

"Think I'll hang on to my money. Maybe they will put out some cigarettes soon."

"I haven't got any money left. Tell you what I'll do, Bill. I'll swap you that piece of soap I've got for four bottles, if you'll buy them."

"That soap isn't enough to wash your face with a single time. I'll give you one bottle."

"Hell no! That soap is valuable."

Each prisoner who made a purchase was proud of his little brown bottle, the cork stopper, the bit of cotton that held the pills in place, and a hundred tablets of dark and crumbly texture. Long before supper time, the men had carefully scrutinized every part of their newly acquired possession. The meaning of the characters on the label was hotly debated. The irregularities in the glass bottle were sneered at. The bit of cotton was carefully preserved for some hoped for future usefulness, and the pills were cautiously tasted by some or hurriedly swallowed by the impatient ones.

Sykes, when he had dropped down on the bench with his bowl of rice in front of him, conservatively poured two pills from his bottle, carefully recorked it, and held the tablets in the palm of his hand uncertainly.

"Go on, eat 'em," grumbled Blake, who had observed the meticulous operation of Sykes. Wherewith, Blake dumped out a large handful and powdered them by crunching them between his fingers and palm. He sprinkled the dust on his rice and, with relish, began to eat.

"How do they taste?" asked Cameron as he laughed at Blake.

"Swell! It's something to eat, anyhow."

"Sort of dry, aren't they, Blake?" Paul questioned.

"Sure, but that doesn't hurt anything." Blake took a drink of water.

"Until I know more about them," Cameron said, "I think I'll take about two for each meal. They're supposed to be vitamins."

Ashley looked at the actions of the others and, without uttering a word, followed Cameron's example.

In the morning, as soon as the prisoners leaped out of their beds and switched on the lights, an uproar of unusual magnitude swept through the barracks. Something strange had occurred. The tumult meant that a vast disappointment had been met with.

"Look at then goddamn ants!" shrieked Blake.

Each one in the room quickly glanced up at Blake's portion of the shelf to see what he indicated. He had left the cork out of his half-filled bottle of Wakamotos, and a thick stream of thousands of tiny red ants spread from the interior of the bottle, down over the side, across the shelf, straight down the wall, and out through a crack where the flooring met the sideboards. Blake snatched up his precious bottle and shook it violently to get rid of the pests.

"Hell!" he declared, "they have chewed up every pill, and they are only powder now." By that time the ants had covered his arm and had begun to sting him. With an oath, he dropped the bottle and ran for a water faucet on the back porch.

Paul and Cameron howled with laughter. While Blake's loss might be pathetic, the scene was comic.

"The little rascals got into mine, too, Cameron announced after he took a look at his own part of the shelf. "They went right through the cork. Look at the holes they gouged out." A similar condition like Blake's existed there. A thick parade of ants ran all the way to the floor.

"I can fix that and keep the ants out," Paul said. He searched in one of his pockets for a piece of twine that he had been saving. Making a loop around the neck of his bottle, he tied the other end of the string to a rafter over head. The contraption swung down in pendulum fashion.

"That should work all right," Cameron said when Paul had completed his task, "but I have another idea." He grabbed his mess kit and rushed out to the sink. In a moment, he was back with the utensil partly filled with water. He placed it on the shelf and rested the bottle in the middle of the pool. "That will fix them. They can't swim."

Before they fell out for tenko, all the prisoners in the barracks had adopted those procedures or similar ingenious ones to combat the new menace that had come upon them. Depression was relieved for hours thereafter by sudden opportunity for lengthy and detailed discussion on the arrival of the ant army and the most effective means for overcoming the assault.

"Those ants are going to be an awful nuisance," Cameron said to Paul.

"But not as bad as the rats. Remember the other night how they spoiled every banana that we all had saved because they were too green to eat?"

"And how!" Cameron replied. "Those damn rats make a fearful racket every night, running through the barracks the way they do."

"That benjo is the worst place," Paul remarked. "I'm almost afraid to go in there at night. The little devils run all over the place, up over you and around your feet. Somebody is going to get well bitten one of these days."

"Do you know the Nip soldiers eat them?" Cameron asked with a shrug of disgust. "Not out of the benjo, but they capture them alive in the warehouse where the rice is stored."

"Aren't they the same rats, only in a different place?"

"Of course they are, but the Nips don't seem to know that much. They are a strange crowd. They think if they get them alive out of the place where they feed on grain and then kill them that they are clean and edible."

"Well," Paul said philosophically, "maybe we'll come to the same conclusion some day."

"What will the folks back home say when you tell them that?"

"We have stooped pretty low in many other respects; that may not be as hard as it sounds right now."

The prisoners were lined up in front of the barracks, waiting for the Taiwanese soldiers to bring the farming tools from the warehouse and for the sergeant from headquarters, who would be the work overseer for that day. Without warning, like the undulations of successive waves, heads turned to the side. There had been no noise to attract, but a mysterious something had beckoned to the men on the flank. Their turning was a signal to be passed from man to man until all standing there were staring aghast in a new direction. The little two-wheeled food cart was being pushed into the compound and across to the cookhouse.

"Pretty slim today!"

One could wager with safety his life savings that those three words would be used by at least one POW whenever the cart was rolled into the compound.

"No different from any other time."

"A handful of 'walking sticks' and a bunch of sweet potato leaves for the whole camp."

"Looks like we are going to have soup to add to the rice today."

"Soup! You mean a little swamp water. I'll bet we haven't even got salt to put in when they boil the stuff."

"What the hell is that back stuff down on the bottom?"

"Christ! It looks like meat!"

"No such luck!"

"It's shark meat!"

"No! It's whale!"

"You're a lot of smart guys! Know all the answers! Not a one of you ever saw that kind of stuff before. But with your brilliant minds, you can tell the crowd what the stuff is."

Paul nudged Cameron and whispered, "You are a deep-sea fisherman. What do you think that black, stinky stuff is?

"It's too far away to tell. But I'd risk a healthy guess that it was porpoise or dolphin. That white underside seems to identify it. But it may be something similar. I'm not sure just what they may have in these waters around here.

"Not shark?"

"Hell, no! But I wouldn't argue with these wise guys here who know everything."

"Looks like we might have a few proteins for dinner," Paul commented.

"And how we need them!" Cameron returned.

"Like Bataan, where we rounded up all the loose carabaos when the food ran out."

"The cavalry horses went next."

"Including the old man's pet charger," Paul recalled.

"After that the pack mules that had been hauling supplies up the mountains."

"That was the best tasting meat of the lot, I thought."

"Fish! Say, that gives me an idea," Cameron suddenly cried.

"Don't tell me. I believe that I can guess what you mean," Paul said.

"What do you say we try to do something about it when we come in from work today."

"Righto!" agreed Paul. "Maybe we can get a chance with the interpreter out on the farm."

"Let's keep our eyes open for an opportunity. We could have a lot of fun out of that little project and perhaps bring some real bacon home for the hungry boys."

When two nimble-minded Americans have a common thought, it is not too difficult for them to find ways and means. So, when the Nipponese interpreter in the middle of the morning wandered through the farming area where the prisoners were exercising their ingenuity to produce the least amount of work, he was spotted by Paul. *This is a good moment*, Paul thought to himself, and he began to ease over in the interpreter's direction.

"Good morning," Paul said in an allaying voice when he reached the side of the interpreter.

"Ah, good morning," replied the interpreter.

You are an ugly little mutt, Pussy, Paul told himself. Then aloud he said, "There are many fish in the sea around Taiwan."

"Oh, yes. Many fish."

"All fine Nipponese fishermen go to war, I guess."

"Yes, all go to war."

"Nobody fishes much then, I suppose. Too bad."

"No, not many fish."

"Some prisoners here are very fine fishermen. Maybe they could get lots of fish for Nipponese soldiers and people who live in the village."

"So?" the interpreter asked with considerable interest.

"That POW over there leaning on his kuwa. See him? He is the finest fisherman of all. If you could get a boat, you ought to make him fish for you. Then you would have lots to eat."

"Maybe good idea."

"I'm sure the captain would think you a very smart soldier if you could arrange that. Perhaps he would raise you in rank. That would be fine."

"Perhaps! I will see what can be done."

Paul discreetly moved away. He felt that he had said enough. Later, the next time he had an opportunity to talk with the interpreter, he could remind him of the matter. *Better not push these sensitive people too fast. Let them get the feeling that it is their original idea. Ego, you know.*

For weeks thereafter, Cameron and Paul pecked away at the interpreter, trying to get a favorable decision on the proposed fishing expedition. But they met with the same Japanese delays and procrastination that had always rebuffed the prisoners whenever an effort was made to improve their lot.

On one occasion Buddha had been enticed into Cameron's roost. He had been wandering down the hall with little apparent purpose in mind, and it seemed like a fine moment to Cameron to invite him in. Perhaps the conversation could be brought around in the desired direction. At the same time, Cameron felt a certain pang to his conscience. Here he was doing the very identical thing for which he and many others criticized the sycophants in the camps. However, he had no selfish interest in the situation; he was making an effort to assist all his colleagues. That altruism, as he well knew, would never be understood by the majority of the prisoners. He would have to bear their certain censure in silence.

Buddha had sprawled his bulk out on a cot. *Wouldn't Blake snort*, reflected Cameron, *if he should walk in and find this detested person using his bunk.*

After exchanging a few idle remarks, those coming from Buddha being limited to little more than grunts, Cameron opened up the subject he had on his mind. "We had a rumor around here, lieutenant, that you would like some of us to go fishing for you."

"Maybe," replied the officer without moving from his relaxed position or displaying any particular enthusiasm.

"I believe that some of us can help out on the food situation," Cameron said, pursuing his objective. "You can easily get a sampan for us and some tackle. There is plenty of fine fish close by. We wouldn't have to go very far out. Could be back in a few hours."

Buddha was shaking his head. After a short hesitancy, he countered Cameron's argument. "Need many guards. Cannot spare to be seaman."

Cameron tried in vain to penetrate Buddha's mind. What was the real reason behind his obstinacy? Was it merely fear over the possible escape of prisoners? "POWs would have to come back. There is no place for them to go. The sea is very great."

"People in the village," continued Buddha, "do not want to give up their boats."

That does not make sense, Cameron reasoned. There had to be hundreds of boats lying idle because the men were at war. For some reason the womenfolk were not fishing. Yet they were perfectly capable. *It appears that the Nips do not want the boats out at sea, even with their own people in them. They do not want to chance one of our submarines making contact. That is likely the underlying reason.* If this was right, it was most obvious that none of the prisoners would ever be permitted to cruise around in those waters. *I believe*, Cameron insisted to himself, *that we have some of our Navy slipping in and around this area. At least that is a most encouraging thought. And what a rumor it would make if I dropped the least hint of that notion.*

"What was all the commotion about last night?" Cameron asked his roommates in general one morning as he was disengaging himself from his blankets. "There seemed to be quite a stir, but I was too exhausted to wake up."

"I know all about that," Sykes announced while he folded his mosquito net. "Happened to be out in the benjo last night and heard the story."

His roommates stopped their various tasks and looked at him in expectation that he would continue the story. Everything was quiet except the noise Sykes made in bustling about.

Finally, Blake could contain himself no longer, and he blurted out, "Well, what the hell happened?"

"Why? Don't you know? It is a very serious thing."

"You stupid clown," cried Blake, "of course we don't know, or we wouldn't be asking you."

Cameron and Paul chuckled to each other in the corner. "Isn't that just like that pair?" Cameron whispered to Paul.

"Like a couple of comedians on the stage."

"I wonder if they have been that way all through their careers."

"Easy now, Cam. Give them the benefit of the doubt. You may be old and decrepit yourself some day."

"Okay! You old fossil," Cameron retorted, giving Paul a gentle poke in his stomach.

"It was Grayson," Sykes continued. "You know, he has been having a lot of trouble with his throat the past couple of days. Last night, it seems, the condition got rapidly worse, and he couldn't breathe because his throat was swollen closed. Doc got hold of our interpreter and explained the thing to the sergeant of the guard. In no time, they had him removed to someplace outside the wall."

"Where to?" asked Blake.

"I don't know exactly where," replied Sykes. "Probably to a Nip hospital in the village. They certainly work fast when something serious happened. Maybe they intend to treat us better from now on."

"Wait a minute, Sykes. Wait a minute." Cameron felt obligated to stamp out a wild rumor in the making. "Who took Grayson out of the compound?"

"Some of our people. They carried him out on his cot."

"How soon did they came back?"

"In about ten minutes."

"Did you talk with any of them?" Cameron continued to pump Sykes.

"Oh no. I haven't had time to do that."

"Very well then," Cameron analyzed. "Our people were gone about ten minutes. There is not a house or building between here and Karenko, which is at least four kilometers away, except the little warehouse just outside the wall. Obviously, that is where Grayson was taken, unless he was left out in the middle of the farm."

"Probably so," admitted Sykes.

"And the other part of your deduction, I think, is just as sour. The little yellow bastards have stabbed POWs and beat the hell out of them and left them lying where they fell. They must have been in a serious condition, because some of them died. But did the Nips take them out for treatment? You're damn right they didn't! The reason they rushed Grayson out so fast was because he had a contagious disease. If there is one thing the Japs are fearful of, it is that. I've lived with them too long not to know."

At the tenko formation several minutes later, Cameron was proved right in his contention. Pussy stood before the prisoners and made an announcement. "It is the order! All POWs will wear face mask. Three times a day, they will gargle with the fluid. The waste will not be made. Dismiss!"

By the time he had returned to his room, Sykes was wearing his handkerchief tied across his nose and mouth.

"Look at the old desperado." Blake laughed. "What are you going to do, rob a stagecoach?"

"They ordered us to wear face masks, didn't they?" came Sykes muffled reply.

"I'm sure," Paul advised, "that with so many prisoners here and no facilities to make masks, they will bring around something more suitable in a short time."

Sykes was unimpressed. Still wearing his mask, he rushed out of the room. In a moment, he was back, out of breath from his hasty effort. "I've looked all over the barracks and the benjo," he cried, "and there is not the least sign of any liquid to gargle with. The interpreter couldn't have meant water, could he?"

Blake gave him a sneer, and Ashley screwed his face up in disgust.

"Relax, Sykes," Cameron said. "Just be a good little boy and wait. Everything will turn out all right. You are the only one in camp who is getting excited about the matter. They'll bring the stuff around for all of us."

Within an hour, the Taiwanese guards lugged in large pails containing a purple-red solution of potassium permanganate. They set the pails on the rear porch near the water faucets and posted a crudely printed sign, which said, "Three times day."

Shortly thereafter, the squad chiefs were issued rectangular pieces of cotton, which were to be worn across the face. A piece of cord was attached to each end to loop around the ears and hold the mask in position. Sykes's worries on that score were ended.

"All this bother," Cameron announced, "may be for the benefit of the Nips. But, believe me, it may help to hold down an epidemic in camp. If that ever occurred, I can see the guards pulling out and locking the gate and leaving us in here to live it out."

"You may be right," Paul said. "It could be a disastrous thing. But have you had any report on Grayson?"

"Yes, I saw Doc a bit ago, but he can't learn a thing. The Nips wont tell him how Grayson is doing, and they refuse to let him go near."

"I'm afraid, Paul, that means one less POW."

"May God help him! We can't." Paul bowed his head and was silent.

A few of the men entangled in the tentacles of the wall sustained themselves and others with their sense of humor. Any new situation that arose had to endure the banter of the witty ones. There was O'Reilly, for instance, who could draw a dozen laughs a day from the crowd. But it was his regular weekend cry that not only brought guffaws from his neighbors, but also served as a reminder of the passage of time. On the dot, he would slowly force his ungainly and emaciated frame up from his cot, raise a clenched fist in the air, and shout, "Me Gad! 'Tis me sixty-second sober Saturday night!"

But a man did not necessarily have to be an accomplished joke smith to retain his sense of values. If he was fortunate enough to see the ridiculous side of events, he was in a fine position to maintain his mental equilibrium. Tragedy could hardly be laughed at, but scores of events each day could be lightly passed off with a feeling that "it just can't happen that way."

Once Cameron was loitering on the rear porch with little to occupy him. Another POW came out of the benjo and hobbled up the short flight of steps to the porch. *Poor devil,* reflected Cameron sympathetically. *In spite of his age, he was a pretty good man when he came into this camp. Now look at him. He's white-haired, and his bones stick out all over. The rigors of this life have been mighty hard on him. I should have been more alert and hurried over there to give him a hand up those steps.*

The other POW sauntered up to the bucket of gargling fluid, swept one hand through the liquid, and brought up a palmful of the chemical, with which he calmly proceeded to wash his hands.

"Good God!" Cameron cried aloud. "You filthy son—" He checked himself abruptly. The entire episode suddenly took on a different aspect. It was so absurd, so out of keeping with normalcy, that Cameron had to turn his face and shake his head with laughter. *I don't believe it,* he tried to convince himself. *I'm having daydreams. It's a delusion!*

Men living far removed from the influence of civilization, whether it be in the frigid polar regions or in the sticky tropical jungle or deep under the sea, will withdraw from the niceties of life. Inclined toward simplicity, with purpose and sometimes without, they grow beards. Men behind the wall were no exceptions. When the last razor blade was no longer effective and attempts at sharpening it on the inside of a bottle, whose neck had been broken off, produced no results, the only alternative was to forego shaving. A well-trimmed imperial or a neat Vandyke would appear to amuse the prisoners.

Spurred on by a spirit of competition, some other POWs endowed with inherent hair-growing qualities, produced handsome sideburns and flaring muttonchops, to the envy or joy of their comrades. Then those men of restricted imagination brought forth howls of mirth from their fellows by turning up, proud but guileless, with scraggly goatees, ragged chin whiskers, and bushy long beards.

It was that large latter group that felt obliged to follow leadership blindly, and without understanding, that finally brought an end much of the hairy-face episode. It was too much for the others when those unkempt beards and whiskers grew foul from rice accumulations or shivered with the movement of maggots.

"Deliver me from ever growing a beard," Cameron announced.

"I rather think you would look very aristocratic," Paul responded, "with a close-cropped and well-brushed set of whiskers."

"You don't think any such damn thing." Cameron laughed back some at his tormentor. "Why don't you step out with some nice, fluffy side whiskers?"

"At that, I could not look much worse than some of the men here."

"Outside of a few, they remind me of smelly backyard goats or a shaggy Saint Bernard that has just rolled in a mud puddle."

"At least you limit yourself to a small, discreet mustache, Cam. You have gotten many shaves out of that one blade, you have."

"Yes, I've been using it for a year now. The trick is in keeping it in shape."

"You are lucky to have that sharpener," Paul said.

"That little gadget cost me a lot of bowls of rice, but it has done noble service for everyone here who wants to use it."

"The boys come streaming in here by the dozens every day to grind out an edge on their blades."

"That chump from whom I got it," Cameron explained, "is a typical example of the selfishness that exists here. He had that sharpener for months and never let another soul use it. He was so afraid it would wear out. But when he raised a beard, I was only too glad of the opportunity to tempt him with some food. He fell for it. Now he hasn't got either the food of the sharpener."

The squad leader said to Cameron one morning, "Say, soldier boy, the Nips have called for one POW from each squad for a detail. Just what it is for I do not know. But your name is next up on the roster for any dirty job assignment."

"Okay, pal!" responded Cameron.

"I don't suppose you want to inspect my roster to see if I am completely honest about how I keep it, like the other POWs do."

"Hell no!" Cameron laughed back at him. "I haven't sunk quite so low that I would argue with you over such a small matter."

"That's some encouragement. I have more trouble from my own people running this little corporal's job than I do from the Nips. They are a bunch of crybabies who refuse to carry their own weight."

"You do have a nasty job," Paul interpolated. "Few persons realize or care what a thankless task it is."

Cameron joined up with the others who had been called upon to perform the task, whatever it might turn out to be. "Gee whiz, general," he said, "what sort of a formation is this going to be, with all this rank?"

"I'm not certain myself. But I got the impression that we are going out of the compound."

"To see the world, I suppose," Cameron remarked flippantly. "It looks as though the Nips picked most of the generals to go. I don't see what we little fellows are here for, unless it is to fill in and make a larger crowd."

"They will let us know only too soon."

In a short time, Scurvy and the interpreter with a dozen armed guards arrived. The prisoners were lined up for inspection and at the command of, "*Bango*," were required to count off. That formality was always necessary in Nipponese procedure, even though there might be but one person in the formation. The group was then marched out of the camp gate and down the lane toward the village.

"At least it is refreshing to get out from behind that wall," Cameron spoke to the officer at his side.

"I'm pinching myself to see if I am actually awake and doing this."

"You don't know what is up?" asked Cameron.

"Haven't the least clue. But it appears that we are bound for Karenko."

"Just another of those things the Nips do, without ever letting one know what it is all about. Everything seems to be a secret mission with them."

"I always have a dread of small parties being taken away from the crowd. Anything could happen, and they may not return."

"That's true," agreed Cameron, "but I hardly believe we need have any concern over this formation. A couple of expressions I overheard when Scurvy had us lined up seemed to mean we were going to do something that Tokyo wanted. Something was to be sent back there. I could not understand it all."

"You know a little of their lousy language?"

"Just a bit," admitted Cameron. "It helps a lot to be able to listen in without their knowing it, even though I am not too proficient. We have been able to pick up a lot of interesting things that way."

Pussy halted the prisoners in front of a neat and clean home on the main thoroughfare. "This is house of mayor. We go in very quiet like."

He led the way up the several steps; through the door, which he opened without knocking; and into a home that was fitted out in occidental style. The party was taken directly to the dining room.

One look and the POWs recoiled in astonishment! A large table had been set ready for a meal. There was a place for each prisoner, and in front of each chair rested a plate of luscious fish and assorted vegetables. In bowls along the center of the table were small cakes of many varieties and bananas, oranges, and mangoes. In the corner of the room stood three civilians, quiet and suppressed.

Scurvy clumped into the room with his samurai sword slapping at his ankles. A kiotsuke was called, and the three men in the corner stiffened and bowed with their arms and fingers stretched and straight. The lieutenant waved his arm toward the center chairs, and the civilians took seats. At a command from the officer, Pussy indicated to the prisoners that they were to align themselves on either side of the mayor and his staff. When all were seated, the POWs strained their eyes to scrutinize the appetizing food spread before them. Temptation stirred in their souls to plunge into the banquet without further ado, but normal politeness and the fear of bayonets retarded them.

Scurvy surveyed the table, made several adjustments to better satisfy himself that its contents were as he desired, and then slowly glanced from diner to diner. When all was as he wished, he called into an adjacent room. Cameramen came rushing in and worked frantically at their equipment to put it in adjustment with the least loss of time. Scurvy marched to a position in rear of the mayor and gave a signal. Cameras ground and shutters clicked.

Well, all right, pondered Cameron. *Have your little propaganda party, but get it over soon. Each of us here is licking his chops to get started on this delicious food. I guess that having our pictures taken for your papers, which we could not avoid if we wanted to, is little enough price for our first real meal in a year.*

The photography terminated with the same abruptness with which it had commenced. The newsmen bowed and left. Pussy announced, "All will now stand."

What's he going to do now, ask a blessing? Cameron questioned himself. *Strange for Nips to stand in this fashion before they commence to eat.*

Then came the startling command from Pussy. "All now march to front street!"

At no time to the knowledge of Cameron had man wanted to murder another with more relish than the prisoners wanted to dispose of their captors! *Of all the low meanness that these little yellow bastards can display,* Cameron cried to his soul. *You have had your fun; now let's get back to our jail.*

Another alignment, another roll call, and the prisoners were marched off. They were taken down a side street to the waterfront. Pussy called to the three senior officers present and directed than to sit on the stone wall facing the sea. A soldier brought up fishing poles, and the trio of worn warriors had to sit and dangle lines while the cameras whirred again. One of the guards dropped over the wall to the narrow strip of beach several feet below, where he fiddled with one of the fisherman's lines. Scurvy bellowed, Pussy translated, and the general hoisted his line. While the newsmen ground their machines frantically, the officer dramatically raised his pole and displayed, dangling on the end, an eighteen-inch dead pompano!

Without giving a thought to a possible murderous reaction toward his reacting violently in that solemn moment, Cameron laughed loudly and lustily. The episode was too ridiculous to do otherwise. But, amazingly enough, Scurvy grinned and Pussy uttered a light chuckle.

They had taken Cameron's guffaw of derision as an indication of delight at the cleverness of the Nipponese to have put on such a grand performance.

Hard labor, brutality, and starvation were quickly forgotten after the group returned to the compound and quickly spread the news of the day's episodes in Karenko. Even the sickest man and the most cynical man enjoyed the tales that were told by the participants, each of whom had his own version. Some of the listeners howled with delight at a good story; others provided a more sadistic impression, because their companions had thought for a moment in Karenko that they were getting something that those back behind the wall could not have, only to have that anticipation plucked from them.

"Paul," Cameron confessed, "the whole thing was a mess. Some of the POWs who had that disappointment of seeing wonderful food only within their grasp, only to have it whisked away from them, will never recover from the shock."

"How did it effect you?" Paul inquired solicitously.

"Hell!" Cameron honestly replied. "I was duped like the others. It was a tough moment to restrain myself from grabbing a bite until they gave the signal. But when they rushed us out of that dining room without a single bite, I nearly went mad. Only the bayonets kept me under control."

"It's amazing how they can act," Paul said. "That food will spoil sitting around without refrigeration."

"Anyhow, we can't sit around and mope over it. The whole crowd here is conjuring up immense banquets after hearing our experience and will be having a further mental letdown."

"That is only too true," Paul agreed. "When the imagination runs wild, a lot of harm can be done."

"Wonder if we are smart enough to figure something out to relieve the situation and get these people thinking about other things."

"Perhaps our minds have not deteriorated too far for that," Paul replied. "How about stirring up a foreign language class?"

"That's a swell idea. Why didn't you think that one up long ago?"

"I needed your stimulation to prompt me, and you have been a little laggard in that respect lately."

"What do you think of Spanish?" Cameron inquired. "You and I both could start off with a class in that, and then look about for someone more expert to take over."

"Done, my boy," agreed Paul. "The first thing after supper tonight, we'll go the rounds and drum up some customers."

The thought of having a language class several nights a week met with immediate responses. The following day, that was the chief topic of conversation. It had a bolstering effect on the POWs. The enthusiasm of some carried over to others who were in need of a little urge to overcame their lethargy. Consequently, the first meeting of the class was highly successful.

Everything went along quite smoothly among the responding prisoners, for the first hour. Cameron explained to the group the plans that had been hastily thrown together. Then Paul took over the responsibility of refreshing the minds of the class members on pronunciation.

"Kiotsuke!" bellowed the POW nearest the door. Each prisoner jerked himself promptly to a stiff standing position. The sergeant of the guard, with his bayoneted rifle, strolled in. He wandered among the men, pushing his way past where the space was limited. For many minutes, he was silent, while the prisoners waited for the onslaught. After all, were they not assembled in groups larger than two without authority of the camp commander?

The sergeant stopped in front of one officer. "Sitting on bunk," he said. Raising his arm, he snapped his finger on the point of the culprit's nose.

A faintly audible chuckle came from a POW in rear. It was funny to him. On the sergeant's face was the slightest trace of a smile. Only a prisoner long accustomed to scrutinizing with the utmost care the face of a Nipponese guard could have recognized it. The tension relaxed.

"Smoking without ashtray," the sergeant said to another man. Flick went his finger on the end of the man's nose. One by one he accused prisoners of similar derelictions and administered like punishment.

"Who in charge? Who is honcho?" he asked.

Before the involuntary movement of heads toward Cameron occurred, as might be expected under the circumstances, he spoke up and accepted the responsibility. "Sergeant, I guess am."

"What are you doing?"

Here comes the deluge! everyone thought.

"Well, Sergeant," Cameron drawled slowly in a time-consuming effort to allow his mind to develop a satisfactory response. "Prisoners must be good prisoners and not get into trouble. Not good to think about the war. Must follow Nipponese orders." *Yes, yes,* Cameron thought he read into the mind of the sergeant, *but what has all this stalling got to do with my question?* "So, prisoners believe they can help camp commander by going to school and study."

Cameron casually tossed his hands forward in a gesture indicating that his answer was a complete reply to the sergeant's question. There were smiles and shakes of the heads among some of the other prisoners. A few merely stood there with their mouths hanging open.

"Study? What study you make?"

"We study foreign language, Spanish. Maybe tomorrow we study mathematics. All very good so prisoners will not make trouble."

"No more study," the sergeant said with finality. "All must go. Cannot come together like this. Only two POWs talk together one time."

Those nearest the door waited no longer but quickly slipped out. It required no urging for the others to follow. They had violated one of the regulations against assembly, but fortunately, they had been caught by a sympathetic guard, at least one with enough authority to take the action he felt was proper. The light punishment he had administered gave him a high rating with the prisoners. Never in their experiences had they received such kindly treatment.

"One more effort to help the crowd out has gone to pot," Cameron said with a note of sadness.

"It's difficult to get anything accomplished," replied Paul. "But let us keep after it. Something else will turn up if we keep on trying."

"I think we got out of that little difficulty with ease. That nose-snapping sergeant could have been mighty tough if he had been so inclined."

"He seemed to be more intelligent and have more consideration than the average run of Nips."

"Maybe he is an American bred Nip and has some respect for us."

"It is possible," replied Paul. "However, I would not set that argument up as sound logic. The way we treat them back home, kicking them around as we do, may give them a great reason for revenge and resentment now that they have some of us Americans under control."

"Say, I have an idea," Cameron said, suddenly changing the subject.

"An idea! Most amazing! Just what is it this time?"

"Take it easy, you old fossil. It isn't much, but I believe it will attract some of these weakened minds into doing something other than merely sitting around and twiddling their thumbs."

"I am very interested, Cam. Go ahead."

"You know a couple of these POWs have found great interest and entertainment in collecting recipes. They have a whole box full of cards."

"But probably not a single one will work."

"Maybe not," Cameron agreed. "But it will be a stimulation. The big objection is that it will keep the thought of food alive in everyone's mind."

"You're looking at the matter backward. The thought is ever present, so why not give them an outlet?"

"You agree with me then?"

"It is a fine idea. Only I hope you will not suggest that I run a clearing house."

"No, no," argued Cameron. "The thing to do is to get Sykes in here to run it. He's already started a collection. Without his knowing it, we can talk him into a centralized agency where everyone comes with their recipe to swap for another."

At the first opportunity, Sykes was approached. Cameron mentioned, "You know, Sykes, that little box of recipes is quite an idea. You seem to be expanding it almost every day."

"It's something to do to keep busy," replied Sykes. "What amazes me is how readily I can recall the ingredients and quantities."

Cameron glanced down at the card Sykes was holding in his hand. It was a recipe for an elaborate cake. There was no requirement for sugar written on it. He looked up and caught Paul's eye. The two men shook their heads in understanding. Another mind was commencing to slip.

"I suppose in a large group like we have here, Sykes, there must be many more who have a knowledge of cooking like you have." said Cameron.

"Probably not," agreed Sykes, unabashed.

"Without a doubt," Cameron continued, "you could have the best collection in the camp."

"How's that?" he inquired.

"By setting up like a big businessman. Pass the word around that you will accept any new recipe that you do not already have in exchange for one of yours. In no time, you would have more cards than that box would hold. You start showing enthusiasm over a project like that, you will have half the camp joining in. You know how the tendency is to follow some other person's bright idea."

"Why, I never thought of that," admitted Sykes. "That is a grand way to increase my collection. And the more I can get, the better selection I'll have to chose from when I get back home, because I expect to publish the best of them in a high-caliber cookbook."

After that initial success, the well-meaning conspirators moved afield, discretely planting throughout the barracks propaganda seeds, which quickly sprouted and bore fruit.

"It's amazing how many POWs have suddenly become gourmets," Cameron suggested a little later.

"Yes," Paul confirmed. "I believe that half the barracks have taken up a collection of recipes. While I may be a patient man, I'm about to succumb to this constant barrage of prisoners coming here to discuss them with Sykes."

"Our effort to be helpful seems to have ricocheted. But I guess we asked for it and will have to bear the annoyance."

"Of course, Cam. A great deal of joy has been brought to many prisoners, even though nothing will be gained except the momentary relief in having something to occupy them."

"Sort of gives me the creeps to think about it—about the sort of thing that goes on in an asylum."

"We are not much different here, Cam, and growing worse every day."

"Believe it or not, I haven't read a single card that has a recipe of any value. Wonder what some of their wives will think when these prisoners take those things home."

"You can count on them to be understanding."

Blake had a secret. His roommates tried to pry it out of him with sly glances, innuendos, and even direct requests for an answer. Yet Blake refused to commit himself. Every several days, he would slip into the room with a spare ball of rice. Confined behind the wall, one could never expect to obtain any more food than anyone else had issued to him. The distribution was too carefully observed by many POWs, who spent their waking time in prowling around the compound with no other thought in mind.

So, when the unheard situation arose where a man obtained more than his allotted portion, it was news indeed. The conversation, discussion, and analysis that went on behind Blake's back testified to the vast magnitude of the event. Accordingly, the third time that Blake slipped into his room, surreptitiously carrying a ball of rice in his bare hand, Cameron, at last, thought he had the answer.

"I know where his extra rice is coming from," he whispered to Paul. "His regular timing has given me an idea. Tomorrow I'll find out for sure."

The next afternoon when the supper rice was being distributed, a moment when no prisoner would ever think of being any place except close at hand to protect his interests, Cameron deliberately left the barracks and strolled down toward the pens where the few pigs were kept. Just ahead of him, three other prisoners were headed in the same direction. Up at the Nipponese kitchen, one of the enemy cooks was about to enter. He was carrying what appeared to be an empty bucket, and Cameron sensed that he had just returned from the pens. *So far so good*, Cameron told himself. Carefully permitting the other POWs to precede him in order that he might learn all the procedures of the new game, he sauntered slowly along. Each of the men in front of him was given a handful of rice from a large bucket by the POW who was on duty at the pig sty.

"Did the Nips bring much leavings tonight?" asked Cameron, hoping to bluff his way into the good graces of the man who had the rice scrapings at his disposal. "Guess the yellow boys were hungrier tonight than usual," the man replied. "There was only a little left when they got through eating. The poor pigs won't have any chow tonight. Here you are." He scooped out of the bottom of the pail the dregs that remained and handed them to Cameron.

"What do we owe you for all this help?" Cameron asked, hoping to obtain all the details.

"The others have been giving me checks that will be good when we get back home," replied the keeper of the swine.

"Well, much obliged. I'll see you." Cameron had no wish to become a party to such transactions. He was not too proud to enjoy the additional food, but he felt that he should not be an accessory in an event that might bring trouble to someone else. It was obvious that, when the enemy discovered what was going on, and they surely would learn of it, they would administer severe punishment to all those who were implicated. His worst fear was that some well-meaning prisoner, in talking with one of the enemy authorities, and there were many who were constantly doing that in an effort to advance their position, would mention the rice matter and unintentionally get his companions into trouble. Then, too, a POW having a number of checks found on his person during one of the irregular enemy searches would bring down an investigation, the consequences of which might be far-reaching.

Cameron hastened back to the barracks and entered his room. "Look what I have for you," he cried, carefully placing on the table the rice he carried in his hand. "Let's divide it five ways."

The reaction to his remark was electrifying. Not a word was said, but in the soul of each person present an inexplicable twinge seemed to shock him. How could anyone give away food? was the question each asked inwardly. Is there more to this life than battling against everyone else for one's own gain? A new thought had been injected into their existence!

"This present 'reign of terror' seems to be more intense and lasting longer than usual." Cameron was stretched out on his cot with his arms folded behind his head.

"Yes," replied Paul, "it is. But be patient; they will tire of it soon and slack off."

"I can't put my finger on what annoyed them so much this time. It must have been quite serious to them."

"Don't lose sight of the possibility of something having happened elsewhere which might have caused them to take their spite out on us."

"Probably a lot to that," Cameron conceded. "Reverses in the military campaign down south are likely the very things for which they need an outlet. The poor devils can take their revenge out on us."

"If we could have news from the other camps, I wouldn't be surprised to find that they are taking the same punishment at the same time. One of these days, we can check up on that."

"We could then conclude that such treatment is directed from Tokyo," Cameron analyzed.

"Too bad we do not have more guards around here like the nose-bopping sergeant."

"You will find only one in ten thousand like him."

"Not to change the subject, Cam, but have you ever eaten snails?"

"No! And that is only half of it."

"Wouldn't you be interested for the proteins?"

"This crowd would eat anything if it could, even by the greatest stretch of the imagination, be called food. That includes me, too."

"I'll tell you what I have in mind, Cam. I've noticed early in the morning, while the dew is still on the ground, that there are snails moving through the grass. I believe we can gather up some and arrange to have them boiled. If they can be eaten, it might help out some, at least as long as they last."

"It's a deal! The first thing in the morning, I'll go out with you and see what luck we can have."

Immediately after tenko the following morning, Paul and Cameron wandered through the grass near the edge of the compound, looking for snails. "Here is the first one," cried Paul.

"So that is a snail. Let me have a look at it." Cameron took the small shell in his hand and turned it over several times. "How do you cook it?"

"You must take the animal out of the shell and clean it well. Then boil it in hot water until it is done."

"Sounds simple enough. Let's collect a good batch and have a try at it."

"There is a good-sized one; pick it up."

"Look at that scamp going up the tree! Come to papa!" Cameron reached up and picked the mollusk from the trunk of an adjacent tree. It did not take many minutes to gather all the snails the two POWs could carry without a container. They made their way back to their room and bounced in on the others, who were getting their bowls down from the shelf for the morning meal. When Paul and Cameron plunked the little creatures down on the table, Ashley and Sykes stared with awe. Blake, however, leaped forward with the greatest of interest. He picked up one of the little animals, but hastily dropped it.

"What the hell is that slimy thing?" he cried. "I got that mess all over my hand."

While his roommate howled at Blake's amusing plight, he stomped about the room trying to find some means of drying his hand.

"That's a snail, Blake," Cameron was finally able to announce, when he had brought his hilarity under control.

"Well, I suppose you need a rabbit now in order to have a race," Blake growled.

"That was a tortoise, Blake, according the fable," Ashley tossed at him.

"Well, it's all the same, only another name," Blake tried to convince his companions.

"Blake," Cameron chided, "there's food in them there shells. And we aim to get it."

"Food! Hell, nobody can eat that stuff."

"Will you help clean them, if we guarantee you some first-class proteins?" asked Paul.

"I ain't much of a hand at gettin' food ready for the table," complained Blake. "Anyhow, I've got some mighty important things on for today."

"Very well," remarked Cameron. "Let's put them in confinement so they will be here when we return from work this afternoon." With the assistance of Paul, he dropped the animals into a bucket and fitted a washbasin on top. "That will keep them fresh for the rest of the day."

After Paul and Cameron returned from the farm late in the afternoon, they collected their charges and went out to the back porch where the wash rack was.

"Paul, you start cracking the shells, and I'll run over to the kitchen and see if I can get a pail of hot water."

"Right! But get it as hot as possible. We'll need it to get the slime off."

An episode such as they were engaged in could not be withheld from the rest of the camp. As a matter of fact, it had been discussed at length during the day at the farm. Now that the mollusks, about which so many prisoners had heard, were actually on exhibit, many POWs hovered around to see and learn. Paul was unmindful of his observers and their humorous remarks while he carefully broke the shells and extracted the animal inside.

In a short time, Cameron returned. He had been successful in evading any of the guards and carried a pail of steaming water with him. With the edge of a piece of tin that he had picked up, he cut the wiggling snails into small parts and removed the entrails. Assisted by Paul, he washed the parts carefully in the hot water. Try as they would, they were unable to remove completely the sticky substance. Finally, they gave up with disgust.

"Come on, Paul," Cameron said. "Let's try to get them cooked as they are."

"That is the next problem."

"I've made arrangements with the cooks to use a corner of the fire, so long as the Nips don't come around."

They were back in the barracks by the time the rice was being served. The little gray bits of meat did not appear very appetizing. They had been cooked without salt or any other seasoning. Paul shook his head with uncertainty. Cameron smiled with the same feeling.

"It's food, ain't it?" Blake had no qualms.

Cameron, without further ado, divided the dish of snails into five portions and placed one part on each bowl of rice. Blake did not hesitate but wolfed his share down. The others watched him carefully before they discreetly selected a piece and nibbled on it.

"No flavor to them," Cameron commented.

"Mighty flat taste," said Paul.

"A little salt would have improved them," Sykes testified. "But you can't have everything."

"Don't believe I can go with them," said Ashley, squeamishly. "Do you mind?"

"Hand them over here!" called Blake.

As might be expected, the word traveled around the barracks as fast as a rumor could. In the early morning, many POWs were out in the moist grass seeking food. Day after day, to the dismay of the guards, who raised no objection but tried to convince the prisoners that snails were not edible, hungry men scoured the compound for snails until the time came when they were completely exterminated.

"Now that the snails are gone," Paul told Cameron one day, "I believe we can get another windfall."

"What under the sun have you run across this time?" asked Cameron.

"I was snooping around at the pig sty, and the POW in charge there gave me an idea."

"Yes?" Cameron prompted him with impatience.

"The Nips told him that this was the butchering season in the village and that they were getting some of the offal sent out to fatten up the pigs."

"To feed the pigs!" exclaimed Cameron. "While human beings starve! How can we get our hands on it without getting some bayonets stuck in us?"

"If you would calm down, Cam, maybe you could figure out the same answer that I did."

"Put it up to the Nips?"

"Why not?"

"Hell, they would never concede that. Let their darling little piggies miss out on those choice morsels? It's asking a lot."

"They will never offer it to us; so the first step is to ask them for it."

"Let's get busy, instead of sitting here twirling our thumbs," said Cameron.

"Do you want to talk to one of the lieutenants about it?"

"I better lay low. It will be less disconcerting to them if we use the usual channels and get our own interpreter to take it up with them."

At the urge of Paul and Cameron, the POW interpreter was convinced that there was at least a small chance of success. Hardly a man behind the wall, in the general discussion that followed, felt that the enemy would make a concession of that nature.

Accordingly, the next day the prisoners were completely dumbfounded when the word came down from headquarters that the offal would be turned over to the camp. Rejoicing was loud and long for the balance of the day. "Meat! Meat!" was the cry far into the night.

The Nipponese authorities were true to their promise; many a prisoner wished they were not after the first sight of the delivery made from the abattoir. Several buckets filled with loathsome potpourri of waste entrails were brought to the kitchen. The contents were the castoffs that had been rejected by Orientals for consumption. However, they made their way into a caldron; and the prisoners later carried them, without upsetting a single bucketful, to the barracks at mealtime.

"This is quite a change," remarked Sykes with optimism, "to have some fine-looking soup."

"I drew some floaters," Blake exclaimed, scrutinizing his bowl. "Wonder what they are."

Paul spread his face into a grin and said, "Try them, Blake and give us a report."

"It's food, ain't it?" Blake quickly took one of the gray pieces in his mouth. He brought his teeth down on it several times; then, in consternation, he stopped chewing and looked at the others in the room.

"Can't you make it, old man?" Cameron asked.

"You guys play a joke on me? This is a piece of rubber." After appropriate sound and action, the chunk of food was sent scooting across the floor, while Blake's roommates howled their delight at his predicament.

"Blake, that was merely a piece of the cow's lung," Paul explained.

It turned into a game from that point on. Each chunk of food was picked from the liquid of the soup, and a debate raged as to its identity. Agreement was eventually reached on every exhibit, but not until laymen had been made familiar with heretofore unknown parts of bovine anatomy.

"The Nips told the kitchen force that we would get this same stuff each day this month," Cameron commented, "because this is the slaughter season."

"I …I don't believe I can go it," Ashley sheepishly said.

"Come, son," Paul gently reproved him. "It is not nearly as bad as it appears to be. We get used to it, and this soup is not without some nourishment."

"The lousy food is only part of the trouble," Ashley replied. "This penitentiary life just about has me whipped down."

"Penitentiary!" guffawed Blake. "I only wish we were living in the luxury of a penitentiary back home."

"It is quite a contrast," Sykes chirped. "Think of the grand life a murderer has back home."

"Especially while he is waiting for the electric chair," Cameron said with sardonic humor.

"But he has radios and books and magazines," continued Sykes.

"And three square meals a day," Blake grumbled.

"Doctors and hospitals and no bopping," Sykes asserted.

"And he is not denied opportunities to practice his religious beliefs," Paul mentioned.

"I dare say," Cameron broke in, "that the finest thing that a convict has back home in contrast to what we dirty crooks have behind the wall is the lack of uncertainty. He knows to the hour of the day when he will be released and does not have the worries of an indeterminate sentence as we have. He has contact, even though limited, with his family and knows whether they are still alive, instead of his constantly wondering and hoping."

"You are right, Cam," agreed Paul. "It is the uncertainties of life, the not knowing, that puts fear into a man's soul."

"Our families are in the same predicament about us as we about them. They don't know and must live on hope and prayer."

"They will, rightly, conjure up all the horrors possible to the imagination," Paul said.

"And the odd part of that," continued Cameron, "is that their fears for us are greater than those of ourselves for the simple reason that they live in uncertainty, while we actually do and see these things from moment to moment. We know exactly what is going on, horrible though it may be. The people back home know only through their imagination, which can deal you some ragged blows on occasions because you never know the real outcome of the thing you are worrying over."

The conversation was suddenly interrupted by unusual cries from the outside. The men in the room rushed to the window to find out the cause of the disturbance. A squad of enemy soldiers was forming up on the parade ground outside. Commands were being issued, and the soldiers were responding with calls in unison.

"How do you like that?" Blake asked, pointing up the hill to the headquarters building.

"Do my eyes deceive me?" Paul queried.

Coming down the steps was a yellow man, larger and heavier than the average Japanese. He was nude from the waist up. Each step was taken by extending a leg outward as far as possible, squatting down on both heels, and then repeating the process with the other leg. A long and heavy piece of bamboo clutched tightly in both hands was raised overhead with each squat. The whole procedure was much like a weird dance, accompanied with harsh cries from the performer.

"Who the hell could that monkey be?" asked Blake.

"He is the new sergeant major," replied Sykes. Sykes always knew everything that went on in Nipponese circles, so he thought, on matters of which he did not know, giving the impression of being informed. "Just reported in yesterday. They say he is quite an athlete."

"Mr. Wakamoto himself, I dare say." Cameron had a sense of humor.

The others laughed.

"With all that energy, he must take plenty of Wakamoto pills with every meal," Blake asserted.

While his antics were being carefully observed, the sergeant major made his way down to the waiting squad. He then put them through a strenuous drill, bellowing his commands in a loud and dramatic voice.

"What kind of ballet dance is that?" inquired Blake.

The troops were parading back and forth with arms and legs stiffly flailing up a down.

"That is some version of the goose-step," explained Cameron.

For some time, the drill and the antics of the Nipponese troops continued. The prisoners from behind their windows viewed the activities humorously. It appeared to them like a vaudeville show or a concerted effort to display what the enemy thought to be military efficiency.

Satisfied with the footwork of his troops, the sergeant major turned to bayonet exercises. From a distance of twenty-five yards from several straw dummies, he had each subordinate in turn execute a maneuver. The operation was to rush toward the dummy with a bayonetted rifle clutched tightly in both hands. When facing the target, the soldier would come to a complete stop; thrust his arms full length ahead; and, with a horrible scream, jump forward stiff-legged until the tip of the bayonet struck the stuffed dummy.

"That kind of stuff would be fatal," Blake remarked after keen observation. "They would not have a chance against one of our soldiers."

"Believe you are right, Blake," Cameron commented. "They are not able to maneuver when they hold themselves so stiff. They are off balance as a matter of fact."

"Well, it sure looks like poor training to me," continued Blake. "We had a couple of minor hand-to-hand fights up in my sector. The Filipinos didn't know anything about bayonet fighting. But I always trained them to remember that the guy with the most guts always won, and the guy with least guts ran before the steel actually clashed. So that way, we always had the best of it, and nobody ever got a scratch."

Dusk was hovering over the compound when the sergeant major suddenly put a stop to his drill master activities. He dismissed his troops and, in raucous tones that echoed through the compound, called for the prisoners' interpreter.

The two men went into a huddled conversation, which was punctuated by the antics of the Nipponese as he swelled out his chest and rocked his shoulders to and fro in a strutting manner.

After receiving the instructions Wakamoto had imparted, the interpreter hastened into the barracks and went directly to Cameron's room. "Sorry, but the sergeant major has called for all the POWs in this room to report out front," he advised.

"What does the strutting bastard want?" asked Blake.

"He feels that he has a complaint about not being saluted properly," replied the interpreter.

"Saluted?" Ashley queried. "Why, we haven't had an occasion to salute him. We have been right here in this room all evening."

"That's correct," Paul spoke up. "He must be in error. No one has been outside since he started his drilling. Can't you explain that to him?"

"He knows that," responded the interpreter. "It seems that he expected you to salute him through the window."

"Why, the guy's nuts," declared Blake. "They have already said we are not to salute between rooms and parade ground."

"If you don't mind, gentlemen," pled the interpreter, "I am merely carrying his instructions to you. I suggest you all come out to where he is waiting, and I will do my best to present your side of the matter."

"That is all we can do in the circumstances," Paul spoke up. "So let's go out and find out the bad news."

Wakamoto brusquely ordered the little group to stand at rigid attention. Then he gave a quick order to stand at ease. In rapid order, he continued the sequence many times until he was well satisfied with the click of each movement. He walked back and forth of the formation with his hands clasped behind his back. His pompous and affected actions were disgusting to all his observers. What he was shouting at them as he strode in front of them was not understood, and he made no effort to have his remarks translated. When he had finished his invective, he struck each of the prisoners hard in the face with his fist, checked their stiff posture, ordered the interpreter away, and marched off up the hill to the headquarters.

"Now what do we do," Cameron asked angrily.

"I'm afraid we'll have to stand here at attention until we get further directions," Paul suggested.

"The dirty little yellow bastard!" grumbled Blake. "I suppose the length of time our punishment depends upon how well we retain this stiff position."

Cameron had noticed how passing guards cast an eye in the direction of the five prisoners, keeping them under close scrutiny. A short time thereafter, Paul began to sway. His feet stood still, but his body would not conform.

"What's the matter, you old fossil?" Cameron whispered out of the end of his mouth.

"This is a tougher job on an old man than I thought," Paul replied.

"It's getting me to," admitted Cameron. "A little of this goes a long way."

"I'm getting goddamn tired of this," bellowed Blake, while his colleagues cringed for fear that one of the guards might overhear him and report the lack of discipline. They did not wish to have the time extended.

"Hey, Jim," Cameron called in a loud whisper to one of his friends, who among others was standing by, helpless to be of any aid.

"Get the interpreter and ask him to see Wakamoto or one of the officers and get us out of this. Two hours is about long enough."

"He has forgotten all about us," Blake wailed bitterly.

"Watch your step!" Jim suddenly cautioned. "Here comes the old man from the kitchen now."

Paul swayed against Cameron, who reached an arm out to steady him.

At the same time, Cameron risked a turn of his head to check on the movements of the camp commander. "He's coming our way," he reported. "When he comes close, I'll give a loud kiotsuke! If we all make a snappy about-face and a very proper keirei, maybe we can influence him to let us out of this mess."

The prisoners had been left facing the barracks, but the captain was approaching from their rear. It would be their responsibility to turn and face him and render a military courtesy. When the camp commander had approached reasonably close, Cameron cautioned his colleagues. "Steady!" Then he called out, "Kiotsuke!"

At that command, each of the POWs attempted to execute a military about-face in a punctilious manner. But a peculiar thing happened! Their knee joints were locked, and their leg muscles refused to respond. Paul threw his shoulders around, but the motion was too much for his remaining strength. He fell flat on the ground. Cameron and Blake, who were at his sides, moved clumsily around and stooped to assist him to his feet. It was painful for them, because their legs and had become stiff and difficult to move. The others in the formation shuffled around to face in the new direction. Their inadequacy to perform the maneuver properly was not noticed by the camp commander, who had been distracted by Paul's fall.

"Why you here?" the captain questioned the prisoners.

"The sergeant major made us stand here," Cameron quickly spoke up.

"Why that?" continued the captain.

"There was some misunderstanding about a proper salute," Cameron explained.

"We have been here a long time," grumbled Blake, with little respect in his tone.

"Perhaps we have been punished enough," Cameron suggested. "The prisoner who fell is a very old man and cannot stand this kind of punishment."

Without further comment, the captain moved off in the direction of the guardhouse.

"He'll tell the sergeant of the guard to release us now," Sykes chirped.

"Too bad he couldn't do that little thing himself," Ashley commented.

"I'm afraid you are a little too optimistic over the matter," explained Cameron, "He'll never overrule a subordinate. That is not in the Jap code. It would tend to lose face for the sergeant major."

Some time afterward, the interpreter walked up to the prisoners and said, "Wakamoto just sent word to me by one of the guards that I was to give you a lecture and then release you."

"Well, thank God! The yellow bastard finally came to his senses." Blake was angry and did not hesitate to show it.

Each of the POWs moved his legs and bent his knees in an effort to restore circulation and loosen up joints and muscles.

"I was to instruct you—to use his words—in the necessity of prisoners displaying every military courtesy. So," the interpreter continued, "consider that I have done so. Sorry that I could not get you out of this mess any earlier, but Wakamoto would have none of it."

"It all goes to show," Cameron remarked as he stumbled along while steadying Paul with one arm, "that these people are absolutely unpredictable. Each one operates on rules of his own, and you have to outguess each one separately."

Cameron had been observing Blake for a good part of the morning. Something was different in the actions of that hulk of a man. He did not seem to be the belligerent person this morning that he usually was. As he worked in the field preparing mounds for the planting of sweet potatoes, he appeared more shy than normal. The guards seemed to disturb him, for he frequently glanced in their direction and made a greater display of activity when he noticed any one of them looking his way. That was not his accustomed method. Always in the past, he had ignored them and extended himself only when they came up to him and grumbled over his inactivity.

"What's happened to you today, Blake?" asked Cameron. "You seem to have the jitters. You're not your old tough self."

"Nothin' wrong with me," countered Blake.

"The hell there isn't. You can't fool me that easy. Something is bothering you, Blake. Can I help you any?"

"Naw, I'm okay. I admit these Nips have sort of gotten my goat lately. Maybe this damn hard labor with no food is telling on me."

"You know, Blake, this is not the first time something has gone wrong with you. Each of the other times, you snapped out of it in good shape."

"You must have been mighty observant."

"I have been, Blake. Paul and I had quite a discussion about it the last time. We were going to talk to you about it, but you came out of it in a day or so and were your old grumbling self. If it is something that recurs. It will probably get worse before it gets better—unless you can put your finger on the trouble and conquer it."

At that instant, an unintelligible and loud bellowing came from immediately behind Cameron, and he received a hard knock on the back from an enemy rifle butt. The tone of the guard had only one meaning, and Cameron caught an expression that meant "lowly dog"— the Japanese have no oaths that are so dear to the heart of an American. So Cameron and Blake moved their way up and down with more vim until the guard moved on to reprimand other laborers who were not working hard and fast enough to satisfy him.

When the POWs were marched back to the compound at noonday, Cameron took a position in the column where he could watch Blake. The doughty old soldier, whose physical courage in combat was indisputable, gave a complete reversal of form. He marched along quietly with military precision as far as his weak condition permitted. *Never before*, Cameron reminded himself, *has he done that*. Blake always refused to knuckle down to the Nips demands unless they made a point of insisting upon it. After the men had lined up in front of the barracks for the final tenko to assure the guards that no one was missing, Blake stood erect and counted off his number like any recruit.

Cameron studied the strange manner of Blake with interest as he slowly wandered back to the barracks. *He has lost his grip for some reason or other*, Cameron told himself. *And I can't understand why*, he continued to meditate.

Back in the corner of his room. he talked the situation over with Paul.

"There is no question," Paul agreed, "but that we have a little problem here to solve."

"We have to get to the source of the trouble first," Cameron explained. "The wall is getting him beaten down."

"Cam, you know Blake has lots of friends here in camp. But does he have anyone with whom he is intimate enough to unburden himself?"

"No, I don't know of anyone. We here in the room are about as close to him as any other POWs, yet we have never had his confidence."

"Oftentimes," Paul spoke as though he was thinking aloud, "a man will develop a complex that boils up in him. It grows worse as he keeps it to himself. But if he can release it out of his system by confiding in somebody, a healthier condition will come about."

"That condition of isolation that you speak about is a problem that I have met before. I noticed during combat a man who would fight like hell when he had a little organized group simply fell to pieces when the support of the man next to him was taken away. On his own, he was not worth a damn but wanted to get away from whatever he was faced with. The average man seems to collapse when he is unsupported."

"That is one of the great principles of warfare," Paul asserted.

"Without question! And that same condition may be working against Blake. He may not realize it, but down in his soul somewhere, he has developed the feeling that he is alone with the problems he has to face. He has lost his courage."

"But he would be the last man to admit it."

"He would be fighting mad if we ever suggested it to him," declared Cameron.

"That may be the answer. Accuse him of it, and build up the fight in him. Otherwise, he will languish."

"Well, let's try it at the first opportunity."

"What better time than right now!" suggested Paul, getting up and walking over to Blake's cot.

Cameron stood up and waited.

"You act as though you had a business proposition to put up," said Blake when Paul had taken a seat alongside him.

"I have," replied Paul, "but I have been wondering if you are man enough to handle it."

"Just what do you mean by a crack like that?" Blake asked.

"Once upon a time, you were a hard-fighting soldier, Blake. And here in camp you have maintained a sort of pugnacity, until recently. Lately, however, you have grown as docile as a little lamb."

"That's a lot of baloney! I just haven't been feeling too well."

"You are letting something get your goat, Blake. And if a big, stout hombre like you starts slipping, there is small chance for the others who look up to you for guidance."

"One of us ought to take you out and beat the hell out of you, Blake." Cameron had jumped into the conversation because he knew that Paul was too kindly of heart to get belligerent, and some incentive must be shown if the fight in Blake was to be built up. You are folding up on the rest of the crowd here and letting us down."

"Aw, pipe down," demanded Blake, turning his shoulder to the two prisoners who were trying to goad him.

Cameron realized that he had gotten in a light jab to the jaw. A swift uppercut as a follow-up would be most effective. "All this hero stuff about you on Bataan that I have heard of probably never happened."

"That's about enough out of you, Cam, before I get up and work you over."

Cameron exuded delight at his success. "I have an idea that you started those stories yourself. Did anybody ever see you do anything worth commenting on?"

Blake clenched his jaws hard together and unraveled himself from his perch. As he slowly got to his feet, everyone in the room knew that a fight between two stout antagonists was about to occur. It was Paul, however, who realized that the matter had gone as far as it should. He was not certain in his own mind that he could intervene and pacify Blake. Why, Paul asked himself, had Cameron gone so far and riled Blake to the point of physical combat? Anyhow, Paul thought, he would grapple with Blake until he could explain to him what the plan had been. And at the same time, he knew that Cameron would not take advantage of the situation. So when Blake had straightened up and was about to make for Cameron, Paul stepped in front and placed his hands on Blake's chest to withhold him.

"Wait now, Blake," Paul cried. "This is all my fault. We came over to your bunk to try to help you and never expected the matter to go this far." He looked into Blake's face and saw there the most amazed stare going straight over his shoulder toward Cameron. Paul had to turn his head to see what was going on behind him. Cameron had flopped down on the bench and was howling with laughter.

"Poor Blake." Cameron laughed. "Finally snapped out of it. It was so simple. A couple of thrusts at his sensitive spot, and the heat in the old man came right to the front."

"I don't see the joke," Blake grumbled. "I still think I should sock that grinning face of yours."

"Now, Blake, take it easy," cautioned Cameron. 'You well know that an old skeleton like you wouldn't get very far with a young man like me in the peak of condition. Set him down on his cot, Paul, and we will let him in on the secret."

Paul gave Blake a push that was more than gentle, and Blake felt that it was discreet to sit down and let it go at that.

"That's right, Blake," Paul explained. "Cameron and I were trying to bring you out of the fear or worry that you had slipped into. It was our purpose to make you fighting mad, and I am afraid we succeeded too well."

Cameron stepped over to where Blake was seated and slapped him on the thigh as he slumped down beside him. "Listen to me, you big lug," Cameron commenced. "You never had two better friends in the world than Paul and me. We have had our eyes on you for some time and came to the conclusion that you needed some help. So we are going to give it to you, whether you want it or not."

"Now, Cam," Paul cautioned, "do not talk so rough. Blake understands."

"You can't talk to a big Joe like that," Cameron said in a friendly manner, putting an arm around Blake's shoulder. "This is the only way he understands you. But seriously," he continued, addressing Blake directly, "we want to lend a hand to pull you out of the depression you seem to have settled into. The first thing you must realize is that there are at least two people here in camp who are on your side and willing to go to bat for you. If you will accept that fact, you have won half the battle. And I guess it is perfectly obvious to you, or we would not have taken the trouble to stir you up."

"Thanks! "Blake was grateful but not too articulate.

"Yes, Blake," Paul spoke quietly and seriously. "We must be close friends and rely on each other to keep up our courage and sustain ourselves. Without a feeling of kinship, anyone of us will perish. Only the knowledge that there is someone interested in our welfare and willing to stand shoulder to shoulder with us can pull us through these dark moments."

"I see what you mean," Blake answered thoughtfully. "Sort of makes you feel stronger and better here." He tapped his chest.

"There is nothing finer in times of stress," Cameron asserted, "than the strength you get out of close companionship, the feeling that there is someone who supports you. It has done me a lot of good. When you can feel that satisfaction, then you can laugh. And when you can laugh, all hell can't beat you down!"

Blake grinned without restraint. Something new had seized him within. There was buoyancy and joy in his soul again. He may grumble at things that displease him, but no longer did he feel isolated.

"Everybody stand by for fire drill!" The call came from the squad leader came as he walked down the hall. "Your instructions later."

"I'll go see what the orders are," volunteered Sykes, rushing out the door.

"That will be a good idea, Sykes," called Cameron. "You are the only one who gives a damn about Nip orders."

"Cam," Paul spoke softly, "you are a bit gruff today. Didn't your rice set well this morning?"

"Why, I didn't think I said anything out of the way. I was merely having a joke."

"It may have been meant to be a joke, Cam, but it is the way it is received, rather than the way it was said. You were not your gentlemanly self."

"My error, I guess, Paul. I meant no harm."

They discussed the matter a few minutes more, and then Sykes burst into the room filled with enthusiasm. "I have all the orders," he cited, out of breath from his haste and excitement. "At the bugle call, we are to hurry out of the barracks to the parade ground. Each man is to carry one Nipponese blanket and some other article that will represent extra clothing. It must be made very realistic, as though there were a real fire and we would save nothing except what we carry with us. The men in the hospital will be carried out on their cots. A detail of men has been formed to do that."

"Aw, pipe down," muttered Blake. "They will tell us what they want. After they have changed the orders six times, we can begin to think seriously about what to do."

"A bucket brigade has already been appointed," continued Sykes, with little heed to the interruption, "and those men have to collect all the buckets in the barracks and rush out barefooted. Another group has been detailed as a destruction squad."

"And what do they do, pray tell?" Blake asked with sarcasm. "Perhaps they put a match to the dynamite to blow up the barracks."

"How ridiculous!"

"Didn't you say they were the destruction crowd?"

"But they are to help avoid destruction," explained Sykes, innocently. "They will carry the fire brooms that the guards put on the porches."

Blake yelled with mirth, and the others had to join in. "You mean those bamboo sticks with the dry rice grass tied on the end?" asked Blake.

"I've always wondered what use we could make of those fire spreaders," Cameron commented. "The Nips made those things to put out magnesium fires if any bombs were dropped on this dry, wooden barracks. And the damn wisps of hay would be the first things to burn up."

At that moment, the bugle sounded outside, and the prisoners felt obligated to take some action. Some few tore with mad intent to follow precisely what they understood the slipshod instructions of the enemy to be. At the other extreme many stood up and looked about to see if any guards with flashing bayonets were at hand to enforce the orders. Seeing none, they flopped back down on their cots to relax. Confusion reigned. Confusion always reigned whenever the Japanese soldiers were involved. Even after they had gone through a maneuver a dozen times, they engaged in rushing about without direction, shouting and screaming.

About half the POWs finally got out to the parade ground; the others remained inside to await the final and proper directions on what to do. One of the enemy noncommissioned officers out in the compound waved his arms frantically over his head and shouted orders to his fellows. They took up his directions and waved all the prisoners back into barracks.

"We change our mind." Cameron laughed, repeating the often heard expression of the Nipponese, which they used when they wanted to change their actions.

"Did you get some good exercise?" Blake asked when Sykes sheepishly returned to his room.

Additional instructions were passed through the barracks, and guards stationed themselves in the hall to exercise direction to the formation. When the bugle sounded the next time, the growls of the sentries gave impetus to the movements of the POWs as they hastened off.

The barefooted bucket brigade formed as directed and started to pass filled buckets out toward the parade ground, while the empties moved from hand to hand in the opposite direction. The destruction

squad assembled and waited for instructions. Another small group
was hastily gathered, required to remove their clogs, and forced to
run toward one of the small warehouses. While these groups were
being disposed of, the larger number of the prisoners received orders
to cluster together in the center of the parade ground. Rapidly, the
guard detachment surrounded them. Bayonets shone and machine guns
turned in their swivels.

"Sit down," shrieked Pussy, motioning with his hands. "Take off
the clogs now."

The sound of wheels and the laughs of Occidentals forced the seated
POWs to turn in the direction of the sounds.

"God Almighty. I don't believe it!"

"We've gone back one hundred years!"

"Slapstick comedy!"

As the prisoners stared and passed droll remarks, down the incline
from the warehouse rolled an ancient hand pump fire engine. It was
pulled and pushed by a band of prisoners, who were thoroughly enjoying
their task. The hilarity they showed was accepted by the enemy as
interest in their work.

When they arrived in the center of the parade ground, they needed
no further instructions, but fell to the task of pumping with a will. They
were enjoying themselves fully. Though the guards shrieked orders, the
prisoners poured their buckets of water into the tank, and the squad at
the pump raised and lowered the horizontal bars with vim. The show so
far had been high comedy, but the best was yet to come. Two Nipponese
held the end of the nozzle, clutching it as if their life depended upon it.
A noncommissioned officer stood stiffly near them in command of the
nozzle crew. All of them faced the barracks at which the stream was to
be directed. They waited and waited! It was their intensity that was so
amusing to the watching prisoners and that rocked them with hilarity.
For minutes, the nozzle squad waited with the greatest expectancy.
Eventually they had to turn to see the cause of delay in the appearance
of the stream. The length of hose between them and the pump was
filled with holes, and the water was gurgling out of them in tiny jets.

"They haven't had that hose out of the barn in twenty years."

"Typical Nip! They know nothing about repair and upkeep."

For the rest of that day, harassed prisoners forgot their difficulties of the moment and continued to enjoy the theatricals they had witnessed. It was Saturday the following day, and that meant a weekly inspection. Floors were mopped, and windows were cleaned. Cameron finished making his bed up in the required manner. He carefully smoothed out the last wrinkles and left for the benjo.

Several minutes later, a heavily bearded POW entered and sought out Paul in his corner.

"Say, I haven't got your home address in my book yet," he said to Paul. "How about letting me have it?"

"I'd be happy to," Paul replied and gave him the information he wanted.

At the other end of the room, Blake fumed to himself. *Another one of those damn pests*, he murmured inwardly, *running around with a notebook and jotting down addresses. What the hell he ever expects to do with them, I'll never know. He's a pain in the neck.*

In order to write down the information Paul had given him, the visitor sat down on Cameron's cot. And it was at that precise instant that Cameron walked into the room. He gave one look at the man who had violated his privacy and saw that it was a POW whom he had little respect for because of his attitude in camp. Cameron's heat flared up instantly, and he took impetuous action.

"Get the hell off that bunk!" Cameron yelled.

The suddenness of the assault caught the visitor without the quickness of wit to make a reply. He merely raised slowly to his feet as though in a fog. "I didn't hurt your damn bunk," he finally drawled.

Paul looked up at Cameron, and on his face was an expression of astonishment. He slowly shook his head at Cameron, who brought himself quickly under control and dropped his head momentarily.

"I beg your pardon," Cameron said honestly. "Sort of blew up. Sit down again and relax. It won't hurt the cot."

"Wouldn't be interested!" the visitor retorted. "I can find a lot better places to sit." He shoved his notebook in his pocket and strode out of the door.

Paul smiled at Cameron knowingly. Words were not necessary to convey his thoughts.

"Guess I'm weakening," Cameron admitted. "Maybe the wall is getting to me. It had to come some day."

"No, son. You're not weakening. No man is weak when he makes an error and comes back with a quick apology. That was one of the few apologies that I have heard since we were confined."

"But he wouldn't accept it."

"That was his error, not yours. You made a great stride forward; he slipped back a notch."

The "reign of terror" that had been in progress for the past week was developing into a pressing situation. It was getting completely out of hand and was no longer restricted to so-called punishment for violations of the innumerable regulations set up by the Nipponese. Every POW was being manhandled or struck—*bopped* was the term prisoners applied to it— and no questions were asked. Efforts of the POWs to talk with the authorities in order to find out what rules were being violated were of no avail. No audience would be granted. Because the men behind the wall were not able to determine the reasons for the general aggressive action by the guards, they were in a quandary and unable to extricate themselves from the condition with which they were faced.

The only means of contact with the authorities left to them was the method of writing a formal letter to the camp commander. In the past, while that procedure was authorized, it had never produced results, for the simple reason that those communications never arrived at their destination. They were stopped someplace in the chain of progress, from the prisoner to the interpreter to the noncommissioned officer of the guard to the lieutenant to the captain.

Now, there was great concern throughout camp. No one was safe from assault, and no one could find out why he was subjected to punishment. Consequently, the last resort was attempted. Prisoner after prisoner wrote a letter asking for an understanding.

"Hey, Cam," the squad leader called in the door with a voice that was not much more than a hoarse whisper, "the Nips have called a meeting up at headquarters. I just can't make it with this cold and temperature that I have. How about taking over for me?"

"Hell, yes, old man," replied Cameron without hesitancy. "Sorry to hear about your cold. You better take it easy. I'll go up and listen to them. Do you know what they have on their minds and what time they want us?"

"Up at headquarters, right away. My only guess on what dope they are going to put out has something to do with this damn 'reign of terror' they have on at the moment."

"Leave everything to me, my good man," chided Cameron. "It will be a pleasure to sit in on such a conference, if they only give us a chance to speak our piece."

"They won't," called the squad leader as he turned to leave. "And thanks a million, Cam."

"Think nothing of it."

"That was nice of you. Cam," said Paul after the POW had left. "Looks like you have a good reputation around here. I doubt if he could have found two men in the whole squad who would have come to his rescue."

"Guess you are right. He would only have received a lot of grumbles, excuses, and vehement refusals."

Some minutes later, the squad leaders were seated in a room at headquarters. The interpreter and Scurvy were present. It would have been too lacking in dignity and would have been a lowering of his prestige for the camp commander to be there in person. Japanese authorities had strange ideas about their association with prisoners of war. The conference was unilateral, as all such gatherings had been in the past. The general principle in the transmission of information was for the Nipponese officer to issue his instructions in his own language, which were then translated and announced by the interpreter. That was the form used regardless of how well the officer might be able to speak in English. It had merit in that the responsibility for the correctness of the order was placed on the interpreter, and the official representative of the Imperial Nipponese Army could never be held accountable. It had the advantage of giving the officer time to collect his thoughts should a question be asked by a prisoner. By the time the interpreter had relayed the thought and had held a conference with the officer in his own language, the matter would be well thrashed out between them. If a reply was suitable, it could be given; if not, it could be brushed aside with the comment that the question was difficult to interpret and therefore could not be answered. Yet, while the interpreter was presumed to do all the talking in English, Scurvy would either forget himself or because of his impatience would take over the conversation himself on occasions.

"Many letters," Pussy started out by saying, "from POWs have been received about assaults by the brave Nipponese soldiers."

The adjective used by Pussy caused Cameron to smile.

"All have been investigated."

You are the sweetest little liar in Japan, thought Cameron.

"They are full responsibility of sentinels and all justified." Placing liability on the soldier to the exclusion of the commander was typical in the enemy hierarchy. "When prisoners break the rules, they must expect sentries to punish. Soldiers read about bad treatment on internees in America. Many people in Japan think all prisoners should be killed. But to gracious majesty, the emperor, you owe your lives."

I've heard that one before, Cameron muttered to himself.

"Internees in America have only one bowl of rice in two days. Many have hands tied to neck so cannot sit down or lie. Some shot because go too close to fence. Very bad! We know that soldiers were not ordered to do that."

That is certainly a great concession to make, thought Cameron. *Can it be that these little yellow people have some spark of decency after all?* The tiniest thought that they may have same humanity entered Cameron's soul at that moment. Actions were by uncultured and irresponsible soldiers.

When Pussy stopped for breath, Cameron seized the opportunity to make a remark. That chance may not come again. "Those matters are to be regretted," Cameron commenced. *But we don't believe a damn word of it*, was the thought that ran mind through his mind. "But the treatment here is not according to International Convention. Isn't it possible to put a stop to all these assaults? And isn't it possible to have a little more and a little better food?"

Pussy and Scurvy went into a huddled conference to discuss those matters that had been injected into what was intended to be a one-sided conversation. Cameron was able, unbeknownst to the enemy, to interpret to his own satisfaction much of what was said. Accordingly, he was ready to respond when Pussy questioned him.

"Is treatment here cruel?" asked Pussy.

"You would not want us to say the treatment was cruel," Cameron replied innocuously. "But it would give us more strength to work harder on the farm if we could have more food."

"Nippon has many problems," Scurvy angrily blurted out. "Prisoners must know difference between guest in first-class hotel and being POW. Must know between war and peace. Cannot expect food better than gallant Nipponese soldiers have."

Cripes, meditated Cameron. *If we could get only a fraction of what these enemy troops get. It's criminal the way they carry those heaped-up buckets of fried fish and rice and thick soup around under our noses.*

"Does any of the prisoners wish to write letter, voluntarily, to his government and ask that internees be given better treatment? If not, then cannot expect better treatment than internees get. You all go back and tell other POWs that to write letters for better treatment for internees is good thing. Dismiss!"

Before any prisoner present could make a remark, Scurvy and Pussy slipped out of the room, and the conference was concluded.

Cameron brought the information back to the barracks. In his own room, shortly thereafter, the outcome of the conference was the main theme of conversation.

"I'm not going to write any letters for the bastards," declared Blake. "Hell with 'em."

"I believe they meant that as an order," suggested Sykes, "and we have to comply with it. Think how much easier that could make our lives if we do what they want."

It was difficult for the others to tell whether Sykes wanted to please the enemy or was willing to sacrifice morality to gain preferment in their sight.

"You would make a fine spectacle," cried Ashley with heat, "writing the secretary of state and asking him to change the national policy because you want better treatment."

"That has nothing to do with it," replied Sykes in defense. "We are on our honor to follow their orders and directives. Seems to me, if they order us to write letters to our government, we have no alternative."

"At least," Paul broke in, trying to keep the discussion from becoming caustic, "we have learned what the intention of the authorities was in calling the conference. They always have some neat little plan up their sleeves."

"That is the right answer, all right," agreed Cameron. "I know because I heard them talking it over in their own language. They said that Tokyo had ordered all camp commanders to get the POWs to write home complaining about the bad treatment the internees were getting and asking that it be immediately improved if the prisoners were not to suffer in consequence."

"It is interesting," Paul commented, "how the Nips hope to reach our people back home through us. They are clever rascals."

"Their effort will not amount to much," said Cameron. "I doubt if many of the POWs will be influenced to write such tripe."

"We may find ourselves in one of those inextricable positions that they set up for us—'no write as we say, no food.' That situation has happened before when they put the pressure on us."

"Life is none too rosy in Nip control; that is true. But we have to resist them as long as possible. I doubt if the matter is worth starving over, however."

"Hardly that extreme," agreed Paul. "Even if we are finally forced to accede, our friends and relatives to whom we write would understand what we are doing. We could choose our words with care."

"At least it would be one way to get some news home—if the Nips ever send the letters."

"I suspect that we shall hear from them again on this subject."

The thought of writing letters stirred something up in the soul of Ashley. That evening, he sat at the table with a pencil in hand and some scraps of paper before him. To jot down his feelings for the one to whom he was devoted was the only release he had. It was a release from a claustrophobia that, unbeknownst to him, had engulfed him and that worsened with each passing day. He wrote:

Dearest,

While I shall never be able to mail this letter to you, I know that my thoughts will somehow seek you out and that you will learn of the troubles that are bearing down upon me.

I have some friends here who have made a definite effort to help me overcome some of the obstacles that exist, but their assistance has been so feeble. That aid does not penetrate deep down into my being where the trouble rests, and their help lingers for such a short time.

Otherwise, everyone here is so hateful and so anxious to take advantage of me. They pursue me constantly in an effort to even take my little rice away from me. And the enemy guards, I know, have been instructed to seek me out and do me harm at every opportunity. I am convinced that they have cagily sought out each prisoner's past and that anyone who was a part of the destruction the enemy suffered on Bataan will be made to pay for the part that they played. That, without a doubt, is the reason for their relentless pursuit of me. It is their mad intent to make me suffer and endure, a little at a time but without letup, until they drive me into insanity or worse.

If I could only have a chance to get outside, even for the briefest of moments, and enjoy the freedom of the open space, it would do wonders for me. I want to breathe the fresh air out there and be able to walk in peace without these ugly heathens assaulting one constantly.

They will goad me on until I can stand it no longer; then I will leap on one of them and tear him to shreds with my bare hands. That shall be my great moment, but it shall at the same time be my last. I am fighting hard to avoid such a situation. The temptation is present on frequent occasions, but I never can muster up the courage needed make the decision. Nor do I find the strength to carry out that purpose.

If I only had some release from this persecution that prisoners and enemy alike are inflicting upon me and with which they pursue me endlessly! If there were only some outlet for me whereby I could force these feelings out of my soul and meet my tormenters with courage.

But they are too formidable, and I do not have the strength. My mind is befogged. I do not see the issue clearly. I am unable to find a solution. If this goes an much longer, I fear that I am lost.

Yet I cannot give up. There must be a solution. If I only could get the help I need. No more of this, my darling.

My love to you always,

A

Paul and Cameron had watched young Ashley as he wrote with great intensity. They had observed his blanched face and his quivering hand and realized that something was amiss.

"Cam, that youngster is losing his grip again."

"Yes, I agree," Cameron replied. "For a while, I felt that he was normal again and would bear up under the strain. But the past few days have proved otherwise."

"It looks like we should take some drastic steps to help him out of the difficulty," Paul surmised. "Unfortunately, he has reached the stage where he will not talk freely with us and tell us his problems. It would be a great help if we knew exactly was bothering him. This way, we have to guess at it and may miss it a mile."

"You know, Paul, this is one time when a man pays the penalty of respectability. If we were not so damn honest, I could find out what ails him."

"You are way ahead of me, Cam. Just what do you mean by that?"

"Why, you old fossil, don't you see? What is to hinder us from taking a peek at that letter he is writing the first time he is out of the room? The only obstacle is that damn respectability that we profess to have. And I wager you a goodly sum that that letter will tell us what we want to know."

"The letter will tell us; I am certain," replied Paul, rubbing his chin with his hand. "But we would have to be some sort of crooks to take a look at it. It would hurt my conscience."

"True! Yet to be logical, we should consider the matter further. If our purpose is to help Ashley, should we be too finicky in finding out what his problem is, so that we can give him the best assistance we have?"

"I succumb to your argument."

As soon as Ashley left the room shortly thereafter, the plotters, feeling like two criminals, set to work to find the letter. Paul stood guard at the door, ready to give an alarm, while Cameron reached the letter down from the shelf. He stood with his back to the window and quickly glanced over the written pages.

Nothing occurred to interrupt, and Cameron, with a deep sigh of relief when he had finished reading, carefully placed the paper back in the same position in which he had found it.

"Now what?" Cameron asked after he had given Paul a quick summary of the letter.

"He sounds like a mental case, all right," replied Paul.

"We knew that already," Cameron answered. "What are we going to do about it?"

"Give me time; give me time."

"I thought we had helped him solve his problem the last time this matter came up. It looks like it is going to take more than we have to offer."

"Possibly so," Paul agreed. "But that doesn't mean that we can leave him in the lurch. Somehow or another we must bring him out of these thoughts that are disturbing him. They are false and imaginative."

"That appears to be the crux of the matter. If there were something tangible to put one's finger on, we might be able to fight the thing out for him. But, with the difficulty wrapped up in his own mind, you and I are mighty helpless."

"Mm," hummed Paul. "There is a possible answer. I'm afraid that you are too practical to respond, though."

"I'll be damned! Why, you old fossil, you have no confidence in me. Surely, I am not that stupid." Cameron was smiling. He realized that Paul had an idea he wanted to advance and was baiting him, Cameron, into a receptive mood.

"Well, relax, my little schoolboy. You have forgotten it years ago, but there is something we mortals can grasp on to when all mundane things are against us. It is something we ignore and refuse to accept until everything in this world fails us. Then, as a last resort, like a deathbed repentance, our conscience catches up with us. Because there is nothing left to us, we are willing to go out of this world to seek succor. Timid at first, like a babe taking its first uncertain steps, we let our thoughts dwell on the supernatural and begin to wonder whether there might not be something to be gained there. Once that question is raised in our souls, we take encouragement because no one can answer that query in the negative. Little by little, a stimulation takes hold of us; and the greater the earthly pressure on us, the more rapidly the encouragement grows. It is but a short time, then, until we begin to believe and build up a faith in that possibility."

"I understand what you mean, Paul, and I am not qualified to debate that issue with you. Nor am I ready to accept all you say on such short notice. Unfortunately, I have grown away from such matters over the years. But there is no immediate solution there to our problem with

Ashley. We must be realistic with him. He is a definite mental case and needs same practical treatment."

"That is exactly what I am leading up to, Cameron."

When Paul used his full name instead of the invariable "Cam," Cameron looked up in Paul's face. What he saw there quieted him and gave him pause. Paul's voice had been intriguing, with its mellow and kindly tone. But his face was enraptured; something shone out from it that entranced Cameron. It possessed a glowing light. Paul's beautiful soul was seeping out into the open!

Paul! Cameron exclaimed to himself. *You must be the real Paul,* he thought. *In all my wanderings, I have never seen a face as glorified,* meditated Cameron. No human being could be transformed like that without supernatural help. Fearfully, he shuddered. Was he a witness to something too awful to contemplate?

Paul's voice interrupted Cameron's meditation. "I am trying to be realistic and give you something specific and definite—some actual thing that we can do."

"Yes, Paul." Cameron's voice was weak, and his entire body slumped as though enervated from a strenuous effort.

"We must convince Ashley that there is hope. We must direct his thoughts in the other direction—away from these conditions that face him daily."

"You mean that, if we can convince him to have confidence in a spiritual and intangible force, it will override concern over the brutal treatment that he sees every day?" Cameron was no scoffer. Nor would he let his realism becloud the great values of that projected thought, which the highest qualities of the human mind develop. At the moment, Cameron was in a quandary. He was trying to redeem a colleague from a mental torture that was partly real and partly imagined, and his first judgment was that Ashley should be convinced that his problems were no different than those of any other POW and were normal, under the circumstances. But now Paul had quickly swept all that aside and had offered an entirely different approach. Cameron was trying sincerely to find the best solution. He knew only too well that all phases of a problem had to be studied and considered. Moreover, he had confidence in Paul, and he felt that Paul was among a very small handful of POWs whose mental and emotional stability had not yet been seriously damaged by the pressures of the wall.

Paul answered Cameron's question with one sincere word. "Yes!" he said.

The two men looked steadily and earnestly into each other's eyes. Confidence and admiration were exchanged.

"Paul," Cameron commenced, "I think we might try your way. It could help Ashley, although I am not completely convinced. I don't see how it will divert him away from these things that physically touch him."

"That is very simple to explain, I believe. I am convinced that the greater the pressures a man is enduring, the more he needs and the more he will respond to spiritual condolence. The problem is to convince him that such succor is available to him, and all he has to do is grasp it. Some day, if our situation continues to deteriorate, you may find yourself in that same position. And when that time comes, remember my words today. They may save you from your own destruction."

Cameron shuddered. "Enough of this conversation," he said, slapping his hands on his thighs and rising to his feet. "I have faith in you, Paul. I am going out to the benjo and find Ashley. There is nobody here in the room at the moment except ourselves, and it should be a good time to have a long talk with Ashley. But," Cameron said as an afterthought, turning back to Paul when he had stepped out into the hall, "the burden of this will have to fall on you, as I feel completely unqualified to help. Perhaps I had better leave you two together."

"No, Cam, you are not as unqualified as you think. Come back with him, and we will all thrash this out together."

Ashley showed no reluctance in being included in a discussion of matters that deeply concerned him as well as all other POWs. Cameron had diplomatically guided him back to the room without letting him realize that he was to be the one about whom the conversation was to revolve. And Paul, with the smoothness of matured judgment, had carefully directed the discourse from the general to the specific.

"But it is true with every one here," Paul was arguing. "No one POW is able to save himself from this situation of imprisonment, where everything is against him, without aid of some sort. It may be enough for his friends to counsel him but usually, as we have found out, requires much more help than they are able to give. They have the same weaknesses as the ones they are trying to help. They have the same pressures placed on them. It is like two drowning men trying to save each other when neither of them can swim. All they do is flounder, and the demands of self-preservation finally override any desire they had to help the other fellow. So one must look elsewhere for sustaining values."

"Paul," said Cameron in an effort to make a contribution to the conversation and to urge his friend on, "what ails many of us is that we have not taken our religious education very seriously."

"Probably so," agreed Paul, trying to give the impression that he was studying Cameron's remark. "There is much in what you say. Like so many other things in life, we have to learn the hard way by actual experience. Most of us are so enwrapped with worldly matters that we are unwilling to lift our thoughts out of this mundane mush. Consequently, we miss the beauty and glory and stimulation of those higher values."

"Or we wait until that is the only thing left to us." Cameron was doing his best to be of help, and he repeated the lesson he had learned earlier.

"Everyone here has reached that point." Paul laid the cards on the table.

Ashley and Cameron glanced at each other. When their eyes met, it was in shocked agreement. There was only one course of comfort left to them.

"Consider anyone of us—you, for instance, Ashley. Your difficulties here are just like mine or Cameron's. The same things trouble you and disturb you; you are no different from the others. But you may feel that you are. It is but natural for anyone to think that his problems are different and greater than those the others have to contend with. Until one realizes that each one of us is in the same boat, he is not being honest with himself."

When Paul hesitated and stared at him, Ashley felt that he had to comment. "What you say is true in general, yet I know that these Nips are after me more than many others."

Cameron felt completely tongue-tied. He wanted to say something to keep the conversation from being diverted out of the channel he and Paul had agreed upon, but he felt so completely out of his element that he was unable to contribute any intelligent remark.

"You know, Ashley," Paul said in his mellow and kindly tone, "one of the great mistakes that we make under these conditions we live in and that may lead to our downfall is to let our thoughts dwell on the rough treatment we receive, instead of using our intelligence to think our way out of these difficulties. We may not believe that there is a circumstance greater than ourselves that directs our destinies. But I will tell you this, young man—if you have the courage to try to find out, you will get the greatest surprise of your life."

"Just what do you mean?" Ashley asked with impatience.

"You will get the greatest awakening you ever had in your life," Paul replied with sincerity as he drove a fist into his palm to emphasize his statement. "Your whole mind and body and soul will be lightened with the load taken off them, and your thoughts will be clear and free from the pressures that beat down on you. You will be a new man, stimulated and exhilarated far beyond what any power in this world can give you."

"But ...but ..." Ashley tried to say something.

"No buts about it," interrupted Paul.

"What I was trying to say, is that maybe I've gotten too far away from that sort of thing. I wouldn't be listened to."

"Who are you to pass such judgment?" snapped Paul. "If you have any doubts, there is one sure way to find out. Try it"

"You mean that you will pray for me?" asked Ashley in an expectant voice.

"I'll be damned if I will!" Paul's words may have frightened Ashley, but his tone did not. "You get down on your knees right there and pray for yourself. It is you, yourself, that you are concerned with, and you are the one who has to reach out and get the help you need. I can do no more for you. So get busy! Cameron and I will leave you alone here for fifteen minutes. We will go out in the hall and close the door and allow no one to disturb you."

As they stood guard in front of the closed door, Cameron asked, "Why wouldn't you give him a little encouragement by just a little prayer? I know you are capable of that."

"That is not the idea, Cam. It will do little good for someone else to kneel there with him and say a few mumbo jumbo words in an effort to pacify him. That is too superficial. He is the one who has to feel the thing down deep in his soul. It has to generate in his mind. He must build up a belief and a confidence in what he is doing. The more he does that, the more he will receive."

"Do you mean that he will actually be heard and that action will be taken to give him what he asks for?" Cameron asked.

"Now you are asking me how far I go in my faith. That has nothing to do with Ashley. But to answer your question, the intensity of man's faith and belief is an individual matter. It builds up from those who are convinced that each thought and act is directed to those who merely *think* there is some such direction because they have been so told since childhood and have never taken the trouble to find out for themselves. Anyone lower down in that scale is either disinterested or a nonbeliever. And you, Cam, can decide for yourself where you stand."

"I admit, Paul, that I am like most other men. We retain a remembrance of such matters because of earlier instruction, but the affairs of the world have kept us too busy to give serious thought to them."

"Maybe you are also like the many others who have no interest until they find themselves in a spot where no earthly help can be of value. Then they are willing to lift their eyes elsewhere."

"That is only too true, Paul. I realize it now. It is the one big reason I don't jump into the fold and accept what you say. I would feel like a hypocrite."

"The longer you wait, the more you will feel that way. And before we are out of this mess, you may wish you had 'jumped' long ago."

Move! Move! We are going to move to a new camp! It was no rumor this time. Pussy had told one of the skud leaders that everything was to be packed up. Just that—nothing more. The news rapidly spread throughout the camp like lava that flows in haste down the mountainside, seeping into all the crevices as its fingers stretched outward and onward. It moved across the small parade ground in haste as one POW called excitedly to another. It rushed from room to room in the barracks, out to the wash rack, and on into the benjo. In the space of seconds every man behind the wall had heard the statement and had repeated it to himself.

Then the rumors flew. We have been repatriated! We are going to Tokyo! We are to be released! Our troops have landed on Taiwan! On into the night speculation prevailed. Each man knew he had the answer and knew that the conjecture of a colleague was faulty.

One of the effects of the wall was to instill in the breast a wisdom far superior to that held by any other POW. Because of his responsibilities and his competitive life, for obscure reasons, an army man often develops a fanciful self-esteem. He believes that he knows more and can do a better job than his superior. The restrictions of group imprisonment will aggravate that feeling in the individual, and ego will run rampant. Added to that is the firm belief that any man holds that, when matters go wrong, it could never be his fault. This is especially true when one has suffered military defeat. The ignominy is too great to permit analysis of the reasons therefor. It is too simple a solution to mouth criticism of others and particularly the top commander. It is he who has to endure the scorn and derision of those who insist upon reclaiming their prestige and ego.

The debate continued as to where they were to be sent and the reasons for the move. Each POW was convinced of his own views, and no logic could dispel that feeling of assurance. Meanwhile, the Nipponese authorities fumbled along with their preparations for the transfer. Everything was to be taken along. Rough wooden benches, worn smooth on top from the rubbing of fleshless human seats, were collected on the porch. Rickety tables ware grouped similarly. Pieces of luggage belonging to POWs were piled in a motley stack. Each one had been lovingly packed by its owner with his possessions of tin cans, bottles, bits of clothing, and the other useless things that a man in restricted confinement will hoard. Oriental grass rope had been graciously distributed in small quantities to bind those packages. The filthy timbers, retrieved from the pigpens where they had been torn down, had been preserved with the utmost care and marked for identification in reassembling and were piled along with the other items. The pigs themselves had been taken to the village and were never seen or heard from again. That was a painful moment because, for months, those porkers had been carefully watched over and nurtured as they grew larger and fatter. Someday they would be found in the soup, everyone believed.

There was little if any intrinsic value in the whole pile of debris. But it was all there was in this poverty-stricken camp, and it was all that could be expected in the new location. So its useful value was great, even though to occidental eyes, which were accustomed to the luxuries of life, the sight of those possessions was sickening.

Then the usual oriental delays set in. It was rush, rush until the preparations had been completed; then it was wait, wait until the higher command gave the order to march. From the viewpoint of the soldier in his low echelon, such clumsy procedure was typical in most any army. It gave rise to the common complaint of "hurry up and wait."

At least there would be no forced labor on the farm and in the rice paddies. The tools had been packed; without exception, each POW was vitally interested in learning what his next location was to be. There were several who, for reasons of their own, tried to be friendly with those enemy guards who were willing to exchange greetings. Several words spoken in the other man's language, accompanied by readily understood gestures, gave a feeling of kinship. That, associated with the fact that no brutality was being shown, made the POW believe that be had established warmer relations and was being given very confidential information. Those POWs were quick to seize upon what they thought was information and interpret it according to the preconceived thoughts they held. From that time on, it was gospel to them, in spite of the fact that their impressions might be completely foreign to what was intended, if anything was intended beyond idle banter.

I have the complete story now," cried Sykes on one occasion as he rushed into the room where his friends were idling. Each of the others glanced up and moved into a listening position. "It was given to me secretly by Mullet Face, and he cautioned me not to repeat it to anyone."

Blake looked at Ashley, and Paul exchanged glances with Cameron. *The same old approach*, each one thought. The way to generate your own rumor and make it sound impressive and to gain prestige is to start off with a statement about the confidential nature of the subject.

When Sykes hesitated and looked about at the others in a dramatic fashion, someone with little sympathy for Sykes's effort prodded him, "Skip the frills! What did the goddamn Nip say?"

"That's what I'm trying to tell you," replied Sykes in a pout. "He risked his life to give me the information because, if he was caught talking to me, it would be too bad for him. We are going to Shima!"

"Shima!" Blake repeated. "Where the hell is that?"

Cameron turned his back to Sykes and stifled his chuckles by holding his hand over his mouth.

"Well, I don't exactly know, but I think it is a Portuguese possession off the coast of China. Isn't that where the exchange ship we heard about is going to come in?" Sykes was struggling to defend the piece of information he had, and in his deteriorated mental state was tying together unrelated bits of knowledge he had in his mind.

"That Nip was very kind to you," Cameron commented, "in passing on that dope."

"We have an understanding. I gave him the ornament off my cap as a present, and he was very pleased and told me what I wanted to know."

"But you don't speak his language," the skeptical Blake interjected.

"You don't have to be an expert on that. We made signs; so he understood. He told me Shima, when I asked him by motions where we were headed for."

Blake poised himself to ask another question, but Sykes sensed it coming and abruptly flew from the room, muttering something about going to the benjo.

As soon as he had left, Cameron gave a shout of laughter. "Shima!" he howled in glee. "Do you know what *shima* means? That is 'island' in Japanese, and it is used in connection with the names of all the hundreds of islands around Japan, just as *maru*, meaning 'circle,' is hooked on to the name of every one of their ships."

"For no good reason, I dare say. Looks like Sykes trying to 'handshake' with the Nips didn't amount to much." Blake dismissed the incident without further thought.

It was days later when the orders to move actually were received. Late one afternoon, all the POWs were lined up in the standard tenko formation. Pussy and Buddha stood out in front and observed the roll call. The reports were made by the squad leaders to the Nipponese officer, who immediately called for another count. There was no change in the figures reported, and suddenly great excitement prevailed. Buddha called Pussy into conference, and there was an exchange of loud words amid much gesticulation. It seemed that they could not arrive at a conclusion; so Buddha bellowed for the sergeant of the guard, who came running to the front. More alarming words were passed back and forth, and finally the soldier took off in the direction of the guardhouse, with several of his subordinates at his heels.

The prisoners craned their necks to see what the disturbance was all about, for this was excitement of the first magnitude. Something was amiss, and it must be something very serious from the commotion it occasioned.

All was quickly explained in a short time when three skeletons in ragged uniforms were led out of the guardhouse by the sentries. The first was an officer who sometime before had asked the authorities for permission to write a letter to the officials of the Red Cross. When asked what his reasons were, he had innocently said that he wanted to inform them that the POWs badly needed some food and perhaps they would send some if they only knew what conditions were like here in camp. The poor fellow was unceremoniously thrust into the eso and forgotten. One of the other tattered and bedraggled prisoners suddenly pushed out into the light of day was a POW whose arm had flown up from the impact of a hard blow in his face that a guard had administered. That was apparently an error according to the code of *bushido*. Evidently, one receiving punishment must stand erect until felled by the blows of the gallant followers of that chivalric class. The last of the three forlorn men was a soldier who had been caught taking from a garbage can those rice scrapings that the enemy soldiers had discarded from their meals. That was an unforgivable offense. Those scraps were intended for the pigs.

The three POWs were pushed into the ranks, and a new count was made. It was complete this time, and Buddha was content. All the prisoners were present!

The beaming lieutenant turned to a soldier who had joined him during the commotion over the lost prisoners and gave him same directions. After pushing his cap back from his forehead, the newcomer called out in loud and idiomatic English, "Now you fellows are going on a trip to a better camp across the mountains."

The perfection of his accent made all the POWs pay special heed to his remarks. This was the first time they had heard their native language spoken by one of the enemy in the same accent they used themselves. It seemed to have come from an American in disguise.

"We're gonna issue you your rations ahead of time. So don't pull that old soldier trick of eating it all the first meal. It's supposed to last for five meals, and there won't be any more. Do you get it? Everyone be all set to pull out at six in the morning. Reveille will be early enough to give you plenty of time for breakfast and to go to the latrine. Now be on your toes so we can make connections."

"Christ! Who is this guy?"

"That's the clearest English I've heard since the Japs took over."

"That Joe was born and raised in the USA."

"Sounds like a San Francisco accent to me."

"Frisco Freddie!" A new character entered the lives of the POWs, and he was named the first time he had appeared.

It was the middle of the following morning before the column of prisoners, flanked by many enemy guards armed with bayonetted rifles and machine guns, started through the gate on the first leg of a journey that led to an unknown destination.

The eyes of each man took a final sweep across the compound. It had been a hellish place, with its squalor and scarcity and brutality, but it had been home. Regardless of hardships endured, departure from the place where a man rested his worn body and where he had seen his fellows die and where he had made associations of other white men from all over the globe sent through his soul an emotion of sadness at having to turn his back on that spot forever. Over there at the far side of the compound was the cookhouse, which played such a vital part in the lives of the prisoners. There the pittance of rice was boiled each day, to be fought over from the second it was issued out by the enemy until the last grain had been consumed by the hungry. Behind the barracks, only one end of which was now visible, was the benjo. For the rest of his life, a prisoner would always question himself as to why the benjo had been of such great importance during his imprisonment. Perhaps it was because so many varied things occurred there. Enemy guards could always be expected to be prowling there, looking for trouble. True, too, that was the spot where many rumors made their way into the expectant ears of those who were starved for news and information. Many times during the darkness of the night, a man living on a liquid diet would have to leap out of bed and run the gauntlet to reach the benjo in time. "When you gotta go, you gotta go!" There was peace and comfort there as well. It was always a joy to feel the seclusion behind the closed door of a tiny cubicle. A prisoner sitting on his heels with his feet planted on the floor, oriental style, could enjoy several minutes of complete relaxation, while he listened to the rantings of a sentry as the little yellow man inflicted punishment on an unfortunate POW. The prisoner squatting there often overheard a whispered rumor that was not meant for him, and that very fact made the rumor more impressive to him.

The unsightly prisoners, marching two by two, passed through the gate and beyond the stout brick wall, the top of which was made inviolate by bands of glistening electrified wires. Few of the prisoners realized the importance to their lives of putting the wall behind them and moving farther from its influence with each step they took. Nevertheless, a mass feeling of relief spread through the column. The air smelled more stimulating when it was not restricted by the confines of a compound.

Cameron spat at the wall as he passed under its arch. The only gesture available to him at the moment, it epitomized his intense hatred and resentment toward that symbol of suppression and ruthlessness. In his soul, there could have been no greater satisfaction if he had, by that act, dynamited the wall and every person and institution associated with it. He was bitter, in spite of his effort to control his feelings. He had a white man's feeling against oriental domination; he had dignity in himself and pride in his nation. Such feelings were entirely compatible with the brotherhood of man and with high moral values.

"It's a relief to get out from behind that wall," he whispered to Paul in a serious tone.

"Indeed, yes," Paul answered. "I thumb my nose at it!"

"Maybe it will not be for long, but we can enjoy the open spaces for a spell."

"What a difference it makes to feel free again, even though we are marching here in a column with guards all around us."

"Just look at all those skeletons ahead of us. They seem to have lost their prison slouch and are stepping along like free men again."

"God, help them! I hope they can be free soon. At least they have a few moments of freedom of spirit."

Paul and Cameron, as had all the other POWs, had discussed at length the possible destination to which they were headed. There was no dispute on the length of time involved. Because they had been given five little buns before departure, they would be on the way for five little meals. That meant about two days.

There was another circumstance about which the two friends were certain. Karenko lay near the east coast of Taiwan in an elongated rectangle of a plain, which was hemmed in on three side by steep mountains, whose peaks rose high into the sky upward to fourteen thousand feet. The sea bordered the fourth side, and its floor suddenly dropped off to make some of the deepest ocean in the world. A short railroad ran the length of the rectangle, and the roadway along the coast had generally been cut through the mountains at the north and south to connect up with the other side of the island. Travel on the short railroad did not fit the amount of time involved, so that means of transportation was discarded in the discussion. Even though the roadway linked up with the west side, its use was not considered, because Paul and Cameron felt that the enemy did not have adequate trucking facilities to move hundreds of prisoners of war. It was physically impossible to march that group of emaciated men by foot any great distance. That meant that the sea was to be used.

"I don't relish being packed down deep in the hold of another Nip vessel," Cameron had said as he shuddered over the prospect of such restricted confinement, with poor air and darkness and the increasing probability of being bombed or torpedoed by his own side.

It will be mighty bad if we have to be shoved down in another coaster like that *Hozan Maru* that brought us up here from Takao," replied Paul with misgivings. "There are no joys in traveling around the Orient below the waterline."

"The very thought of that makes one wonder if it would not be better to try to make a break for liberty."

"I doubt if there is a single man here who has enough strength for that," Paul had thoughtfully answered.

"He wouldn't get far. There are many guards constantly around us. We are in enemy country, and even though there are probably many Chinese who would hide us, the Nips would scour the area. And a lot of Chinese would pay the penalty."

"Those mountains might be a fine hideout, Cam, because the Japs are afraid to go up there. But a sick man without food or clothes would have a hard time with the headhunters who live there."

"The worst thing would be that every man who got away would sacrifice ten of his colleagues. They would be executed within hours. No man in his right mind could be so selfish to deliver deliberately ten of his own friends up to the samurai sword merely for his own advantage. I've often wondered what the people back home will think of us when they learn that no one made an effort to get away."

"We will have to suffer that ignominy in silence, I guess. After all, we learned the hard way. After all, we saw in the early days the Japs proved to us they meant business about escapes. Just think back on how many of our people they cut to shreds merely on a suspicion that someone was planning an escape."

The last small rise of ground on the four-kilometer march to the town of Karenko finally came under the weary feet of the slow-moving men. From its top, the prisoners had their first view of the town and its harbor. Every pair of eyes roved back and forth in search of the vessel that was believed to be there waiting for its cargo of humans.

"There it is!" cried Paul. "I can see its funnel."

"Where?" asked Cameron. "I don't see a thing big enough to take this crowd."

"Look down here to the right," replied Paul, pointing. "You can see just a small part of it. Behind that concrete warehouse with the rusty roof. Just half of the funnel shows and the tip of the stern."

"Oh, yes! I see it now." A feeling of relief went through Cameron. This was not like the dingy little vessel that had been used on the trip from Takao. This one seemed to gleam in the sunlight from a recent coat of paint, and it appeared in the distance to be of respectable capacity. But any feeling of relief was quickly dispelled by the knowledge that he would be at the mercy of his own bombers and submarines, locked down deep in the hold without even the benefit of a life preserver, an item the enemy always overlooked when they moved prisoners by water.

"I don't quite understand that new white paint," Paul said, trying to make an analysis. "Maybe this war is not moving along as fast as we have tried to make ourselves believe. If the Nips can afford to paint up their ships like that, and not even camouflage them, they must occupy a fairly secure position on the seas hereabouts, as well as having plenty of resources that we didn't believe they had."

Cameron shook his head with concern. "Well, this is only the early starter of 1943. It takes one hell of a long time to build fleets of warships and airplanes. And the distances from home over here are unbelievably great."

"We have a little war with Germany that might be taking all our attention. They were making some mighty good headway the last time we heard."

"Good God, yes! They may have overrun all of Europe as well as Russia by now. The only reason, Paul, why I feel that things are not quite that bad is because the Nips have not tantalized us with crowing over such a fact. They love to break down our morale gloating over those major events that are disastrous to the nations we represent."

"Yes. They are nice people, I must say. In their own minds, that is about the only real contribution they can make here, to harass the poor defenseless prisoners."

The *Otari Maru* had already taken aboard its cargo and civilian passengers when the POWs arrived, and the pier had been cleared so that no one could come in contact with the prisoners. Tenko was necessary before boarding. There always had to be a roll call formation at every possible occasion. Even though the march from the camp was made under the closest scrutiny of many guards, the suspicious authorities felt obligated to make a final check before the prisoners left the pier.

There was a surprise for the prisoners after they cleared the gangplank and filed below. The interior of the vessel gleamed with fresh paint. New matting had been installed on the low platforms that served the Orientals for squatting and sleeping in group fashion. Such cleanliness and respectability made an unexpected contrast with the holds of ships in which the POWs had been herded on other occasions.

The men were happy to crawl up on the matted platforms and rest, but the guards bellowed for them to remove their shoes and drop their kits in the passageway. The first ones to arrive followed the well-known principle of making themselves comfortable at the front, which made the later arrivals scramble around and across them in order to get to the rear. There was more than discourtesy that caused that action. It was fear of water travel under these conditions, and should anything go wrong the men who were seated nearest the ladder felt they had the best advantage to get to deck. What happened to the others in an emergency was of no concern of theirs.

Cameron took a look at the platform in front of which his squad had been stopped. He stood aside while the others scrambled for position. Perhaps be could set an example, he thought, by showing some forgotten gentlemanly characteristics. But, no, it was to no avail. Yet Cameron smiled at the way unthinking men would act. When all had found spots for themselves, he tried to step around the others and find a small opening where he could sit and rest.

"There is no space here," someone objected.

"Go find another spot," cried another.

"Don't step on me. Can't you see this place is full?"

Far be it for me to argue with them, Cameron told himself. He was amazed at the self-control he had shown. On another occasion he might have asserted himself and shown a bit of anger and later have been distressed over his display of temper. But now he merely smiled to himself. It mattered so little, he concluded. So he sat down in the passageway and leaned against a bulkhead.

A short time after the ship was under way, several POWs called to someone in friendly pidgin English, evidently trying to get some information. Cameron looked in that direction and noticed that the guards had moved on out of sight.

"Hey, Cam," someone called, "why don't you see what this chink knows. You can probably understand him."

Cameron got up and walked over to the Chinese. "Hello," he said in the vernacular. "You understand Japanese?"

"Only a little," replied the other.

"What are you doing here?"

"I am the steward. This is a ferry that runs between Karenko and Suo, where the railroad comes in from the north."

"You like this job?" Cameron inquired.

"Oh, no. I am businessman in Taihoku. When war comes, all Chinese have to help Japanese."

"Japanese treat your people well?"

"No, no! We have very bad time. They hold us down. Can earn only so much; must give all else to them. But now that we have war, we earn nothing. Must do as we are told. So am steward. Get no pay, only ration coupons. Not very many of those. This shirt I have on is my only one."

"Where is the battle going on now?"

"Many big fights on big islands. Japan says she always wins great victory. But Chinese know she can not whip America. Many ships and airplanes and soldiers go to the south, but they never come back."

"Here comes a guard. Return after awhile."

"Okay! And I bring you some hot tea."

As soon as the steward left, many of the prisoners called to Cameron and crowded up to him. They were all impatient to hear what news he had been given and thoughtlessly ignored the approaching guard.

"Kora!" barked the sentry in an ugly-sounding tone. Then he jabbered at length in his own language, while he pushed the prisoners back on the platform and made threatening motions.

Another guard poked his head around a turn in the passageway to see what the commotion was about. He stood there watching with his bayonet thrust to the front but said nothing. From his throat came a low growl like a frightened dog might make.

It was many minutes later before the sentry finished his tirade and sullenly moved off out of sight. The Chinese steward must have been observing, for he immediately hove into sight, carrying a metal teapot, which he tried to keep out of sight by carrying it awkwardly in front of him. He placed it on the deck near Cameron, slipped a small object in Cameron's hand, and hastily retreated.

Cameron glanced at the item in his hand. It was a small box of safety matches. *Matches*, he said inwardly, *worth their weight in gold!* He knew only too well the penalty of being caught with contraband such as that—a stiff blow in the face, a trip to the eso, maybe something far worse. Quickly, he thrust the box into a pocket, looking around to be certain that none of the enemy had seen him. In the few seconds that had transpired, someone had grabbed the teapot and carried it up to the platform, and every man seated there was reaching a cup forward and calling in demanding tones for "his share."

The quick temper in Cameron flamed up at such conduct.

Before the hasty words he was about to call out, Paul, faithful old Paul, spoke quietly to him. "It is only something that a hungry man wants to put in his stomach, Cam, so control yourself. Don't drop down to their level over a little something to drink."

"Thanks, Paul. I was surely going to blow up over that."

"It's too hot down here to drink that anyhow."

"Hot! Yes, it is mighty hot down here with little ventilation," Cameron reflected. *But that gives me an idea*, he said inwardly.

Without a word to Paul, he walked down the passageway in the direction the Chinese had taken. It was simple to find his little galley. Cameron looked in both directions and then asked a question. Yes, indeed, the steward could do that little favor for the American. In a few minutes, Cameron strolled back where his own squad members were seated. He handed Paul one of the two objects he carried. Paul's eyes opened wide at the unexpected offering.

"Iced tea!" he cried. "Where under the sun did you ever find a piece of ice? This is the first ice we have seen since the war started."

"I thought you would enjoy that, Paul. Now, stand here and drink it in front of these nice people. Rattle the ice around in the glass so it will tinkle, and lick your lips with glee over the sugar in the glass."

"You are brutal, all right, Cam. But I guess these men deserve it this time."

It was a five-hour run up the coast to Suo. Instead of berthing in a dock, the vessel came to anchor well out. Many sampans hovered close by, and one by one, they closed in to the ladder. The POWs were lined up and in a column. In turn, each had to climb down the ladder and, when he felt it was safe, step or drop into the smaller vessel, which rose and fell with the heavy swell. It was not a severe undertaking for a nimble man in good health, but it was no simple matter for those undernourished prisoners whose minds and bodies would not respond to the demands of the occasion.

Those who were not fortunate in their timing fell into the hold of the sampan and were jarred and bruised and cut. After two of the small boats were jammed with prisoners, a motor-driven sampan took them in tow and headed for shore. It cut them loose close in, and the native in charge took them up on the beach. To disembark was simple. All one had to do was to drop over the side into two feet of water and wade ashore. The beach ran back a hundred feet, but its smooth sand was littered with the filth that is peculiar to a small oriental fishing community. Flotsam, decayed fish, and debris of indescribable variety littered the beach. The odors were nauseating. *Let us out of this*, each one spoke to himself.

But such was not to be. Prisoners had to be collected, and the open beach was the ideal place. So as each boatload arrived, the occupants were required to sit down on the wet and dirty sand and wait for the others. As the last ones came in, the word was passed around that the prisoners would now have their evening meal. One of the small biscuits was hauled out of each man's kit or pocket and, with no visible gratitude, quickly eaten. There was always hope, in fact expectation, that even on an occasion such as this, the enemy would show compassion and produce a little rice or perhaps some bits of fish or anything that might appease hunger. But nothing of the sort happened. If a man had some water in a canteen or a bottle, he could partially quench his thirst. If not, he had to do without or be taken care of by a friend.

Darkness covered the land when the word was given for the POWs to rise and line up for tenko. The invariable recounts, to convince the meticulous authorities, bored the tired prisoners, who were anxious to be on their way. It was a short march through the village to the railroad depot, while the natives stood in silence along the road and observed the strange sight, which was symbolic of the power and might of Nippon to conquer the white man.

At the command from the guards, the prisoners rushed for the steps of the cars. There was no order or system or courtesy. Nearly every man there had but one thought in mind. It was, *Hurry, hurry. Get there first, so I can have the best choice for a seat.*

The effort was pathetic. Bearded old men, wobbly under the influence of malnutrition and encumbered by bundles trying to squeeze two at a time through a door that was built for the passage of only one put on an exhibition that would have been a howl as a vaudeville skit. But this moment was too serious for humor—and too disgusting.

"This coach looks just like an American railroad car in miniature," Paul said after he had been pushed into a seat by the force of those in rear.

"Its doll size, all right," replied Cameron, trying to make himself comfortable in the seat that faced Paul.

"These seats are too narrow for two men to sit together," Paul said as he moved closer to the window so that his neighbor could fit into the space adjacent.

"Too bad they couldn't build these with upholstery instead of plain hard wood," he replied.

"Wonder why the backs are straight up and down and not tilted a little for comfort?" queried Cameron.

"And all the seats face each other with little enough space for your legs."

"This ride will be no comfort," Paul admitted. "But I will choose it in preference to the hold of one of their little freighters."

That remark stopped further complaint over their discomfiture. The comparison brought to mind many terrible hours below the waterline. It was well that the future remained unknown to them.

Four Americans crammed in a space about one yard square, where they had to eat, sleep, and store their luggage. There was a common feeling of disgust over the lack of comfort, but the situation was not serious and would have been accepted as humorous by well-fed Americans. To make matters more disagreeable, enemy guards stood at each end of the coach and would allow no one to rise from his seat. Every hour, tenko was taken. The Nipponese harbored great suspicion, even though the windows were kept closed and the blinds drawn.

Cameron was beginning to feel miserable from the effect of an uncomfortable journey in the hot and airtight coach. The air was foul from sweating men, and where it could leak in from the outside, it carried to the nostrils of the prisoners the sickening odor that comes from the burning of soft coal. He glanced over at Paul, who was not faring any too well. "What the matter?" Cameron inquired of his friend. "Can't you take it? You're all slumped down there with a sad expression on your face as though you didn't enjoy this lovely excursion at the expense of the emperor."

"I admit I have enjoyed more pleasant journeys," Paul replied, forcing a little cheer into his voice. He squirmed around in an effort to change his position to a more comfortable one but nudged his neighbor in the process.

That person stirred in his seat and glowered at Paul as though to indicate that he resented being jostled.

"It is rather severe on an old man like me, and my bony buttocks are pushing hard down on this wooden seat. But somehow I'll stick it out."

The night dragged, as nights do when a man can find neither rest nor sleep; and the POWs were tossed back and forth in a heap every time the train jolted to a stop or jerked forward. What little water there had been in an overhead tank at the end of the coach had long since disappeared. The men had learned that, by attracting the attention of the guard and asking for authority to go for water, they were able to leave their seats for a few minutes at a time. But as always when conditions are severely restricted, the early ones thought only of themselves and had little regard for the others. They guzzled water to quench their thirst and then slopped more over their faces and hands for the cooling and refreshing effect. When the tank ran dry, it stayed dry.

By this time, every POW had learned of the economy of scarcity under which Nipponese lived and that there was never any replacement or addition to the original supply. There must have been something amiss in their souls to treat their fellow colleagues in the abominable fashion that seemed to delight them. Those who were chagrined at such behavior, if they were charitable, said that such actions resulted from the severity of the unusual pressures they met with. Those less charitable, and perhaps more realistic, claimed that the culprits never knew any better and that they would act the same way under any circumstances.

Cameron had been attentively observing two of the guards, who lounged at the door directly behind him. He listened hard to catch their words. One of the guards would open the door at the end of the coach, look around, and then quickly jump back and push the door closed. The two men would then jabber together for a moment. When they ran out of conversation, they again opened the door and, with great curiosity, again peered out. When they had finished staring at what was going on, back in again they came and, with giggles, bantered back and forth. Cameron strained his ears to catch the words.

"We have just passed through Kagi," he whispered to those who were seated in his little compartment. "It must be a rather large town from what I gathered from the sentries. They were bantering about it and the girls that they knew there. The place where we are going is some few kilometers inland from the railroad. The name sounded like Shirakawa, and from what they said it is a former army camp that had been abandoned because of being in a malarial swamp. They have been there before and are afraid to go back this time. They said that all the soldiers get malaria there."

"That sounds none too promising," commented Paul.

"They are sending us there intentionally so that we will all die of malaria," cried the POW sitting next to Cameron. "Then they will be able to say we died from natural causes. The dirty yellow bastards!"

"Not so loud, old man," Cameron begged. Always trust a Nip to know some English. Nearly all of them got some of it in school.

The word was relayed back through the car by devious means that only imprisoned men learn how to do. With it went the thought that had been expressed by Cameron's neighbor, and every man who heard it repeated felt a great doom encircle him. Men lived by emotion, not intelligence.

Just as all train rides do, this one finally came to an end. At a command from the guards, the prisoners filed out from one end of the coach, pushing and sweating, impatient at the slowness of those in front. Down on the ground again, the men stretched stiffened muscles and joined their colleagues from the other cars.

"Tenko! Tenko!" cried Pussy, who had appeared suddenly in spite of the thought and hope that he might have been left behind.

"Damn perpetual tenkos," grumbled Blake, giving voice to the common thought. "Every time we turn around, we have to have a goddamn roll call."

Slowly and with little interest in the matter, the POWs moved into their squad formation and counted off. After Scurvy was content that all were present, he called the sergeant major over to him. The two huddled together in conference. Pussy joined them after several minutes; and the three discussed something that seemed to be of vital importance.

While the fatigued prisoners stood restlessly in ranks, suddenly from the side, the soldier who had been labeled Frisco Freddie stomped over to the lieutenant. His face showed disgust and impatience. For a minute he listened to the conversation going on between his compatriots. Then he turned toward the prisoners and issued a command. "Right face! Forward march!" he bellowed in loud tones.

The astounded prisoners hesitated a moment at the unexpectedness of the new situation but quickly recovered and executed the orders. If he was wrong, they would witness an interesting episode of Nipponese discipline. If he was right, it would be a grand relief to get started instead of standing dumbly by while the authorities tried to make up their collective mind.

The outcome was amazing. No sooner had Freddie put the column into a forward motion than Scurvy and Pussy and the sergeant, without the least concern, turned and marched along at the side of the prisoners. They seemed completely content at the course of events, as though that action on the part of the soldier had been a part of a play.

"Don't get it," growled one of the prisoners. "Some young squirt comes up and takes over the lieutenant's command, and nothing is said about it."

Paul, who was marching nearby, ventured to explain. "That is typical Nips. Anyone can do anything he cares to, it seems, in their army. The senior officer present can't afford to do anything about it because he would cause the junior to lose face. And nothing could be worse than that."

"It seems to me that the senior is the one who loses face by letting some soldier barge in like that and take over the command."

"Perhaps when they get back to camp and out of sight of these white men, poor Freddie will get a good going over."

"Detail halt!" commanded Frisco Freddie in clear and understandable English. "Left face! Now pay attention to what I have to say. When I dismiss you, I want all you guys to climb aboard those cars behind you and sit down in the bottom. No standing up because someone will only fall out and get hurt. Get me? We are going to take a short ride through the cane field and then a short hike to the new camp. Everybody on their toes now. Fall out!"

A wave of mirth and interest swept through the group of prisoners—mirth because it seemed funny that one private could steal the command from the high and mighty officer and interest because, down in their souls, the prisoners felt stimulated, as soldiers, to hear some snap and precision in commands given to them.

For two hours, the little engine and the jerky cars behind it wandered through the fields of sugar cane. It was almost like riding the kiddie car in an amusement park back home. The resemblance occurred to everyone there, and comment on it lightened the journey by idle talk. Even the weak whistle and the tinkle of the bell on the engine gave those childish minds something to enjoy.

The prisoners dismounted alongside a dirt road that was cut by the railroad tracks. They grumbled while another roll call was taken. The weather was hot, the men were exhausted, and the road was dusty. When ordered to march forward, the POWs strolled at a slow pace. For no understandable reason, the guards made no effort to hasten the slow step. Even at such a dragging pace, the exertion was too much for many, most of whom were men of considerable age.

Oddments of luggage carried on shoulders and under arms grew heavy and burdensome. Yet they could not be discarded. That empty tin can and that glass bottle were too precious. Someday, something may turn up that could be kept in one of those containers. Those small scraps of cloth held great value. Soon they would be needed to add more patches to an already badly patched shirt. One kit may have contained an extra pair of worn shoes, which eventually would have bartering value. An acquisitive society will not discard its birthright; property ownership is relative. There are times when mere scraps are as important as is great purchasing power on other occasions. Such conditions are amplified in diseased minds.

It was inconceivable that any prisoner would discard his pack. He would have done that quickly enough on the first day or even during the first hour after being plucked out of his normal life of luxury. But not now, not after months of trying to eke out an existence under conditions of scarcity. The most meager possession was a stimulation to the ego. And men quickly adjust to a new set of conditions but are invariably influenced by self-interest. Only a few will retain their standards of dignity and respectability, with a touch of altruism and decency.

"There is something wrong here," Cameron ventured to Paul, "when these Nips don't take advantage of a fine situation to dispose of a few more of their hated prisoners."

"They have that chance, with most of the POWs ready to fall down," Paul replied thoughtfully. "And this unusual consideration for us must be due to one of two things; the war situation or diplomatic consideration must have caused Tokyo to issue orders to the local camp commanders to go easy on us, or the captain himself must have had a change of heart."

"Yes, you are right. And on that subject, I'm interested in knowing more about this Frisco Freddie. He suddenly appears on the scene. Undoubtedly, he is a native born American. I don't believe we can dispute that. For the first time they have sent a Nip who knows something about our way of life into our camp. One could speculate a lot on that. Is it something insidious? Or is it an effort to advise the captain and give him a better understanding of the people under his control?"

"That is quite a question, Cam. We have seen too much and have been through too much to be gullible, but at the same time, I am among the first to be willing to concede the authorities are trying to solve this prisoner problem with honesty."

"You concede that with caution, of course."

"With the utmost of caution, Cam. I will never be blinded by a single instance of reasonable treatment to us. It will take a long period of time to even begin to overcome the suspicion we have built up regarding their hatred for us and their desire to do us harm at every turn."

"Yes, Paul, it will be hard to make us ever believe that they have any respect for us as humans with rights and dignity. But we cannot condemn them completely. Their concept of life is so entirely different from ours. If they could understand our viewpoint or at least make us see theirs, we might have a chance of getting together and overcoming this feeling of intense hatred and suspicion."

"All that is fine for long-range relationships, but we have an immediate interest that concerns us vitally."

"Right! We want to live through this mess and get home alive!"

Rest periods were called frequently by the guards, to the great comfort of the prisoners. It was a joy to hear the command to halt and to have the chance to flop down by the roadside. But it was agony to have to get up again and plod along with no certainty of how long it might last. At one rest period, Freddie strode along the column and passed the word to the POWs that those who wanted to leave their bundles in a pile could do so, and the bull carts coming up from the rear would bring them on into camp.

"He is a hell of a decent sort of guy," cried a tried prisoner.

"That is just one way of stealing our luggage," grumbled Blake, who had overheard the remark. "I wouldn't trust any of these little yellow bastards."

"I'll risk it," replied the other. "I'm going to drop this pack anyway. I've reached the end of my endurance. If it gets to camp, I'm that much better off."

The men sauntered along, eyeing with hope and expectation the long rows of mango trees that lined the sides of the road. With so many trees bearing fruit and the scarcity of population evident, surely some of the harvest would reach the prisoners' camp. Too bad the fruit is so hard and green now. It would be a wonderful treat if a person could have several of them to eat.

In time, a turn was made down a small lane, which twisted around some low hills. Then suddenly a split bamboo fence, twenty feet high, appeared after one of the turns in the lane. Directly in front, a large double gate entry yawned, ready to swallow up the marching column. The sentry box nearby and the guards loitering there left no doubt that this was the end of the route.

"So this is the malaria spot!" cried Blake, looking about as soon as he cleared the gate.

"Looks to me that it hasn't been used for a long time," replied Ashley in a disconsolate voice.

"There must be an awful good reason," continued Blake, "when they have so many troops on Taiwan and so few places for them to live."

"It's ominous," agreed the younger man.

"These buildings seem to be in fair shape," commented Paul, who had overheard the conversation.

The others were observing their new home with keen scrutiny.

A compound was formed by the bamboo fence, and paralleling it on all four sides within was a lower fence of barbed wire. It might have been a hundred yards from side to side, but the area seemed cramped with the several long, one-story barracks that took up half of the space. Open wash racks had been constructed at one end of the barracks, while along the fence a single building with a chimney indicated the cookhouse and a plain frame structure adjacent was identified as a warehouse where the few rice sacks were probably stored and where the farm tools, the kuwas, were waiting.

"We are going to have a nice job cutting this grass," muttered Blake as he surveyed the hip-high weeds that had been growing for a long time without attention.

"Look at those hills," Ashley complained. "Right against the fence on three sides to cut out any air and light."

"Can you imagine the water sweeping down through this place every time it rains?" Blake grumbled. "Why, we are in a regular well."

"No wonder they moved their soldiers out of here. This is nothing but a swamp filled with mosquitoes."

"Who the hell would ever build a camp here in the first place?" asked Blake. "Nobody but a damn dumb Nip," he continued, answering his own question.

The POWs were lined up in a row between two of the barracks. Tenko was taken, to the disgust of the exhausted men who had to stand there in the hot sun.

"Benjo! Benjo!" called several of the prisoners, waving their arms to get the attention of the guards.

One of the soldiers pointed his bayonet at a deep drainage ditch in front of the prisoners and grunted several times. It was a signal for all the POWs to move forward to relieve themselves. *Fine sanitation we are going to have here*, was the thought that went through the minds of those who cared.

From over one of the hills just outside the fence, a darkened sky appeared. Then thick black clouds followed. A peal of thunder and a stroke of lightning broke over the compound. Before the men could be moved into the barracks, the storm broke. It was a tropical burst of heavy rain that fell straight down in a tremendous volume.

"I have an idea," said Cameron, nudging Paul, who followed him outside.

After quickly kicking off his shoes and slipping out of his torn uniform, Cameron stood under one of the eaves and splashed in the torrent that cascaded down. It took but a twinkling for other POWs to follow his lead and revel in the volume of water that was pouring off the roof. But there were some who could not be interested.

"Refreshing!" said Cameron.

"Indeed!" replied Paul.

"Let's have a look inside and see where we can find a place to bunk."

A dark wooden hall ran the length of the structure, and rooms opened up on it from both sides. Each room was partitioned off by a siding that ran only partway to the roof.

"Notice the construction of that roof, Paul," Cameron said, pointing up to a tangle of rafters that ran in many directions. "What do you make of that?"

"That has certainly been constructed to withstand a lot of rough treatment. It's surprising, too, because this building is so low. Hardly seems necessary to have all that heavy framework."

"Earthquakes!" cried Cameron in explanation.

Paul and Cameron looked into different rooms to find space that had not been taken over by those who had arrived there ahead of them. Finally, they located a room that was empty. It was the first one they saw that had two cots unoccupied. As they wanted to be together, they quickly pounced on the opportunity before the bathers came in to fill the remaining space in the barracks. Several cots and nothing else were in the room. They were made from a bamboo frame. Smaller diameter bamboo had been fitted into the side pieces.

"That will be hard to sleep on without some sort of a mattress," Cameron commented.

"It looks almost as bad as one of those beds of nails the East Indian fakirs sleep on," Paul retorted with humor.

"Pick yourself a spot, Paul. The first man on the ground gets first choice."

"I would prefer this side, with the light at my head so it won't glare in my eyes."

"But wouldn't you be more comfortable in that spot?" Cameron asked, pointing to a cot that was placed against the large screens at the end of the room. "You will have more air. And look, here are windows that slide into place."

"Really, Cam, it will suit me better here. My eyes do not relish the glare. I know that might be considered the choice spot in the room, and you are thoughtful about it. But you take it at once before the next POW arrives, or he will grab it first."

They tossed their small kits on the cots of their choosing. That constituted ownership to a degree, but they knew only too well that they would have to remain in the room to defend their priority. It would be an awkward situation if someone else in their absence claimed possession by virtue of being seated on one of the cots of his selection. Only physical force would settle that debate. That was one thing Paul and Cameron had not yet stooped to, and each had vowed to himself in his mind that he would not sink to that level. The example shown by too many others had nauseated them.

"Why don't we try to get Ashley and Sykes and Blake in here with us before some other POWs take over?" Paul asked.

"Can you take any more of them?" Cameron tossed back at him.

"Well, Cam, there are many who are worse. At least we know how each other lives, and it will not take too much adjustment to get along with them."

"You guard our cots, and I'll go find them," replied Cameron, hastening from the room.

Several minutes later, the other three men came into the room, followed by Cameron. "Here we are again," he said. "They thought they had better spots where they were, but they knew that their roommates would never be as understanding as you, Paul. So they came on down here."

Paul smiled. He knew he was not the only one who had an influence on the others. Their life together had been freer of disagreeable incidents than that of any other group. It was far from smooth because of the constant irritations that existed, but at least there had been no really angry words. Nor had it ever come to fisticuffs.

Buddha waddled down the hall shortly thereafter. Each of the POWs sprang to his feet and gave the customary bow when he poked his head in the door. The lieutenant looked about and rubbed his head in meditation.

"You biggest," he declared, pointing a finger at Blake. "You room corporal." That decision having been made, the Oriental slouched on to the adjacent room.

"Now you are a big shot, Blake," Ashley chided. "You will have the weight of the world on your shoulders."

"That is a very distinct honor, my colleague," Cameron laughingly declared. "You should not fail to appreciate the trust and confidence that Sloppy Belly has shown in you. In truth, you are a marked man and destined for great honors."

Blake ground his teeth. To have any dealings with the Orientals galled him. It was some time before he spoke, after he had mentally surveyed the situation and looked over the room. "Well," he finally drawled, "if I am in charge of the room, I'll have to choose the bunk that suits me best. That one!" He stretched out his arm and snapped a finger at the cot where Cameron had stretched out.

A shudder ran through Sykes. *Now there will be a battle*, he thought to himself. No prisoner would dare to claim another cot that had already been occupied by another person. Only physical prowess could succeed. *Cameron can hold his own, even against Blake*, meditated Sykes. *So there will be a terrible row, and the Nips will hear it and came running. And then all of us will wind up in the eso. Oh my! Oh my! Why do I have to be in the middle of this row?*

"Why, Blake, it would be a pleasure to let you have my place," Cameron's smooth voice declared. His sincerity could not be mistaken;

he really meant what he said. If the truth be known, he did not expect Blake to confiscate his cot after such a generous offering.

But Blake was unable to respond in kind to such graciousness.

There was a light smile at the corners of Paul's lips. It was an indication of contentment and understanding.

Sykes held his breath. *This matter is not settled yet*, he told himself. *There is sure to be an argument.*

After picking up his kit, Blake strode over to the window. In his mind, the matter was not settled. Cameron tossed his belongings onto the cot vacated by Blake. He was not defeated as a lesser man might have felt in the circumstances. Cameron, without realizing it, rose to great heights of character at that moment. His graciousness might have meant little to Blake, but the act saved Cameron's conscience from wallowing in the mire.

That night, the prisoners used all their ingenuity to sleep with comfort. No arrangements had been made by the authorities to supply straw for bedding. There was plenty of high grass growing about the compound, which could have been made use of under other conditions. But now it was sodden and muddy from the heavy rains.

Cameron laid his few bits of clothing across his bamboo cot, hoping that the ladder-shaped device would not cut ridges into his body. Even such a rack of torture as that could not keep a weakened and exhausted man from slumber. *Maybe I should have slept on the floor*, he meditated, just before he fell asleep.

Sometime during the night, Cameron partly woke up and groaned. *Damn these crossbars on this cot*, he spoke inwardly. *They have gouged creases in my back, and the pain is awful.* In his half-asleep condition, he turned partly over, hoping to relieve the pain. Try as he might, he could not fall off into that slumber that he wanted so badly. The aches in his back would not leave him but pestered him continuously. *Gosh! It's hot in here*, he told himself as he rubbed a hand over his brow. Little by little, sleep moved farther away from him, yet he fought against the wakefulness that dominated him. *If I only had some water*, he said to himself. Yet he recalled that, in spite of the rains, no water was available in the faucets outside of the barracks. The prisoners had tried in vain to get water for drinking before they had gone to bed, but without avail. *Why the hell does everything have to happen at once?* he complained. He ran a thick tongue over his dry lips. By that time, he was not sure whether he was merely drowsy and needed sleep or whether something else was wrong with him. Every muscle in his body was painful, and any position he took was agonizing. Years seemed to roll past. His thoughts told him that he was in hell, and the fires burning around him made him drip with sweat.

"Oh!" Cameron uttered partly under his breath.

"What's the trouble, Cam?" Paul asked, hearing the groan. "Time to rise and shine. The bugle has blown."

Cameron raised his eyelids. It was daylight, he realized. The others in the room were hustling about in preparation of rushing out for tenko. "Something hit me, Paul. I can't make it."

An admission of that sort from Cameron could not be lightly cast aside. There was something wrong, and Paul quickly sensed it. He stepped over to where Cameron was lying and gently placed a hand on his forehead. "Brother, you are right; all is not well. You have a temperature that feels like a blast furnace. And you are soaking wet! I'm going to call Doc."

It was after tenko when Doc could get there. He had nothing but his professional knowledge to guide him in a diagnosis—neither stethoscope nor thermometer. He questioned Cameron at length and then finally gave his opinion. "It could be dengue, Cam, breakbone fever!"

"Must be," panted the patient. "Every bone in my body must be broken. I'm so damn sore all over."

"Better get you off that gridiron bed," suggested Doc. "The floor will be easier."

He looked around, but the other prisoners sensed what he was after and produced what rags and remnants of clothing they possessed. Doc and Paul quickly spread them on the floor, smoothing them out to make as comfortable a bed as possible. They eased Cameron off his cot onto the mean pallet.

"That's better," Cameron cried, "but awful hard on my sore muscles."

"I'll do what I can at once with the Nips to get you some sort of a mattress," Doc volunteered. "They are hard rascals to deal with, as you know and so slow in getting any action."

It was midafternoon when Paul and Doc dragged in a sack filled with straw. "We finally talked them into a little rice straw," Doc said. "They kept putting me off and saying that they would investigate."

"The sergeant was in during the morning," Cameron groaned. "He looked at me and poked me. Finally decided I was really sick, I guess. Just grunted and stalked out. Tried to get me to stand up. Was too miserable to give a damn what he did. Could have used his damn bayonet, so far as I was concerned."

"What can we do, Doc, to keep him from being molested by every guard who comes stomping through the barracks." Paul was realistic. He knew that each sentry who came in, and there were many every day, would want to know why one of the POWs was lying down and why he did not leap to attention upon the entry of the emperor's representative.

"I'll tell you," Cameron whispered between gasps. "Make a card with 'sick' printed on it in Nip. Hang it over the bed. When a guard gets tough, I can point to that."

For a week, Cameron lay there, grumbling over the ill fortune that had laid him low. Nothing could be done for him, other than to try and make him as comfortable as the limited facilities allowed. The first three days he was too ill to even think of food. His ration was allotted to him from the cookhouse, and the disposition of that rice became a subject of bitter controversy among many members of the squad. Some thought the proper solution would be to draw cards for it. Others insisted that it should be pooled among all. Another thought advanced was that each of the tiny bowls of rice should be allotted to one member of the squad after another in turn. In that fashion, a prisoner would get at least one double serving instead of spreading the allowance out among many where it would hardly be noticed.

But it was Cameron who settled the heated discussion. *The vultures disgust me*, he told himself. "Paul," he cried aloud, "bring me my rice as usual. I'll eat it myself." When it came in, Cameron continued his instructions. "Close the door, Paul, so the others will forget about fighting over these few grains. Now divide it up among you in the room."

The extra spoonful of rice for the next several meals made a different man out of Blake. He unbended and acted in a courteous manner toward Cameron. Several times, he even brought in a drink of water for the sick man. Cameron noticed the extra attention, and he said to Paul on one occasion, "I hope that Blake is becoming a human being again."

"Perhaps he has some respectability left after all."

"That fellow is just playing his cards close to his chest," chimed in Ashley, who had overheard the conversation.

No sooner had the POWs settled down in their new camp than the rumors began to fly again. Other times, new conditions, and different guards made the crop of rumors particularly choice. Repatriation was around the corner! POWs were to be exchanged for the Nipponese interned in America! A Red Cross ship with supplies would soon dock at Takao! Tobacco was to be furnished! Vegetables, sugar, and fruit were being grown on Taiwan in far greater quantities than the available shipping could carry to Japan, and they would be issued to prisoners! A dentist was to be assigned to the camp! Medicines, especially quinine, were on the way! But rumors they were, and rumors they remained.

"What's the matter, Ashley? You look sort of beat down?" Cameron slapped his young friend lightly on the back in an effort to cheer him up.

Ashley was sitting on the grass outside the barracks, watching the enemy airplanes that passed by overhead at irregular intervals and that caused considerable speculation among the prisoners as to their destination. "Those damn planes worry me. What if one of them dropped a load of bombs down on us? We wouldn't have a chance. Sometimes, that is exactly what they intend to do."

Some emotional perturbation here, thought Cameron. He realized in a general way that something was wrong with Ashley, but the complexities of a man's mind were too much for him to fathom. "You have the jitters, man."

"If I could only fight back at those damn planes and those Nips here on the ground," declared Ashley as he shook his fist in the air with an oath.

"Take it easy, old man. One of these fine days, our turn will come."

"I'm sorry, Cam, to blow up that way," Ashley answered in a quiet voice. "Sometimes it is more than I can stand, and my temper gets away from me."

"You have had a lot of those spells lately. Can't I do something for you? There ought to be a way out of your problems."

"Oh, I'll be all right."

"It will take a lot of hard effort and willpower, Ashley. I believe if the rest of us lend a hand to cheer you up, we might get results."

"Don't worry about me, Cam. Thanks just the same. I'll conquer it."

But Cameron was not so sure.

One morning, several days later, Cameron was standing stiffly at attention while the roll call was being taken. He began to weave back and forth, and try as he would he could not control himself to remain still. A strange feeling permeated his whole body. *Now what the hell is the matter with me?* he queried of himself. Fortunately, the formation ended at that moment, and Sykes and another prisoner stepped forward and seized Cameron by both arms.

"We have been watching you, Cam, just in front of us," Sykes spoke. "It looked like you might topple over any minute."

"I'm all right," he replied. "Just had a little dizzy spell."

"Hope you aren't getting malaria. You know that about 20 percent of the camp has it already."

"We'll all have it before we get out of here," Cameron declared. "Even the Nips say that this swamp is the worst mosquito-infested area of Taiwan." With that, his knees gave way, and he would have tumbled to the ground if his two friends had not had a firm grip on him.

"You are either having a recurrence of that dengue you just got over, Cam, or else the malaria has hit you. Come on, let's get to your room."

When he was able to flop down on his cot, Cameron gave up. He relaxed completely and knew that he was in for another siege of illness. Sykes went down the hall and came back with Doc.

"Not again?" the medical man asked Cameron. "We just got you back on your feet, and here you are falling by the wayside again.

"I'm really in foul shape, Doc," whispered Cameron. "This is something different. I can tell it is not the same thing I had before."

"Maybe we can do a little better by you this time," Doc replied with a smile. "The Nips finally let me have a thermometer. At least I can read your temperature. And they have promised us a small amount of quinine because of the many cases of malaria."

"That's mighty damn human of them! The little yellow bastards!" Cameron was in no mood to control himself.

"Here, get this under your tongue," ordered Doc, shoving his precious thermometer into Cameron's mouth. "Run it up as high as you can, because the Nips have told me that no one can stay in bed unless he has a fever of 104."

A few minutes later he removed the instrument from Cameron's mouth and took a reading. "That the best you can do? It's a shade below 104, but I'll have to take the risk. You stay here in bed. I don't doubt but that you have malaria, although I wouldn't swear to it without a laboratory examination. I'll keep after the Nips for the quinine they promised me. It will not go far with the scores of cases we have already."

"More coming up," muttered Cameron hazily.

Paul hovered close to the sick man and did what he could to make him more comfortable. There was little else that either he or Doc could do.

The promised quinine finally was delivered.

"Here, Paul. See that he gets five of these today and tomorrow," ordered Doc as he handed some pills over to Paul.

"Why, this is silly, Doc," argued Paul. "This is no effective treatment for malaria."

"You are right, Paul. That small quantity will have little if any effect. But that is the dosage the Nips prescribed. My hands are tied. Each one of those tablets has to be accounted for. They check on who is to receive them and give me just that many. It's an outrage! I argued and argued. They finally slapped me in the face and ordered me out of the office."

"They have been bragging a lot about having conquered all the quinine-producing islands, but they don't seem to have the product."

Cameron soon floated off into the land of the opium smokers, intoxicated by a condition that he could not and did not want to control. He no longer cared what might happen. His dreams were grotesque; they made no sense. Try as he did to cast them away from him and to replace them with something of beauty and of peace and contentment, they persisted in being a kaleidoscopic array of Nipponese bayonets and oriental mud and of little yellow men with shaven pates. It was grotesque and horrible. Nausea and headaches and chills and sweat!

When the severity of his illness abated, Cameron slowly felt a clearing of his thoughts, like a patient coming out from under the influence of ether. *God*, he breathed to himself, *I'd give an arm for some little comfort from home—a sip of orange juice, a thimble of milk, a spoonful of ice cream! Anything to relieve this dryness and thirst!*

It was only a stout body, refusing to succumb, that brought Cameron through. Others were also fortunate; some were not.

Days later, he rolled out of bed for the first time. His knees were too shaky and his body too weak to stand alone. So he piled back on his cot unceremoniously. It took time, too much time, to complete his recovery. For some unknown reason, the authorities did not rush him into activity. Probably because they had settled in their own minds that he was sick, and from that point on, they lost interest in him.

It was a sad moment for him when Paul caught him up on the news of all the events that had occurred during his illness. Cameron listened with astonishment as Paul called the roll of those who had gone on to happier surroundings while Cameron had slept through his agonizing sickness.

"It's a shock," he declared, "to hear of so many at once. A single case is bad enough, but you sort of know that it is coming. The shock is not so sudden. Well, I hope the poor devils are better off wherever they may be. They found no joy here."

"If these losses keep up, none of us will ever get back home."

"That is the first time I ever heard you talk like that, Paul. Have you had some premonition yourself?"

"No, no! I was just idly speculating." But Paul's voice had a faraway sound.

For many days, Ashley had been brooding to himself. Everything seemed to be all mixed up in his thoughts. He knew that some sort of a struggle was going on within him. It was becoming more acute, he sensed, and that meant a serious situation. Some vague thing was threatening him, but in his ill condition, he was unable to understand what it was.

One day, he was sitting on the edge of his cot, stirred up by the thoughts that were racing through his mind. As he meditated, he spoke to himself at length. *Why, why,* he asked, *are these Nips constantly picking on me? I have given them no cause to treat me as they do. I have always tried to follow their silly rules and regulations, but nevertheless, I seem to be their target. They are after me constantly.*

And the POWs are just as bad. They hound me to death the same way. I don't get it! They're yellow, all of them, and pick on me just because they see the Nips doing it. They think that will give them a position with the damn guards. Their annoyances have reached the point where I can't even eat anymore. Maybe that is one of the reasons they are after me all the time, so I can't eat and then they can grab my portion.

Ashley brushed a hand over his head, which was aching. Then he rubbed the back of his neck. There was a great soreness there too. His chest hurt, and he could not draw a deep breath without suffering. He was frightened. His hands shook, and he ran a tongue over a parched set of lips. As he contemplated, his anger grew more violent. The world was against him. He was caught in a trap from which he could not extricate himself. A pair of arms of tremendous proportions seemed to encircle him and bind him tighter and tighter and tighter. There was a scream in his throat, which he managed by the greatest exertion of willpower to suppress. Yet he realized that he was losing ground. That pounding of his heart and that dripping forehead and that haze that was overcoming him told him that he was contending against more than he could overcome. His condition grew rapidly worse. The climax was near!

"They will not do this to me!" he screamed aloud as he dashed at full speed from his room. "I'll get out of their goddamn clutches! They can't stop me now! I'm going home!

"Cam," cried Paul when he saw Ashley run out of the barracks in mortal fear, "run and stop him! I'll get Doc!"

Ashley raced straight for the high fence at the end of the compound. In his mind, there was only one thought. *Freedom! Freedom from this oppression*, he told himself. "I'm going home. I'm going home," he kept whispering to himself. *Nothing stands in my way but a little fence. That will be easy to clear, and then I will be out in the open and away from all this horror.*

The wind flew past his hot forehead; his legs took on a burst of speed; his eyes saw the beauty of the world beyond. There were clouds, beautiful and fluffy white pillows, hovering just over the top of the split bamboo fence. Set in a sea of blue, they made an inviting picture, just like the sky back home that held so many lovely memories. In the seconds that followed, a thousand remembrances of the peace and joy of home raced through his thoughts—his home of childhood, lying between the hills, with the cluster of elms that engulfed it; Marie in flowing organdie skipping down the lane, her arms extended to welcome her returning soldier.

The high fence was before him now. It was the only remaining obstacle between him and liberty. He looked high above it as he ran those few remaining strides. The lazy white fluffs, slowly moving in a sea of blue, spelled peace and quiet. *There is where I'm going*, Ashley told himself. He saw himself take a floating leap to clear the fence, and he felt a gentle breezy as he glided outward ...

Horse Face was patrolling the fence, on the inside. He had been well named by the prisoners, and his soul was as ugly as his outward appearance. At no time had he neglected an opportunity to show the meanest of traits toward POWs. There was a good reason for that. Horse's Face had been denied the privilege of fighting with his comrades against the terrible white man who must be annihilated by command of the emperor. Being kept in rearward areas to guard prisoners rankled him to the core. Somehow he must fulfill his destiny. Banzai!

Suddenly he was confronted with a prisoner running madly through the compound. *He must be off in the head*, thought Horse Face, *and he is running straight toward the fence. It will be a huge joke to see him bounce back when he crashes into that twenty-foot high, springy bamboo fence.* But that mood impulsively changed. *A detested Occidental coming my way,* he chanted inwardly, *trying to escape!*

Up came his rifle, the bayonet on the end twinkling in the sunlight. He peeked through the sights. His finger twitched. *Pin-n-ng!*

"Banzai! For the Emperor! Bushido! What a famous warrior am I!"

"The Fourth of July! No work in the rice paddies! I don't follow the Nips reasoning," Cameron said, shaking his head. "They watch us every minute to make sure there is no display of patriotism or nationalism, and then they recognize this day."

"That is difficult to explain," replied Paul. "I doubt if a white man could penetrate the oriental mind to that extent."

"It may be they consider it Independence Day, when we broke with Great Britain—"

"And in their minds, it is one more effort to drive a wedge between our present friendship."

"Precisely! But it is silly reasoning to me."

A noisy commotion down the hall interrupted further speculation of the ways of the Nipponese. Paul and Cameron leaped to the door with curiosity. The wooden building seemed to shake from the disturbance.

"They're at it again," said Paul in a grieved voice. "It seems that idling in the barracks brings these rows on."

At the intersection of the two halls, a lively battle of fisticuffs was on. There was a degree of humor attached to watching a pair of skeletons doing battle. Neither had the strength to hurt the other. Nor did the engagement last long. The friends of the gladiators forcibly pulled them apart. Yet the pugilists continued to fume and snarl at each other. Their tempers were high. One finally wrenched himself free and quickly grasped a stout bamboo pole from a corner. Before he could be stopped, he had laid several blows on his antagonist.

"The end of another beautiful friendship." Cameron laughed.

"It's a shame the way they get on each other's nerves under these conditions and cannot control themselves."

"I believe that is only part of it, Paul. It seems to me that one of the weaknesses of the military service is that officers develop a high degree of ego. They too often think that only they can be right. It would be a loss of prestige to them if someone else should prove them in error."

"Each time a prisoner makes a comment, another POW immediately contradicts him. That is about the only way that one can give a release to his ego in close confinement like this."

"Then the dispute is on! And it is only a small step to the point of swinging their fists."

"And to keep up our average, there will be exactly five more such battles before the day is over."

Blake strode into the room. "Guess there would be less rows if they had a chance to discuss Topic A."

The others smiled. That was the first time that great subject had been mentioned in camp.

"Maybe you are right, Blake, but the subject of food is paramount now," offered Cameron.

"They would have to import some monkey glands." Blake grinned.

"If they did, they would go into the soup, I bet," came from Cameron in quick repartee.

"Did you hear that the last of the bunnies passed on last night?" asked Paul.

"That's too bad," Cameron consoled. "They have the same difficulties of living under these starvation conditions as the POWs do."

"That is a damn outrage," grumbled Blake. "We started off with twenty of them, and one after another, the Nips let them die. I believe they only brought them into the compound to tease us and never had any intention of letting us have them in our soup."

"You may have a good point there, Blake," said Cameron without committing himself. "They were cute little white balls of fluff to look at, however. We can always remember them."

"Why not go down and have a look at the rest of the farm," Paul suggested.

That was a daily event with the prisoners. There was some joy in looking at the few hogs, a dozen or so goats, and a small flock of chickens. The anticipation of some day having a little meat or fowl in the soup was constantly before the POWs. At Paul's suggestion the prisoners got up from their cots and strolled out the door. Each gave a look at Ashley's empty bunk, but no one said a word.

Over in a far corner of the compound, the small herd of black goats was being kept together under the supervision of one of the prisoners who had been detailed by the authorities as the goatherd. Formerly, the animals had been allowed to roam at will through the compound. But ever since the day they had stampeded through the benjo, where one had fallen into one of the openings in the floor, the Nipponese had ordered that they be herded together under guard.

"Look what I see over there." Cameron laughed, nodding his head in the direction of the herd.

"I would like to have a picture of that to send back to jolly old England," Blake said with sarcasm. He had little love for his British cousins.

A former governor of a British colony was bending over and, with a stick and a piece of cardboard, scooping up the droppings. Somehow or other, as only POWs can do, he had gotten hold of a couple of tomato plants. They were planted alongside his barracks, and by meticulous care, he hoped to someday have a tiny harvest. Fertilizing his crop was a part of that care.

Cameron and his roommates strolled past the little boxes that had been built from pieces of scrap lumber for warrens for the rabbits. All was still and quiet. The enclosure was empty of life. The men did not linger long; the place reminded them too much of the barracks with its empty places.

Behind a netting of wire, scrawny white leghorns scratched in the sandy loam. The reason for their shabby feathers had always been a source of argument among POWs. The debate between lice and pecking at their own feathers from hunger would go an endlessly.

"A sorry mess, I must say." Blake shook his head woefully. He recalled his years on a well-cared-for farm back home.

"Too bad the Nips have to enclose them in that cage," Paul pondered. "Think of the fun they would have roaming around the compound. Even the chickens are denied freedom."

"Guess our people are responsible," Cameron reminded him. "When they did run loose, the occasional egg they laid was always picked up quickly by a POW. And a couple of boys are sweating it out in that filthy eso now for having stolen one of the hens."

"Onto the pigsty!" commanded Paul as he strode away.

"This is without a doubt the smellingest pen I have ever ran across," cried Blake, rubbing his nose.

His colleagues did not need to be reminded of that. The odors were stifling. A prisoner had to be of hardy constitution to stand near that sty for more than a few minutes, in spite of an intense desire from curiosity or anticipation to watch the porkers. But the condition that bothered the watchers most was the swarm of flies—huge black flies, thousands of them—that lingered like a matting an the backs of the swine, in the empty feed trough, on the ground for yards around, and even on the faces of any hardy prisoner who might stand nearby.

"They are not getting any larger or fatter, are they, Blake?" asked Cameron,

"Those hogs are going backward," he replied. "And what can you expect? The Nips bring in to camp a few pounds of those lousy vegetables and divide them into two equal parts. The hogs get one share, and the thousand prisoners get the other half."

"Well, Blake." Cameron grinned. "We can't show any partiality around here. Anyhow, the pigs are probably more important to the Nips than this crowd of POWs."

"Well, here is Old Mary," called Paul. Old Mary was a sow, huge in frame but so undernourished that her flesh hung downward, showing a sway back and a belly that dragged the ground. She was kept in a separate pen, and all the prisoners hoped that some day the authorities would bring in a boar to keep her company. Perhaps then the herd would increase in numbers. At the moment, poor Old Mary was lying on her side and panting.

"The poor thing," sympathized Sykes, who heretofore had had little to say. "The hot weather must be hard on her."

"Say," Blake called in a startled voice, "that sow is sick. She is in a bad way. That's not a hot weather complaint. I tell you, that sow is gone."

The others crowded closer, while Blake pointed out in detail the reasons for his judgment. His farm experience had told him at a glance the seriousness of Old Mary's complaint.

"Is it old age?" queried Sykes.

"She sure is powerful old, that critter," Blake replied.

"I believe she is dying of 'lover neglect,'" ambled Cameron with a sober face.

"Maybe we'll get some pork in our soup after all," chortled Blake. "This is one way to beat the Nips."

During the night, Old Mary escaped from all the problems that oppressed her—starvation, confinement, abuse, and lack of love. While the prisoners had a sentimental attachment for her and recognized the symbolism of her departure, their bellies dominated their thoughts and emotions. The authorities sent word down that a detail of men should take the carcass out and bury it. Never would it occur to the Nipponese, well fed to the point of hardened muscles and rotundity, that meat was meat in whatever condition it might be.

Consequently, Old Mary's remains were tossed up on a handcart and surreptitiously moved to the back door of the cookhouse. With unaccustomed speed, a cook's knife slit her, disemboweled her, and hacked her into bits. The level of the contents of the soup kettle rose upward.

News of such tremendous importance raced through the camp instantly. A few squeamish POWs attempted to remove the pieces in uncertainty, but that made no impression on the great majority. When the authorities realized what had happened, it was too late. Old Mary had already made hundreds of white man happy and contented.

"Say, Paul," Cameron suddenly tossed at his friend one day, maybe we had better check up on some of our squad leaders to see what they are doing with the Nips about our observing Memorial Day."

"Yes, you are right. It's only a few days away. It will be a good chance to get our cemetery put in shape, too."

With a common purpose, the two men strolled down the hall of the barracks. It was their plan to corner one squad leader at a time and convince him before he could obtain the support of one of his colleagues. "Slippery" was the first one they met. He was one of the more adequate and dependable squad leaders, but he had successfully resisted the assignment on so many occasions that he had become known throughout the camp as Slippery.

The authorities always lined the POWs up in sequence of the numbers printed on a bit of cloth and attached to the shirt. His number was an odd one, which always threw him into the front rank. Because of his size, he stood out among the others in the squad. Frequent readjustments of squads were made because of losses and a desire of the enemy to keep filled all rooms nearest the guardhouse. Perhaps control and administration were thereby simplified.

So it was an easy solution for the officer arranging the new squads to merely point to Slippery and designate him as squad leader. But Slippery had other ideas. He had no desire to have any dealings with the enemy, and he did not care to be put in a position where his own people could accuse him of enemy leanings. That was a very common complaint among prisoners. However, somebody had to be squad leader; and so long as there were a few prisoners who felt that by so serving they might gain a personal advantage, Slippery felt justified in standing aside on their behalf. When selected, he would respectfully ask to be excused because, "My hearing is so bad that I might not be able to hear all the important Nipponese orders," or, "My malaria is returning, and I might find myself in bed for a long time."

But one day Scurvy caught up with him, and to Slippery's complaints, he merely said "No! No!" and walked away. Slippery's luck had run out, and he found himself saddled with the job.

"Slippery," Cameron inquired, "what's the score on Memorial Day? Have you, in your great position of leadership, done anything about it with the Nips yet?"

Slippery threw himself back on his cot and chuckled. He and Cameron were close friends, and many cutting remarks could pass between them without any feeling of acrimony. "Yes, Cam, we have already tried to talk with the captain about it. We probably caught him in a vile mood; and while he did not refuse, he sort of changed the orders on us."

"How was that?" Paul asked with interest.

"He dismissed us rather abruptly by saying that he could not listen to complaints coming from squad leaders. He said that each man had to stand on his own and do his own talking—that no one was permitted to speak for another man or any group."

"It looks like he has things that were all mixed up in good shape now," replied Cameron.

"We were asking for a favor, not making a complaint," Slippery continued, "but we just couldn't get that point across."

"Then it was left that some individual POW had to bring the matter up?" Paul inquired.

"Now wait a minute, Paul," Cameron cried with a twinkle of enlightenment in his eye, "you need not get me mixed up in this."

"Why, Cam," Paul answered with a tone of banter, "your accusations really hurt me." The smile he gave Cameron belied his words.

"That I believe," Slippery said with seriousness, "would be a very effective way of handling the matter. Who better than you," he continued, addressing Cameron, "could get results out of the Nips?"

Cameron was caught in a vice, and he knew it. Shirking a duty or refusing to help others were matters he could never be accused of. "I merely asked a simple little question, and now I find myself completely enmeshed in the matter. Why does this have to happen to me?"

"I suggest, Cam," Slippery said, "that you catch Buddha and put it up to him. He'll be OD tonight."

"All right! All right! I'll talk with him after tenko tonight. It may get better results to see him instead of that damn exalted camp commander."

"Well, Slippery," Paul said as they got up to leave, "we certainly put our little scheme over in fine shape."

"Indeed, yes," he replied. "He fell for the whole works." The two men laughed together.

"Now what the hell are you talking about?" inquired Cameron with a suspicious voice.

"It was arranged between Slippery and me," explained Paul with a sober face, "to stage this little act and get you to agree to handling the matter for us. But the problem was to get you to make the original suggestion so you would not be suspicious. It has taken me two days to direct our conversation in the groove for you to make the suggestion as your own."

"I believe you two are the most accomplished liars in the whole camp," Cameron called over his shoulder as he strode out the door.

Amid the laughter between Paul and Slippery, Cameron overheard Paul's whispered remark, "Perhaps we are."

Certain tactical maneuvering had to be arranged in order to give Cameron time to leave his place in the tenko formation and reach Buddha before the Nipponese lieutenant departed. It was the custom for the officer who received the reports from the squad leaders to depart for headquarters as soon as the last report was made and the guards had personally made their own count. While the officer was walking away, the sergeant would dismiss the formation. So the prisoner OD who accompanied the lieutenant was delegated to find some subject of conversation to delay his departure until Cameron could hurry over from where he was standing. It worked just as the scheme had intended.

"Good evening, Lieutenant," Cameron greeted him with a salute.

"Hello," replied the officer.

Cameron quickly opened up his subject. He suggested that it might be a good time for the prisoners to put their cemetery in better shape, more in keeping with the appearance that the Nipponese authorities demanded. Memorial Day was a short time away. That was the day that respect was paid to the dead.

"Nipponese have many dead, too," Buddha replied, none too friendly. "Americans have no courage! They bomb island and kill half, wound other half! Then send scouts in to see. But they are quickly driven out. Then more bombings and kill the other half. Easy to land and take over after that."

Poor Buddha, thought Cameron. *In his wrath he is giving away all the news that the Nips have so carefully kept from us.* "We are very sorry for bombings," he said soothingly. "But POWs can do nothing about it. We are far away. Both sides bomb, and it is very bad." Cameron was cautious not to disturb Buddha.

By diplomatic remarks, and with his tongue frequently in his cheek, Cameron eventually obtained Buddha's reluctant acquiescence. "Okay! Okay!" he agreed impatiently at one point in the dialogue. "Borrow Nipponese bugle and sound 'Taps.' But it must mean that and not mean signal!"

The damn suspicious rascal, Cameron declared to himself.

According to arrangements and under the direct supervision of the interpreter and several guards who were detailed to observe, a little ceremony was held in the compound on Memorial Day. The other nationalities among the prisoners joined the Americans in a gesture of goodwill. Cameron had been the intermediary between the authorities and the POWs. Because of that, the direction of the ceremony fell to him, although he tried on several occasions to pass it on to one of the squad leaders. But the interest was lacking in most of the POWs. It was too much trouble for them.

From a prayer book, which was one of many things that had turned up in camp, Cameron read a few simple prayers. A hymn, which had no patriotic implications, was sung. Then one of the POWs sounded "Taps" on the borrowed bugle to end the ceremony. That particular bugle call on that solemn occasion tore at the hearts of every man in uniform. It was not only the effectiveness of the music itself that impressed, but it was also the first time since imprisonment that an American call had reached the ears of those prisoners, who were starved for anything from home.

For some time, the authorities had been irritated by the reluctance of the POWs to accept gracefully the forced labor requirement. The matter had been argued back and forth at length, but the result was always inevitable. Because the prisoners dallied at their tasks, the amount of completed work was less than the Nipponese could justify to their superiors. In addition, many of the POWs refused to carry their share of the work requirements and feigned illness. It finally reached the point where the guards insisted upon turning out for work all except the kitchen force. The sergeant in charge would pass down the formation and, after a cursory glance, decide for himself which prisoners were too sick to labor. His overzealous desire to make a work record for himself resulted in many who were manifestly ill being ordered to labor in the rice paddies.

The camp commander must have felt the matter was getting out of his control, because he unexpectedly announced one day that the commander of all camps on Taiwan would visit the camp to discuss the situation.

So on the appointed day the colonel, Wild Bull, blustered into camp with all the fanfare due his exalted position. When the squad leaders were summoned to headquarters for a conference with the colonel, they insisted that Cameron accompany them. He had had certain successes with the authorities earlier, and it was thought he might lend support to whatever arguments were presented on the POWs' behalf.

The bulky form of Wild Bull leaned over the table that separated him from the prisoners. He glared at each one in turn, twisted the ends of his heavy mustache in a slow manner, and ran a hand over his closely shaven head.

Dramatic, thought Cameron. *And he seems uncertain of himself, sort of nervous like. Maybe if we are discreet and avoid an argument, we can gain the upper hand. But what of some of these stupid POWs sitting here with me?* he contemplated. *At least one of them will agree with whatever the colonel says and thereby weaken our argument. At least one more will say something most undiplomatic and arouse his ire. If they will only keep their mouths shut, which they have never done in the past, we might have a chance.*

Wild Bull growled a command. His interpreter stepped forward. After clearing his throat, the colonel barked out instructions to the soldier at his side. "There is misunderstanding about work."

Cautious silence from the POWs attended his statement.

"Do you volunteer to work?"

Because the question was addressed to no one in particular, there was no immediate response. The colonel squirmed in his chair, while the face of the interpreter took on a what-do-I-do-next appearance.

Somebody ought to give him the answer, Cameron told himself. Not being one of the squad leaders, he was hesitant about speaking up. Yet it was a strategic moment to direct the thought, before someone else might blurt out a reply that did not represent the attitude of the vast majority. "No, sir," Cameron said.

Wild Bull was taken aback by hearing an answer different from what he had anticipated. He stroked his chin several times as he studied the situation. Then, with suddenness, he made an unexpected reply. "All right! You don't have to!"

This time, the prisoners seemed at a disadvantage. They moved in their seats groping for an understanding of this decided change in the policy of the authorities.

It occurred to Cameron that some clarification was needed. He chose his words carefully as he asked, "Sir, will we be punished if we do not volunteer?"

"No!" It was an ugly grunt.

This matter is far from settled, Cameron said inwardly. "Does the colonel," he began with trepidation, "fully understand that no one refuses?" He hesitated. *That needs greater accent*, he told himself. "That no one refuses," he repeated, "to obey any orders. We are merely expressing our desires in reply to your question."

There were several minutes of conversation between the colonel and the interpreter, while the prisoners waited in anticipation. The matter seemed to be satisfactory to the two, and the interpreter replied, "He understands."

A wave of the hand by Wild Bull meant the conference had ended and that the POWs were dismissed.

They rose, gave a stiff and formal Nipponese bow to the colonel and then to the camp commander—etiquette must be preserved, especially at a moment of tension—executed a sharp about-face to the rear, and departed.

The results of the conference raced to the ends of the compound in the space of minutes. As fast as men could run and scream, the news floated through the barracks, swept in one door of the benjo and out the other, slithered past the pig farm, and reached the prisoners working in the rice paddies beyond the enclosure.

After Cameron had related the events in detail to his roommates—it was always such a thrill to hear someone who had been an eyewitness and to be able to ply him with direct questions—Sykes spoke up with a voice lacking in assurance. "Don't you believe that you were a little hasty? Maybe we should have tried to placate him without making such a definite commitment."

Count ten! Count ten! Cameron cried to himself. On many occasions he had been disgusted with Sykes's wishy-washy attitude. *Where is the man's character and dignity?* Cameron had inquired inwardly. There were hasty words on his lips, which he was struggling to control.

But someone else spoke up and gave Cameron a moment to collect himself. "Hell no!" shouted Blake. "That's the way to treat the little yellow bastards! If our people had used some guts from the very beginning, we would be getting decent treatment now."

The following morning, the situation moved rapidly forward. It had always been the custom for the authorities to open the big, swinging double gates in the fence each morning after tenko. They were left open for the day and guarded by a sentry, so that working parties could pass back and forth as needed. Today they remained closed. The feeling in the camp was one of ominous stillness, like being enclosed deep in a mine after the elevator had gone back up or being locked in the hold of a ship when the bulkhead doors had been slammed closed.

"Do you sense what I do?" asked Paul, staring at the unexpected sight of closed gates.

"Yes," replied Cameron with his eyes fixed in the same direction. "It can't be that the Nip guard forgot. They just don't forget such things. Nothing but a definite order from the old man could make such a change."

"It probably means a change in our lives here at Shirakawa, too."

"Well, we asked for it," Cameron consoled. "And I reckon we have the courage to stick to our guns."

"All but a couple in this crowd. I'm a little concerned about their courage. They would do most anything to avoid having their rice ration cut, even sell out the rest of us."

The first order of business for the day was the coming of Pussy with a bundle of papers under his arm.

"More things to sign," grumbled Blake when he caught sight of Pussy. "All we do is sign things. A guy is lucky enough to get a letter, and he has to sign three times for it. We signed in groups of ten that we would not attempt to escape, and if anyone did, the others in the group would be executed. We signed dozens of papers that they made us write on every possible thing about why America is fighting and what we are going to do after the war—" Blake was in his element in his verbal castigation of the hated enemy. He would have continued on except for the abrupt interruption by the howls of laughter from his friends.

Pussy's instructions to the squad leaders, as he passed out the sheets he carried, were clear, at least in his own mind. "Each POW who volunteers to work will sign in one column and those who do not volunteer will sign in the other column."

Without comment, the squad leaders read the heading on the papers, which said in English: "I declare that I work voluntarily in prison camp." One column was headed "Yes"; the other, "No."

True to form, the POWs standing before Pussy began asking questions. "Shall we put a date on the sheet?" "How soon do you want them back?" "Does this mean past work or future work?"

Pussy stood as much as his patience permitted and then blurted out, "You will sign and shut up! Dismiss!"

For the remainder of the day, the air in the compound was filled with the murmur of conversation. Very few minds were made up on the action to take—not that there was much divided opinion on whether to volunteer for work or not but, rather, the indecision hinged primarily on the vaster subject of just what the enemy had in mind by requiring the signatures.

"Something must have come up," surmised Blake, "about this forced labor. Maybe something international that makes the Nips feel they have to have this for their own defense."

"That is quite possible," Paul quietly replied, "but that raises the other side of the question. Do the Nips have to have a piece of paper to justify forced labor when they have so many more serious things to account for? Anyhow, they do not expect to lose this war. Didn't the camp commander say in his speech the other day that the glorious soldiers of the emperor would fight an for one hundred years and that each Nip would take ten Allies down to the death with him?"

"There was lots of big talk, all right," agreed Cameron.

"But what if all that is true?" asked Sykes in a frightened tone. "If the war will last that long, maybe we had better be careful not to antagonize them."

Another POW with an anxiety complex, Cameron whispered inwardly. *Perhaps he needs our sympathy instead of our antipathy.*

"Calm yourself, Sykes," said Paul in an effort to pacify him. "When they make such wild statements, it indicates they are losing the war, and fast. Spitting at the sun!"

"If they get our signatures," analyzed Cameron, "the Nips could use them for their clearance later on, like Blake says, although I doubt if they can be worried about a small detail like that. There is another angle that we should not overlook. If you sign up for volunteer work, you might be signing away your life. They could then call you out for any sort of work they chose to, perhaps laboring in the salt mines or some other work that you couldn't survive. If you rebelled, they would love to stick you like a pig, because they have your agreement to work."

"That's the big thing, I believe," Paul declared after deliberation. "You probably have hit the answer right there!"

"Maybe I'd better go around and see each of the squad leaders and pass along what we think about it. Nobody should sign up for a thing like that when it can mean nothing good."

In spite of the efforts of the majority to present a unanimous stand against the enemy, Sykes and three other prisoners would not be influenced. They signed to volunteer for work and then slithered off to their cots like whipped puppies.

"No guts!" declared Blake with an oath.

"Maybe it is their guts that bother them," Cameron replied with a feeble attempt at humor. "But I think it is something else. Take a look at each of them. Are they particularly fine samples of the military profession? Would you risk placing them in command of troops in combat? Do they give the impression of having real courage, either physical or moral?"

"Be patient, Cam," came the considerate voice of Paul. "They have been through a lot, you know."

Cameron bit his lip. It was better to remain silent than to let his heart speak out and thereby condemn another man, even though he might be right. It was unplanned and unpremeditated, but the feeling was abroad that the four had let their colleagues down when an issue of character was at stake.

The matter had a most peculiar outcome, when later Sykes asked the interpreter when the volunteers might start to work so that they could have a better ration. The reply Pussy gave struck the camp as most ironic. "Since the POWs do not volunteer, you will not have privilege of working. No special favors to you!"

The reaction to the refusal of the prisoners to be docile and submissive came with severity and certainty. Tenko was called late in the morning, a most unusual time. For three hours, the prisoners stood in ranks while the guards romped through the barracks making a minute inspection. All of the possessions collected by destitute men over a period of months were confiscated—bits of wire, pieces of string, empty tin cans, precious notebooks, strips of bamboo, and even the cards that had been issued to the sick to show they were excused from work temporarily. Under such circumstance, it could not be expected that the guards would leave things in any sort of order. Bedding was torn apart, the few clothes that had been hung on pegs were tossed into corners, and cots were turned over in an effort to see if anything might be hidden beneath.

When the inspection had been completed, the POWs were sharply called to attention. Scurvy, dragging his heels, appeared in front of the formation. Officers never gave instructions to a formation. Those orders had to be transmitted through an interpreter. That always gave the officer an alibi, each prisoner was convinced. So Pussy read the new instructions. "POWs must not have shoes in possession at any time, only clogs. All regulations must be strictly complied with. At no time except after lights are turned out may prisoners lie on bunks. Cards may not be played. Walking in the compound will stop, except alone. POWs may not visit in other rooms. No more smoking will be allowed. Many inspections will be held every day. Barracks and compound will be always prepared for inspection. Entire squad will be punished when any member violates rules. Bathing cannot be permitted. When prisoner attempts to escape, ten will be executed."

"What do you think of all those rules, Cam?" asked Paul after they had been dismissed and had returned to their room.

"They are the same old things; only the Nips have not always enforced them in the past. But there is no doubt that they are going to be mean. Oh no! We will not be punished if we do not sign for voluntary work. Nice honest person, that colonel!"

"He did not say anything about cutting down the rice," Blake stated in a worried tone, speaking of the chief subject in his thoughts.

"I'm afraid they couldn't cut the quantity down any," Cameron rejoined. "It's so microscopic now that it is no longer divisible."

"They may do that gradually," Paul stated, "as a more subtle and oriental means of ruthlessness."

Prisoners were not permitted to retire before the final bugle call, which defined the end of the day, and they had to be in bed with lights turned out by the termination of the call. It could be done easily in the time allotted, because the men were invariably so exhausted by evening that they stood beside their cots waiting for the first note of the bugle. Usually they were asleep within a very few minutes.

"Good God!" exclaimed Blake as he was awakened from a sound sleep. "What's that horrible sound?"

Just outside the door, a Nipponese voice was calling, "Tenko! Tenko!" A similar voice was making the same call farther down the hall. Heavy soldier boots crashed on the floor as other guards raced through the building.

"Something terrible must have happened!" cried Sykes, leaping form his bunk and wandering aimlessly about the room in his partially awakened condition.

"Now what the hell!" exclaimed Cameron disgustedly, reaching up to turn on the electric lamp.

Paul, unruffled and smiling, slowly put one foot on the floor. But the next one came down in amazing haste, for at that instant, the door was kicked open without ceremony.

A shiny bayonet was thrust in, followed by a guard, shouting, "Hully up! Hully up!" His angry attitude and gestures were readily understood.

The prisoners made haste in dressing and rushing out to the hall.

The guards lined them up, and there they stood for many minutes waiting for instructions. In time, the sergeant arrived. He ordered a roll call, but the sleepy and disgusted POWs had to make many attempts at counting off their numbers in the enemy language before they accomplished that task without error. After grunts and growls from the sergeant, the men were dismissed.

"The dirty yellow bastards!"

"Why, Blake," chided Cameron, "if you get all riled up like that, you'll have a hard time getting back to sleep."

"I must say, that is something new, after all." Paul could not analyze the reasons for the night call any more than anyone else.

"They must have had a very good season," Sykes broke in, "to disturb us in the middle of the night like this."

"Reason, hell" shouted Cameron. "And it is not the middle of the night. It's only ten o'clock."

"You mean we have been asleep less than an hour?"

"Just that! And I'm going to be asleep before you people get through worrying about it. Good night!"

One by one, the POWs crawled back into bed. The regular customers made a visit to the benjo, now that they had been awakened. Gradually the lights throughout the barracks disappeared. Peace and quiet prevailed. Rest was one of the few comforts the men could claim, and they enjoyed it.

Crash! *Bang*! "Tenko!, Tenko!"

"Christ! Not again!" cried Blake, mad enough to throttle anyone who got in his way.

"Why, it is not even midnight yet," grumbled Cameron after the light was turned on and he glanced at his watch.

"This is going to be interesting," commented Paul, "a sort of gradual wearing down process. Neat and subtle oriental trick."

Three more times that night, the rapidly crumbling prisoners were called out for tenko, and it was a happy moment when daylight finally arrived and the activities of the new day commenced.

"I wonder if a man can get used to that frequency of being disturbed at night," Sykes said.

"And why not?" Cameron asked optimistically. "You get up a dozen time a night to go to the benjo, don't you? All you have to do is to regulate your kidneys to meet the tenko call every couple of hours."

Blake was sitting on the step leading to the door of his barracks, his eye roving in all directions to see the approach of an enemy guard before he himself was seen. It was a better procedure, whenever possible, to keep out of the way of the guards. One got into less trouble with them that way.

"What's the dope, Blake? It seems awful quiet out here." Cameron had come down the hall and had taken a good look outside before he ventured forth.

Blake was seated at his feet. "A couple of Nips just came through the compound. Bopped only one POW. They've gone now."

"They're still at that digging, I see." Cameron referred to a number of trenches being carved into the tops of two of the hills that enclosed the camp.

"Doesn't make sense to me," replied Blake, casting his glance in that direction. "They ought to put the trenches on the other side of the hill if they intend to use them against any effort to rescue us. And what about those trenches we had to dig here in the compound? They aren't enough for even a small part of the POWs to take shelter in in case of an air attack."

A smile crept over Cameron's face, but he quickly dispelled it. He was about to chide Blake on the poor analysis he had made but thought better of it when be realized that no purpose would be served thereby. It would merely tend to embarrass Blake. "You know, Blake," he said finally, "I've been thinking about those things, too. It sort of strikes me that these trenches down here are not for our protection but for the Nips to use should there be any attack against us. Look how they are lined up. They make a pattern like a defensive line against an attack from either of those two valleys, where an advance would probably come from. Now, those trenches on the hills are something different. Notice how they are arranged. A couple of machine guns planted there could sweep the compound and especially the entrances to the barracks. They could drive us inside if they felt we were about to mutiny on them and could mow down anyone who attempted to leave the building. What do you think?"

"Yeah," drawled Blake. "I see what you mean. Maybe you are right."

"Here comes Doc. What is he grinning and shaking his head about? For once in his life, something other than worry is on his mind."

"What do you say, Doc?" asked Blake when the medical officer reached the steps.

"I've really got the last word in Nip brilliance to tell. Come on inside where we will not be observed."

Such an invitation needed no urging. News of any sort was of magnitude to POWs, especially any comments from Doc, who was held in high esteem and could occasionally get a choice bit of information from the Nips. His news was accepted as Gospel. Accordingly, Blake leaped to his feet and, with Cameron, hurried into his room.

"You know the Nip corporal who has been in charge of everything I do," commenced Doc.

The others nodded.

"He makes all the decisions—tells me when a man is sick or not, determines if he should be in the hospital, issues out the quinine, and keeps a finger on everything. Well, apparently he has been getting interested in medicine. He has been keeping me and our interpreter busy for a long time answering his questions. That broken-down stethoscope they issued us had intrigued him, but he seemed to be afraid of it. However, one day last week, he rushed in and said he wanted me to teach him how to use it. He had only twenty minutes to spend but wanted to know everything in that time. It has taken me about twenty years to learn what I know about it, but he wanted the dope in twenty minutes."

"How did you solve that?"

"Did the best I could in the time, of course. But I could not understand it at the time. The other day, he gave me some instruction in the gall bladder—drew me a picture and told me how he thought it functioned. Daylight hit me, and I realized that probably he had gotten hold of a book on general medicine someplace and was reading it. But now the climax occurred. He came into the hospital and told me he had been appointed a doctor and was going to leave to take over his duties in some small town nearby."

"What?" Blake and Cameron shouted in unison.

"As I understand it, Nip doctors here on Taiwan are classified by some sort of rating. The lower the rating, the smaller the town you practice in."

"So, he is going out to doctor to all the helpless Chinese in the town where he will be." Cameron moved his head back and forth in bewilderment.

"It could have been worse," added Doc. "Once he said he thought he would operate some day on one of the POWs. He wanted to see what the inside of a man looked like."

"Good God!"

From the rear of the barracks came a call of alarm. "Hey, Butch!" someone called. Without thought or plan, that term had grown to be part of the lives of the prisoners. It meant only one thing—that a Nipponese guard had entered the building, and the POWs were warned to be on the alert and not be caught violating any of the rules. The first man to see the sentry always called out at the top of his lungs, and the warning was passed on down by others. Everyone felt safe in calling out in that manner. The dumb Nips would think that some POW was calling to one of his friends.

The guard Nip wandered down the hall, peering into the different rooms, satisfying himself that all was well. Eventually, his step was heard at the other end of the hall, and it was thought safe to relax. No guard had ever retraced his path. Paul flopped down on Cameron's cot, while the others in the room took comfortable positions. Conversation returned to Doc's experiences, and the prisoners were enjoying the outcome of that discussion.

"Hey, Butch!" suddenly sounded at the window. It did not have a familiar enunciation or accent as coming from a POW. All heads quickly turned in the direction of the call. There stood the guard who had recently passed through the building. He pointed to the cot where Paul had been seen resting and uttered unnatural-sounding words.

After all the POWs had sprung to their feet, the guard left the window and rushed around through the door into the barracks.

"How the hell did he get wise to that call?" Blake inquired.

"Probably heard it often and thought he would use it like we do, to get attention," Paul responded.

At that moment, the guard burst into the roam. He was angry; there was no mistaking that. He pointed at the POWs standing before him and then to the cot where he had seem one of them reclining, against orders.

Paul took a step to the side, so he could face the guard. He was about to speak and acknowledge himself as the culprit. Lying on a cot was a serious offense and meant a period of time in the guardhouse.

All that ran through Cameron's' mind in quick order. *Damn it!* he cursed to himself. *Why did he have to catch this old man? He can't stand up under a siege in confinement. Why could it not have been someone else?*

Before Paul had a chance to say a word, Cameron impetuously raised his voice and said, "I," pointing to himself. He knew that the dimness in the room kept the guard from recognizing who actually had been on the bunk.

"Eso! Eso!" bellowed the Nipponese and pointed to the door, indicating that he wanted Cameron to precede him. There seemed to be no alternative. The yellow man was intent on following up on the situation he had discovered. He was complying with his orders, and—who knew—promotions sometimes grew out of such attention to duty.

Cameron walked toward the guardhouse, with a bayonet dramatically held at his back.

In an excited voice, the guard reported to his sergeant what he had seen. Cameron was accused of deliberately violating the orders of his imperial majesty. The vernacular was understood by Cameron. The situation was against him. In the space of minutes, he was accused, tried, and convicted. The sergeant walked up to him and gave him a hard blow on the face. That was a little personal touch that showed the importance of the noncommissioned officer, who then grunted some commands. Cameron was roughly seized and hurried off to the eso.

The American strained his eyes to see, but had to wait until they became accustomed to the darkness into which he had been pushed. After a while, things took on shape. The only light was a thin sliver that peeked through a tiny aperture high over his head where two boards did not quite meet. When he strode across the room, he counted three steps. The opposite direction was the same. The room was empty, without windows, and the door was built solid.

Cameron sat down in the corner and pulled his knees up to his chin. *This is one hell of a mess to be in*, he contemplated. *I thought I was smart enough to keep out of here. But, no, I had to play the big hero stuff and stick my neck out. What a damn fool I am. Maybe not, though,* he continued to meditate. *Poor old Paul could never have gone through a week of this. That is a long sentence in one of these Nip esos.*

A small shaft of dimmed light suddenly shot into the room from the direction of the door. Cameron glanced in and saw the face of a Nipponese guard peering at him through a small opening. Evidently, Cameron thought, a peephole with a removable covering. He did not have time to give it much thought, because the sentry bellowed at him and demanded that he get on his knees in the middle of the room. Cameron obeyed. The sentry was satisfied and closed the opening. In another minute it was again opened, and the guard looked in. Fortunately, the American had not moved from his kneeling position, and the guard grunted and left.

The prisoner's position grew rapidly more difficult as his muscles became cramped. In spite of the frequent inspections made by the guard, Cameron felt he must do something to relieve the pain he was suffering. He decided to try to out stretch one leg at a time for a few seconds to straighten the muscles. He rested his hands on the floor to balance himself and to avoid any noise. Cautiously, he started to shove a leg backward, but the stiffness was too great, and he dropped over on his side. Before he could recover, the guard's face was at the opening. When he saw Cameron's position, he became violent and rushed in through the door. With a heavy boot. he kicked the prisoner several times and growled instructions. Cameron was now made to squat down on his heels and clasp his arms in front of his knees.

At least I got my position changed, he told himself with good nature. *This must be the second stage of punishment, now that I failed to measure up with the lighter one. But this is not so bad*. He smiled. *Fortunately, I have long since mastered the oriental squat. Would that monkey be surprised if he knew that I have been doing this for years, just like he has? An hour or two should not be too bad.*

Must be about supper time, Cameron told himself a little later. *Wonder if they will remember me and let me have some rice?*

The time passed on, and nothing, but the regular investigations of the guard broke the monotony. Later, Cameron heard the bugle announcing the end of the day. He wished for his cot and the chance to stretch out for a night's sleep.

The door crashed open at that moment—*Nips always crash and bang*, thought Cameron—and the guard entered. He gave the prisoner a push and motioned for him to lie down. *Well*, the American debated with himself, *we keep the same hours here as the POWs do who are in good repute. At least it is a change to be able to stretch out, hard as this wooden floor is.*

If I had only had a few minutes warning, Cameron meditated, *before I was shoved in here, I could have put on some extra clothes. They would soften up the hardness of this floor. And a piece torn off the bottom of my mosquito bar and tucked in my pocket would come in mighty handy to cover my face and keep these hundreds of damn mosquitos off me. Nothing can aggravate a man more than a continuous pestering by mosquitoes*, he said inwardly, waving his hand back and forth in front of his face.

Many things raced through his mind before sleep overtook him. The foulness of the room was suffocating. Cameron's predecessors had taken the only possible course and had relieved themselves in the corner. Scraps of rice were scattered around attracting flies. *I have to get this place cleaned out in the morning*, he told himself as he slipped off to sleep.

The bugle woke him, but the bellows of the guard made certain that he leaped up on his feet. There he was required to stand. *"Mizu?"* he called to the guard, asking for water. A drink would help, and maybe several drops on his face would freshen him up. The only encouragement he received was a grunt.

Shortly, the door was opened, and the guard set two containers down on the floor. He withdrew and closed the door without speaking.

Cameron walked over and carefully reached for the vessels, fearful that, in the darkness, he might upset them. Rice, yes there was rice, and a cup of water. He had to use his fingers to carry the grains to his mouth or try lapping up the food as a dog might do. His thirst was so great that he swallowed the small quantity of water in two draughts, without remembering that he wanted to put several drops on his face and hands.

Today was like yesterday; tomorrow, when it came, was the same as the day before. A pittance of food arrived at mealtimes. During the normal working hours, Cameron was forced to assume strange postures. Rest was permitted only when the other POWs were sleeping. The prisoner's effort to obtain a broom to clean out the room was scoffed at, and his pleas for more water in that hot, unventilated, and tightly enclosed space met with clubbing.

There was plenty of time to meditate. Cameron's uncontrolled emotions developed an intense hate. *I'll kill every Nip bastard I ever meet when I get the chance!* How many times had he heard that from other

POWs? Now he had declared it himself. Was he slipping to their level? Where were all the good intentions he had set up for himself? He was suddenly shocked at the thought he had expressed. *Wait a minute, Cam,* he addressed himself. *Let's calm down. What was the reply I got from that chaplain who spent a few weeks in our camp when I asked him how a man in his profession would deal with these monkeys when he got the upper hand?*

I remember. He said that he would exact justice—just Christian justice!

Days later, Cameron was released from his private chamber of horrors. There were no preliminaries to give him advance notice that his incarceration was nearing its end. At no time could he get any information from his guards on how long he might have to linger and rot away in that horrible eso. The order came suddenly, while he was on his knees with his arms pushed back and a stick thrust through the crooks of his elbows. Each new guard on duty had a different type of gentle torture that he reveled in imposing upon the prisoner.

When the American heard the order to get up and leave, he found it most difficult to straighten out his legs and arms. He massaged his sore muscles and painfully stepped forward. The sudden brightness of the sun pierced his eyes and forced him to keep a hand over them until he could adjust himself to the new condition. Rubbing a hand across his face, he felt a ragged beard, sticky and unkempt. His body felt uncomfortable from sores and bruises, and his patched uniform, stiff from sweat and dirt, irritated him as he walked.

His unexpected appearance in the compound created a wave of comments from all those who saw him, a wave that spread out from wall to wall as fast as sound travels. Those prisoners nearest him joined him and prodded him for comments.

"The only thing I'll say now," he parried, "is that take care you don't get shoved in there. It's no picnic! After I get cleaned up and rested, I'll give you all the details."

Cameron knew that under imprisonment conditions only a handful of friends could be expected to be loyal and to have a real interest in one and that the many others were living only for themselves, and their questions were merely to satisfy their curiosity. At the moment, Cameron was too much concerned about getting back to his barracks to nurse his wounds. There would be plenty of time later to talk at his leisure.

Paul met him at the door. He shoved a hand forward, which grasped Cameron's in a tight and brotherly manner. "My heart has been most heavy, Cam, and I—"

That was as far as he got before his friend stopped him. "Not another word, Paul." But the affection that was transmitted when he put an arm around Paul's shoulder was the most that one man could give another.

There was a strain in the room. No one seemed quite sure what might be the best thing to say. Both Blake and Sykes acted as though they wanted to say something more than the mere greeting, cordial that it was, that they gave Cameron when he arrived. Cameron himself was not in the mood to carry on a conversation. His first thought was to care for his bruised body, but the strained atmosphere could only be broken by himself.

"How are the night tenkos coming along, Sykes?" he asked with a wan smile, trying to be cheerful.

"Oh, those!" replied Sykes with alacrity. "For two nights now, we have not been disturbed."

"That certainly is encouraging. What happened? Did the Nips finally tire out?"

"I suspect that is what happened," Paul offered. "When they start a thing like that, as you know, it peters out before too long a time."

"That fern is what interests me," Cameron declared, addressing his remarks to Blake. "It was about ready for the harvest when I went into the eso. Have you begun to get those good old *imos*, those sweet potatoes yet?"

"Hell no!" cried Blake with disgust. "Do you know what happened?" Without waiting for a reply, he answered his own question. "We dug up imos by the hundreds of bushels, fine, big, fat, luscious potatoes. They made us carry all of them over to that old stables, where we shredded them and spread them out on the floor to dry."

"But listen to our tale of woe," Paul cut in, prodding the speaker. "Go ahead, Blake, tell him the bad news."

"They didn't give them to us," complained Blake. "Finally, we had to ask the interpreter when we would have some to eat. Then he told us that they were very sorry but all imos had rotted and had to be thrown away. Oh-h-h!" Blake finished up with a wail that brought a laugh to the others.

"The Nips are masters at that game, all right," replied Cameron. "That is the third farm we have completed, the third time that we have been solemnly promised to be given the produce, and the third time they have failed. But who brought in the imos? Did you people go back to work?

"Not by a damn sight," declared Blake. The poor devils were never given a chance to say whether they would volunteer or not, and the Nips have been taking them out every day to work."

October 1st! A day of magnitude at Shirakawa! Buddha stepped through the gate, motioned to the first POW he saw, and beckoned him to approach. "Tell all prisoners they leave tomorrow!" He was excited, and he transmitted that emotion to the POW listening to him. "Twenty kilos baggage for each."

"But ...but ..." stuttered the prisoner, trying to get additional information. He was too upset at the tremendous change about to enter the lives of the prisoners to bring forth an intelligent question.

Meanwhile, Buddha had turned and slipped out the gate.

"Pack up! Everybody, pack up!" he screamed, running to his barracks. "We are leaving tomorrow. I personally was informed by the officer." In spite of his intense excitement, he could not suppress his ego.

After a while, some of the other POWs were able to calm the man down and receive a more lucid statement of just what had been said and what was intended. But it was an assured fact. The lieutenant had definitely said the camp would be moved, and at once. Tomorrow!

Why? Where? Those were the vital questions each POW was asking and thinking about. Soon, each had his own answers. Whether those answers were absurd and illogical made little difference; the point was that no prisoner could be without an answer to a question because his colleague with an answer might occupy a position of superior prestige.

Sykes came bouncing into the room, tripping over the doorstep in his haste. He was beaming with enthusiasm and could barely wait to speak his piece. "I have finally gotten the lowdown on where we are headed. All these rumors floating around are wrong."

"Quit talking so much and say something," cried the impatient Blake.

Paul and Cameron exchanged glances. *Here it comes again*, they thought. Whatever rumor a man had to pass on became in his mind the absolute truth. It was his rumor, his property, and he was obliged to defend it to the end to maintain his prestige.

"We are going to Shikoku!" Sykes proclaimed with great assurance.

"Where the hell is that?" Blake quickly inquired.

"Why, don't you know? I thought everybody knew where Shikoku was."

"No, goddamn it, I don't know!" Blake vehemently declared. "Why all this argument to get a little bit of information out of you? Do you have to give us your entire biography first?"

"No," replied Sykes, almost in a pout at having his excitement dampened. "Shikoku is one of the major islands on Japan, the one just east of the Inland Sea."

"That should be a nice quiet place," Cameron told the others. "I've been there. It's the least exciting one of the islands. Should have plenty of food there and probably less bombing, once our people get started."

"One of the guards told me," continued Sykes with an air of superiority at having been singled out for the honor of being the recipient of that information. In reality, he weakened his position, as the others well knew. The guard was probably telling Sykes where his hometown was or giving him some other information wholly unrelated to that which Sykes was wishing for.

"We shall know in a short time," said Paul, trying to terminate the discussion in a peaceful manner.

Sykes's story about completed the number of possible places where the POWs could be sent. When he had left the room to joyfully tell his rumor to his friends elsewhere in the barracks, Cameron said, "Somebody has to be right, Paul. There is no place left that has not been included in one of the rumors. All the Jap islands, China, Korea, Manchukuo, South America, Africa, even home."

"My guess is that we are not going anyplace right away," replied Paul, "that is, not tomorrow or the next day."

"Yes, I'll stake my money on that same thing. Never yet have the Nips ever done anything at the time they announced. No reason to think that this will be an exceptional case."

"What do you make of the reasons behind the move?"

"It seems to me that we can safely fall back on the analysis we made the other day," Cameron replied. "All we had to go on were a flock of rumors. Without a doubt, some of than are logically true. Add to them the news that is brought in by new POWs from other areas, and some sort of a sensible picture can be formed."

"I agree. Something also can be gained from what we see here. The Nip air activity has been on the increase. But we have yet to see one of our own planes, unless that mystery ship a week ago could have been one."

"It may well have been," Cameron stated. "It was certainly like nothing we had seen before."

"He must have been twenty thousand feet up and was streaking along faster than anything we ever saw before."

"True!" Cameron continued. "It could easily have been one of our reconnaissance planes getting pictures and having a look at the island. There's lots of that to be done before our troops can land."

"It would seem sensible to me, Cam, that, if any sort of threat of landings on Taiwan appears, the Nips would pull this camp of senior officers farther back as soon as possible."

"If our deductions are right, and they probably are, that the Nips are losing island after island on the drives from the south and east, they haven't much left to point to with pride except these bodies here, the colonels and generals and governors of colonies from all the Allies. At least this crowd is symbolic of something, although it isn't of much value otherwise."

"We could also be of some minor trading value in the end."

"No doubt, but you know what the end will likely be for us when that other end comes."

For a week, the camp was in a turmoil. The authorities set the departure ahead from day to day. The time would arrive and then be cancelled. A POW was as temperamental as the traditional prima donna over his meager possessions. All he had were several empty tin cans and some rags of clothing, but he unwrapped and rewrapped than meticulously and with loving care.

Eventually the big moment came! Long before daylight one morning, the prisoners were called out and lined up. It was difficult for the excitable enemy troops to satisfy themselves in the daytime that tenko showed all prisoners present; but now at night, with only the occasional lights along the fence to illuminate the compound, the commotion showed the fears of the authorities over the loss of a single POW. The roll was called many times, and the guards counted and recounted. A few sputtering army trucks appeared from out of the darkness and parked at the gate. Luggage was loaded on; the POWs from the hospital were given the privilege.

"What's that big furnace hooked onto that truck?" asked Sykes, who saw a strange contraption strapped on, running and belching smoke.

"The Nips are undoubtedly short of gasoline," replied Cameron, "and have to improvise. That could be a charcoal burner."

"I hope it doesn't blow up while we're around it."

The dawn was breaking when the prisoners finished their march and drew up alongside the miniature railroad running through the sugarcane fields. That was the way the POWs had arrived, and that was the way they were to depart.

"At least we can safely say that we are going over to the main railroad," Paul told Cameron. "Then it will be anyone's guess whether we go north or south."

That point was soon settled. Hurry! Hurry! Hurry! The train will not wait. Prisoners must be there on time. The Nipponese were worried. If the detachment were late in arriving, it would go hard with the authorities. Yet there was time to spare at the station before the train showed itself coming around a bend far to the south.

Keelung! The thought ran through the mind of each prisoner. They were headed for the northern port of Taiwan. From there, it was a short water journey to either the China coast or to Japan itself. Better not to look too far ahead, the wise ones said.

The rail journey to the north was hot and tiresome. Nothing could be seen from the windows, because the guards required all blinds to be drawn. Something big must be going on, defenses and troop movements, everyone felt.

At the end of the trip, the prisoners were lined up and counted and then marched to the pier. Looking out over the dock from the upper floor of the pier shed, the POWs saw a magnificent sight. Lashed to the pier rode a liner of huge proportions. She gleamed with a fresh coat of white paint. On the bow, contrasted in black, the name of the vessel stood out. *Oryoku Maru!* At that moment, it was merely the name of another Nipponese ship to the prisoners. They were to hear from her again, on another day!

"Paul, finally we are about to take an ocean voyage under Nip supervision on a luxury liner," Cameron declared.

"I trust you don't mean, Cam, that we will be berthed in the bridal suite."

"No, my good friend. Hardly that. We'll no doubt see the Orient from a porthole."

"I'll be thankful if even that is true. It will be a joy to be above the waterline."

"Now it is you who is assuming things, Paul. Do you think we will not be locked down in the hold as in the past?"

"From the size of that vessel and by the fact that I see no influx of passengers, I might rashly guess this crowd might enjoy some stateroom above the waterline."

"There seems to be plenty of space, six decks that I can count."

"One look at that ship makes me feel that perhaps this war is going too well for the enemy, Cam. How can the Nips afford to use such a huge liner to haul detested prisoners around? And where did they ever get paint to trim her up like that in the middle of a life or death war?"

"Those, Paul, are some of the unanswerable questions. Never be surprised at anything the Nips do. I know one thing, though, and that is that more than one of these POWs will by now have reached the conclusion that the apparent luxury of a voyage in that vessel means that it is an exchange ship and that we are going to a neutral port for repatriation."

Paul burst into a laugh. "It is pathetic how many will arrive at such conclusions merely because such matters are their fondest wish."

"Anyhow." Cameron sighed. "It would be a wonderful thrill to be surprised with a condition like that."

The prisoners were formed into a column, which snaked over the gangplank to the deck. The head of the line was directed through a passageway and down a ladder, down a second ladder, and finally down a third one. Words were not spoken. Each POW held his breath. Too many times before, they had been crammed into a dark and unventilated hold. This time they had come to the conclusion that conditions would be more desirable. Each step down, down, down brought them closer to the disaster they knew must come someday. A man's luck could not hold up forever.

As each tired and sweating prisoner readied the last step, he was met by angry guards who demanded that he push on to the far end of the compartment. Bayonets were freely shifted stomachward to add speed to the orders. The center of the compartment in which the prisoners found themselves consisted of a steel shaft about a dozen feet across on a side. Surrounding that were shelves for sleeping, with a narrow passageway between them and the shaft. The shelves were deep enough for two men to sleep end to end between the passageway and the steel hull of the ship.

"How the hell do they expect five hundred men to live in a place like this?" grumbled Blake. "It can't be done."

"It certainly looks that way to me, too," replied Cameron. "But don't forget these Nips are masters at packing things and people into small spaces. Somebody must have figured this out beforehand."

Blake's feeling was the same as that of most of the other prisoners. Too many men and too little space! They resisted the circumstances because they did not want to accept them. But somehow or other, with no small amount of enemy threats and prodding, the prisoners squirmed and crawled onto the shelves. They had to lie shoulder to shoulder; and if two tall men were end to end, their legs overlapped. On the upper shelf, a man could sit up only if he could put his head between two steel girders. Below, it was a little better, as the planking overhead gave a few inches to spare. Several small electric bulbs, shining yellow, gave enough light to see what one was doing. The air was dead from lack of circulation and stifling from the sweat of men. Clothes were quickly stripped off tired bodies, and the men looked about for a better knowledge of their surroundings. The uppermost thought in each mind, although it was never mentioned aloud, was how to get out in a hurry in an emergency. That situation would surely arise, each one felt. The war must be pretty close now. Submarines were undoubtedly slithering along under the surface. Planes would attack before the ship's destination was reached. What about mines? Our people, of course, would have sown those at strategic spots.

The only exit was by the small ladder and two steel bulkhead doors at the end of the compartment. Where they led to, no one yet knew. High up above the upper shelf ran a row of closed portholes. It was not long before a courageous POW had unscrewed a latch and opened one. It was refreshing to see the daylight and get a whiff of fresh air. Others were quickly opened; many were too tightly bolted to operate without a hammer to loosen the bolt head.

"How far down is the waterline?" That was an important question. These men feared being cooped up below the waterline. They wanted a chance to get out of the hold—when the time came.

"Right in the middle of the compartment!"

The prisoners huddled back in mental torture. A hole in the side would let the water in, not let men out! The portholes were too small in diameter to permit the passage of a body, unless it was rather small. Each POW who could see the opening silently compared its size with that of his own body. How many men will be fighting to get out before I can get a chance?

It was not long before one of the ship's crew, accompanied by a guard, came through the compartment. He crawled over the prisoners lying on the upper shelf and, with a heavy hammer, tightened up the screws on each port hatch so that no man without a tool could unloosen them.

"The little yellow bastards!"

Blake's comment was echoed by many others.

All was not misery and depression. Several prisoners nearest the bulkhead doors were called out by one of the sergeants. They followed him through the passageway to a galley where they were given food buckets and told how to make the distribution. A wire container with bowls of different sizes was passed into the recumbent group of men, followed by the food buckets. One of each group was delegated to serve. Rice, a piece of fish, a few new potatoes, a tiny piece of ginger, miso soup with seaweed, and a bowl of hot tea.

The prisoners looked at each other in astonishment. Such food as this they had never come their way before. It was out of keeping with their living conditions.

"I don't get this," cried Blake with his mouth filled with delectable fish.

"They must have been forced to comply with the International Convention," replied a POW at his elbow.

"Perhaps it is because we are in the hands of the Nip navy again," Cameron offered as a solution. "They have a reputation of being more cosmopolitan than the army and knowing more about Occidentals."

"Whatever it is, I am for it," murmured Blake, unconcerned with any further debate on the subject.

When the meal was finished, the well-scraped bowls were collected in the wire containers and carried up on deck, washed, and returned to the squads. That became the procedure, and it was a choice detail, one to be fought for, to carry the dishes up in the fresh air. When the morning meal arrived, a similar banquet was spread before the prisoners. In spite of the crowded quarters and discomfiture, better food raised the spirits.

Scurvy, hated and rated the cruelest, was the lieutenant in charge of the guard detachment. He must have been picked, many a POW thought, because of his harsh treatment as an assurance to his superiors that the prisoners would be kept in line. If he treated his own subordinates in any such manner as he handled the prisoners, undoubtedly those soldiers were hoping that disaster would overtake the *Oryoku Maru*. His handiwork seemed to be destined to pursue the POWs to the end.

When the call was sent down to come for the noon meal on that second day, it was Cameron's turn on the roster. With the other food carriers from the different squads, he strolled down the passageway to the galley. He watched one of the mess attendants fill the buckets. The food had fallen off materially in quality and Cameron, like the others who were watching, realized that their day of luxury had drawn to a close. He glanced about him and saw that none of the guards was near, so he decided to speak to the man who was filling the buckets. Cameron was always careful not to let anyone with whom he came in daily contact learn that he was proficient in the NIP's spoken language.

"The food for the last two meals has been fine," he said to the man in the vernacular. "You have a very good cook here."

"Ah, thank you," the man replied. "Aboard ship, the food is better than ashore."

"Maybe not quite so good this noon," Cameron added, pointing to the buckets.

"The lieutenant said to make the change," the attendant returned. "He was afraid it was too rich for men who had not been accustomed to it. Didn't want to have any sick people on his hands."

"I see. The lieutenant ordered the change."

"Yes. We have to reduce the meals to rice, a little soup, and tea."

Cameron relayed the information to his colleagues. There was murder in their eyes. When the news reached the POWs in the confined compartment, they seethed over a situation that had gone against them and left them with no recourse, no means of fighting back. Their emotions surged up within them but could find no outlet against the enemy. There must be a emotional release, so it took other forms.

There were other matters to report when Cameron returned to the compartment with the food buckets for his squad. When the tempers began to cool down from the disappointment over the food, Cameron announced, "The ship appears to be filling up rapidly, from what I could see."

The prisoners withheld their eating for a moment, looking at the speaker with expectation.

"There are many civilian families coming aboard," Cameron continued. "I saw a number myself, and the attendant in the galley told me that many Japanese were being evacuated from Taiwan."

"Looks like we should feel honored," someone quipped, "to be included with the nationals that they want to save."

"It does point out a fact that we already suspected," Cameron reported, "that the Nips are having some concern about landings on the island."

"You are a good reporter, Cam," Paul complimented. "What else did you learn on your expedition down the deck?"

"One other thing I can state from actual observation," he replied. "There are hundreds of wounded Nip soldiers coming aboard, too. They make quite a sight, each one in a white kimono."

"Where could they have come from? They weren't wounded on Taiwan."

"I tried to find out in the galley, but there wasn't time. When we went past them, however, they all seemed quite docile. There wasn't a single belligerent look on any of their faces when they saw us occidental prisoners."

"Don't see how their wounded could get off the islands we capture," Blake pondered. "One of the things we are doing is pounding their shipping, what comes in and what tries to leave."

"That is likely very true," agreed Cameron. "But in spite of our efforts, undoubtedly a vessel now and then escapes. How about these casualties having come from the China mainland or having run the gauntlet from Singapore and Burma? Then again, they may have been here for a long time—since the early actions in the Philippines, maybe."

"If they get loaded today, we ought to sail tonight."

Shortly after the evening meal, which was as meager as the noon meal had been, one of the guards pulled the light switch. The compartment was thrown into utter darkness. Not a flicker could penetrate through the steel that encompassed the compartment. It was an eerie sensation, lying there in complete blackness, with men crowded together shoulder to shoulder, a solid barrier overhead that kept a man from standing upright, and bayonets just outside the closed bulkhead doors. The air was hot and difficult to breathe. What action would panic-stricken men take? There was some consolation knowing that the vessel was still tied up to the pier. Soon she would be on the high seas with no solid construction to keep her propped up.

One by one, the POWs slipped off to sleep, that peaceful and restful sleep that helps to melt the fears and worries of the day. Sometime during the night, vibrations of the ship aroused the sleepers. They sensed a motion. They were under way!

For a while, the forward motion produced little more than a sensation of lightly gliding through quiet waters as the *Oryoku Maru* cut her way through the harbor. But once in the open sea, she took on full speed ahead, and the vast change in the speed was recognized by men lying in the hold. Suddenly, she turned on her side, righted herself and rolled far over to the opposite side. The cycle was repeated time and again, and the sensation was like riding a toboggan down a slide of many sharp turns. It seemed as if that motion kept up for hours before the ship finally righted herself, reduced her speed, and finally came to rest. Sighs of relief could be heard from many directions throughout the compartment.

Whatever the ship had been running away from no longer was a threat. But on second thought, what was the meaning of the stopping of the vessel? Had an Allied destroyer caught up with her and demanded her surrender? Could it be possible that she was about to be taken into custody by the Allies? Every waking man waited for one of two things—a torpedo or gun volley would come this way if the *Oryoku Maru* did not behave herself, or the master would order the opening of the sea valves and sink his ship. Didn't the Nips always die to the last man? If they had to go, what value were some evacuees and wounded soldiers? Prisoners did not even count. The disgrace of capture and losing a ship to the enemy without a fight could never be lived down. Banzai for the emperor!

But there were red faces in the morning! Horrible thoughts that pass through the mind in the darkness of night appear so silly in the light of day. The *Oryoku Maru* was back in her berth alongside the pier in Keelung Harbor!

"What to make of all that?" Paul asked Cameron, who was lying beside him, after the news had been brought into the compartment by the POWs who had gone for the breakfast rice.

"Brother, I was scared last night, and I make no bones about it. What happened I'll never know."

"I confess I prayed a little, Cam. But you did not answer my question."

"Well, since you expect me to know all the answers," Cameron began in a light vein, "my guess is that one of two things happened. The ship went out of the harbor for a 'dry run,' just to see how well she could run the gauntlet if she had to. She was certainly doing some bucking and twisting, I must admit. The other possibility is that she was making for her destination and ran afoul of a submarine—surely we have submarines around here by now—and got chased back into the safety of the harbor."

"Very plausible. Now we still have to make our getaway."

"Hang on to yourself, Paul. Remember that you are the one I have to lean on to get through this mess. You have two of us on your shoulders, so don't fail us. I admit that I am weak."

"Sure, and you are a sissy," Paul flung back at him, "after all the gladiator stuff you pulled off during the campaign. If you don't receive the greatest number of decorations of anyone out of this campaign, I miss my guess."

Cameron sat up. His sudden move did not take into consideration the girder above him, and he banged his head against it. "Goddamn it!" he cried, massaging his bruise. "Excuse me, Paul," he said after several minutes. "I know you do not approve of my swearing, but just crash your head into that steel sometime and see what you do!"

Paul smiled in an understanding way, and Cameron continued. "Paul, anybody can have guts when there is a job to be done. When you are out in the open and can meet your opponent man-to-man, that is one thing. You have a chance! You can fight him or you can run! That is your decision of the moment. But when you are cooped up here where you can't fight back, your mind is liable to go screwy."

"Wow, don't let yourself get out of hand, Cam. You are no different from anyone else. The man of real courage is the one who can control himself and be an example to the others. Can you imagine what would happen down here if there was no leadership, no one to show the others what real 'guts' were?"

"I shudder to think about it. They would tear each other to pieces in the stampede and then all jam up at the ladder trying to be the first one to get out. What horror! But you have given me a jolt, Paul. It is sort of like a dash of ice water to bring me back to normal. I'll try to be a man through this." Then, suddenly, in a burst of humor, he added, "But damn it, Paul, if you ever weaken or show the least sign of fear, I'm lost!"

"My faith is strong, Cam. It'll bring me through."

Another day, followed by night, came and went and then another and finally another. The *Oryoku Maru* remained in harbor. None of the prisoners were able to pry any information out of the guards. Because of the expertness developed by POWs after a long period of time, the thought was prevalent that, if they could not learn anything, it was because the Nips themselves had no information.

The utmost care was exercised in guarding the men in the hold. They were kept far below hour after hour on pretext that the ship might steam out of the harbor any minute. But that moment kept being delayed and delayed. The prisoners grew more restless by the hour in their crowded and stagnant quarters. Appeals to the authorities met with little concern for the comfort of those who were closely imprisoned. Boppings and mistreatment were administered whenever a favor was asked.

"Paul," Cameron whispered to this friend as the two were lying on their wooden shelf. "I've been turning this situation over in my mind for a long time."

"Mm-m-m!" replied Paul. "With what result?"

"I'm convinced that the officer responsible, whether it is Scurvy or the captain of the vessel, has no idea of what we are undergoing down here. Neither one of them has ever poked his nose into this compartment. Our only dealings have been with these half-baked guards who have no authority to change our lot and are afraid to let us talk with Scurvy because we may make a complaint."

"Mm-m-m!" Paul hummed again. "Sounds plausible to me. Any one of the guards feels that, whenever he can't handle what comes up, it reflects on him."

"True! So uses his own judgment in making a decision, which is usually a bopping to the POW who raises a question."

"Well, Cam, you have raised the issue. Surely you have thought of a solution," chided Paul.

"I'm not too sure. The problem is to get to someone beyond the dumb sentry on duty."

"Yes, and that means we have to be smart enough to present him with something that will frighten him into going to his sergeant, who will be frightened into going to the lieutenant."

"Now we are making progress, Paul. Let me think what we might figure out. How about your being sick?"

"Wait a minute now," Paul hurriedly called over to his neighbor. "Don't get me mixed up in a bopping affair. I'm still sore and bruised from the last time they worked me over. Let's tell them a mutiny is developing. We wanted something to frighten them into action, didn't we?"

"Yes, but hardly that kind of action. I'll tell you, Paul, the sickness thing might work. You don't want to be the guinea pig, but we still could use the sick argument. Le them think an epidemic is breaking out!"

"That's a real idea! Now you have struck on something that will frighten them without fail. They may not be too concerned with us, but they will fear the consequences from their superiors if an epidemic started that might jeopardize the heath of their own people."

"Let's talk it over with some more POWs and get their idea."

Paul and Cameron selected a number of other POWs in whose viewpoints they had confidence and discussed the matter with them. Agreement with the plan was unanimous. But as Cameron knew only too well, he would be the one to put the plan into action.

It was easy to get the other prisoners to agree to a suggestion that might benefit them, but to induce them to carry out the action was a far different matter. Get as much as possible while giving as little as possible became, by rapid stages, an obsession. An existence beyond an economy of stringency and deprivation needed a stimulation from beyond his mundane life if a man were to have a thought and consideration beyond self. Regardless of the insouciant effect of malnutrition, the spark of life fights against extermination. As it flutters toward extinction, it becomes less altruistic and more self-concerned.

"Joe," said Cameron, with a sense of defeat even before he made his suggestion, "you are one of the more senior officers here. We believe that you should be the one to put this scheme over. You know, leadership and all that sort of thing."

"Well, of course, Cam." Joe hesitated, fumbling for words to counter Cameron's argument. "Uh, uh … Since the Nips have refused to recognize seniority among us, I'd not be the best one to do it. Why, I might even get in trouble for that very reason."

"Your rank and seniority are things you'd cram down our throats only too fast back home. It's easy to exercise leadership when the going's easy. But it takes a real soldier to assume command when he has to take personal risks!" Cameron surprised himself with a tongue that could lash out so effectively.

His goading of Joe had no effect, however, because Joe crawled back to his little niche without a word in rebuttal.

"That's the sort of a bird the government supports for thirty years," Cameron cried to Paul. "And when an emergency arises, he folds up."

Reaching a hand over to Cameron's arm, Paul said, "Shh! Take it easy. Nothing will be gained by such caustic remarks, even though they may be true," he added in a whisper.

To hear Paul say anything unkind of another individual was so unusual that it brought forth a smile from Cameron and calmed down his emotions. *He is human after all*, thought Cameron.

"Well, what's next?" asked Paul.

"All right! All right! I'll go do it! But, it certainly gripes me to put myself out to help some of the POWs who wouldn't raise a hand to even pull themselves out of the mire. If somebody else didn't do things for them, they'd probably lie down and rot."

As Cameron squirmed off his shelf and dropped down into the narrow passageway, Paul said quietly to himself, *Cam will get a real joy out of that act. I think he knows it, too. He never expected that old Joe would take any action. In fact, Cam would have been disappointed if Joe had.*

As he squeezed his way past the prisoners who were standing in the passageway, Cameron was preparing himself to make a favorable impression the guard. He looked ahead and saw the soldier standing beyond the partly opened bulkhead door, ready to slam it shut if any POWs came too close. Cameron spoke to him and sauntered toward the door. He hoped that his action would not be disarming and that the guard would not become alarmed. *I'll to have to talk to this fellow in his own language*, Cameron said inwardly. *He doesn't understand English.*

At Cameron's next comment to the Nipponese, the guard drew his bayonetted rifle to a position of readiness and placed a heavy boot against the door. The growls that rose from the sentry's throat sounded like the warnings a watchdog would give at the approach of a stranger.

Cameron stopped and casually leaned against the framework that supported the sleeping shelves. "We have some sickness here," he said to the guard in the vernacular. When the soldier shrugged his shoulders in disinterest, Cameron continued, "Maybe all prisoners will get very sick, and gallant Nipponese soldiers may catch the disease." He clamped his jaws tightly together and declared to himself, *What a damn hypocrite I am! The little yellow bastard!*

Something ran rapidly through the soldier's being that jolted him into action. He left his post unguarded and hastened to his leader. "Sergeant of the guard!" he bellowed in a frightened voice, while

Cameron stood in front of the bulkhead door and smiled at that first step toward his success.

He listened attentively to the loud dialogue between the Nipponese. *Why do these damn monkeys always shriek at the top of their lungs?* he asked himself. *They get mighty excited it seems. But they weren't that way during the campaign,* he continued to meditate, *the way they prowled through the jungle like cats. Maybe having the leadership of an officer at hand makes the difference, and they grow fearful when that encouragement is not present.*

The conversation between the two soldiers was audible to Cameron, but its rapidity and slurring of words limited his full understanding of what was being said. He gathered that the sergeant had ordered the guard back to his post and that the epidemic was too serious for him to handle. The officer must be called!

Now we are getting someplace, Cameron said inwardly. *The lieutenant will come here with the thought that an epidemic is about to start, and it will be easier to speak with him than if I had to convince him from the start—that is, if he comes at all,* he reasoned. *He may be frightened to death of sickness, as most of these Nips are, and slam the bulkhead door in our faces—forever!*

In time, Scurvy appeared halfway down the ladder, his samurai sword dangling and interfering with his progress. Hanging on various parts of his body were other articles of equipment, which all the guards on the vessel constantly wore—a steel helmet, sidearms, a life preserver, and a coil of rope.

What magnificent courage these damn Nips have! growled Cameron within himself. *All equipped for an emergency, even though we are tied up a the pier and at the same time refusing to give us a single life belt. Bushido!*

"You have bad sickness?" Scurvy called to Cameron without leaving the safety of the ladder. He was not risking contamination by coming too close.

"No, Lieutenant," returned the American, shaking his head to amplify his words. "Not yet, but I would like to talk to you about it."

Taking courage from Cameron's assurance, Scurvy approached the door and asked, "What is it then?" His voice now had a tone of anger.

It gave Cameron a feeling that Scurvy resented being called when no emergency existed.

"Sickness may break out, Lieutenant. I thought it my duty to inform you before it happens."

"Well, well ..." sputtered Scurvy, uncertain as to what he should do or say, while the sergeant and guard stood in respectful silence, wondering how the conversation was progressing.

Cameron followed up his advantage and said, "The POWs have been down here many days, Lieutenant, and it may be a long time yet before we reach our destination. We thought that, because you are concerned over the prisoners' welfare, you wouldn't want them to get sick."

"No! No!" cried Scurvy. "But what is it you want?'

"Perhaps you could let us come up on deck for fresh air a little while each day."

The officer stroked his chin while turning the request over in his thoughts. "Very well!" he decided. "It will be arranged."

"That is very kind and thoughtful, Lieutenant," returned Cameron, while he wanted to kick himself for his sycophancy. "And a bath would be helpful, Lieutenant. We do not ask for one every day like the Nipponese soldiers get, just an occasional one."

"Very difficult to get bath on board ship."

"Yes, sir! We understand that. But we knew you were in command and could find some way to have it done. Perhaps we could go out on the wharf and use a fire hose from the pier shed.

The suggestion was too sudden for Scurvy to assimilate without some deliberation, but the subtle compliment paid him had its effect. "We will arrange," he finally agreed, nodding his head.

"Arigato! Arigato! Thank you very much! That will surely keep POWs from sickness." Cameron gave the Nipponese a bow of courtesy and turned back toward his shelf.

He crashed into a group of prisoners who had pushed close up to him to hear the discussion. Before he could weave his way back, the whole story was being told throughout the compartment. The listeners conveyed the information to all corners of the hold in a rapid manner.

As Cameron hoisted himself up alongside Paul, his friend said, "The news has already swept past us up here; you have arranged for fresh air and bathing. That was a magnificent job, Cam, and you can feel the raised spirits all through the compartment. Listen to the joyful jabbering!"

"It worked out pretty well, Paul. I never got bopped once!" Cameron stretched out and dismissed the incident from his thoughts.

"Of course, the POWs were grateful and thanked you for what you did for them."

Cameron was silent. He had not even thought of that. Finally, he said, "Strange thing, isn't it, Paul? Not a word was said by anyone. Quite a commentary on the life of a POW!"

"Well," he added later, "I'm sure they are appreciative but a little negligent."

"You are developing a more understanding nature, Cam, and showing more patience toward others."

"I can't be too sure of that, Paul. These damn POWs certainly rile me on occasions. Sometimes I wonder if it's worthwhile trying to help them. They are so ungrateful and snarl among themselves to gain the slightest advantage."

"Some of us here must keep our equilibrium, you know, Cam. Otherwise the whole thing would go to pot. Perhaps a good example will set a standard and get results."

"Too late for that, I'm afraid. Deterioration has gone too far."

"Well, don't give up. You can save yourself by holding on to your dignity and trying to help others, even if you can't influence them to save themselves."

Cameron said nothing, but he let Paul's remarks seep deep into his soul.

It was a gala day on the morrow! Word was sent into the "rattrap," as the POWs termed their compartment, that the different squads would line up at ten-minute intervals for bathing. An incoherent uproar filled the hold of the ship, as each POW scrambled for a post position. Some few who still possessed a chunk of soap scratched into the bottom of their kit to find that luxury. They clutched those bits of soap in their hands as though someone was about to grab them away. The real fear was, however, that a colleague might ask to use someone's soap. It was easy to refuse the request, but it was difficult to live with one's selfishness afterward.

"Come on, Paul," chided Cameron. "Get that crusty, old carcass of yours down in the aisle."

"Our squad hasn't left yet. They are still standing in the passageway—"

"Where they have been standing since the call came," Cameron interrupted. "They could not wait to get there, even though the other squads got to go first."

"They have been blocking the passageway, and the others can hardly pass by them. Two POWs, with their normal weight, couldn't get past each other in that narrow passage."

"First time I ever heard of any advantage to being a skeleton. But come on! Get going! They are moving up, and we have waited to be the last. If we linger any longer, the next squad will squeeze us out."

In spite of themselves, impatience welled up in Paul and Cameron as they followed what appeared to them to be the dallying of the others in front of them. "They move very slowly," Paul called over his shoulder to Cameron.

"I'll bet you one thousand worthless Nip invasion yen that some stupid POW has stopped on the gangplank to gape around while everyone behind has to wait for him."

Some minutes later, they reached the main deck. Sunlight and fresh air suddenly struck them like a piercing tonic and stimulated their whole beings. There was no need to talk. Each knew from his own glorious experience how the other felt. Deep draughts of good clean air, a glance at the blue and cloudless heavens above, and then to the business at hand!

One man seized the end of a short length of frayed fire hose. The others pushed up as close as possible, waiting. "Turn on the water, Bill, behind you!" Cameron called from the gangplank. "Can you beat that, Paul! They'll all rush up to get their share of water, but not a single

POW would take a second to turn on the valve. They're so damn afraid someone will get an advantage."

Clustering close around the end of the hose, which a POW held upright so that the sizable jet of water could act as a powerful shower bath, the prisoners rubbed themselves gleefully and splashed to their hearts' content; the sweat and filth of many days accumulation flowed down to the edge of the pier and disappeared into the harbor.

"Good God! Here comes a Nip woman!" cried a POW.

Splashing stopped. Consternation prevailed. Blake saved the day. "Hell with her!" he laughed.

Back to their joyful task! But each white, glistening body faced toward the vessel, while the woman, with her offspring strapped on her back, continued unconcerned on her way behind the POWs and up the gangplank.

It was the day after the bath on the pier that the big event occurred. Suddenly, and unexpectedly, a new sensation swept over the POWs down in the bowels of the *Oryoku Maru*.

Blake had just returned with the hot tea that was part of the noon meal. "Gee! They make this stuff in the bathtub, Cam. Have you see that place?"

With a prisoner from each of the other squads, Blake had been lined up by a guard and marched amidships. The men were directed into a compartment, but when the door was opened, they leaped back in fright. Steam poured out of the opening. It took but a few seconds to realize that, while the room was filled with steam and a loud, hissing sound was coming from the interior, there was no danger lurking there.

Once inside, Blake noticed that the compartment was a bathing room, tiled on floor and sides, and that a sunken bath at the far end was filled with hot tea. A steam pipe had been improvised and ran from the wall into the tub, where the steam ran into the liquid and kept it bubbling and at a high temperature.

He filled his canteens with a ladle, asking himself all the while if the tub had been thoroughly cleaned since the last Nips had bathed there.

When Blake asked him the question, Cameron pondered for a moment and then said, "You mean they use the bath to make the tea in?"

"Yeah, they sure do, with a stream pipe belching into it. Do you think it's clean?"

"Oh, yes!" replied Cameron. "That steam would kill any germs. But that sounds like a good idea though, since they have to make great quantities of tea for a large passenger list."

Then, without warning, the bulkhead door was slammed shout! The clang of the metal and the push of the air in the compartment had ominous impacts on the prisoners.

For seconds, no one spoke. Men looked at each other in wonderment.

"Wuz that?" asked Blake, slurring his words in his excitement. He had tossed his canteens on the shelf and was climbing up the framework; but he remained suspended there, waiting for the next event.

Cameron gave a deep sigh of uncertainty. Something was up! The slamming of that steel door forecast a portentous moment! He looked over at Paul, who lay in a partly reclining position, his weight on one elbow. His other hand was finishing a movement from forehead to chest.

Far above, a soft, regular sound repeated itself. It was a man running across the open deck. He must be wearing a pair of those rubber-soled shoe the Nips use for quiet jungle work. Strange how that soft sound would penetrate so far below. It was the only noise in the silence of the tomb. Or was it the faint vibration that could be felt through many layers of steel?

Boom! A distant cannon shot mellowed by the intervening insulation of sheets of steel.

"That must be the stern gun we saw on deck," announced Cameron.

"Anti-submarine guns though," argued Paul. "Surely no sub could get into this harbor."

"It would be mighty risky."

Tat-tat-tat! Ping-ping-ping! Boom-boom-boom! Zip-zip-zip!

"For Christ's sake!" swore Blake. "Did you ever hear so many different calibers at once?"

"From all around the place," added Cameron. "They must be on the tops of all the buildings and all the hills in the area."

"And no two alike," continued Blake. "How they hell do they expect to have an air defense with all that assortment of junk. Not even a single '75.'"

No one had to be told it was an air aid. The motley array of small caliber weapons from all sides spoke loudly enough for all to know.

Zoo-oo-oom! *Swish-swish*! *Crash*!

Dive bombers! Christ Almighty! They have finally come! The first goddamn action we have seen since Bataan!

In minutes, it was over, but the men in the hold had lived an eon. Their feelings were mingled. It was a tremendous thrill to hear, for the first time, your own people in the sky—to know the war was finally being carried to the homeland of the little yellow bastards. *Courage! Maybe someday soon this mess will be over and we can be free again!*

But God! What if they had dropped one on the middle of this ship? How deep is the water we're lying in? Will they be coming back?

In due course the bulkhead door slowly opened. That was an assurance to the POWs that the raid was over. Where had they come from? Was a landing on Taiwan imminent? This is October 1944! Surely our task forces have gotten this far by now. But oh! They are so slow, so slow in coming.

Hold on! What has this raid got to do with our sudden move from this island? Why, of course! It's all clear now. The navy is just outside—ready for invasion! No wonder the Nips want to rush this camp of POWs out of the way. These are the senior officers of all the Allies. The Nips could never afford to lose them. Why, that's all they have left that they can point to with pride. One by one, their islands are being snatched away from them. A batch of skeletons. But they do represent the great occidental nations!

Carrying the rice bowls and tea cups up on deck and washing them after each meal had the compensation of looking around and a few breath of good fresh air. But in spite of that, it was a task not sought after. For some unexplainable reason, a starved and beaten POW had no desire to contribute to the common good. He invariably wanted to restrict his mental and physical effort to those things that brought him personal gain. Consequently, dishwashers had to be detailed in turn.

It was Joe's turn this time, but Joe usually had to be reminded when his turn came around. Then again, his little sleeping spot was far back on the upper shelf, making it awkward for him to crawl over those nearest the passageway.

A thought struck Cameron. He reached over and dragged the basket of dishes toward the edge of the shelf. In a moment, he had slipped over the edge, dropped down to the deck, and was gone with the basket in his arm. That basket of dishes was his visa to leave the compartment and climb up to the deck above. The guard never questioned the POW with an armload of dirty bowls. It was taken for granted that he was bound for the deck and the guard above.

Cameron dallied in every motion. He wanted time to look around and investigate and to find out what had happened. Out in the harbor a few hundred yards away, a small vessel was burning and sending up clouds of smoke. Beyond and over the small hill that dropped down to the wharf and warehouses that bordered on the water, long stretch of many faint wisps of smoke rose skyward. *The airfield*, thought Cameron.

When he had a chance to look over the side adjacent to the pier he noticed a large section of the pier shed had been blasted out. The planking of the wharf at that point was covered with a large, dark red smear, and bits of white cloth were mingled therein. Far back up on the hillside, many white-robed figures were moving about. The ship itself appeared completely deserted, except for the occasional guards—and, of course, the men far below.

Paul knew what Cameron was up to. Most of the others in his squad called him a sucker for doing another POW's work, while Joe relaxed and did not do his share of the common task. It was not the fact that old Joe got out of his duties that disturbed those who observed everything; it was the fact that Joe thereby got an advantage over them. He had gotten out of something, thereby accomplishing what each of them would have liked to have done—jealousy, selfishness, perhaps; call it what you will. If one of them had been asked why he resented Joe's recalcitrance, he would not for the life of him have been able to explain his feelings. Analysis of one's emotions was not a part of the average POW's life.

Cameron slipped into his position alongside Paul, who asked in a quiet voice, "What did you find out, Cam?"

"A lot! Those dive-bombers tore up a lot of things—the airport, ships in the harbor, warehouses. We were lucky! Their bombs didn't miss us by much. I think they have evacuated the ship—all except us and several guards. It looks like some of the Nip patients got it on the pier. The rest of them seem to have been taken to an inn up on the hillside."

"Guess we won't be moving out tonight then."

"Probably not! We can keep our eyes open. And when they bring back the passengers, we'll know they intend to make an effort to run the gauntlet."

"Looks sort of bad now. If the air crowd is nearby, the subs must be too. And there is lots of water to traverse before we get wherever we're going."

"Now, listen, you old fossil! Don't weaken on me. I'm depending on you to support me."

"All right, Cam," said Paul, dangling his offer. "I'll stand up under whatever comes." But the old tone of sincerity and confidence was not there. "By the way," Paul continued, "better tell the others what you have found out. It will give them some stimulation."

"Well, maybe so."

That night the men in the rattrap slept well, in spite of their aroused emotions of joy and fear.

But it was the excitement from those very emotions that had exhausted them to the point when sleep took hold with little delay.

"Another day, Paul," Cameron said when the two men were awakened by the slight motion of the bulkhead door being swung back by the guard.

"I wonder what it will bring forth," replied Paul, rubbing his eyes.

"Ought to have another raid. If they are close enough to hit Taiwan from the air, they'll probably come frequently."

"I'd like to see them come again, Cam, but, at the same time—"

"You'd not like to have them come," interrupted Cameron as he finished Paul's sentence. "I'm willing to admit I feel the same way about it. I don't claim to be any big hero, stuck down here in this sardine can."

"Just like a cornered rat!"

"Right," agreed Cameron, "but with a difference. When you push a rat into a corner, he can turn and face you and fight. With us, it's not the same. The Nips have us in a corner, all right, but the situation is as though they had us blindfolded and handcuffed and facing inward."

"It would be a tremendous mental relief if we only had a chance to fight back, or if we could only be out in the open."

"There will be a day—a day when all these Nips who have beat us and gloated over us will be torn to pieces by the bare hands of every POW!"

Paul glanced over toward Cameron and saw a fire in his eyes. "That's what they all say, Cam," he softly replied. "But I wonder."

About noontime, the great excitement occurred again. The American Navy bombers struck. The feeble sounds of the air defense gave the POWs a moment of humorous exhilaration. But it was fear—fear accentuated by not being able to see and by uncertainty—that preyed heaviest on them. Men cringed in their restricted spaces; their bodies involuntarily shuddered when a bomb hit close by. No one spoke. Each man waited for the inevitable. Questions were asked to oneself. Would I be safer sitting or lying down if one of those steel girders were thrust down on me? Horrible thought to be pinned down by one of them while the cold seawater slowly climbed up toward my chin. Should I stand up in the passageway? There is more headspace there. Ah! Maybe it would be safest if I stood by the ladder and be ready to rush out that way ahead of the others. But I wouldn't dare wander over there now. Every man here would know it and call me "yellow." Well, maybe I am, but I'm not going to let anyone know. I'll wait for the alert, ready to rush when the time comes.

"Hope that is the end of it," Cameron said, breaking the deadly silence that followed the last bomb and the end of the firing.

Paul ran a hand across his dripping forehead. "Some of those close ones gave me the jitters. I was never too sure."

"Brother, they scared the goddamn hell out of me! I wouldn't broadcast it, but I'll tell you. Christ! I've got to get out in the open where I can see what's going on."

Paul was beginning to collect himself. "You're not going to get out in the open and see anything until this sea voyage is over," he chided Cameron. "So sit back and take it easy. If you can't resist, relax and enjoy it."

"Paul, you're a great help to a man in distress." Cameron laughed, thoroughly composed by now. "Take a look at all these POWs around us," he cried in a burst of affected humor. "They look all washed out, as though they had been through some dreadful incident. They couldn't be scared, could they? That's silly! We're not!"

"Oh, no! Not at all!"

There was one more day of American bombs tossed indiscriminately at the *Oryoku Maru*, one more day of dread with all the fears of the preceding days again entering the souls of the POWs.

"What a hell of a bunch of bombardiers!" shouted Cameron at attempted levity when calm again prevailed. "If that is the best training we are giving them back home, we'll never win this war."

"Maybe they weren't trying to hit this ship," countered Paul in defense of the airmen.

"To be serious, Paul, I probably agree with you. Even though this may be the biggest ship in this harbor, I'd say there were more strategically important targets at the moment."

The following night, Cameron was aroused from his sleep by a gentle nudge. "We're moving, Cam. We're underway." Paul spoke in a whispered tone.

Cameron rose up and rested his weight on his elbow, alert and attentive. "No mistake about it, Paul," he whispered back. "This must be it!"

"I hope the skipper can make it."

"We can count on him to do his best, but that may not be good enough."

"Hope our Navy is not asleep at the switch and will fail to see this vessel."

"How'd you like to wake up in the morning, Paul, and find two beautiful American cruisers steaming southward with the *Oryoku Maru* in tow?"

"You're wide awake and dreaming."

"If that happened, the old shaved-head skipper would open his sea valves and we'd sink before the cruisers could throw us a line."

"Go on to sleep, Cam. You'll give me a nightmare."

For some hours, the vessel moved forward at reduced speed, its movements readily identified by the men below, lying awake in the blackness of the hold, listening and sensing. Sometime early in the morning, the speed was suddenly increased, and the additional thrust of the screws, the increased vibrations of the ship, was immediately transmitted to the human cargo in the rattrap.

During the day following, the bulkhead doors were left open. That gave a greater sense of security to the POWs, who had learned that, in an emergency or in a moment of danger, those doors would be quickly and conclusively banged shut.

So long as they remained ajar, no danger threatened the *Oryoku Maru*.

As the hours sped by with no sign of danger, the courage of the prisoners picked up. Hope increased in their souls. With the revolutions of the screws, the safety of dry land was brought closer to them. They began to move about in the restricted compartment, stretching their legs in the narrow passageway, squeezing past their colleagues to visit friends in other squads. The few dim and yellow light bulbs lent encouragement. One could see, after a fashion; and where one was not encased in that eternal darkness of a tomb, spirits rose out of the despondency level.

Cameron sat in his tiny space, looking at nothing in particular. His eyes roved from one POW to another, out of natural curiosity. They rested on the basket of rice bowls lying on the shelf. A short while before, the bowls had been returned from the deck above, where they had been washed and were now at hand and ready for the following meal. *Strange,* he meditated to himself, *how many of those china bowls have been broken already by those heavy-handed POWs who have so little consideration for the others in the squad. So long as they have a piece of mess equipment of their own, they give no worry to how many dishes are broken and who had to do without.*

The bowls are none too sanitary, Cameron continued to contemplate, *merely rinsed off and brought back here to dry by evaporation in this hot oven.* Then a thought suddenly struck him!

Without attracting attention, he quietly picked up his canteen cup and reached forward for the basket of dishes, which he pulled toward him. That move caused all the prisoners within sight to adjust their positions and attentively stare at him. *Just like animals,* thought Cameron, *lolling around a circle with a bone in the center. Each one wants it, but every one of them afraid to pounce on it for fear that the others will all jump on him. Someone will probably ask me what I am doing even before I show them.*

Picking up one bowl at a time, Cameron allowed the remaining moisture to drip into his cup. When he got down to the bottom, he was happy to see several bowls sitting upright that had already collected the drippings from those on top. In the end, he discovered, to his satisfaction, an inch of water in the bottom of his cup. Reaching into his little kit, he retrieved several articles. Before his observers could break the silence, to inquire what he was up to, Cameron had his face fluffy with soapsuds and his razor with a well-worn blade sliding across his chin.

Out of the corner of his eye, he saw his neighbors rub fingers across their stubble. It had been more than two weeks since anyone had been able to shave. No water had been available since leaving Shirakawa. The small amount of water or tea the POWs could get aboard ship was inadequate to quench the thirst produced by the torrid and stuffy hold.

Paul laughed and said, "Leave it to you to find some ingenious thing to do."

"The amazing part of it is that a man can shave with about two teaspoons of water. I'll need only half of this, so get busy and scrape that Santa Clause stubble off your face."

"There'll be a fight for drainage after each meal now. Someone will be injured in the rush, or I'll be badly mistaken."

The evening meal had been finished. It must have been about dusk, according to the few watches left among the prisoners. Shortly they would have tenko, when several guards would stand at the doors while only one entered the cage and observed the counting. *Of course, they are scared of us,* each POW agreed, *afraid we'll pounce on them and maybe take over the vessel.* So only one guard ventured inside.

The few scattered blankets were being rearranged to afford the greatest available comfort during a long night's sleep on stiff boards.

Then, a surprising thing happened. *Boom!* The field piece on deck was discharged! Before the sound died away, the lights in the rattrap went out. The prisoners were instantly alert and tense. The heavy sighs that were heard around the compartment meant that the fear of uncertainty had swept through the souls of the prisoners.

Before the men could collect themselves and make an intelligent analysis, the steel bulkhead doors were slammed closed! Cameron's body involuntarily jumped, like a man experiencing a nightmare. The sudden closing of the doors compressed the air in the compartment with a thud that was sensed rather than heard. It had the feeling of finality to it, as though the entrance to a tomb had been closed and cemented over, while the ones within were too amazed to shriek out. Then, through the blackness of the rattrap, a new sound—one that had not been heard before—penetrated the sensitive eardrums of the prisoners.

Clang! Clang! Clang!
Clang! Clang! Clang!

Metal striking metal! Heavy metallic blows echoed through the vessel in a rhythmic three-at-a-time.

"Can you figure that out, Cam?" whispered Paul.

"They are hammering closed the steel hatches that cover the bulkhead doors!" Cameron whispered back.

Paul knew what was happening, but he felt it necessary to speak to relieve his tension. Everybody else knew the meaning of the metallic hammering. They were penned in now, watertight and airtight! No human hand could or would help them! An oriental enemy who hated them and a friendly navy unaware of their presence were in control of their destinies.

Very few words were spoken. Only those emotion forced out or the whispering of those who thought that they were talking to their own souls penetrated the quiet.

"Goddamn yellow bastards!"

No one this time could even give a smile to Blake's outburst.

"Hail Mary!"

When the doors clanged shut, Sykes twitched. His body felt numb and rigid. He opened his mouth to gasp the foul air, but he found it necessary to breathe rapidly to survive. Sweat flowed freely from his nearly nude form.

I've got to die! he cried to himself. *Will I be blown to pieces or will I suffocate? There is no way out now. Death is near. I am encased in steel. I can't breath. Why must the end be such torture? To go through it, slowly engulfing me and tormenting me and not being able to do a thing to save myself.*

As it became more difficult for him to get adequate air, Sykes felt the vital force of life flicker and wane within him. Moisture beclouded his eyes, and he wanted to scream—to get a release from the pressure within him.

Hold on for one more second, he spoke to himself, *before you cry out. Save your strength; save …your—*

He felt himself going. Far off, he saw the faintest speck of light. What is that, a pinhole in the steel bulkhead? Slowly, it grew larger. A tiny figure of a human being appeared in the opening, as a dark silhouette with a strong light at its rear. The figure moved forward, gradually increasing in size as it approached. It had a long dark robe draped about it, while in one hand it carried a sickle. The other hand was moving. It was beckoning to Sykes; it was motioning for Sykes to come to him! *No! No!* Sykes sobbed, between his noisy and rapid gasps for air. *No! No!*

Something touched his foot in the darkness, and then a human hand was laid on his hip. It patted him in a reassuring way. There was encouragement there. A quiet voice with calm firmness spoke to him from out of the dark.

"Get hold of yourself, old man. Nothing is wrong. They have merely offed the lights."

"We'll never get out of this!" he sobbed. "A torpedo is on the way!"

"Hell no! Those damn sailors of ours couldn't hit a ship standing still, let alone one that's dodging them. They haven't the guts to come near that gun on the deck above. If they had, they would have got this ship months ago.

Sykes quieted down, as though he was getting his disturbed emotions calmed and controlled.

"Nice going," the voice continued.

"But what if they do send a torpedo into us?" Sykes feebly asked.

"Well, hell, what if? It has to hit us first. If it does, it will just blow a hole in her side, and we'll all swim out."

Sykes made a sound. It might have been a chuckle. "Thanks, Cam," he said.

Fear had struck Cameron when he'd heard the metallic clatter of the doors being shut. That fear quickened him like an electric shock with each stroke of the hammer on the metal hatches. As he sensed those hatches dogging down the doors against the bulkhead, so that no one within could ever release them, he felt his life was being squeezed into a smaller and smaller crypt. Each hammer blow forced the sides and top and bottom closer and closer against him. Soon, it would be impossible to even move.

The stifling air distressed him, and his realization of that fact was the little event that saved him from going mad. His mind refused, without Cameron realizing it, to accept defeat. At no time did a man have less in his favor than now, but some little cell demanded that Cameron fight to the end, be aggressive, take the initiative, not lie in one spot huddled up in fear.

Air was the immediate requirement—air to breath—more air! Food, clothes, shelter, Cameron recalled, were the fundamental requirements of man. He had learned recently that water was of even greater importance if man was to survive. It required but a few waterless hours of torrid heat to make a sufferer go mad and his tongue swell to strangle him. Air now showed itself as the most essential requirement for life. To be denied breath for but a few minutes meant disaster.

Well, damn it—an involuntary urge prodded Cameron—do something about it!

His body suddenly straightened up to a sitting position, with his head between two adjacent steel girders that formed part of the deck above. In springing to that posture in the blackness of the rattrap, his head struck the edge of one of the girders. Although it was a stinging blow, the injury was not serious. The result was to sober him from the onrush of hysteria.

Collect yourself, he meditated, *and try to do some rational thinking! Anyhow, the air seems to be clearer up here close to the upper deck. Now let's see,* he told himself, *only a clear mind can act intelligently in an emergency.*

What could happen? In the first place, some sort of alarm would be sounded. They must have sighted or thought they'd sighted a bomber or a warship or a sub. If it had been one of the first two, we should have heard from it before now. So I suppose the chances are in favor of a sub or a pack of subs. This careening of the vessel from side to side gives weight to that suspicion.

Now, what may happen, Cameron continued to ask himself, *if a torpedo hits us? It will strike below the waterline, which is where we are. There is a lot of ship forward of us, but not much aft. A hit forward would probably not injure anyone in this compartment, yet in the space of minutes, we would be thrust high in the air and the prow would begin to sink. We would be dragged down and this would become a rattrap indeed. That's bad!*

Should a hit be made amidships or aft, a lot of POWs would be torn to pieces! Was there such thing as a torpedo dud? Cameron had Never heard of one. *Wouldn't that be a tale to take back home to our navy, if one of its warheads failed to detonate? Maybe if it strikes us here, there will be a hole in the side large enough to get out of—that is, for the fellows still alive; the others would have no interest.*

No, damn it, he reasoned. *That has little possibility! Any sort of a hole like that would be letting the water rush in so fast that we would be swept way from it.* He envisioned the cold, black, salty water that would push you rapidly to the far side and fill the compartment rapidly. The higher you would rise to the surface of the water, the less airspace you would have between the water and the upper deck. A few feet and then a few inches only left to keep your nose dry and then—

What is that horrible sound I hear over there? Cameron asked himself as a human sound of distress reached his ears. The broken silence jarred his senses, and his thoughts were diverted. *Sounds like Sykes,* he spoke inwardly, *just in front of me. Better go over and see what happened. He many need help.*

In the morning, the bulkhead doors were cautiously opened, and the dim, yellow lights again glowed. The sensation from too abrupt a change was strenuous on the emotions of the POWs, who had suffered mental torture for hours. Reactions were not normal. There were some tears, inaudible prayers, and prolonged sighs. Speech was slow in coming. A man choked when he attempted to mutter any words. It was not until a guard screamed to come for the morning rice that any real action or talk was possible.

The next night, someone brushed against Cameron in the darkness of the rattrap. While the few electric bulbs were turned on during daylight, except when an emergency existed, they were always snapped off by the guard immediately after the evening meal. For a POW to get from the inside of the shelf to the passageway, he had to crawl on his hands and knees toward the center of the compartment. It became an acrobatic feat because the men adjacent to the passageway were packed in shoulder to shoulder and made their feelings known in loud and angry voices if a prisoner jabbed a knee into their ribs when he crawled over them.

"Now what's up?" Cameron asked of the form that was passing him. His tone was one of affected anger but had subtle undertones of levity.

"Got to go to the benjo," came the whispered reply. The voice of Blake was readily recognized.

"You'll have a hell of a time convincing the guard to let you past him. Latrine hours are by the clock, not by the necessity."

Blake made no response but clumsily let himself down over the scaffolding and disappeared. Because it was too early to drop off to sleep, Cameron listened for Blake's encounter with the sentry. Light would show at the top of the ladder if the guard opened that door for Blake to leave. Silence continued. No sound of rapping on the door to attract the attention of the guard came to Cameron's ear. *Strange*, he thought. *What has happened to Blake?*

An hour or so later, the sound of a light touch on the uprights of the shelf framework attracted Cameron's attention. That was the way, the only way, a POW prowling around in the dark could identify his berth. He counted the number of uprights with a touch of his hand and then crawled up.

"Couldn't you make it, Blake?" asked Cameron when the bulk of Blake appeared at this head. While he was curious to know what had happened, his speaking to Blake was more for the purpose of letting his colleague know that he was at the right spot and also to keep Blake from crashing into him.

"Aw, I changed my mind," replied Blake, scrambling off in the darkness.

Hours later, Cameron was disturbed by a muffled oath, which awakened him. "Goddamn it, watch where you're going!"

"I gotta get out, I guess," Blake whispered back.

Now what is that fellow up to? Cameron inquired of himself. *Some more of that latrine bluff?* He lay and listened. *It must be close to morning*, he thought. He possessed the feeling of having had a complete night's sleep.

Later, the dim lights were suddenly flashed on. That was the signal for PWOs to wake up. A new day had arrived. The breakfast rice would be ready in a few minutes. Blake strode down the passageway and clambered up. Cameron looked at him carefully but said nothing.

"Did you have a good sleep last night, Blake?" Cameron lightly asked later in the morning. He wanted a clue as to Blake's actions of the night before.

"Petty good," Blake replied with a curt sentence.

"We got through the night without any submarine alarms," continued Cameron in an effort to keep the conversation alive.

"Probably won't have any sub attacks during the nighttime," answered Blake. He was speaking like a typical POW now. There was something stored away in his thoughts that he had to release to show his erudition.

"Yeah? Why not?" One his neighbors entered the dialogue. This was a good moment to satisfy his curiosity as to what Blake referred to or to dispute his statement. Nothing like a good argument. It was dangerous for a POW ever to make a statement. He would always have to defend it.

"I've always known that the best time for subs to attack as either at dusk or dawn," answered Blake.

The argument that followed was lost to Cameron. The "dusk or dawn" mentioned by Blake struck him as important. Somehow or other, those times were related to Blake's actions of the night before. *Why, yes,* Cameron debated with himself. *It was just after the lights were switched off last night that Blake crawled over me. That was dusk outside. Then this morning, just before the lights were turned on, he crawled out again. That was about dawn. What could he have been up to?*

I know. Cameron smiled to himself after several seconds of contemplation. Those two times being the danger periods in his mind, Blake was not going to be caught at a disadvantage if anything happened. He wanted to be close to the ladder in the event of an emergency so as to be the first out of the rattrap. He wanted to be close to the ladder if the Nips opened up the door above for the prisoners to leave. But they would never do that. Instead, they would have a couple of machine guns there, so no one could make a rush and get out. What a tragedy if such a rush did occur? Panic-stricken men would clamber for the exit, heedless of their neighbors' or their own safety. The first to arrive would be trampled to death by the others. No system or orderly departure could be put into effect then, even if the Nips should open a door. It would be too late.

The shock of suddenly realizing what a calamity there might be forced Cameron to burst out with an excited expression. "Paul, we'd be in a hell of a spot here if something did happen."

"What do you mean, Cam? Slow down now. Tell me what you have in mind."

"If disaster struck, every POW still alive would make a rush for the exit. Can you imagine what horror there would be? Fighting, clawing, crazy men trying to get there first!"

"Yes, only too true. That would be a holocaust, even if this compartment wasn't hit."

"It gives me the creeps to think of it."

"There has been no thought or instructions given in what to do in an emergency."

"No, Paul, for the simple reason that the Nips probably don't give a damn what may happen down here—so long as we don't try to crash through a door."

"Probably true, for the same reason that they have not given us any life belts."

"Whether they let us out or not, these POWs will go mad and make a rush if something is not done ahead of time to avoid it."

"What would be proper procedure to empty this rattrap in an emergency, Cam?"

"Well, any sort of system. Just so long as everyone knows what it is and follows it. Let's work something up. We should leave by squads and not all rush at the same time."

"That would be orderly. What sequence of squads?"

"The men in the rear would be the most impatient ones, Paul. They should come out first and on down until those nearest the exit. They should lie quietly on their bunks and leave last."

"I agree with you," Paul admitted. "Why not see each squad and get their reactions."

"It would be better if we went to each one and told them that is the way the Nips ordered it. That would save arguments and a thousand different ideas. Maybe the POWs would get some encouragement out of the fact that the Nips were interested in working out a plan."

"Fine, Cam! Let's tell them a little white lie for their own good. If you crawl over to the shelf and discuss it with the squads, I'll go down below and pass the word to the others."

"Right! But don't let any dumb POW try to change the system," cautioned Cameron. "Each one will try to do it, so that he will have the best advantage for himself."

For the next hour, Cameron and Paul crawled around the compartment, careful in their first statements so as not to unduly excite the POWs, explaining the need for a system and urging each one to follow the plan carefully. One prisoner rushing excitedly for a jump start could easily start a fatal stampede.

For once, some common action was agreed upon. The feeling that the enemy was interested in their welfare gave the POWs some security of mind and willingness to adopt the plan without the usual bickering. More than one prisoner was so appalled at the thought of disaster that they accepted the plan in a daze. Their emotions advanced to such a high pitch that they could find no words to argue the matter!

"Blake," Paul called over across his shelf in a friendly way later in the day," do you still have that watch compass Joe once had?

"Yeah, I got it," returned Blake with little concern.

"What direction are we moving in?" asked Paul.

"North! We got to be going north," affirmed Blake, making no move to get the compass out of his kit.

"How about checking our direction?"

"All right," Blake grumbled as he fumbled for the little instrument. He laid it down on the planking and leaned over close to read the result in the darkness. "Looks like it is pretty much northwest."

"That's interesting," announced Cameron. "Must be headed for Korea. We've been under way long enough to have reached Japan, it seems to me."

"Why not plot our course?" Paul suggested.

"That's impossible," an objector immediately growled.

"Too much steel in this hull to get an accurate reading," cried another one.

"Let's see now," said Cameron, coming to Paul's support. "The compass may be only a cheap affair and may easily be thrown off by the steel ship, but I believe can get some knowledge from it."

"How?"

"Yes, how?"

"Well," returned Cameron, thinking rapidly. "How would this work? Let's get an average estimate on our speed first. We can hit that within reason from the feel of things. Then we can see how long we go in one direction before a turn is made. Plot it roughly on a piece of paper. Each time we swing in a new direction, plot that distance. It will be an interesting game, and we might be able to figure something out."

While Cameron was talking, one POW produced a scrap of paper. Another loaned a pencil stick, and Blake took over control of the compass reading, while Paul kept an eye on his watch, one of the few that still remained among the POWs.

For endless hours, the little group played at the game of navigation. Other prisoners crawled in to observe over their shoulders. The line on the chart grew in a zigzag path but formed a general direction toward the northwest. Suddenly, the needle of the compass wobbled in a peculiar fashion and, after several seconds, came to rest in the opposite direction. Blake picked it up to examine it more closely. He struck it lightly against his hand.

"The needle must have stuck," he said, gently placing it back on the flooring.

"Maybe the steel of the ship threw it off," one of the observers suggested.

"But it is still pointing 180 degrees off," Cameron said. "Why couldn't the vessel have shifted her course that much?"

"Be going back to Taiwan if she did," Blake declared.

"Not by any means," countered Cameron. "We could have gone past Shanghai into the Yellow Sea to avoid interference and are now headed back toward Kyushu. Or don't you remember your geography?"

One morning soon thereafter, a slowing of the ship's engines and a slow movement forward in what felt to be a calm sea gave the men in the hold a feeling of security. Gone were the racing of the engines and the vibration of the vessel. No longer did the careening and lurching of the *Oryoku Maru* shake the prisoners around in the rattrap.

The bulkhead doors were opened to each one's astonishment. Something had happened; a port must have been reached. Now it would be possible to find out how accurate the navigation with the aid of a cheap compass had been.

"Say, Sykes," Cameron impatiently called, "you have the only pair of heavy shoes. How about crawling over to one of the portholes and using a shoe as a hammer to unscrew the latch?"

"Oh, no!" Sykes replied with fear in his voice. "They told us not to touch them or it would go hard with us."

"Now, Sykes, wait a minute. You haven't learned much in the last two years. The only Nip rules you have to comply with are those that they enforce. Let's check up on this one. I venture that they are too busy with their thoughts on many other things to remember about the portholes." Cameron crawled over toward the side of the ship, picking up one of Sykes's shoes on the way. "Let me borrow this a minute," he said. "I want to see where we are and what's doing."

He hammered hard on the latch, using the boot as a tool. Finally, it moved slightly on its screw thread, and Cameron rapidly began to move it around with his hand. The other locking device operated as easily. Many POWs moved up to assist. In a matter of seconds, the circular door was swung back on its hinge.

"We are in harbor, all right," called Cameron gleefully. "And it looks like Japan."

The rush of the other curious POWs swept Cameron aside. Everyone wanted to see the light and smell the fresh air, as well as to learn what was outside. The shoe was used on the adjacent porthole, and others across the compartment were pressed into service as hammers. One of the feelings of security among the prisoners was the safety of numbers. It took either a stupid or courageous POW to assert his initiative and test out the Nipponese reaction. But, by all following suit, they felt that no one individual would be punished. It was easy to sit back and have no responsibility for the first act.

Slowly, the vessel moved through the smooth water toward the pier. The POWs pulled on their clothes and arranged their kits. Of course, they were to disembark here. Orders would surely be sent below soon. But what about safety? The high seas were dangerous, yet a port city might be bombed at any moment. Best to get out of this hold as fast as possible and back on dry land.

It seemed hours to the impatient men before instructions were received to move out. "Squads in rear move out first!" someone called.

What a temptation to slip into the slow-moving column and gain an advantage. Why are they so damn slow? Some fool up front is blocking the whole column because he wants to gaze at the sights! Hurry up before we get caught in a bombing raid!

Climbing the ship's ladder and walking along the deck to the gangplank consumed the last bit of energy. Weeks crowded in a stifling hold with little chance to move one's muscles had played havoc with the prisoners. Their legs failed to respond promptly, and breath was short. The expected joy of finally rushing out onto the pier was not there. The trip was slow and plodding.

"Look behind you, Paul," said Cameron after he had stepped off the inclined gangplank onto the firmness of the pier.

"My God!" Paul replied reverently, staring in amazement.

He watched the prisoners ambling down the gangplank as they leaned heavily on the handrail for support. They were bearded; their wide-open eyes stared straight ahead, while their drooping lower jaws told of their exhaustion. One man stumbled from weakness; another slowly sank to the flooring when his knees gave way under him.

"I've never seen a group of human beings in such misery," Cameron commented, moving on under the rude direction of a guard.

"That sight sort of makes me sick right here," replied Paul, placing a hand on his belly. "First-rate Americans, white men, so beaten down from fear and ruthlessness that there is nothing left of them but an animated shell!"

"I doubt if they can move on to the next stop, unless they have a chance to get a complete rest."

"God bless them!" murmured Paul.

"You're not so much to look at yourself," Cameron chided, relaxing the tension.

Moji! That fact was quickly learned. On Kyushu! The POWs were marched a few hundred yards to an open square beyond the pier shed.

"Uh! Uh!" grunted the guards, motioning for the prisoners to sit down.

Such glorious relaxation! The dangers of the war zone while locked in the black and airless hold of a ship were behind them. Here was the sunshine and the distant blue sky overhead, spotted with blotches of white that shifted with the wind. All around, the fresh and invigorating air softly played on distended nostrils. A man again had elbow room and freedom to shift his body. And the solid, yet soft earth beneath stimulated a tired soul after the restriction of being penned tightly between heavy steel plates.

Quiet relaxation and relief from anxiety restored bodies and tired minds. But a few minutes passed before men began to perk up and look about. There was much that they wanted to learn about. *What sort of place is this Japan? The storybooks tell of it in one light, but the native soldiers encountered in battle and prison camp denies all that.*

War activity was energetic. Across the way, office workers were engaged in a ceremony. They raised a flag, white with a large circle of solid red, and then formed for mass calisthenics. Near the pier, many crates with noisy police dogs had been placed. They must be for shipment to the battlefront. Imagine these little yellow bastards having enough sense to use dogs in combat. Strung along the curb on a street that ended at the wharf rested military trucks and light tanks. Well, good news! The shipping must be limited. Surely that sorely needed equipment had been standing there unused for many a week. The paint showed hard wear from weather; many of the tires were flat; debris from wind and rain had collected on the ground around them. Far in the distance, the wisps of smoke spoke of factories hard at work for the war effort. Behind, on the water in the harbor, which no POW cared to look at, a half dozen freighters rode at anchor. They told the story of the hazards of the sea, for they rested there rotting and rusting. The silhouetted funnels were clean cut against the white sky, with no smoke belching upward. Not even a solitary sailor strode the decks.

Strength and courage returned slowly to the prisoners by reason of their carefree lounging on the ground, removed from the horrors of the unseen and the uncertain.

Expressing a deep sigh and shaking his head, Cameron said to Paul, "This is one of the greatest moments of relief I've ever experienced."

"Those were most difficult days. You can be proud of yourself, Cam, on how well you weathered them."

"Don't let any superficial observations fool you," Cameron apologized with lowered head. "More than once I was on the verge of completely blowing up. I'll never know how I held on that last fraction of a second each time. I had to grit my teeth and grab my body with both hands to restrain myself from leaping up and shrieking out like a madman. There was a feeling within me like I was a balloon with too much air being pumped in."

"Guess we all were pretty much that way," admitted Paul. "The dull ones with no imagination probably came through best because their thoughts of potential disaster were limited. I received great stimulation from my faith. Others no doubt came through because they had something beyond the powers of man to cling to. That sort of thing is a powerful influence and mental relaxer in time of stress."

"I reached the conclusion, Paul, during those terrifying moments, that a man would be sort of a damn fool to ignore those values. But my conscience sort of bothered me. I felt that, by not exercising my belief and confidence when matters were going well, I had no right to call for help when I was in dire need."

Paul looked at Cameron, smiled in his influencing way with a countenance lighted from within, and replied slowly, "Cameron, that is the real value of faith. You can kick it around and scoff at it when you do not need it. But in an emergency, it is there waiting patiently for you to grasp it. It is the one thing in life that never fails you or lets you down regardless of what your attitude has been before."

"You make it sound very impressive, Paul."

"I suggest that you do something about it then. There are two important steps that you should follow. However, be sure to express your gratitude afterward, just as you would thank any man for a favor bestowed on you. That is just plain courtesy, as a matter of fact, but of great importance for permanency. The other matter for one to remember is that he has an obligation to his fellow man. If one has found an answer to his problems, he should pass on that course of conduct to others. There is plenty for all. It does not matter only in prison camp, where there is only a limited supply of even the basic fundamentals."

"Well, Paul, why haven't you enlarged upon this before? We've been close together for years in this mess, and I've heard you mention these matters only in a casual way once or twice."

To reply to that gave Paul no concern, as he said confidently, "There are, of course, two ways of handling that. One is to shout it from the housetops. But with practical men, busy with the realism of this world, such action is unimpressive. Actually, that might have the opposite effect from what was honestly intended. A more subtle procedure will give far better results."

"Sort of like a propaganda program." Cameron laughed.

"Well." Paul smiled in return. "That is hardly the proper term. The real thing is that the spark must be self-generated in a man's breast. There must be a real need for something beyond himself to bring him aid and comfort and to a fuller life."

"And a life hereafter?"

"You are going too fast. Consider it only from a purely selfish standpoint at first. One should ask himself, being constituted as the human animal he is, 'What can I get out of it? What good will it do me?' If he sees a real value in it for him, the first difficult step has been taken. From then on, it races forward with rapidity. The 'hereafter' angle you mention will solve itself in due course. The whole matter is far too complex to grasp at one sitting. Take it step by step. It'll be more fun that way—always something greater just ahead, waiting for you when you are ready for it. You can't expect to be a general your first day in the army, you know."

At that moment, their intimate conversation was disturbed. The POWs at the edge of the group were being motioned up. Progressively, the others took like action. Kits were slung. Tenko, the inevitable tenko, was next. Following a short march to the railroad siding, the men clambered into waiting coaches with drawn blinds.

Sometime later, the train drew up before a fair-sized depot, and the command to line up on the platform was sent through the cars.

"Big doings!" announced Blake. "What's next, I wonder."

"Can't see much here in front of the station," his neighbor commented. "Maybe the name of the berg is on the end of the building, and we can find out what it is when we march out."

"Hey, Cam," called Blake with impatience, "where the hell are we, do you know?"

"This is Beppu!" Cameron replied. "I was here once before. It's a hot springs resort town. See those buildings back up on the hill there?"

"Jeez! You mean the Nips have huge places like that?" Scattered among the distant hills were modern-looking hotels, and their presence in the Orient was amazing to Blake.

"Those are the first-class hotels that the Occidentals and wealthy Nips use. I had a weekend in that white one with the red-peaked roof."

"Do you think they're going to put us up in a place like that?" Blake asked with enthusiasm.

"I rather doubt it," returned Cameron. "There are dozens of inns packed in throughout the city. We'll probably go there. You'll find them more comfortable than any place you've been in since the campaign started."

Another tenko occurred, followed by a march down the main street; a turn into a narrow lane, which carried the group over a short but high-arched bridge; and a halt before a three-story frame building squeezed in between a profusion of like structures. The head of the column was turned at the entrance. Shoes were ordered removed and stored on the tiny porch.

For the next half hour, the prisoners lived in a jubilant daze. Each of the many rooms that opened off from diverging halls and narrow porches had a sign in front. It told in Japanese characters the number of occupants it would hold. One by one, the rooms were filled as the guard at the head of the column peeled off the proper number and motioned them inside.

The flooring was soft straw matting; there were ample, luxurious downy quilts to sleep on and under. The walls of the rooms slid back and opened up to the great world outside.

"Look at the flimsy way this is built," scoffed Blake as he inspected the narrow strips of light wood that made the framework of the walls. "Why, it's nothing but paper," he called, pushing a finger against a panel. It went through and left a gaping hole where he had experimented.

"What do you know about that," answered a curious POW, who likewise pushed a heavy hand against the paper panel to satisfy himself. Another tear was the result.

"You must be very careful," cautioned Cameron. "These Nip houses are the flimsiest things. Any rough handling will tear them to pieces."

"What a mess if a fire should start," observed Blake. "The whole town would go in a few minutes!"

"That is true," Cameron agreed. "Fire is about the most frightening thing the Nips have to contend with. Notice outside how every house has a tile roof. You may wonder how that weight can be supported by such flimsy understructure. But they use tile so that any sparks falling down will not set the house afire."

Blake laughed aloud. "Imagine one bomb, just one little tiny American bomb!"

Cameron laughed back. The thought was indeed interesting.

There was one benjo on each floor, wholly inadequate when the inn was filled to capacity. It was enclosed for privacy and consisted of a rectangular hole in the floor over which a native squatted. But the benjos here had an added touch, a thing of beauty. The sides of the rectangle were bordered with a narrow framework of blue porcelain, while an upright of the same material stood at an end for protection against a careless person. The opening went straight down to the ground, and the fumes rising from below were adequate to make a man hurry in his task and depart.

Nearby, a washbasin with a single faucet completed the plumbing facilities on each floor. There was a rush for water. Men wanted to feel the cool comfort after weeks of a splash over their faces and a wash of their soiled hands. Maybe, later, when all had had that privilege, a man could get a shave. At least that might be the accepted thought among normal men. But not among POWs!

The first four men to get there, all that could cluster about the bowl at one time, had the faucet wide open and were splashing water all over their nude bodies. The famous unsung POW anthem prevailed: "I've got mine; the hell with you!"

Ire rose in those waiting behind. Angry words were called. Physical encounter was but seconds away.

However, the forthcoming fray was delayed by the arrival of a guard. He howled and growled, pointing to the growing pool of water on the floor. His fist swung four times, and four hard blows were rained on the culprits.

Three times a day, rice was served to the prisoners. The dining room was small, and the men ate in relays. The low floor tables were intended for natives accustomed to kneeling, but to an inexperienced Occidental that posture grew painful after several minutes.

Twice during their stay, the POWs were permitted a hot bath. In a far wing of the inn, a small pool had been built from which hot water bubbled. A man would splash water over himself after dipping it out of the tank with a cup. If he was fortunate to have any soap, that process was next. Then came more splashing and rubbing until time was called and the next group came in.

On Taiwan, the guards had been well indoctrinated by Wild Bull and Evil Eye in the refinements of brutal and ruthless treatment toward the hated occidental prisoners of war. Even in Japan, well removed from that source of barbarism, the POWs were still hounded by Taiwanese guards. The Kempeitai, the Japanese military police of Beppu, had jurisdiction within their area, and consequently were overseeing the operation of transferring the prisoners' camp through their district. They strolled about the inn but left the guarding of the prisoners to the troops from Taiwan.

One day when a POW had incurred the wrath of one of the guards, the Nipponese proceeded to bop the hapless man unmercifully. That had been the accustomed procedure for a very long time, and no reason occurred to the sentry for any different action. But this time, one of the Kempeitai military policemen wandered past while the punishment was being administered. He said nothing but turned about and flew down the stairway. No one gave any particular thought to the matter. Yet within the space of half an hour, all the Taiwanese guards were called from the inn, never to be seen again by the POWs.

From then on, the military police guarded the doors of the inn and appeared within only when taking tenko twice a day. The change was a major event in the lives of the prisoners. Conversation on the subject carried on for a long time thereafter. Now they were alone to enjoy the comfort of the inn, to stroll about the building at will. The constant fear of running afoul of an antagonistic guard was gone. The furtiveness of life, important once, became a thing of the past.

Early November had crept up. It was 1944. Something of major strategic importance had happened last month and might still be going on. That much was certain to every POW. The quick transfer of the camp to Japan, even though there was a two weeks' delay at Keelung, the attacks by the American Navy, and perhaps even the change in treatment here at Beppu all pointed to a major action going on somewhere.

Meanwhile, there was joy to be had at Beppu. Even if one could not leave the inn, there was plenty to be seen out beyond. In one direction lay the beautiful hills with hotels of different hues tucked away between foliage and promontories. Closer in, a massive statue of Buddha attracted attention. He sat silently with his knees curled up, looking out over the town and meditating. Northward stretched the Inland Sea, peaceful and calm, smooth and alluring. An antique cruiser came and went. A training ship, everyone agree. Twice a day, the ferry for Shikoku steamed in and out amid whistle blasts and commotion throughout the town. Around to the south, the hills rose abruptly and high. Where they met the water, a railroad track wound around the contour.

Across the street the flat roof of a building, originally built as a municipal bathhouse but now used for housing, gave the prisoners a sight of native life in congested surroundings. Mothers scoured their babies here, while older children played at their games. An old man cooked over a charcoal burner, and a housewife dabbled in a garden. She had hauled dirt up from below and outlined it with small boulders. Elsewhere on the roof, ropes sagged under the multicolored clothing of the occupants as it dried in the sun. Seaward, but adjacent to the inn, flowed a small stream. The tide rose and fell and gave the POWs many a happy hour watching the rush of the water upward and then downward. What mystified the Americans was the sanitary condition of the stream. Not an empty tin can nor a broken bottle or debris of any sort was ever tossed into the water.

On the far side of the brook, a family conducted a dying business in the rear room of their tiny home. Yards of material changed color and design and were suspended on high ropes. When the air raid alarms sounded, work stopped. The old man and his wife changed into what passed as uniforms, doffed light helmets, and hurried off to their new tasks.

There were no young men anywhere in the town. All must be away fighting the detested white men, a fight from which many would return encased in little white cubicle boxes.

"How the hell can these Nips fight a war on a shoestring like they do?" inquired Blake of no one in particular.

"They don't need all the fanfare and impedimenta like we do. One soldier, one uniform. They keep them darned and patched until none of the original material is left. They get replacements from the casualties." Cameron was speaking close to the truth.

"Anyhow," Sykes broke in, "they have finally changed our treatment for something more decent. I knew they would."

"Yeah?" questioned the unconvinced Blake. "All I want to do is get my hands on those little yellow bastards from Taiwan someday. I'll wring their damn necks—especially Horse Face!"

Cameron laughed. "I had a chance to talk with Fish Face before he was kicked out of the inn. He was a tough little rat and deserves plenty of punishment. But he broke down one day and wanted to talk. He was frightened about going back on the *Oryoku Maru*. The trip up here had frightened them almost as much as us. So I took a chance and used my best Nip talk on him. He blabbered a lot because he was scared. I gave him a note to take back to the other POWs on Taiwan. He promised he would get it to them. It was to get word to some of our people where we were in case we disappeared from this point on."

"I hope the damn *Oryoku Maru* sinks with that hyena," growled Blake. What a forecast Blake unknowingly uttered!

Speculation on where they would be sent next consumed the thoughts of the POWs. When all the answers were collected, there remained no territory under Nipponese control that had not been mentioned. Cool nights, when the prisoners were wrapped up in warm and soft quilts, was the time for meditation. Then a man's thoughts were his own, unmolested by the whims and antagonisms of his neighbors. That was probably the most enjoyable period of all, quiet comfort in the darkness before slipping off into sleep.

In time, information on the new destination reached the inn. The prisoners had been told that they were awaiting the Nipponese detachment that was to escort them. But to where? They would be told in the proper time. So when a commotion was heard in the front street, the POWs rushed to the windows to see what it was.

A company of troops marched down to the front entrance of the inn and halted. The soldiers made a better impression from their appearance and soldiership than any other troops the POWs had seen. They wore heavy woolen uniforms and carried blanket rolls.

"Umm," pondered Paul as he watched them maneuvering below, "my guess is that they have come from either Manchukuo or Hokkaido. We know that they have been at least a week on the way, and they are wearing winter uniforms."

"That is better than a guess," Cameron confirmed in part. "But I believe we can narrow it down further."

"How so, Cam?"

"Well, the heavy uniforms undoubtedly mean a cold climate. Your two guesses there could not be improved upon. Yet I read something more into what we're seeing. They appear to be well-trained troops, probably regulars, or a long time in the service, which is the same thing. My hunch is that, because the Army of Manchukuo is undoubtedly the pride and joy of the empire and is being readied for the last stand, these fine-appearing soldiers are a part of that command. I can't imagine any troops left in Hokkaido as well trained as these. All they need up there at this stage of the campaign is some home guards."

"So then we're bound for the really cold country, you feel?"

"That is my best estimate from very limited information."

On the following morning, the prisoners were ordered to prepare for departure. There was the expected scramble to find one's own shoes. The first POWs to reach the porch where they were stored stirred them up. Subsequent ones added to the confusion. No one had any consideration for the others. It was fortunate if a POW had thought to tie his two shoes together. At least he would find both of them at the same time.

The guards were patient. They stood quietly in the street, observing the scramble and the tossing briskly aside of any shoe a man picked up and discovered was not his. The procedure was different than had many times been observed by the POWs, when the enemy soldiers had occasion to stack their shoes or clogs in a common place. Then, each pair was laid down in a particular spot that the owner could identify, and no other soldier would even think of disturbing them.

The same train ride back to Moji occurred, followed by a transfer to other coaches and a further trip to Fukuoka. At mealtime, by prearrangement, the train stopped at a depot, and lunches were put aboard for each prisoner. Eyes opened wide in astonishment at the luxury of the lunch served. It came in a box made of thinly shaved wood with a lid and a removable tray. Inside was a meal of unbelievable quantity and variety—hot rice, fried fish, pickled vegetables, a piece of a sweet.

"It's about time these Nips got wise to themselves," declared Blake, "and began to treat us decently. This war must be drawing to a close, and they know it."

"I hope you are right, Blake," Cameron said. "But this lunch procedure is just the routine way here. They use it instead of dining cars. Nevertheless, there has been a change toward better treatment, now that we are out of the clutches of the Taiwanese crowd."

That night, the POWs took the ferry across the straight for Fusan on the southeast coast of Korea. For the first time on a sea voyage, they were issued life belts and instructed in their use. When they were ready to set sail, orders were given to don the overcoats that had been issued at the pier and any extra clothes one might have. Put on the life belt and wear it constantly. It would be cold, mighty cold, if one were dumped into the sea.

"Hear that?" Blake cried, shortly after the ship sailed.

"Sounds like bombing. No mistake about that," Cameron authoritatively confirmed. "And it is the port we just left."

"Close call," said Paul. "We were fortunate to have gotten away just before it happened."

"But they will hit us next," cried Sykes in a state of alarm. "They can't help seeing a big boat like this nearby."

"I doubt if our fliers will consider this ferryboat of any particular importance," Cameron suggested. He raised a hand where only Paul could see it. There were two fingers crossed. "Those pilots get a mission and maybe a secondary one. I doubt if a stray ferryboat would be included when they have to come so far. Of course, they are out for big game, not a handful of civilian passengers."

From the looks of Fusan, it had taken at least one load of bombs. The prisoners did not linger long there but were hustled onto a waiting train, which started for the north.

"There it is again," declared Sykes. "We are being pursued it seems."

"Yeah," agreed Blake. "They're bombing Fusan. And we just got away in time."

"That makes the seconds count." Cameron laughed. "Any of you superstitious people can now worry about the third time being unlucky. For myself, I'm going to sleep." He leaned back in the coach seat and closed his eyes, hoping that the jostling of the train, the small cramped seat in which he and three others were crowded, and the increasing chill in the air would not keep him awake.

For three days and nights, discomfort, assuaged by spectacular sights, filled the prisoners' time. The men, crowded into small seats, endured the increasingly cold weather and the badly regulated heat from the engine that sometimes made the coaches unendurably hot but too frequently rendered them icy cold. They suffered the parading through the train of pompous military police from each district and devoured the cold lunches distributed from the railroad depots, where they had been stacked for hours on the platform. All these factors contributed to a life of misery. Yet misery could be complained of only in a superficial way when it was compared with earlier experiences of downright fear and uncertainty.

In Fusan, at the far end of a spur line, the train came to a bucking halt at a tiny community that might have been the Texas panhandle in mid-January. Crates and boxes that had filled the vestibule of the coaches on departure spewed forth their contents from time to time when Nipponese guards had slashed away the bindings. Gray flannel shirts confiscated from the Indian Army, British woolen uniforms from Hong Kong, and socks and silk-wool long underwear issued to Nipponese troops in cold climates were gratefully accepted. The new duds replaced cotton khaki uniforms worn since Bataan and Corregidor and long since turned to rags.

The POWs stumbled from the train, happy for the opportunity to stretch their cramped muscles and lined up for tenko. Outside, tiny flakes of snow swirled in a nearly horizontal direction from the effects of the high winds romping through mountain passes. The natives bustled about their winter tasks. The men were garbed in white robes and wearing high hats, white and of a truncated cone design. All of this, along with the many solid occidental type buildings in this distant oriental community presented views that would intrigue any tourist!

"Now where the hell are we?" asked Blake, squirming in his heavy clothes, several sizes too small.

"There is the station sign, but it has been painted out. Can you still make out the old letters? They're in English." Cameron nodded his head toward a small board nailed horizontally on an upright.

"Chang Chia Tun!"

There was a march of one kilometer through the little village and beyond to the wire fence that enclosed a large and substantial Russian-constructed barracks. In the open compound, the POWs were arranged by name after the confusion of shuffling about. A smart-appearing enemy lieutenant arrived, holding, with difficulty, in his hand posters that fluttered in the stout winter wind.

"I will call the roll," he announced in English without the least trace of an accent. The astonishment on the faces of the prisoners was apparent to him, and with a smile that had a touch of a sneer, he explained, "I am a graduate of Duke University."

Name by name, he meticulously called the roll, requiring the prisoners to remain standing in the zero-degree temperature and on frozen ground. Guards strode by, and any movement by a POW trying to stir up his blood circulation was a signal for reprimand. Such lack of attention was discourteous to the representative of his imperial majesty!

Further ceremonies were in order, following the roll check. A lumbering, stocky colonel, mustached and limping, strode out in front. Two guards quickly brought forward a table. A third man swung a chair into place. "Gimpy"—the nickname was inevitably and unanimously prescribed—placed one foot on the chair and hesitated because it rocked under his weight.

The American-educated lieutenant, with formality and courtesy, moved forward and offered an arm to his superior as a measure of safety. The POWs needed some comic relief, and a resounding fall on the hard ground by the colonel would serve that purpose well. However, Gimpy awkwardly stepped from the wobbly chair to the firm footing of the table without mishap.

His address consumed many minutes as he harangued the prisoners in the same manner that his predecessors had done at previous camps. At the end of his tirade, while he was descending from his dais, Old Joe crumbled to the ground where he had been standing at rigid attention for so long. Like a man shot in ranks, another POW repeated the action. The commotion attracted the attention of the lieutenant, who ordered adjacent POWs to carry the two men into the barracks.

Doc had sidled over to Joe and to the other prisoner on the ground.

"What's the dope, Doc?" Cameron called to him after he straightened up from his quick survey.

"Malaria!" Doc replied.

"Up here in the frigid zone?"

"Yes," answered Doc. "A sudden change in climate will often cause a recurrence."

"That's a hell of a thing to look forward to," cried Cameron with a grin of embarrassment at finding himself enmeshed in an inextricable situation.

Getting settled in the new barracks proceeded like that on many former occasions. The prisoners filed in and were peeled off by a guard to the capacity of the room. The barracks had two floors. Down the center of each ran a hall onto that opened into the squad rooms. These rooms were closed in on three sides only, the hall end having a railing that separated it from the hall. On the opposite side were two large windows divided into small panels of glass. Between the windows stood a strange object.

"Now what in the hell is that thing?" inquired Blake when he had tossed his kit down on his cot. "It must be a stove."

"That's a *pachika*," answered Sykes. "I was talking with one of the guards while we were standing in column."

"Looks like a pretty good gadget," Cameron announced from a squatting position in front of the stove. He had opened the firebox and peered in. "Made of fireclay," he explained. "Just a huge cylinder of metal to hold the fireclay in place. The heat from the firebox gradually raises the temperature of the sides, and that throws the heat out into the room."

"Don't see how one stove, even though it is about eight feet high, is going to keep this whole room warm," complained Blake. "This weather up here gets awful cold and stays that way all winter."

"It will probably work," consoled Paul. "This is an old Russian barracks, built for their own troops before the Nips came in. I imagine they knew how much heat was needed."

"Wonder if they're going to force us to labor up here," grumbled Blake.

"Doubt if there will be any work," Cameron answered, "now that winter has set in. What do you think, Paul?"

"I agree with you," he replied. "We are in the middle of an agricultural district, and it is frozen up until spring. There are no mines hereabouts to shove us into and no industry, so far as I can see."

"I'd sure like to be sure of it," said Blake, making himself comfortable on his cot. "But I'm afraid they'll dig something up to make slaves of us."

"This entire trip makes me believe that the Nips have change our treatment for the better."

Sykes was not looked on as an optimist by his remark. An entirely different feeling passed through most of his listeners, who were stirred by the belief that Sykes too often sided with the Nips.

Each day saw the temperature fall lower, and that was frightening to many a POW. For years many of them had been serving in warm climates, intentionally influencing the selection of the locations to which they might to assigned. Now, the prospect of a winter in bitter weather filled them with fright. Had not even Gimpy warned them to be careful and follow the instructions of the authorities who, over a period of years, had grown to learn of the treachery of subzero weather?

Happily, a more suitable overcoat was distributed during the first week. "Bond Street special," cried a POW gleefully as he tried on for size the garment handed him.

"They could be camel's hair," Sykes observed, stroking the brown nap.

"You don't look very carefully," Blake complained. "It's made out of small cuttings, and there isn't hair on any of them."

"Probably made out of scraps that couldn't be used for any other purpose," Cameron suggested. "Yet I'll bet it's warm."

"Nice fuzzy collar." Blake laughed. "Dog!"

Everyone agreed with him.

"But you haven't seen half of it yet." Cameron smiled. "Take a look what they use for lining over the shoulders."

"I'll be damned!" declared Blake, turning his coat inside out to investigate. "Pink crepe paper!"

"I know that will be warm," Paul stated. "But you can't afford to get it wet."

"We'll have no moisture here for months," stated Cameron. "It's too cold for snow. We're in for a nice frigid winter if there ever was one."

Prisoners bustled about pasting paper around the sides of the window sashes, which were built double with a foot of space between the inner and outer ones. No fresh air fiend would dare to open them. Sheets, shelter halves, or whatever could be spared were hung up to retard from a man's cot any breeze that might blow through the glass panes. From a pile of coal near the kitchen, containers in the rooms were filled to overflowing. The pachikas must roar constantly. But the guards quickly and firmly settled that. Bank the fire at night, stir it up, and add fresh coal in the morning. POWs with a fear of freezing grumbled loudly. Yet after a night or two, they found out that the heat from the fireclay lasted many hours, and sleeping was much more comfortable in a temperature less than red-hot.

During the day, when the sun was high, the courageous ones took their exercise around the inside of the wire fence. One hundred and ten steps down, one hundred and fifteen across, and then back to the starting point. Yet there were many who would never venture outside the building except when forced out by Nipponese bayonets.

One morning before breakfast, Cameron slipped into his overcoat and pulled over his head the knitted woolen helmet that had been issued to him.

"Where the hell are you going?" demanded Blake in amazement.

"I'm going to test out this cold," Cameron laughingly replied. "Just to find out what it is really like early in the morning."

"Oh, tough guy!" Blake cackled as Cameron strode down the open hallway.

Within the space of five minutes, Cameron came stomping back. On the inside of each eye, where the tears had accumulated, was a frozen cluster the size of a marble.

"You satisfied?" asked Blake.

"Wow!" cried Cameron hurrying to the stove. "That is really cold! Couldn't even make a full swing around the compound. These light shoes are too thin to plant down on that cold ground very often."

"I would think so," commented Paul. "Look what the guards wear, high fur-lined boots."

"Well, here is the cornmeal ready," said Cameron. "Let's pitch in."

Cornmeal, millet, potatoes, and soya beans comprised the diet now. The camp lay far north of the rice belt. With the ingenuity of many minds, the various combinations of those few commodities were concocted into many varieties of tasty dishes. They just had to give us heavier food up in this frigid zone, the POWs agreed, to keep us alive.

"Outside of the cold," Sykes meditated aloud to his companions lolling around the room, "this is the best camp we have had."

"They're sure feeding us better," Blake concurred with reservations. "Only there is no damn reason why they can't let us have meat."

"You know what the Nip officer said at Beppu," O'Reilly reminded him. O'Reilly, tall, bald, lean, and cadaverous, possessed a quick tongue that rolled off witty remarks at the most unexpected times, producing belly laughs when they were most needed. "When you complained to him about not getting enough food, he retorted, 'If they fed you any more, you would want women.'"

Why the others laughed at that observation, probably none of them could say if asked. It was a truism that no POW, undernourished and suppressed, ever entertained a thought of a woman, let alone gave voice to the subject. Ribaldry and off-color stories, so prevalent when men normally gather together, had no place under deprived loving conditions.

"Everybody has a nice warm bed," added Paul, "not like that winter at Karenko."

"So far, they haven't been able to find any work for us," Blake announced, uncertain of the future, however.

"Somebody is going to have to take over the job of administrator," Paul reminded his friends, looking slyly at Cameron.

Since the new camp had been organized, the Nipponese themselves dealt directly with the squad leaders. That circumstance could not be expected to continue, now that the authorities had a camp routine established.

Cameron saw Paul's glance and realized its meaning. While he had no objection to performing those duties as his contribution to the common welfare, he did not propose to be saddled with that task without at least some lightly stated objection. "How about you, Sykes?" he called across the room. "That would be a fine job for you."

On one occasion, Sykes had raised his hand to attract the attention of the Nipponese lieutenant when that official was selecting squad leaders. Cameron's remark at any other time could have been a nasty dig, but he explained the situation before Sykes had a chance to reply. "You know, conditions are not like they were once. No more brutality, no bopping—"

"And a hot bath once a week," O'Reilly cut in, laughing in his breezy manner.

"The job," Cameron continued, "would have none of the hazards it once had. In fact, by pushing with a bit of force, we could easily get the upper hand with this young and dumb lieutenant who runs the camp, now that Gimpy and his staff have gone to Mukden."

"It may be the very moment for you to take on the job, Cam," Paul pressed his point, "for the very reason that we finally do have a chance to make demands."

"I vote for Cam," muttered Blake in an impressive, short statement.

"I'm sure all the squad leaders will approve," Paul said, clinching his point. There was lithe question of that accord, but Paul knew that his announcing the fact would leave little argument left to ratify Cameron's position. "You can come out in the open with your knowledge of the Jap language, now."

Cameron remained silent. There was no reason he should not take on the burden, but he now felt chagrined at having suggested that Sykes take over the task. He knew that Sykes would have welcomed the chance to be intermediary between the POWs and the authorities. Now, poor Sykes had been unceremoniously denied consideration, and Cameron felt the pangs of conscience at having gotten in his way.

It was but a few days later when great news broke and excited all the POWs. One bright-eyed prisoner, prowling around the trash pile in the customary manner of POWs—nothing ever escaped their vigilance—discovered a small tin can. It was obviously of American manufacture, and that meant but one thing to all the prisoners. Red

Cross food packages were somewhere in the vicinity, and the guards were consuming that food!

When the encouraging news reached Cameron, who had been delegated administrator upon the recommendation of the squad chiefs, he hesitated only long enough to plan his course of action. He boldly walked over to the guardhouse, where the lieutenant maintained his offices.

Cameron ignored the sentry and spoke over his shoulder to the sergeant seated behind him.

"The lieutenant," he began in the vernacular, "has appointed me official for the camp, as you probably know. I am to take up matters with him. Will you inform him that I am here to talk about things he wants to know?" Cameron stretched his authority slightly, but this was the time to set a precedent.

The sergeant looked at Cameron in amazement. He was caught in a position where he could not make the customary decision expected of a noncommissioned officer in his imperial majesty's army. Having been addressed in his own language, he felt more inclined to promptly agree with Cameron. He rose without any reply and motioned for the American to follow him into the lieutenant's office.

First hurdle overcome without mishap, Cameron said to himself with encouragement.

While the American stood silently in the open doorway, the sergeant meticulously explained that the prisoner wished to have an audience with the camp commander. Before the official could make a reply, Cameron stepped into the office, saluted and spoke.

"Captain," he began in the officer's own language. His tone was impressive. *No kowtowing now. Meet him as an equal. Stand on your dignity, but take care not to inflame him by acting superior.* Cameron carefully used the word *captain*, as that was the courteous mode of address to a commander, though his rank might actually be a lesser one. "I wish to make my first report to you."

The young lieutenant, inexperienced in the ways of POWs and taken aback by the seniority of Cameron, sat back in his chair, rubbed a hand nervously over his close-shave head, and nodded for Cameron to proceed.

"Everything is going smoothly in the barracks, and you have made the prisoners comfortable."

"Thank you! Thank you!" cried the young officer, beaming satisfaction on his accomplishment. He was thinking of the colonel and the standing he would have in the eyes of his superior if matters went smoothly at the camp.

Cameron sensed that feeling and would not fail to take proper advantage of it when the occasion arose. "Undoubtedly, the American Red Cross has by now, through the kindness of the Nipponese Army, been able to send us some food supplies. Those are only for prisoners, as you know, just as your Red Cross sends similar packages to internees in the United States. We would like to help you distribute them to the POWs, maybe carry them from the railroad station and unbox them."

Cameron had talked with such assurance and a touch of domination that the flabbergasted lieutenant could not deny the truth of his inference. Nevertheless, he knew that he could not concede the point on his own authority. So he stuttered his reply. "Uh, yes! Red Cross food. I will take the matter up at once with the base camp at Mukden. There will be an answer in two or three days."

Drop the subject there, Cameron told himself. *Nothing can be gained by further argument. Other help we need*, he quickly ran over in his mind, *is a dentist*. But that would also have to be a request to the colonel, old Gimpy, and only one thing at a time can be expected. *If he gets a letter asking for two things, he will be floundered*, Cameron told himself. *Save all that for the next time, after the food matter has been settled. Otherwise, bring up anything the lieutenant can handle here locally.*

"The hot bath once a week is very enjoyable and healthy."

Again, the camp commander beamed and nodded.

"I'll have some POWs run the boiler, if you agree, so we can bathe twice a week."

"But, that will take more coal," the lieutenant countered, "and I am allowed only just so much."

"Ah, we understand. We will not use any more coal, just the same amount. The extra coal for the hot water we will get by saving it from the heaters in the barracks." Cameron knew he was lying, and he also knew he was on dangerous ground. The lieutenant might insist the POWs reduce the use of coal in the pachikas rather than transfer it for use at the bathhouse. However, he was willing to risk that the stupidity of the lieutenant would not pick that point up. Cameron also knew that, if the POWs could get freer access to the coal pile, it would be possible to use it fairly much at will.

"That will be all right," the lieutenant agreed.

"Now, we can help you some more," continued Cameron. "You keep one of the Nipponese guards at the coal pile all day. He gets very cold standing there. I will arrange for a POW guard and set certain hours to draw coal. He will be on duty at those times, and I will make him keep a record of the amount taken away." *Even the most stupid POW,* thought Cameron, *can keep a record if I tell him ahead of time how much coal he must show.*

"I think that is fine idea," said the officer.

"Very well then. Suppose we start tomorrow morning. If you tell your sergeant that he need send no sentry there any more, we will take over the responsibility for you."

The lieutenant nodded acquiescence.

Cameron very properly saluted and hastily departed.

That procedure, instituted by Cameron, became the criterion for the future.

Yet in prison camp, where no direction or control of prisoners existed, discretion was not always one of the virtues of the captured. Like water in a sieve, many of the men discarded any centralized effort to deal with the authorities and attempted to seek personal favors and preferment. After seeking advice from the more substantial squad leaders, Cameron's efforts were making strides forward for the greater comfort and contentment of the camp. Red Cross supplies in limited quantities were distributed, all the coal the prisoners could use became available under the new procedure, hot water for tea became a reality, heavy socks were issued, precious soap became available, a distribution of mail was arranged for, and a POW letter was authorized to be sent home.

But impatient men under stress could not or would not control themselves and take advantage of a circumstance that was working in their favor.

They noticed that Cameron had ready access to the camp commander and that he seemed to have little difficulty in gaining his point. *Why can't I do the same?* many a POW asked himself. *Cameron never gets bopped when he approached the lieutenant*, they told themselves. *There is no reason to think that I would either*, they thought.

So one after another, the recalcitrant ones stopped the camp commander whenever they found him in the compound. Individual wants were expressed without any relation to what was best to the group as a whole. One POW requested to change his overcoat for a larger size, another wanted a pair of warm boots such as the guards wore, and another thought that he should have more soap.

The attitude of the camp commander changed toward Cameron, who noticed that he was not as well received as he had been on earlier occasions. In spite of Cameron's pleas through the squad chiefs for other POWs to avoid bothering the lieutenant, he received very little cooperation. Individual POWs acted ugly when spoken to. "I've got as many rights as anyone," they replied. *What you mean to say is to hell with the rest of the camp*, was the usual unspoken rejoinder.

Associated with the change of attitude of the camp commander and the gradual loss of the improved conditions the POWs had enjoyed, appeared those two fearsome specters of forced labor and ruthless treatment. The change unfolded slowly but relentlessly. Guards no longer showed a friendly curiosity toward the occidental way of life. Carelessness of the prisoners toward observation of the regulations brought quick retribution from sentries who prowled about the barracks seeking violations. The greater freedom of action once enjoyed by the prisoners grew more restricted daily.

"Captain," Cameron said during a conversation with the camp commander, "the prisoners are behaving very well in the barracks. I thought it would be important to inform you of that, because it would save the Nipponese soldiers lots of bother if they could reduce their inspections to once a day."

"What do you mean?" asked the lieutenant in an obvious effort to avoid accepting the suggestion.

"As it is now, the soldiers have to spend much of their available time going through the barracks. Because the POWs are so well behaved, I thought maybe so many inspections might be unnecessary. Then again, because so many guards come into the barracks, it makes the POWs jump up and salute many times. They all want to follow the regulations," continued Cameron, knowing full well that only fear of reprisal ever made a POW comply with an enemy order. "But they may make a mistake when it happens so often. Then that is very embarrassing."

The camp commander listened attentively while the American made his plea, but he quickly discarded any hope that the American might have. "It is the order from the colonel at Mukden."

"Very well!" Cameron replied, rendering a salute in preparation for his departure from the lieutenant's office.

"One minute," said the Nipponese, rising from his chair in nervous dignity. "Soon spring will come. Manchukuo has little food. It will be best if POWs raise their own farm produce so they can be well fed. We can get plenty of land all around here. That is all."

The prompt dismissal retarded any objection being raised by Cameron at the moment. The blow had fallen. His colleagues would accept that decision most reluctantly.

But spring and the breaking of ground for planting were far away, both in time and events. However, one day, the camp commander sent for Cameron, who felt at once that something new was astir. He ran over in his mind all the possible subjects that might be discussed, but none of them seemed to be sufficiently important at the moment for a hurried conference.

"Have you got any ideas, Paul," Cameron asked the older officer, "what the slant eye may have up his sleeve?"

Paul was thoughtful for a moment, engrossed in thought, before he replied. "Cam, I'm no good to you. Sort of caught me by surprise.

There seems to be nothing to discuss, unless the lieutenant has new instructions from Mukden."

"That's what I'm afraid of," admitted Cameron, shaking his head. "I don't like to get caught flat-footed, without knowing what he has on his mind. I have found that, if I do not have an argument ready, he is likely to issue orders before I can get him to change his mind."

"Oh, he probably wants to line up our forced labor," grumbled Blake, who had overheard the dialogue.

"It's rather early to make plans for ground breaking, and that seems to be the only possible sort of labor he can find for us."

"Do your best, Cam," cautioned Paul, "as we all know you will, to keep the camp from slave labor. It will play havoc with the morale of the POWs, even though they have had a warning that it is coming."

"Well, I have to get going," called Cameron, jumping to his feet. "I've kept the lieutenant waiting too long now, and I might find him in an ill mood and difficult to handle."

"Bombers may come," began the camp commander after Cameron arrived at his office, "and we must be prepared."

Cameron's first reaction was an emotional upsurge of joy at the thought of an air strike so far inland, an impulse that lasted momentarily, before a more intelligent analysis passed through his thoughts. *Hold on now, Captain,* he spoke within himself. *It can't be possible that our bombers would hit so far away from the war zone. And there is absolutely nothing within miles of here that could, by any stretch of the imagination, be classed as a suitable target. Just what are you up to?*

"Much danger exists," the lieutenant continued with slow and cautious statements. "Many prisoners may be seriously injured if not properly protected."

Cameron nodded in acquiescence. "Mmmm," he hummed as an invitation for the Nipponese to complete his narration.

"It will be best if POWs build trenches, enough for all to take shelter when raids come."

The American stared straight into the lieutenant's eyes. *Something is amiss here,* he thought. *This fellow has an idea to put over and it is not for any defense of POWs. Just what is going in in the back of that shaved head of his?* It was certain that there was no anticipated air raid, Cameron determined. The ground was frozen hard and would be nearly impossible to dig in without blasting.

"That is very serious, indeed, captain," began Cameron, partly agreeing with him to throw him off guard. "Many people would be badly hurt in an air raid." Then quickly Cameron, in an effort to get an impetuous response, asked, "Where will they come from do you think, China or maybe Russia?"

"Uh-uh," the officer began but checked himself. "I do not know when or from where. We must be ready. It is my duty to protect the prisoners."

It is your duty, all right, thought Cameron, *and I have no reason to believe you are not speaking honestly. Nevertheless, as a matter of principle, I'm suspicious.* Trying to divert or at least retard the issue, Cameron asked aloud, "Do you mean, sir, that you want me to find out how the POWs feel about trenches and to report to you?" It was a bold request and, on any earlier occasion, would have brought forth serious punishment. Cameron, however, knew that he retained a certain amount of influence, though it had deteriorated in recent weeks. His question was worth a risk; nothing ventured ...

The Nipponese showed in his face and squirming actions that the initiative had been taken from him. Maybe he thought it best not to make too great a demand on the prisoners at one time. If they showed reluctance, there could be trouble. His standing with the colonel might be imperiled. "Yes, yes, he said hesitatingly. "You will explain to them the danger and that I have great interest in their health." That was the face-saving gesture! Now, all was well. Cameron had been given a definite command. The lieutenant sat back in his chair with more comfort.

"The hell with him!" Blake inevitably bellowed when Cameron had related his interview to the prisoners who clustered around him upon his return to the barracks.

"Just an opening wedge to start us back to work," cried Paul.

"That may well be the whole idea behind this trench digging," Paul calmly stated in his dignified manner.

"But, what if he is right and bombers do come?" asked Sykes nervously. "Why, we might all be killed and never get home."

Before any supporter could come to defend Sykes's supposition, the room was filled with the clamor of objections.

"Damn if I vote for any trenches!"

"Me neither. Not a chance in a million getting bombed here."

"What a disgraceful piece of strategy it would be to send bombers away out in the middle of this desert."

"They got plenty to keep them busy where the war is being fought."

"What if they fear the Russians?" Paul quietly inquired. It was a thought that had been discussed before by those who were seriously trying to evaluate all contingencies. Paul's suggestion dampened the ardor of the debate. What if Russians did come in? That was a momentous question!

The group had to disperse quickly when the slow tramp of a guard was heard coming up the wooden steps. However, Cameron was of the opinion that, if the decision on construction of the trenches rested with the POWs, they would have none of it.

The next day Cameron felt obligated to settle the issue with the camp commander, and when he stepped out of the barracks into the cold air that stung his face, he was confronted by a singular sight. Standing near the building was the camp commander talking with Sykes! They appeared to be in one accord on the subject of their discussion, because each seemed to be agreeing wholly with whatever the other one said.

For a moment, Cameron was uncertain whether to join the conversation or wait until Sykes had finished. But when he saw them making motions and point to the open space in the compound, he knew he had to hurry. *Maybe I'm already too late,* Cameron admonished himself. *That fellow has gotten to the Nip and is talking about trench digging. It's too damn bad the lieutenant understands English.*

Cameron reached them too late. He shook his head in despair as he heard the last words of their dialogue. The camp commander had the support of at least one POW in his trench construction scheme, and that moral victory would be difficult to overcome.

"Have you finished?" asked Cameron of Sykes when he came up. "Do you want to go now?" His voice had the stern tones of a reprimand in it, for Cameron was disgusted and discouraged by Sykes's independent action. *No cooperation*, he thought. *No common decision. No thought of trying to get things done of the good of the majority. Every POW for himself, for his own selfish interests. Always the same old story—to hell with anybody else!*"

"The lieutenant was talking to me about the trenches we are going to dig," Sykes said apologetically, wording his statement in front of the camp commander in such a manner that there could be no receding.

Standing there grinding his jaws together, Cameron wanted to throttle Sykes. Anger swelled up in him, and he could feel the heat in his face.

Words coming from the camp commander stayed his emotions and quieted his body.

Another lost cause, meditated Cameron. *I was licked even before I started. Damn such selfishness!*

"Yes, we have agreed," the Nipponese said, showing his pleasure in his voice and by his head bobbing up and down. "Trenches for all will be placed there in front of building. When raid comes, very easy to hurry and jump in."

"Captain," replied Cameron, trying to alter the situation, "we have talked the matter over in the barracks, and many prisoners have had much experience. They all believe it would help you to know that the ground is too hard now to get best results. Many fine Nipponese tools will be damaged. Very soon, spring will be here, and then digging will be better."

"No!" shouted the officer. "Now! Start tomorrow!" He turned and strode rapidly toward his office.

"He means business," declared Sykes.

But into that innocent remark, Cameron read a taunt. Goddamn it, shut up! Cameron wanted to say, but he suppressed the words. *You half-baked nincompoop!* he thought. It was agonizing enough for a man to be defeated in his purpose, but it was inflaming to have one of his own nationals double-cross him to an enemy.

No purpose will be served, contemplated Cameron in his distress, *by saying anything to this dolt. Nothing but an argument will result, and then I will have stooped to his low level by being a party to it. I hope I am a stronger man than that. Keep your mouth shut, regardless of what you may think!*

Not many more weeks passed by, weeks during which conditions grew steadily worse for the POWs, until the word was given to move camp. Some little information leaked in to stimulate the men behind the electrified fence. Because conditions had been relaxed to a degree, occasionally a guard would be friendly. If a POW exercised caution in his questioning, he might get the sentry to drop some little remark on the progress of the war, which was major intelligence to men starving for news.

A tremendous break came one day when Paul and Cameron were down in the basement washing clothes. Adjacent to where they were engaged in their household duties was the benjo. At that time, several Manchus, with a Nipponese guard as overseer, were hacking away at the frozen contents of the benjo, shoveling it out and carting it away. They seemed to be a friendly sort of people and kept looking in the direction of the Americans, probably discussing among themselves the strange appearance of Occidentals and their odd habits.

Cameron, always alert like every POW for a chance to gather information, returned the glance. They were strange to him, too, in their heavily padded but ragged quilted clothes tied up with cords for a snug fit.

"They look mighty like paupers in their rags," observed Cameron, going about his work.

"Guess they are well suppressed by the conquerors," replied Paul in a whispered voice.

"Maybe we can find out some dope, if that guard would disappear for a few minutes."

"He will," prophesied Paul. "They get careless. In a bit, he'll go over to the guardhouse to get warm."

They finished the job they were on, hung their pieces of clothing up to dry, and puttered about waiting for their opportunity. It came. The guard slipped out of the building, and the Manchus, no longer under observation, stopped their labor and sat down.

Quickly, Cameron walked over to the one he thought might be the easiest to approach. In his outstretched hand, he held a cigarette. That was the greatest act of charity a POW could render, to give away a smoke.

"Ah, ah," the man grunted, with graciousness and a smile as he accepted the offering. He quickly hid it in the folds of his clothing; punishment would be certain if the guard caught him with that unusual possession.

"Zzzzz," hissed Cameron, making motions with his hand to indicate an airplane. "Boom! Boom!" he exploded, dropping his hands to represent bombs.

All the Manchus enjoyed the pantomime and laughed. Then they shook their heads. "No!" they meant, but what they meant to convey was not apparent.

Cameron spoke a few words in Nipponese. The laborers grasped some of them and replied in monosyllables. *No progress here*, thought Cameron. We have not the time to establishing a means of communicating with each other. Then a happy thought struck him.

"Newspaper?" he asked in Nipponese, pointing to them and then to himself.

The Manchus lapsed into a discussion among themselves. All that Paul and Cameron could gather was from the nodding of heads and the seriousness written on their faces. Finally, one of the men said in Nipponese, "Tomorrow!"

"Arigato!" replied Cameron, while his heart pounded in his excitement over his success. He walked over to the framework surrounding the separate cubicles and laid his hand up on top, telling his benefactor by motions to hide the paper there.

The man nodded in understanding.

"Got a cigarette, Paul?" asked Cameron. "I have three left, but I need another to give them one each.

Paul always had cigarettes for the simple reason he seldom smoked. On special occasions he would reach into his pocket and cheer up a colleague who was depressed. "Put yours away, Cam. I'll use mine. Never put anything to better use."

There was excitement galore the following day after Cameron quietly slipped over into the corner where the American interpreter was lounging and passed him the bit of paper. Cameron's actions were intended to keep the matter quiet until after a translation was made or that nothing unusual in the barracks would be brought to the attention of any of the guards. But his secretiveness announced to his colleagues that something of major import was astir. Cameron could have called the attention of the other POWs to himself no more surely had he marched down the hall blowing a bugle.

As a mass and as though by prearranged signal, the entire group rushed toward him.

"Hold on!" he cried in answer to dozens of questions tossed at him. "Take it easy! We have a paper but must have absolute quiet before we'll touch it. Everybody go back, please. When we have translated it, we'll pass the dope out. But in the meantime, act normal. It'll mean someone's neck if we get caught."

Cameron's caution was only partly effective. The POWs moved away, but excited discussion went on among them through the barracks, down in the banjo, and out in the kitchen.

Looking out of the window, Paul sensed that the POWs were incautious and indiscreet. "I'm afraid they are talking about it all over the compound. The Nips are sure to sense some strange goings-on."

"Damn it!" swore Cameron. "I'm going to put a guard on each stairway to watch for the Nips. There would be hell to pay if they ever found this out. A couple of us would probably lose our heads, and the whole Chinese community would be machine-gunned."

Eyes were opened in utter amazement at the news when it was finally passed around. For years, only rumors had been available to lean on. Now at last, a real newspaper! It made little difference if it was printed in Nipponese on a small sheet the size of a handbill. It was real, something to get one's teeth into, facts!

Germany was squeezed into a tiny corridor; the Russians were all over the map in the east; the Americans were far beyond the Rhine. A taunt of superiority guided the hands of the Japanese correspondents, it seemed, because the great and powerful Germany had failed, while the Imperial Nipponese Forces still remained intact.

Eisenhower? Oh, yes! We heard about him in Africa. And Patton? I wonder if that is the Bradley I know. Who is Montgomery? What do they mean by President Truman? What happened to FDR?

Ah! The Pacific War! That's the big thing! How near are we to liberation? Kwajalein, Guam, the Philippines! Don't tell me! Where's this Okinawa located? Sounds like a mighty battle going on there.

Emotions were at a high pitch, not only because of the successful conduct of the war but for the greatest reason of all to a POW—freedom may soon arrive!

"To have any news," confided Paul "after these years of restriction is glorious. But when it includes such great achievements it is almost more than my old heart can stand."

"Seems to me it took a hell of a long time," grumbled Blake, without making a proper analysis.

"Only too true, Blake," consoled Cameron. "It has been a very long time. There will be more time passing by before the end of this mess. Not much we can do about that; just sit here and take it."

"And rot," Blake countered.

"We may be in a worse jam than that," cautioned Cameron with deadly seriousness. "When the end comes, these damn fanatics may take us with them. I can't see them letting us live, when they have to go."

"Not a pleasant thought," Paul commented. "Let us not be too disturbed over that yet, however. Perhaps there will be a way to meet that situation when it arrives."

During the period when the thrills of weightier matters held the attention of the camp, the anticipated move to a new area had been practically forgotten. From the upper floor of the barracks, it was possible to look far over the plain toward the distant horizon where the main railroad line ran and to which the short spur from the camp joined. Day after day, from the north, loaded freight trains rolled past, leaving a wispy stream of smoke and distant rumble in their wake.

Heavy military equipment rode on many of the flatcars, and little yellow men in uniforms swarmed over the rolling stock.

"They're sure moving a lot of army someplace to the south," Blake ventured one day. "Maybe China or that Okinawa place."

"Probably cleaning out all the warehouses from the north and getting the stuff close to home." Paul was trying to analyze the strange proceedings, and he made a definite inference.

"You may be right, Paul," replied Cameron, who understood his meaning. "If there is any chance of the Russians coming into the war, they'd better get everything out of the way. But I can't understand how they would dare weaken this Kwantung Army at this stage of the game. That means only one thing to me—that they are mighty hard-pressed down south."

"The military situation is crumbling fast no doubt."

"Can't happen soon enough to please me," Blake chortled.

"There is some connection between this move to the south and our move from here," Cameron stated.

"I suspect so," agreed Paul. "There are two other things that may have something to do with it—trouble here with the Chinese who might try to release us and the fact that this camp sort of got out of hand with the authorities."

"Well," Cameron commented, "maybe we'll know soon. We leave the day after tomorrow."

The destination was not made known until after the POWs had boarded the train. Faulty arrangements resulted in many disagreeable conditions. There were an inadequate number of cars on the train, and when the prisoners squeezed in, they were jammed together worse than on any New York subway. Measures for meals had not been foreseen. One small bun comprised each meal. Cameron was furious, especially so because his colleagues chided and even taunted him over the preparations made for the journey.

When he could stand it no longer, he squirmed his way through the close-packed POWs into the rear coach and sought out the lieutenant. "Where are we bound for, Captain?" he asked in a demanding tone, with little interest in the relationship between captor and prisoner.

"Mukden," the officer replied with an affected smile. "Where the main camp is."

"I wanted to help you plan the trip, but you insisted that you could do it all by yourself. Now look at us! We are packed in here so tight we can't breathe."

"Very sorry," he muttered.

"And no water! We can't even get a drink."

"It was forgotten."

"What about food? You are not going to starve us, I hope."

"Food? We have given you fine bun for each meal."

"For Christ's sake! So, those are the arrangements you made! I'll see that the colonel hears about this as soon as we reach Mukden."

"Ah, but I asked you if buns would be all right for the trip, and you said, 'Yes!'"

"Sure, they are all right. But you know it was never meant that you were only to feed us buns and only one little bun for a meal."

"So sorry."

"You'll have to explain this treatment to your colonel. I don't think he'll like it." Cameron wormed his way back, passing out the information he had received as he elbowed a path through the wedged men.

Entering a new compound as prisoners of war offered no particular excitement. On too many previous occasions, that experience had been endured. It was routine now. Differences existed to be sure, but what counted most in the hopes and expectations of each man centered on the sort of treatment that he might receive.

The base group in Mukden was already in operations, having been set up two years earlier to house those prisoners who were put to work in the adjacent factories, of which there were many here on the outskirts of the city. From the air, the compound resembled any one of a number of such enclosures that enclosed a manufacturing installation. There was something ominous about that. Twenty feet of brick and stone made a wall much too high to scale, particularly so when sentry boxes were spread along each side.

Within the enclosure, extensive barracks filled the restricted space, while at one end the quarters, mess, and office facilities of the Nipponese detachment had been erected. In between, a small area remained that was in use as an exercise area, where men could stretch their legs and rest in the sun.

Greetings between the newcomers and those who had been moved there shortly after their campaign in the Philippines had ended were cordial and emotional. There was no mistake about that sincerity when men met for the first time after their close combat association. After a period of time living together in close confinement, POWs may be expected to build up an antipathy on frequent occasions, but the first greeting after long separation is something else. Handclasps, manly embraces, and tears shed without shame proclaimed the joy of reunion.

Then news! Some facts, many rumors, and much supposition flew back and forth. If report of an identical instance had reached two far removed camps, that information was accepted as confirmed. Swapping of such information and reporting it back to others consumed and made delightful many otherwise dreary days.

The prisoners here, those who had spent years at the Mukden camp, possessed a healthier outlook on life for the simple reason that their daily labors took them outside the wall and across the fields to the factories, where they had surreptitious opportunities to talk with the Chinese who worked in the same compound. Though under the surveillance of guards armed with rifles and bayonets and though forced to labor for the enemy war effort, a POW received a great stimulation when he could pass through the heavy iron gates into the world beyond.

Outside the wall, the air smelled fresher. There was joy in movement, happiness in seeing life moving along from day to day. A smile from a suppressed Chinese, perhaps a quick word from him unnoticed by the guards, sometimes a gesture aided by a facial expression that conveyed information on the war's progress stimulated and encouraged a man. Such things reminded him that he was not alone in a world of suppression and brutality but that there were many others outside the wall who were waiting and hoping and—who knows—preparing for the great moment.

Because Paul and Cameron had tasted success in their episode of smuggling in a newspaper earlier, the thought of repeating that episode stood out dearly in their minds. On frequent occasions, they discussed ways and means between themselves and, with caution, asked questions of the older inmates of the camp. There came a time when they felt they knew all the procedures of a normal day's operation.

After breakfast in the morning, the POWs designated for labor were lined up and carefully counted when they passed through the gate. Under heavy guard, they marched in a column to the factory, where the overseer counted them in and dispatched each man to his task. The guards wandered through the building, prying into all the activities, while others stood at the several entrances to make certain no POW could escape.

About noontime a detachment of prisoners was sent from the cookhouse in the compound to carry food to the workers in the factory. The afternoon activities were similar to those of the morning. At the end of the day, the prisoners were again lined up for tenko and checked over to the guards by the overseer. When the column reached the wall, it was halted, and each POW, summer or winter, was required to strip off his rags and undergo a search for contraband.

Each of these details was laboriously learned by Paul and Cameron in their innocent-appearing interest in the life of the workers who were permitted to leave the confines of the wall. Cautiously, they formed opinions on which of those POWs were most trustworthy and responsible and which ones might be able to make contacts without jeopardy to themselves or others in the camp.

"Paul," said Cameron one day in hushed tones so as not to be overheard, "I believe you and I agree on a half dozen of the factory workers who we can trust."

Paul nodded his acquiescence.

"No doubt, among those, Quade and Johnstone stand out as the two who could best take over the leadership."

"Yes," Paul thoughtfully replied. "Probably I'd pick Quade to handle the job."

"Very well, we'll corner him tonight and have a talk."

After the evening meal, Cameron sought out Quade and inquired, "Sergeant, got anything special on your mind for the next half hour?"

"Not a thing, sir," he replied in an enthusiastic voice. "What's up?"

"Let's take a stroll up to my place where we can talk confidentially."

Cameron and Quade, in a careful manner so as not to attract attention, wandered across the barracks to the small area where Cameron slept on the hard flooring. Paul was waiting for them alone. The other POWs who slept nearby were all out for a stroll in the air before dusk, at which time everyone had to return to barracks.

"Sounds mysterious," said Quade.

"It is," replied Cameron, pointing to the ladder by which they had to ascend to the upper shelf.

"We have a scheme, sergeant," Paul began when they had settled themselves cross-legged on Cameron's blanket, "and thought that you would be the best one to help put it over. Go ahead, Cameron, and explain it."

"Here is the story, Sergeant. You know that this war is coming to a close one of these days soon. At least we all hope so and feel that it will. This camp of POWs may be in dire jeopardy at the end. There is a mighty big chance these fanatics will clean us out when that end comes. And the same thing may happen if there is an assault on their homeland. That would stir them up to a high pitch, to know that these hated Americans had put a foot on their sacred soil. Their officers could never hold them in line then and would no doubt help in the massacre."

"But where do I come in?" inquired Quade. "There are no weapons we can get, unless we overcome the guards."

"Not too fast now, Sergeant. It may come to that, but there is an important step ahead, and that is to know what is going on. That way, we'll not get caught unprepared. That might be fatal, so we must have some plan ahead of time. Now, you POWs have been here a long time but, like those at the rest of these camps, have never had a chance to keep up with news; you haven't the facts or even mere rumors. Someplace in this big city of Mukden, they publish a paper. You have contacts at the factory. We have to get that paper into this compound daily."

"That's really a big order. But I'm willing to bet a solution can be worked out."

"Sergeant, we have the solution!"

Cameron carefully unfolded the plan during the next ten minutes. It was so simple that Quade smiled. Why hadn't it been thought of before?

On a selected day, Cameron put on some borrowed ragged clothing of the sort that hid his identity, as only a practiced eye could distinguish the older POWs at Mukden from the newer arrivals. "This is the day, Paul."

"You are not doing this with my sanction, Cam," responded Paul with misgivings. "You're taking a most unnecessary risk."

"Now, Paul, we've been over that a dozen times. I've got to do it. There is too much at stake."

"You're right, Cam, and I know it. God bless you!" he softly called as Cameron slid down the ladder to the ground floor.

He made his way out into the compound and stood next to Quade in the group of factory laborers getting ready for tenko. "You're sure Johnstone is not here, now? It would be a hell of a note if we turned up with one POW too many."

"You're Johnstone. Don't worry any further."

The roll call was made to the satisfaction of the enemy guards. Then the order to march out was given.

"It'll work fine," said Quade. "I've already been prowling around the gate and Flap Ear is on duty this week all right. He will be the safest bet, because he is the most careless one of all."

As Cameron passed through the portal, he maneuvered his position so that Quade would be between him and the guard.

"Hi there, soldier!" called Quade as a pleasantry, making a playful swing at him with an arm at the same time.

The guard responded in kind, and in a second, Cameron was beyond him, just another POW marching to work.

"That's the Jap Seiki there with the brown cap at the third lathe," Quade whispered to Cameron and proceeded to his task.

Cameron went directly to the machine that Quade had pointed out and began to act as a helper to the man operating the lathe. For ten minutes, no words were spoken, and then Cameron casually raised his head to look about. Each few minutes, he repeated the motion. When he felt secure from observation, he moved closer to the mechanic and spoke.

"You are Seiki? Don't look up. Keep working."

After a short silence, the man replied in English, "Yes, but you are new here. How did you know?"

Ignoring the question, Cameron continued, "You lived for years in America. Your kids were born there. You want to go back after the war."

"But, but ..." stuttered Seiki, keeping busily at his work.

"Okay! I've come to help you do that, but you've got to prove yourself to us."

"I'll do anything," replied Seiki. But how can you help me?"

"My brother is the attorney general of California," lied Cameron. *That should sound important*, he thought to himself. "I can get you back without any trouble."

"What is it I must do?"

"You bring a newspaper from Mukden each day. Start tomorrow. When you first come in the morning, go to the benjo and put the paper up over the top. One of our men will watch and go in after you. He will take it and hide it."

"That will be easy."

"If you ever talk or our man gets caught, I'll turn you over to the military police. You know what that will mean."

"Never fear. I'll say nothing! Never!" He mopped the sweat from his brow.

On the march back to the compound, Cameron walked beside Quade. "Not a hitch," he whispered.

"Nice going!" replied the sergeant.

"Bring your shoes up to my place after supper tonight."

"Right!"

Later, Quade climbed up the ladder and squatted down beside Cameron and Paul. He pulled off a shoe and handed it to Cameron.

"Sergeant, getting hold of this shoe will prove to be the best swap any POW ever made."

"I had to give the bloody Tommy six bowls of cornmeal and ten buns for them. It took a long time to pay it out."

"Only a British marching shoe could serve the purpose," Cameron declared, busy at work.

He had taken from the top of a rafter, where it was hidden, a small piece of metal useful as a makeshift knife. On the bottom of the heel of the boot a narrow strip of steel bound the perimeter. It was held in place by three short screws. In short order Cameron had removed the screws and carefully pried the heel loose. Holding it in his hand, he scraped the leather out of the interior of the heel, leaving a cavity.

"Now if these new screws will only work," he said, removing three long screws from his pocket.

"Where did you ever get them?" asked Quade.

"My shipmate here dug them up. He's being looking for them ever since our first talk here. I think he got them out of some of the framework at the kitchen."

After a few more minutes' work, Cameron beamed at the finished product. "Look now. This is the way it works. The rear screw stays in as a pivot. The two forward ones are loose, just tight enough to hold the heel in place. Give them a twist with your fingers, turn the heel around, put the folded paper in the cavity, and close up the heel. Looking at the heel from the bottom gives no suspicion. The steel plate is in place, and the Nips can inspect your boots as much as they want to. They'll never get wise to a thing."

"Hell, I'll take that chance anytime. All they ever look at is the inside of a shoe and try the edge of the sole to see if something has been slipped in there. But the heel, never! They are much too dumb."

"From now on, Sergeant, we'll have news, real news. No more rumors! If the time ever comes when we'll have to fight our way out of here, we'll be properly warned."

The days moved along to the end of May. Ended was the campaign in Italy. The act of surrender of Germany was duly signed. The Allies from the East and from the West shook hands in friendly camaraderie across the Elbe.

Nearer at hand, stirring events recorded a daily history that chilled each POW, as the news from Okinawa was partly told in the little news sheet being smuggled into the compound. In Japan proper, cities were being systematically destroyed in increasing numbers as the air might of America, no longer needed in Europe, began making itself felt. When would the enemy retaliate in the only possible manner left—by the promised annihilation of her prisoners?

June was warm and comfortable in Mukden. Cameron sunned himself almost daily in the compound, enjoying the thrill of lying on a blanket watching the shifting of white clouds on a deep blue background far overhead. *What a useless human I am*, he meditated, *to lie here throwing away these lives that I may be redeemed. We are fearfully close to Japan. Our land-based fighters are attacking the mainland. When will we make an assault? Will Russia come in?*

July! Air strikes of five hundred, six hundred, eight hundred planes! What is this new B-29 the Japanese press continues to howl against?

An ultimatum from Potsdam! No reply—one day, two days, three days. Why doesn't somebody in Japan come to his senses? We scoff at it all, says the premier, finally.

Headlines of a different sort today. An exceptionally heavy bomb dropped on Hiroshima. A hundred thousand Japanese killed? Those dastardly Americans willfully destroy women and children! But the courageous Nipponese Empire will fight to the last man!

Russia strikes! Around the perimeter of Manchukuo and Korea, her veteran mechanized forces from Germany pour in. Three months since the collapse of Germany—three months well spent in concentrating those forces in strategic areas. What account of itself will the famed Kwantung Army give? The local troops were excited. Trenches around the compound were madly excavated. Was that the way these fanatics would raze the buildings that held their captives and destroy them all?

Cameron stalked into the barracks in a state of excitement. "The Nips have just ordered the kitchen force to bake up five buns apiece."

"That is ominous," said Paul. "It can mean only one thing—a trip of five meals."

"Maybe they are going to take us into the mountains where we will be safe." Sykes continued to believe in the goodness of his captors.

"They'll take us to Japan," cried Blake in dismay. "I'll be damned if those little yellow bastards will ever get me on another boat of theirs. No ship could possibly make a run from Korea or Dairen over to Japan."

"Easy, old man!" Cameron spoke consolingly. "None of us wants to take an ocean voyage around here at this stage of the game. Let's don't try to fight our way out yet. I have my finger on the pulse with some men posted around the colonel's office watching developments. If it comes to the worst, we can yank that Nip interpreter up here and choke him into giving us the truth."

Guards stormed through the barracks in greater numbers and acted more ruthless than ever. A POW was not safe from molestation at any minute of the day or night.

"Let's get out of here," called Blake, "and walk around the compound. The Nips are not bothering any of the POWs out in the open."

"Come on," agreed Paul. "You have a good idea there, Blake."

Blake followed Paul down the hall to the head of the stairs. Each of them from long experience had learned that to be in sight of a Nipponese guard when one could keep out of the way was courting jeopardy unnecessarily. Better to walk around outside until the sentries prowling through the barracks had left. Life under such constant scrutiny was uncertain, especially now. A guard could always find some reason to bop a POW; for that, he did not have to have any reason, just the whim.

Looking at Paul from the rear, Blake observed for the first time that age and a difficult life seemed to have taken something out of his older colleague. *In spite of his age*, meditated Blake, *he was powerfully spry and energetic when the campaign was over. That old man may not get home if he fails very much more. He wobbles along there in pretty sorry fashion, as if he didn't have much stamina left.*

When he reached the landing at the head of the staircase, Paul gave a sudden start, sort of a hesitation in order to make up his mind whether to proceed or not. Blake took the few steps needed to come abreast of Paul and looked down the steps. It was then that he saw the reason Paul had hesitated.

Halfway up was Gertie! Gertie was a character, a hated, abominable Oriental. Of the many Nipponese encountered by the POWs, Gertie was acclaimed as the most inhuman, the ugliest person ever seen. Even the uniform he wore, ill-kempt and ill-fitted, appeared to accentuate his grotesque looks. The protruding ears on each side of his head were not symmetrical. His eyes were set closer together than usual for one of his race. Those defects combined with a scar diagonally across his nose, which must have contributed to the flatness of that organ, to give him a sinister look. If he could force out a smile, much of his deformity might have been overlooked, but his constant frown merely accentuated his ugliness. It is unfortunate enough if a man possesses misshapen figure, but that affects those who see him only in an aesthetic sense. Yet when his actions conform to the hideous sight he presents, nothing but loathing and detest for him can be expected.

So it was with Gertie. He had his own special form of harassment and enjoyed it best when he could inflict it on the more helpless of the POWs, a man sick in bed or an older, infirm prisoner. For his sadistic pleasure, he would tantalize a man lying ill and flat on his back by bringing the butt of his rifle down hard on the POW's abdomen and then watch the tortured man writhe in an effort to regain his breath. Another of his moments of delight came when he could force a prisoner to stand straddle-legged before him with his hands over his head. A quick kick from Gertie between the man's legs was the coup de main that thrilled the guard.

No wonder Paul recoiled at the unexpected sight of Gertie stomping up the stairs. Perhaps it would be best to pass him, with a fastidious salute, rather than wait at the top. So, Paul carefully picked his way down. He saluted Gertie as he passed and continued downstairs. But Gertie, without warning, thrust a heavy boot forward and deliberately tripped Paul, who was unable to recover his balance and tumbled headlong to the bottom.

Directly behind him, Blake witnessed the episode. Something within him brought instantly to the fore all the suppressed emotions of hatred and ferocity that Blake had harbored against the enemy for years. There was no time for deliberation or contemplation. Blake's huge arm, though thinned from malnutrition, moved backward like the driver rod on a steam locomotive and thrust forward with every bit of strength a crazed man could muster.

Gertie grew limp even before his feet left the step on which he was standing. His body did not thud its way down the stairs but, like an acrobat doing a backward somersault, it flew through the air and was saved from being crushed only because Paul's limp form broke the shock.

Nearby POWs, hearing the commotion, came running. To see Gertie lying there still, with his detested face almost unrecognizable from wounds and blood, gave each prisoner a thrill he had waited and hoped for but did not expect.

Cameron joined the group. He spoke to Blake, who was standing stiff and staring with glassy eyes at the destruction below him.

"What's up?" he asked.

Blake relaxed and replied, "He tripped the man, so I bashed his face in."

Cameron leaped down the stairs; straightened out a leg; and, with his heel, pushed Gertie off Paul's body. No one cared to touch Gertie. They left him alone. But many hands quickly reached down for Paul. They raised him up and lovingly carried him to his bunk.

In the vernacular, Cameron spoke to Gertie as he raised his head and put his hand to his face. "Tell your officer you tripped on the stairs and fell. If you do not, you will be turned over to the Russians." Gertie knew what that might entail.

"Okay!" he mumbled in reply, rising slowly to his feet.

Cameron handed his rifle to him in an effort to hasten his departure. "Go to the benjo," he demanded, "and wash your face. Hurry!"

Never had a POW laid a hand on an enemy guard without promptly being deprived of his life for that act of insubordination. To raise an arm in shielding off a blow constituted belligerent conduct on the part of a prisoner. Blake and Cameron had serious misgivings over their parts in the recent drama. Striking a blow and leaving telltale results was of too serious a nature to consume time in conducting a formal trial. Retribution would be sudden and summary. Realizing that, Cameron had impetuously committed a deed that placed him in the eyes of he enemy in the position of an accessory. Further, he had attempted to coerce a representative of his imperial majesty to commit an act of disloyalty.

Yet Cameron had not acted wholly without intelligence. Feeling an obligation to protect Blake and embittered over the assault on Paul, he had rushed into the fray with the intent of intimidating Gertie. It was common knowledge that a Nipponese of the guard level of intelligence possessed little analytical ability. He was concerned first, like any human would be, with his own skin. Anger may influence him to take quick action against his assailant, but Cameron had quickly altered his thoughts to one of the fundamentals of life—protecting himself. Should he report the episode to his superiors, he would be criticized for allowing the situation, disgraceful to the prestige of the Nipponese Army, to occur. That would subject him to severe punishment from his own people. To fall down the stairs and injure himself was a stupid act of carelessness, and any punishment meted out would be light.

Important in the minds of the Nipponese was the precarious position each one now occupied. The Russian Army was rapidly striding through Manchukuo with little resistance. Those relatively few troops in Mukden would be caught in a trap by the approaching Slavic enemy. At the last moment, a banzai charge for the glory of the emperor might be ordered. But what if they were taken prisoner? Nothing in their doctrine could be more disgraceful! To be a prisoner of the Occidental would be one thing. But a prisoner of the Russians? Any condition of life would be preferable!

Among the prisoners, the once obnoxious Blake grew suddenly in stature to heroic proportion because of the resolute and manly character he had displayed. His fellows, with curiosity, strolled past his room just to look at him. One incident in a man's life often alters his reputation from one extreme to another. True, there was some sympathy inherent in this newly developed hero worship—sympathy for Blake because of the assured retribution each felt would come to him. Cameron's less spectacular part in the fray remained unrevealed.

As the excitement dissipated and emotions were allayed, concern over Paul increased. He was badly hurt. Doc could give little encouragement.

There was more involved than obvious physical injury. The heart and soul of an altruistic and helpless old man were damaged. Broken by malnutrition and severe conditions of life in spite of his will and faith, Paul had gradually deteriorated. In recent months, his weakened morale had drained his stamina. Now he was suffering from a severe shock resulting from his recent experience. To him, a Nipponese had always been considered a human being, someone who God had seen fit to place on this earth. In spite of the actions of that human being, Paul had followed the creed of brotherly respect. He bore no hatred or malice. Yet at the same time, he had never been negligent in his soldiery duties. His qualities on that score were never subject to question. A Nip in the field was his enemy and was so treated; nevertheless, there existed a great area for understanding and application of those human relationships that only soldiers of great moral character are aware of, regardless of rank or duties.

Cameron sat by Paul, watching him intently. Long since, he had dismissed concern over himself. There was nothing he could do now to better his friend's position. If the blow fell, he would have to handle it at the time. It was fortunate that he could shake off that worry now. There was a time when he possessed less ability and understanding. But Paul's influence had been a fine thing in his life, sustaining him to grow and develop as only the influence of a grand character can. More than ever before, Cameron consciously realized the tremendous qualities that Paul possessed and that he himself was moving forward as a result of living in close association with those qualities. Now there was fear in Cameron's soul that the beautiful friendship might be brought to a close. In his thoughts, he had always felt an obligation to the older and more helpless man. He had vowed to do his best to assist Paul in coming through prison life and returning home safely. That privilege appeared to be fast slipping away from him. He was obviously worried over Paul.

"Hi, pal!" Cameron whispered when he noticed Paul's eyelids flicker and then open slightly.

Paul returned a wan smile but said nothing as he slipped off into a world of his own. *He understood me*, thought Cameron joyful. And there was much to be understood in those two words. They were packed full of meaning and love and affection, such as could unite only men who had suffered and passed through the valley of the shadow together.

Paul closed his eyes and lay back, relaxed. Life softly assumed a darker and quieter aspect, like one feels when sliding off into comforting sleep. After several minutes, a faint sound churned up in the distance, similar to a smoothly running electric motor. Gaining momentum, the humming grew louder, closer. Soon something was whirring past him like a stout blowing of the wind, steady but increasing in intensity. The sensation was pleasant to Paul and intriguing.

Before long, there was a constant roar in his ears. It was the loudest and strangest sound he had ever heard. *Hurricanes act that way*, he remembered. Yet he felt not the slightest tingle of wind tearing past him. After the sound reached its maximum, Paul sensed things flying across his vision. They were exhibits, momentary glimpses of a stage setting, one following another presented to him in rapid sequence.

An ocean liner had just docked at a flag-bedecked pier. Bands played; crowds cheered; whistles blew. Among the people waving welcome, Paul saw his own family and friends waiting to clasp him in their embrace. Before he had a chance to scrutinize that scene, another rushed before him. This was a bucolic setting, quiet and peaceful, a lovely spot for a tired old man to enjoy in peace his last few years.

The following picture arranged itself suddenly before him and then another and still one more. But they were strange settings. The people looked odd and wore costumes to which he was unaccustomed. Alternating, the scenes showed an atmosphere of great tension in the faces and actions of the characters and then of peace and domesticity and contentment. But there was no presentation of a martial episode.

The rush and whir reduced in volume, grew slower, and finally stopped. Before Paul's startled gaze, old friends sauntered up to him. There was Evans. Behind him came Jenkins. Up strode—of all people— dear old Ashley! But who is that playfully trying to hide behind him? No, it cannot be. Gertie! And he is smiling and extending a hand in fellowship. Gone is the ugliness of his face. Something from within him is shining godlike out onto his countenance. *Welcome*, said his lips.

"We have waited long for you, Paul," Evans said in a soft voice while he gripped the newcomer's hand warmly.

A thrill passed through Paul to be called by his first name. Only a few intimate friends had ever done that before. Now these youngsters of long ago had broken down their reserve and had greeted him as an equal."

"It is a glorious moment to see you all again," Paul finally announced, his voice cracking from his emotions.

"You have many friends here," Jenkins reported.

"How long have you been here?" asked Paul.

"Ever since the march out of Bataan," replied Evans. "Remember, I was one of those who you tried to stop from stealing water from a carabao wallow. One of the guards caught me at it."

"Yes, but—" Paul started to ask.

"Oh, that." Evans laughed. "It was all a mistake. The soldier who did it is here with us. We are the closest of friends. Look, there is hardly a mark left." He pulled apart the front opening of his tunic for Paul to see. Only the faintest of a thin, red line ran across his abdomen.

"The same is true of me, too," Jenkins spoke up. "I never got as far as the end of the campaign, you recall. It was you who helped to find me a comfortable piece of earth back in the jungle. I rested there for a long time, long after the war was only a faint memory."

"And you, Ashley and Gertie, of course. I remember, vividly."

"We hold no rancor here, Paul," said Ashley sweetly. "All the evil things that happened have been explained away. None of us was without sin back yonder. All those things have been forgiven and forgotten out here. You will find it a most pleasant place—no worries, no uncertainties, no ill feelings. Everything is joyful. Brotherly love is our creed."

"Why, oh, why cannot that same feeling prevail back yonder?" Paul thoughtfully asked.

"Ah, but it does!" Evans declared. "Life, back yonder, has undergone a tremendous change in the year since the Last War."

"The Last War?" Paul repeated, inquiringly.

"Yes, the one in which you had a dramatic role and from the result of which you suffered magnificently. After that, there were the expected ups and downs, the strife and conflict between groups and actions as between individuals. Yet a partial blow was never struck."

"Amazing!" declared Paul. "Just how was that brought about? Many a man struggled over the years, back yonder, to perpetuate a common understanding. Did they finally succeed?"

"Yes, success came," said Ashley, taking up the conversation with a polite nod from Evans. "But it came through a different source. Fear, an awful fear of survival spread over the land, back yonder, as the entering wedge. That condition of mind had two parts. One was the fear of physical extermination from the developments of scientific man, which outstripped other factors of existence and threw the equilibrium of life out of balance. The other was that very mundane pressure of finances. The Last War and the subsequent years showed man quite clearly that his pocketbook was inadequate to sustain another conflict of that degree, even though he may be the martial victor."

"Undoubtedly, that factor was one of the most important," Paul stated, thinking back on conditions of life as he had known them. He smiled at what had been so important then seeming so ridiculous now.

"True," continued Ashley. "While there were few moral values involved in the beginning of that vast change, I am sure no man objects to his new and present condition. As I said, the change commenced from selfish and ulterior motives. Man was a realist. He had to look about for some more subtle and less violent method to reach his aspirations."

Ashley pointed to Gertie and stepped aside for him to continue the explanation. "One can hardly believe that such a simple little thing in the life of man became the prod that started him on the way to perpetual peace and happiness. That good was nothing new. Every person, back yonder, had always been aware of its possibilities. Yet ambition, selfishness, prejudice, and bigotry were too ingrained in the soul to take advantage of such a simple and prosaic thing."

"You intrigue me, Gertie," cried Paul. "Quickly, tell me what that neglected act in life was."

"Everyday common courtesy!"

"You mean just being decent and kind, respectful and thoughtful of others?" inquired Paul. "I begin to grasp your meaning. Those things too often, back yonder, had to be earned, rather than being given from the heart to all. They were reserved for only those who had proven their friendship. I see, now, the sequence was in reverse. From courtesy, a friendship develops. We've been on the wrong footing by waiting for the friendship and then extending the courtesy."

"The big impetus in that development and fuller understanding of courtesy came in a spectacular fashion. There was time when nations were hotly wrangling over points of difference. They had reached a stalemate. Another war was but hours away. National prestige and dignity, ideologies, faiths, and many other conflicting factors were so complex and so insisted upon as each side saw and believed that any peaceful solution seemed impossible. The petty humans engaged in the controversy were hotheaded and angry and ready even for personal combat. Then a strange thing happened! One nation's representative stood up before the conference and asked for quiet. When the tumult subsided, he publicly apologized to his antagonists for his past lack of understanding of the problems and difficulties the other nations had. Of course, he would concede this point and that point. Perhaps then the opposition would concede him certain points."

"Rather unorthodox diplomatic procedure." Paul smiled. "Such concessions too often seem to be made only by the little fellow because they were demands made by the stronger."

"You can well imagine," continued Gertie, "the reaction back in his native country. Nearly everyone condemned him heartily. He should be recalled instantly. He was a traitor. He had sold his nation down the river. But he had stopped a horrible world conflict! While the other countries were amazed, they, nevertheless, accepted the changed situation happily. It may be true that their honesty of purpose had suddenly been put to a test; but the point remains. They responded favorably. Calmer deliberations in his nation of the altered status brought about by that one diplomat changed public opinion rapidly. The people, less chauvinistic now, were frightened at the thought of the horror they had just missed."

"From then on," said Jenkins, taking up the explanation, "courtesy became a fetish. Its value had been proven. Everybody, back yonder, had profited from it. Propaganda on the value and necessity of courtesy swept through all nations. Now look at them! Nothing serious ever arises between them."

"Well," broke in Ashley, "that's the end of the story. Shall we go meet the Chief now?"

"I want to, yes," Paul slowly replied. "But I'm not ready, not prepared yet. There is something I must accomplish first. Excuse me for a short period. I intend to return very soon."

Paul's decision started the same faint humming he had experienced earlier. When the crescendo reached a roar, he seemed to be carried back over the path he had traversed earlier. The sensation was a pleasant one.

At the side of the sick man, Cameron and Doc were maintaining a constant vigil. From somewhere, they had borrowed extra blankets to make Paul's bed on the flooring a little more comfortable.

"What say, Doc?" asked Cameron.

"Now that pneumonia has set in, he has little chance. This looks very much like the end."

Cameron turned his head and daubed a clumsy fist at his eyes. A sigh from Paul caused him to look back quickly. Paul's eyes were partly open, and he had a flicker of a smile on his face.

"It's me! Cam! Do you see me?"

Paul nodded, and his smile grew. "I've been away," he managed to say. "I must tell you, alone, all about my trip."

Cameron looked at Doc. Should they permit Paul to expend his little strength in talking? Doc rose to his feet to leave. "Sure," he said sympathetically. "It'll be a fine way to go. Comforting to him to do what he wants to. It cannot change anything."

Cameron leaned over toward Paul to hear his gasping words the better. He laid a friendly hand on Paul's shoulder to give him encouragement. For many minutes, Paul whispered, hesitatingly, to Cameron, who listened enraptured. Gradually, his voice grew less distinct and his breathing became more irregular. Cameron motioned for Doc to hasten to him. When Doc arrived, Paul had stiffened out his body in a final gasp. The smile on his face plainly showed his happiness and contentment.

The Nipponese might make the life of a prisoner of war hectic and uncertain because of their hatred of the Occidental, but their attitude was completely reversed after the death of a prisoner. Solemnity and respect came forward noticeably. Dying and death received different explanations. They were not necessarily the same thing. To die, especially if it could be related in any manner to the glorification of the emperor, was a condition of the future, an exalted honor to look forward to, a resplendent privilege. Associated with that act were the cheers of the crowd, especially those of superior officers; flag waving; and other emotional outbursts to assure the climax. Death, however, was a definite condition, a fait accompli, a situation from which other conditions arose. After death, one's family was honored; their position and prestige were enhanced; the soul joined those of the ancestors and hovered about as an influence over the lives of the living.

Because Cameron had been close to Paul, it was expected and proper that he should attend to the details following Paul's death. Burial must be soon; much had to be accomplished. Paul would have a military funeral if it took the effort and ingenuity of every POW in camp.

"Blake," Cameron said the next morning after he had spent a sorrowful night with his thoughts, "take over the job of digging a grave, will you? See the interpreter about getting a guard to take you out to the cemetery. Pick up a couple of volunteers to go along and do the heavy work. And tools, don't overlook them. The Nips will give a couple of timbers to make a marker."

"Sure thing," replied Blake. "Glad to do it."

"Sykes," Cameron continued, "you are the thread and needle expert in camp. You've been sewing incessantly for a couple of years. I want an American flag, and I want it inside a couple of hours."

"Why, yes," answered Sykes. "But that is quite an order."

"No *buts*!" Cameron tossed back at him. "An American flag! Here, take this Nip bedsheet I'm using. That'll give the white material. It's sort of stained but will do. Blue, blue let me see."

"How about that blue coat that Bates has?" asked Sykes.

"The very thing! Tell that old tightwad to turn that coat over to you, or I'll be down there and tear him apart. He never wears it, just hanging on to it to look pretty when he gets on a ship to go home. Now, about the red. See the mess sergeant. He can put his hands on some red paint. The other day, he wangled a little out of the Nips to touch up some rust spots on the bottom of the rice kettles. Use the rest of that white sheet by painting the same strips red."

"What size do you want it?" Sykes inquired.

"Damn it! Don't start asking a lot of questions. Get going!"

"Okay! Okay!"

"Say, Joe, you're next. You can lend a hand. Get a couple of volunteers who can use a saw and hammer together to make the best sort of box you can."

"Sure," replied Joe "I'd do anything to help."

Late that afternoon, the POWs assembled out in the open compound. Such occasions are always sorrowful, but there is added grief and lament when a friend has to be laid away in the midst of a hostile country with no assurance that he will ever be returned home to join again his own family and friends.

A semicircle was formed by the prisoners, who faced inward toward the bier. It was a rude box in which Paul rested, with warped and irregular boards, but it served the purpose. The fox rested on four chairs, set in pairs with two of each pair facing each other. Measuring up to the demands placed on him, Sykes had whipped together a respectable national emblem. With correct military etiquette the flag lay over the top of the improvised casket, the blue field over Paul's left shoulder. Standing on either side at the head of Paul's last couch were two grotesque easels holding artificial flowers. They had been offered to Cameron by the authorities. Because of the spirit of sincerity and respect intended, Cameron could do no less than accept their loan. He had misgivings, however, for fear those strange and gaudy contraptions would bring forth smiles and humorous remarks from uninformed POWs. This was no moment for raillery. A handful of daisies tied with a ribbon rested on the foot of the box. Cameron had spotted them in a field beyond the high wall; he could catch a glimpse of that field from one of the upper windows of the barracks. Because of the occasion, he had no difficulty in getting permission from the camp commander to pick them under surveillance of a sentry.

Fortunately, there was a chaplain at Mukden camp. While the normal duties expected of him in a prison camp were curtailed by suspicious authorities (though he nonetheless persisted in carrying them out surreptitiously), a funeral ceremony was considered legitimate. He now stood quietly near the head of the coffin, silently waiting.

From the outer fringe of the gathering, a POW called his colleagues to attention. Each prisoner stiffened up and observed. The Japanese colonel, Gimpy, followed by two aides with samurai swords dangling, hobbled up to the cluster of men, passed across the small open space, and stood erect before the bier. He removed his military cap and made the customary low and formal bow as his payment of respect. Upon the conclusion of that act, he faced about and marched to the next of the group of men, where he stood for the remainder of the ceremony.

The chaplain read the service and then called for one stanza of "Rock of Ages." Surely, enough POWs could recall those words to make a credible showing. There was a mouth organ in camp. The owner sounded a pitch and accompanied the singing. It went well. Cameron's qualms were eased.

As a courtesy and to add dignity, the senior officer present had been asked to make a short farewell address to Paul. Because there was a definite ban on ever making a speech, he had to hold the chaplain's prayer book before him as he spoke, to give the impression he was reading from a document previously censored and deemed appropriate.

"Paul," he said, "in the life and career of every man, there are certain moments that project themselves far out and above the rest of his wearisome existence. Today is one of those significant moments for you. You are embarking on a journey, whose end only you will ever know. But your friends are assembled here to bid you farewell and to wish you Godspeed. We are thinking of you today, just as you daily thought of us. Your parting gift, the remembrance of your kindly heart, will linger with us always. We pray for courage and strength and understanding that we accept that pure gift and carry it along our troubled way, using it and passing it on to others.

"From time to time, those of us here will be sailing off on the same voyage you are taking. We know that journey will be the more pleasant, Paul, because you will have eased the path for us, just as you have made the days here more agreeable.

"To that day, then, when we shall come out yonder to join you, we give our final salute!"

Spontaneously, each POW followed the example of the speaker and saluted. Paul was carried on the shoulders of his friends through the gate and across the ridge to the cemetery. There he was laid beside many of his fellow nationals who had preceded him, to wait and hope. No volleys were fired in parting. But as the stony soil being turned inward echoed on the wooden box, a startling sound stirred those present.

Ta-a-a, ta, tah! "Taps!" Cameron's final touch. A borrowed bugle sounded the end of the day. The sun, red and dimmed, was slowly easing out of sight, symbolic of the setting of the Rising Sun.

Daily, Blake waited for a call to report to headquarters. The Nipponese had an account to settle with him. It would be adjusted soon, he felt. This delay was only temporary because of more important things worrying them just now.

"You are acting mighty nervous, Blake," Cameron told him as he watched Blake pace his room and crack his knuckles.

"Making me wait this way is part of their damn torture; I know it!"

"They're not coming for you, Blake. Your friend Gertie was afraid to turn you in. He knew he'd catch hell for letting it happen."

"Why, why ..." stuttered Blake awkwardly. "What do you mean? How do you know?"

To tell his part in the fray was embarrassing to Cameron. The less said the better. But Blake needed assurance of some sort. Why not give him a likely tale? Perhaps, later, some day, the truth could be told. "I'll tell you how I know, Blake. I overheard two guards down by the kitchen talking about Gertie's face. They were laughing because he was so clumsy as to fall down the stairs. His officer transferred him so the POWs couldn't see him and laugh about his stupidity."

"Honest, Cam? Do you really mean it?" asked Blake filled with excitement.

"Sure thing! Now stop worrying. You're in the clear. Take it from me."

"Thanks, Cam. That sure is a load off my mind. I can sleep tonight for a change."

"What about those buns they baked for our trip?" Cameron asked to change the subject and put Blake at ease.

"They've waited so long now that they won't be any good. They'll have to bake some more."

"Say, you give me an idea, Blake. I'm going down to the kitchen and get the mess sergeant to test the Nips out. He can ask for permission to issue those buns because they might go stale and be wasted food. If they give him an okay, it will mean that the trip is off."

When the food was passed around that night, there were extra buns for all. Cameron and Blake looked at each other and smiled in an understanding way. They had something in common, something that was not shared by the others. They grew closer together at that moment than they had during all their intimate association since Bataan. It was to pay great dividends later.

Each hour was of importance now. Stirring events were anticipated at any moment. The smuggled paper told of rapid advances by Russian columns through Manchukuo. The guards were restless and excited. The POWs felt a similar stimulation. Extra caution was essential when men's nerves were tense. Some misunderstood act on the part of a prisoner might bring out also the fanaticism of the enemy. It was also necessary to be quiet and collected if a plan to fight their way out had to be put into effect.

Cameron motioned Blake over to a corner of the room, where the two would be alone and uninterrupted. "Blake," Cameron said, "the time has come to get organized for any trouble that may happen."

"Count me in!" cried Blake. "I've been itching for three years to wring some yellow necks."

"Easy now. This will have to be arranged for quietly. I've got a plan all set up, but I need you to help put it over. When the right moment comes, everything must click. I have some men in each squad all set as raiding parties. One group barges into the Nip storehouse and steals weapons; another goes to the toolshed and gets everything there we can use to fight with. Your job, Blake, is to get each squad lined up on what it is to do and have them ready when the signal is given. You are the field commander."

Cameron went over the details of the plan with Blake, the procedures that would meet any of a number of possible contingencies that could rise. Blake was back on familiar ground now, with something specific to do, especially when the task involved combat, of which he was a master. It was not without forethought that Cameron had selected Blake.

For innumerable hours over many days, Cameron had schemed and planned and plotted against that moment when the prisoners, if precautions were not taken, might suddenly be placed in dire jeopardy by the fanaticism of the enemy. Paul had been his sustaining strength over the years, someone with whom he could discuss and develop an understanding. But, now, Paul was no longer at hand to lend encouragement, support, and guidance.

Cameron felt there were cogent reasons why he should work quietly and without too many POWs knowing what was up. In camp were many officers far senior to Cameron, and he felt it would be lacking in propriety to display any leadership publicly, even though the others were unconcerned or fearful of taking action themselves. Too much forwardness on his part might become apparent to the ever-alert Nipponese. That would be bad! Should many prisoners be admitted to his confidence, without question, haranguing and objections would wile away the time with no accomplishment. Such had been demonstrated so often in the past that there was no hope for confidential and coordinated joint action. And whether he would admit it or not, Cameron was reticent and modest.

There was yet another condition that Cameron felt would work in his favor toward getting others to help him. That happened to be those qualities in a man that intrigued his fellows and gave him a sense of importance to be singled out and confided in. So Cameron convinced himself that, by selecting a POW who he felt could take over a phase of the plan and inviting him into a secluded spot and there whispering in his ear, he could win that POW over. He never told anyone more than what "we" wanted him to do. That mysterious pronoun was never enlarged upon. It gave the inference that cool heads and sound minds were laying great plans. The prisoner called on for help responded with alacrity, in the belief that he alone was being called upon by the planning staff to assist because of the confidence they had in his unique ability.

Though Cameron felt confident in those individuals, unknown to each other who were keeping eyes alert for signs of trouble, he could not relax but paced about the compound and strode through the upstairs rooms peaking out the windows from where he could see beyond the wall.

Then one morning, one of his fellow prisoners hurried in to report.

"A strange airplane is circling around out toward the north," he cried, short of breath from his rush up the stairs.

Cameron hurried to a window to observe. It was some minutes before the plane came into his vision. "Yes, I see it!" he called. "Could almost be one of our medium bombers."

"Probably Russians making a reconnaissance. Haven't they got a lot of our equipment?"

"True, true," he replied with little concern over the conversation. His eye was staring so as not to lose sight of the strange maneuvering in the sky. Suddenly, his lower jaw dropped. He could not speak because of his excitement, could only thrust a finger rapidly forward several times in the direction of the airplane.

"Good God! What does that mean?" his companion called.

With amazement, they watched men parachute down from the plane, five huge white billows slowing taking form and dropping earthward. No sooner had the plane passed beyond them than many smaller and colored chutes followed, red and yellow and blue umbrellas.

"It beats me!" cried Cameron.

"I'm bewildered, too. Could it be Nips making some practice landings?"

"Possibly," agreed Cameron. "If we knew more about how this aerial warfare worked, we could come up with an answer. But so much has been developed in the time we've been in jail that we can't even guess what is going on. Sort of dumb, I reckon."

"If they aren't Nips, why hasn't someone shot them down?"

"Can't answer that one. All I know is that, if they aren't Nips, they have taken one of the damnedest risks in the war."

"Some guts."

"Tell you what we'd better do," Cameron suggested as the plane finally turned and took off toward the west with an open throttle. "Go back to your spot in the compound and keep your eye peeled for anything further. I've a feeling something important is about to happen."

Late in the afternoon of that day, a significant event did occur. A military truck chugged up to the main gate, the smoke from the charcoal burner having been kept under surveillance by an observer in the barracks who had watched it come out from between the distant building and cross the open field in front of the wall. The word was relayed rapidly to the observer near the gate. Cameron was tense. *This may be the moment for our alarm to be given,* he thought. *Be ready, but be cautious.* The signal given too soon would surely bring the wrath of the enemy down upon them.

The gate was carefully opened a few inches, and a discussion between the guard and someone outside took place while the other guards inside the wall stood near, alert for any contingency. A Jap officer was called to investigate. He went through the same motions as had the sentry and hurried back to headquarters. Then the colonel, old Gimpy himself dressed in a kimono, hurriedly hobbled down to the gate. After satisfying himself, he ordered the gate open. The truck lurched inside and drew up in front of the colonel's office. The location was such that a POW could not observe the sequence of events. He would have had to enter onto forbidden ground in order to see.

Word was passed back to Cameron, standing alert in the compound where he could receive and pass on prearranged signals. *Damn it!* he chided himself. *This would happen just when we have to know. We must know! Can't ask someone else to take the risk. It's growing dusk. Shortly it will be dark enough to sneak over the line and find out what this is all about.*

While the darkness was growing, the impatient Cameron gave thought to his plan of finding out what he could. When the time came, he sauntered around to the door of the warehouse in which the hand tools were kept, those kuwas and pick handles that were to be converted quickly into lethal weapons when the great moment arrived.

There was no one near; it was too dark now to be observed from a distance. Cameron worked the screws loose that held the hasp in place. One of the POWs had long since done his job well to make the hasp appear untampered with. But in reality, it could be easily removed in a few seconds time. Cameron hastened inside and drew the door closed. "Gosh, but it's dark in here," he muttered inwardly and proceeded to crash his shins against something hard.

To restrain a cry of pain took every bit of control he could muster. He sat down on the floor and massaged his ailing shins. *Why the hell,* he meditated, *do these damn movie scenes have to happen? Why couldn't I have done this little job without getting into grief?*

When he felt able, he got to his feet and, with the greatest of caution, moved over to the barred window through which he could look across the intervening space and into the lighted window of Gimpy's office. A spectacular sight lay before him.

White men sat there! They were wearing pistols! One was pointing a finger at the colonel as though giving him instructions in a none-too-diplomatic way. Completing this impossible scene—Cameron rubbed his eyes at the incredible sight; such a situation just could not be—was a Nipponese soldier serving tea!

It took careful study of the picture before Cameron, whose excitement and emotions were playing havoc with his thinking, could make any sense out of it. *They are not Nips or Chinese or Filipino and certainly not Russian,* he debated. *Those holsters and belts could be our kind, but I can't get too good a look at them. The dark coveralls they are wearing could be something new. They simply must be home folks! And that plane was certainly one of our models. What's up, I may never know; but this news is too great to keep secret. Every POW is champing at the bit to know what is going on.*

He slipped away from his place of observation and cautiously felt his way in the darkness. A creaking of a door sounded in his throbbing ears. Quickly, he glanced toward the door and saw that it had been partially opened and a head was peeking inside. There was just enough glow from a distant floodlight on the wall to present a dim silhouette. *Christ! This would happen*, he swore almost aloud; the sweat began to form on his forehead, and fear raced through his soul. He remained quiet and watched. The head turned as the owner probably moved his eyes from one spot in the warehouse to another in an effort to see what might be possible in the darkened building.

No Nip cap there, Cameron debated, silently observing the shadowy form. *Nor is the head shaved. That blurred chin could be whiskers.*

"Hey, Butch!" softly called a voice as the head quickly withdrew from sight.

"Hey, Butch!" Cameron called back in a quick but excited voice.

The head reappeared. "What the hell you doing in here?" asked the voice.

"Wait a minute," replied Cameron, relieved, hastening toward the door. "Well, hello there, Sergeant. What a fright you gave me. I've been watching big things in Gimpy's office."

"You gave me a mighty bad fright, too. Ever since you gave me the job of being ready to crack this toolshed if the signal came, I've kept a close eye on this door and the lock. No slipup, you know."

"Sergeant, you're wonderful! That's the sort of reliability that makes our army great. We may not need our plan now. Those are Americans in the headquarters, and they're laying the law down to old Gimpy."

"Hells bells!!"

Little sleep was had that night. When the guards were not tramping through the barracks, the buzz of excited conversation kept everyone awake.

No announcement came from headquarters until the following day, which was to become the greatest day in the lives and careers of many a man. When the news became known, many unexplained matters were made clear. The American parachutists had received a dangerous welcome from an enemy attachment that had rushed to the scene of their landing. For minutes, it appeared that they would be executed on the spot—only the frantic demands of the Nisei interpreter, who had accompanied the landing party, to be taken to someone in authority had saved them from disaster. The war was over, and you goddamn Nips better realize it! That was the theme, and it was played up for its full value in all subsequent dealings the courageous parachutists had with the enemy.

Yet old Gimpy remained a real soldier to the last. He had no instructions from his superiors to release the prisoners. He was responsible for their safety from any actions from his own troops, who may not understand the situation.

"Better watch this crowd," the POWs told each other. "Gimpy may have made the concession that we are free to wander around the compound and that he will keep his troops in their own area as well and retain a guard outside the wall for protection. But they still are armed, and we are not."

Cameron went from man to man who had a part in his plan. "Keep your feet on the ground and don't relax. Our plan is still in effect. Watch every instant for treachery."

Later in the morning, additional excitement came to Camp Mukden. An American jeep raced up to the gate, and an angry voice demanded admittance. There was no delay this time. A solider leaped out of the car and shouted orders at Gimpy, who had come limping out of his office when his sentry had cried an alarm. The colonel, for the first time, cowered! Nipponese hostility and arrogance are quickly reduced to subservience and cringing servility on only one occasion—when a greater physical force than theirs appears.

Gimpy calmly issued instructions to his subordinates. Each one quickly moved to a corner of the compound that had been pointed out by the man in the jeep. There was too much excitement to deny the POWs. They hurried from their barracks as the news spread, and in minutes they, too, had assembled in a mass nearby.

Three soldiers from the jeep, leaving the driver in charge, looked about for a place to stand. The steps on the adjacent building! They mounted and faced the large group of silent and awestricken prisoners. The stage was set for a momentous drama

Years of terror and brutality and starvation had thinned their numbers, reduced them to skeletons, and broken their spirits—those years had stolen from them every vestige of hope—but a spark of understanding still remained in their befogged minds. Before them stood three young officers clad in brown uniforms. Red bands encircled their caps and like-colored stripes ran down the side of their breeches, stopping at the top of the black boots on their legs. Their only visible defense was the small pistol hanging at the side of each. But the sight of the dejected Nipponese at the side of the new arrivals proclaimed more loudly than any blasting radio that there was something unseen, something close at hand that protected them and gave them a superior position. Force!

"Russians!" cried every prisoner aloud. "They're Russians! Redeemers!"

The spontaneous cheer that lifted skyward was lusty and prolonged yet reduced in intensity because of throats choked with emotion and men busy drying the tears from their eyes. Gladness and joy and gratitude were expressed in the manifold ways that would come from a group whose individual emotions were mixed and varied.

The leader of the little Russian party held an arm and hand aloft to call for quiet. It took some time to bring those thousands of dazed men to their senses. Finally, quiet was achieved. Men's ears rang with the intensity of the silence and the anticipation of more stirring moments ahead.

Still holding his hand above his head, the officer removed his cap with the other hand, and in a slow but deliberate voice proclaimed, "By order of the commander of the Russian Red Army, I declare you from this moment *freeeee*!"

What had been cheers and tears earlier expanded into tumult and sobbing as each prisoner released his feelings in his own way. When the excitement calmed down, POWs felt the ordeal, even those who had stood silent and rigid, unable to comprehend the stirring event that had take place in their midst.

Quiet was restored; greetings were exchanged from the improvised dais. Then a touch of friendship, bordering on humor, was shouted to the assembly. "Our victorious armies," called out the Russian officer, "are still a hundred kilometers to the north. We borrowed a jeep made in America and rushed this way, penetrating the enemy lines to seek out this camp. We were in haste to outdo your armies in Germany that released our prisoners when they overran their camps."

The door of the eso was flung open, and POWs who had been there were free to join their companions. Over in the corner of the compound, the Nipponese stood silent and quiet. Their sun had set.

It took time for the prisoners to quiet the upheaval that surged within them. The air smelled purer now; the shackles of bondage and servitude had been burst; emancipation, long sought, restored hope.

The day was moving fast to a close. Much remained to be done. Directions from the liberators to the enemy stirred them into action. Rifles, machine guns, ammunition, and samurai swords were collected and heaped up in an open spot in the compound, each Nipponese carrying out his task at a dogtrot. When that had been completed, the enemy, from Gimpy down to the lowest underling, formed into ranks. There was military precision, even now.

No instructions were needed by the prisoners. There was but one thing for them to do. They assembled in a large circle around the Russian officer. Twenty free men were called from the circle. The Russian reached toward the pile of military arms and selected a rifle and bayonet.

"I congratulate you," he said, handing those items to the men. Twenty times he went through that ceremony. "Line up! You are now in command. Take over your prisoners!"

The circle of men was hushed. A solemn silence fell over the group, influenced by that symbolic moment similar to the baton of a director leading the orchestra. A command from the guard was given for the Nipponese prisoners to march forward, eso bound.

"Oh! Oh!" stuttered a man standing beside Cameron, who paid no attention. But he laid a hand on Cameron and spoke again, which caused Cameron to turn his head. It was Old Joe. "These former POWs will tear them to pieces. There will be a horrible slaughter!"

Joe and Cameron were thinking about the same things, turning identical experiences over in their thoughts, remembering. But they analyzed differently. Insatiable hatred from the treatment received had been stirred up in the hearts of the Americans. Time after time, the threat had been proclaimed that, if one ever got free, he would tear to shreds any Nip he encountered. Years of suffering from barbaric ferocity and malevolence left their imprint, and revenge and retribution were but common emotions inherent in a human being.

Joe was not alone in his fears of a bloody debacle, where scores of angry men would pounce on each enemy and, with heavy boots and clubs, grind his dirty yellow soul deep into the ground. "Cam, we must do something," wailed Joe in a plaintive voice.

"Wait," cautioned Cameron quietly. He had an entirely different thought on the matter. Although his compatriots had acted like beasts among themselves over a long period of time, Cameron still retained faith in them.

The enemy, led by Gimpy, trooped off under the direction of the newly formed guard. A common sigh from the circle of Americans reflected the same thoughts that bothered Joe. Then all was silent! Not a catcall, not a whistle, not a hoot came from the group. These men might have been inside a vast cathedral, hushed by the awesomeness of a great moment. Not a man moved; there was no shuffling of feet even. The decision in each man's soul at that moment paid a fine tribute to the occidental way of life! What a contrast to that day, a long time ago, when the conditions were reversed.

Enthusiasm ran high that night and soon gave way to revelry, such revelry as could be had under restricted circumstances. Lights glared without concern; shouts and singing enlivened the dark hours for the first time; a man smoked where and when he damned well please; the inevitable poker games that sprang up where men were together gave pleasure to many. To hell with the Nips!

Military control must be assumed now. A semblance of that condition had already been set up. Unfortunately, during the years of imprisonment, there had been no internal direction or cohesion. Each POW had pulled away from the center and lived an individual life as he chose. The enemy had stamped out early any thought of command or control by the ranking officer. It was easier for the senior prisoners to succumb to that demand, rather than risk jeopardy to himself by surreptitiously exercising his influence. Anyhow, he would have found it difficult to accomplish because the independence of the American had immediately asserted itself in prison camp. Go to hell! I'll do as I damn well please! That was the attitude that expressed such independence. Loyalty and discipline, as they were known and practiced in a body of organized troops, were overshadowed by the personal demands of an austere life, where a man preferred to fight alone for what little gain there was to be had, rather than join in a common distribution of those limited facilities.

Stretched out on his blanket with his hands clasped behind his head and his knees drawn up, Cameron shook aside the hubbub and the disturbing glare of lights and lapsed into a reverie. His mind was alert, yet the stirring and emotional events he had just passed through distracted his thoughts. Slowly, by concentration, that purpose which he had adopted for himself long ago came into clearer focus. Much could and should be done promptly for the common good. *I've one idea*, he told himself suddenly. Springing up from his reclining position, he clutched his cotton uniform slacks—that garment that he had worn on the day of his capture and that was now barely recognizable. He flipped back the bottom of one leg and tore out the hem. A tiny American flag, about the size of a handkerchief fell into his appreciative hand. *Why, I had forgotten all about this*, he cried to himself, remembering how he had obtained it back on Bataan and had sewed it into the hem of his trousers. He hung it on the framework of the shelf that formed his small living space. From then on, it became an object of interest, a curiosity, or a symbol for man's devotion to every passerby who kept Cameron busy explaining how he had retained it after many searches by enemy guards.

Between interruptions, he lay back on his bunk and pondered. *I haven't been called upon for advice*, he reflected and shouldn't barge in on the problems of someone else. *Yet I may have learned things in my snooping around that should be of value to them. That Nip warehouse is full of food and many sorts of things they would never let us have. And at Nip headquarters there is a room filled with mail that has been collecting for two years and never distributed to us. Damn those yellow hyenas! I'm sure the Chinese on the outside have plenty of food they would be happy to bring in for sale—fish, eggs, meat, fruit, and vegetables, things we need and crave.*

Then there was another difficult problem that needed a solution. Everyone here, including Cameron himself, was wild to get out from behind this wall and enjoy some freedom. For the moment, that was risky, he knew. *Listen to that firing all around. Lots of it close in and over in the city. Why, think of the armed factions all over the vicinity. There are Chinese nationals, Chinese Reds, Russians, uncorralled Nips! Some of our people will run afoul of them, sure as I'm lying here. The poor devils are in such poor physical shape, they can't stand much activity. And their minds after this long interlude may not direct them with too much discretion.*

Some sort of control was necessary for the time being. *I had better go see the top man and risk his resentment over not minding my own business.*

Drowsiness crept up on Cameron. Relaxation gave him a moment to think of the gratitude he owed, the thanksgiving he should express. He closed his eyes and let his heart pour forth. *God in Heaven!* He spoke inaudibly and abruptly. *Accept the thanks of an undeserving man for this deliverance.*

The next two days were too filled with exiting events for the former prisoners to wander very far afield. Thousands of letters, many months old, were passed out to renew love and friendships that had lapsed for so long. The local Chinese besieged the gate with great quantities and varieties of food. And the Nips had insisted always that they could not get any more food because it was not to be had in Mukden. Damn them! Russian officials paid calls and arranged to make life more comfortable.

Then Cameron was called to headquarters.

"Cameron," he was told, "you had some good ideas the other day, and we think, you may have others. So we have an interesting mission for you."

"Why yes," replied Cameron. "I'll be glad to help in anyway possible." In his heart, he was not so sure of that remark. He was a normal human being and would much prefer to sit idly by and relax. Yet there was much to be done, and it would not be done automatically. Somebody here in the compound had work to do.

"You will go into Mukden and maintain close liaison between the Russian authorities and this camp. That assignment is a distinct honor, and you should enjoy it."

Woe unto me! Cameron whispered to himself. *Why didn't I keep my big mouth shut? If it is such a fine assignment, why me? Why not one of the inner circle?* He did not enthuse over the mission. It was much too hazardous. After having come this far without mishap since the end of the campaign, he had no false notions about jeopardizing his safe return home. He had a family that occupied his foremost thoughts, and he was too close to rejoining them to take any unnecessary risks. Anyhow, he was tired and sick like the others and could not stand the strain.

As he stood there momentarily, his eyes seemed to fog over, and another scene flitted across his vision. Paul was there in front of him, and his eyes were looking straight at Cameron, twinkling. A smile broke over Paul's face—that same smile that so often in the dark days had sustained Cameron. Paul's expression was too familiar not to be understood. *Of course, Cameron,* the face said, *you will do it, happily. You may think you don't want to. But down deep in your soul, you know that you will be a far better man for having contributed something of yourself for the betterment of your friends.*

Cameron shook his head quickly to clarify his thoughts and replied, "Yes, sir! I'll get busy on that job at once."

Before Cameron left on his trip to the city, he took a long look at the activities going on in the compound. It meant a sacrifice for him not to be able to enjoy the many things that were making the lives of the former prisoners more pleasant. They would touch him only indirectly. And worst of all, no one would care what sacrifice he was making for them. Nor would they appreciate his efforts on their behalf. They would lie back and enjoy all things that would come their way without a thought of the struggle someone else had to undergo to make those comforts possible. *Those parachutists*, thought Cameron, *they had a lot to tell.* How he wished he could stay on in camp and listen to the many tales of happenings since the darkness of prison life had cut him off from the world. Food! Tons of it coming in from the outside. After waiting and hoping for ages, he would not be able to enjoy it, while those who stayed back would swill it up until they grew bloated. There was the radio that had fluttered down from the skies under a red kimono, along with medical supplies and cigarettes and K rations. One of the men in the parachutist group was an expert radio technician, especially selected to handle and operate that instrument. Contact had been quickly established with China Theater headquarters. The broadcasts from the States came in regularly. But those Cameron would have to give up, or hear them in part later, if he could prevail upon others to forego their own pleasures and repeat what to them was old news.

Relationships with the enemy, now held in confinement, interested Cameron. He had seen one sterling example of how Americans could treat them. A tale of another instance gladdened him; he heard of a guard who had called the Nip prisoners from the eso to go to work. One remained behind cringing in the darkness. He complained of sickness, withdrawing farther back into the corner, awaiting the anticipated blow. What a coincidence, the American sentry had told him. Not so long ago he had been in that identical position himself. And what had happened? He had been called a dirty dog and set upon by blows from the enemy guard's rifle butt. What was to prevent a repetition of that episode now? Oh, no! The prisoner need not cringe in fear. A white man treats his prisoners of war with honor and decency. That is one of the reasons why the white race is superior to the yellow!

The boys are all shaved up smooth again, Cameron noticed. *Plenty of hot water now, and no restrictions on bathing.* He would miss all that.

He wanted to talk at length with the Nip interpreter. There were countless affairs to be straightened out, the opportunity for which may never come again. And the interpreter was willing to talk freely and tell all. One thing Cameron had learned. There was a plan to rush the POWs out of Mukden. The extra buns baked one day were for that journey. Arrangements were made to run the gauntlet, to the west, to Jehol. But one of the Russian columns coming unexpectedly out of Outer Mongolia had severed the route. Another interesting report Cameron had obtained from the interpreter was of the diabolical publicity given out subtly by the enemy. The compound comprising Camp Mukden was an airplane parts assembly plant—an early mission for American strategic bombing! From the parachutists, Cameron had learned that bombers based on the recently cleared Okinawa had the Mukden area assigned for early attention. *What a close call that was,* Cameron meditated. *A couple of weeks more, and we would have been obliterated by our own bombs.*

Airplanes from Kunming were dribbling in with needed supplies and mail. Letters were being taken back to be flown home. Somehow Cameron would have to arrange to find leisure to get off an occasional letter to his loved ones. They were impatient to hear from him just as much as were the families of others. That was the hardest sacrifice for him to make. Now that contact with home was possible, to have it denied him alone among so many, was excruciating.

Then Cameron gave a quick thought to his own condition. *Confound it!* he declared to himself. *I can hardly walk with this painful leg of mine. Doc says it's a result of malnutrition and will take a long time to respond. Meanwhile, I've got to hobble all over town, finding out where the many Russian establishments are located and what the officials can do to assist us. This job will not be simple, and I'm starting off under a great handicap. Why did I ever get mixed up with this?*

In a car borrowed from the Russians and accompanied by a young officer who could speak the language, Cameron poked out of the compound gate and headed for Mukden. On his initial trip through that ancient, sprawling, filthy, war-weary oriental city, Cameron felt and saw and smelled to such variety and degree that all his emotions and feelings had opportunity for full play. Because of that excursion, a permanent imprint was left on Cameron's sensitive nature. For the remainder of his life, remembrances of that day were to influence his thoughts and conduct.

While his car was bouncing over the ill-kept lane leading to the city proper and the motor chugged irregularly because of spark plug failures, Cameron leaned back in the upholstery and intently gazed out of the window. His first sensation was physical. How restful to relax on a soft seat with a pliable backrest that gently conformed to the body. The last time he had squirmed down into such spongy comfort was far back in the days of Bataan. Then he'd had a new model sedan, hastily purchased from a display room floor to augment the dire shortage of military vehicles available. The shining top had been hurriedly sawed off for greater and highly necessary visibility, but the cushions lost none of their luxury thereby. During the intervening years, his body had grown accustomed and hardened by rough planking and bare ground, sometimes eased by a blanket or straw pallet. Attending conditions had hardened his soul likewise.

A feeling of joy permeated his being in finally realizing his long-awaited liberty. Passing through the wall, from darkness to light, from suppression to freedom, marked a symbolic change in his life. Behind him now towered that wall, shaking and crumbling over its loss of power; that damnable wall had squeezed out of a man those fine things of life—the high standards of morality and ethics and the pleasure of their possession, which make for happiness. No need to look back. The wall possessed the diabolical influence of melancholia no more. She was dead, gone out of one's life, and should be forgotten, if a man could ever forget.

The factories just ahead were being patrolled by Nipponese soldiers, Cameron noticed. *Strange!* he thought. Of course, there was a reason. Undoubtedly, the terms of capitulation included a responsibility of the enemy to safeguard those places until the Russian troops arrived to take over. *Or am I*, meditated Cameron, *merely trying to bolster up my courage with such a thought? Here am I, a white man driving past those fanatics with no means of defense, except that little American flag of mine.* He had put the flag on a stick and wired it to the radiator emblem. *Will they know what it is? Will they respect it?* There were many of Cameron's own people back in the barracks who were not impressed when it was hanging over his bunk. How they criticized it! Must have been made in Japan; it was so cheap. Why, it didn't have enough stars. Look at that red stripe; it's only half the right size. The shape is square instead of a rectangle. *The poor dumb devils*, mused Cameron. There were just too many trees for them to see the forest. Keep going, driver; let's don't show any fear.

The pavements in the city showed the neglect of war years. Buildings were boarded up. Wary faces peeked out from upper windows. Here was half the thoroughfare being taken over by some of the more courageous vendors. Bring out hidden stocks of cheap clothing, some vegetables, meats covered by black swarms of flies, tobacco, bad whiskey, and homemade odds and ends. Over there, tawdry Chinese women strolled along the sidewalk, slyly signaling to Cameron as he drove past.

Automatic rifles stuttered on adjacent streets. A single shot cracked close by. Rickshaws, men, and pedestrians, having overcome their fears or feeling that their business of the moment justified a risk, cluttered up the streets and made driving a hazard. Farther along, a body lay distorted across a curb. Should one stop to render aid? Many were passing by on foot, looking, and going on their way unconcerned. Better not stop. Nothing could be done. Where should one call for assistance? Was there a hospital or morgue or police station in operation? Could one make himself understood for a Chinese telephone operator, if such a communication system was functioning? Hopeless!

Ahead, deep holes had been blasted in the pavement, and the dirt piled up in front. Demolished trucks were lined up in front. The Nips had made ready for a meager defense. Beyond, one of their tanks leaned askew, one of its tracks torn off. Cameron's driver bounced over the curb onto the sidewalk, scattering Orientals ahead of him, and bypassed the obstruction.

A sudden roar of motors overhead made Cameron first cringe from habit and then quickly thrust his head out the window from curiosity. A low flight of transports roared past. *American planes, sure as hell,* Cameron told himself. *No, that doesn't make sense. They must be Russian flying troops. But those white stars, just like the ones on that bomber that flew over the compound yesterday and dropped us leaflets? Is every country using the same star marking nowadays?*

There was another dead Chinese lying there, twisted and broken. Nobody cared. Look! A squad of soldiers just ahead! Would they interfere with the only motorcar on the street? Take it easy, driver. They seemed to be concerned with that store whose windows were heavily boarded. They were youthful-looking soldiers, dirty and unkempt. But they had come a thousand miles in a short time. *Hmm! They all carry tommy guns.* One soldier kicked open the door and quickly stepped back, behind the cover of the wall. Then two thrust their weapons into the interior and blasted way. There was no return fire, so they strode in, and Cameron continued on his way.

"Hold it, driver!" cried Cameron with amazement in his voice. "Pull over and stop. There are white people."

Standing at a gate, which opened through a low brick wall, above which a tall, untrimmed hedge rose, were two sad-looking Occidentals. The expressions on their faces changed to astonishment and then quickly to reveal their cordiality at seeing one of their kind.

"Good morning," said Cameron, stepping from his car.

"My dear sir, this is a happy moment," one of the men replied.

They greeted Cameron with unusual kindness and, in a few words, explained that they were missionaries who had been interned in this building ever since the war had come. There were others within. Cameron must meet them all. They needed the sight of a compatriot to cheer them up.

As they strolled toward the British club in which the missionaries had spent the war years, Cameron told them his name and what he was doing here. "We were in a POW camp just north of town. I am trying to find Russian headquarters and get what supplies I can for our people until we leave here."

Greetings of a most affable nature were exchanged all around. Everybody tried to talk at once; there was so much to be asked and so much to be told. Cameron glanced about. Conditions here were the same as back at his camp.

"How have you been treated?" he asked. "Could you get food and other things you needed?"

"The years have been very difficult," replied the father, who seemed to be the one the others looked to for leadership. He was old and worn and showed the results of deprivation. "The Nipponese kept us supplied with millet and cornmeal. Other items have been brought to us by the natives, at great risk to themselves." His voice gave way, and he weaved from the exertion.

A wooden chair was brought from an adjoining room and placed behind him. After he had seated himself, he continued his narrative. "We had blankets and more clothes than just the rags we now wear—not many, but enough for our needs."

"Did the Nips keep a guard here constantly?" Cameron asked.

"They trusted us a little. We were not to leave this compound. Daily, soldiers came to inspect us. They banged their way in and stomped heavily through the buildings, peering into everything and snarling at us. When we did not understand them or did not move fast enough, they would strike us. But they were only children, trained to act that way, and knew no better. Their superior officers were a little more lenient. They knew we had done much in the past years for their nationals in Mukden. Yet it was war, and we were enemies."

"You weren't treated any better than we were, apparently."

"The Nipponese feared us, for some reason or other. A few days ago they told us we were to move out to Jehol. They sent all our luggage ahead, and we were to follow. Now we have nothing."

"But you need food and clothing and blankets. These nights are growing quite cold."

"We have sent word to the Russians of our needs, but they are not interested. They say as long as we are bound to give help to the needy, whether enemy or not, we cannot expect aid from them."

"I'll see that you get what you need," Cameron declared. "That's what I am here for. It was a fortunate meeting, to see some of your missionaries standing there at the gate. We're getting plenty of food out at our camp. Tomorrow I'll have a truckload here for you. Other things will come as soon as 1 can get my hands on them."

"You are so kind. We will be ever grateful to you."

As Cameron rose to leave, a happy thought struck him. "By the way, Father, are there any more white men hereabouts? If so, they are probably in the same predicament as you are."

"There are several groups of missionaries throughout Manchukuo. Their fate I do not know. We have had practically no news. In Mukden here, across the city, there is a French cathedral. We have been informed by the Chinese that the fathers there have not been molested but were required to remain within their own wall. But there is a small group of nuns, of a different faith than ours, who have been interned in their convent. On occasions, we'd been able to slip food over to them by some of our devoted Chinese. They are just a short distance way." He explained to Cameron the route to take.

"Ah, one more matter. I intend to make arrangements as soon as possible for our camp to go back home. What plans have you? Shall we include your group also?

"That, dear sir, is a question each will decide for himself. We had the chance to be evacuated when the dark clouds began to roll in overhead. But those who preferred to stay made that decision after communing with their God for guidance. We felt that, if we were on the ground when the war ceased, our little help would be more needed than any time thereafter."

What physical and spiritual courage! Cameron said to himself. *Damn if I would have had that much selflessness. Never would have occurred to me. They certainly possess something in terms of brotherly obligations and in human relationships that an average man could never understand.* "You mean that you deliberately stayed on in enemy country, knowing what you would be up against?"

"Yes." The father laughed back at him. "Our mission was clear. It is like yours. You soldiers would never think of running away from combat."

"But …but …that is entirely different. We are armed and trained."

"My dear son, we, too, are armed and trained," countered the venerable man, with a softness yet intensity in his voice. "Our armament consists of the greatest force in the world, God's word and His love. And strange to say, that force is not a passive or defensive one. It is offensive!"

Cameron shook hands with all present and silently slipped out the door. He was overawed by the impressiveness of the courage of these men of God. He was preparing to open the gate when he heard the modulated voice of the elderly patriarch behind him.

"Come soon again. You have given us great courage and stimulation from the knowledge of the hardships you have endured."

Cameron's throat was choked. He could not utter a word. To be compared with such men as these!

"God bless you!"

"And may God bless you and all your brothers," he finally stammered.

After he slipped back into the seat of his car, Cameron rubbed a fist across his eyes, hoping the interpreter and the driver did not see the tears that had formed there.

He directed the man at the wheel around the block, along the route that had been pointed out to him. *There, that's the place*, he told himself. He saw a high iron grill fence and a large square stone building set up on a small rise. After instructing his driver to wait for him, Cameron raised the latch of the small gate. A chain and lock lay across the grilling, but they were not in use. Cameron wondered why. He strolled up the incline toward the convent, pondering the propriety of disturbing nuns in their seclusion.

Suddenly, a little Chinese youngster ran out from behind a bush. She saw Cameron, stood still in fear, and then scampered back to the other side. A native mother squatted there with another child, the two of whom clung to her like chicks to a hen.

"Uh ...convent?" asked Cameron in English.

The woman stared at him with an emotionless face.

"Uh ...church?" Cameron tried again.

There was no sign of understanding, so he tried again in Japanese. The woman smiled and pointed to the house.

As Cameron walked off, he wondered if she had understood or merely meant for him to go to the house and make his inquiry. He politely stepped up on the immaculate but bare porch, glancing through the windows as he passed them on the way to the large glassed, double doors that opened into a hail. The bell responded to his touch, but no one answered. A small sign had been pasted on one of the glass panels, the Russian lettering of which he was curiously examining when he heard the doorknob click.

"Good morning," he stuttered to a nun, who stood there smiling.

Her long black robe was spotless but well patched. Behind her spectacles glittered gray eyes, and a long pointed nose protruded toward Cameron.

"Good morning to you," she replied in a friendly Irish brogue, reaching out a long thin-fingered hand to Cameron.

"I have been talking with the fathers over at the British club. They told me about you here."

"Please come in and be comfortable. It has been a long time since we have seen any of our own people. I saw you reading the poster on the door. We have been bothered a great deal by Russian soldiers. They get drunk and come here and make themselves very obnoxious. So we asked the commander for protection. He had that sign put up, which warns all of his soldiers to keep away from this French convent. We aren't really French, you know, but it saves us so much trouble and permits us to carry on our work by claiming to be." She giggled aloud, pointing to a chair.

The room to which she had escorted Cameron while carrying on her rapid discourse was plainly furnished. There was an upholstered chair and several straight chairs. In the center of the room stood a small table with a doily and a cloisonné vase containing pink artificial roses. Framed colored prints hung on the walls—copies of Leonardo's *The Last Supper*, Raphael's *Madonna and Child*, and *La Pieta*. There was no carpeting on the floor, whose stained boards gleamed from recent rubbing. The atmosphere was austere but pleasing.

After Cameron had explained who he was and what he was doing, he said, "If I am trying to help those back in our camp, I must also do what I can to make your life here more comfortable and more effective. What do you need most?"

"We are carrying on our work with those who need us, and we will not differentiate between races. It is the need, rather than who needs it, that concerns us. Food is very essential. So little has been possible for us to get because there are no stores and no normal process of distributing. Many of our Chinese friends will bring us food, but it only means that they have to scurry around to find it and perhaps deny themselves. What little we get, we divide among those who are as needy as we. Yes, it is food we require first, but only with the understanding that we may dispose of it as we see fit, and I assure you, some of it will go to Japanese. No one must be hungrier than we are."

Far be it from me, Cameron announced to himself, *to have a conscience*. Then he spoke aloud, "Tomorrow a truck will bring you ample food for your convent to last some time. No one will check up on you to see what you have done with it. My worry is to see that you and the other sisters here are cared for."

"You have an understanding heart. No more could be expected of any man. You are one of few military men—and I've seen many, Americans, British, Japanese, Chinese, Russian—who possess the milk of human kindness. I have found most of them obtain results because of the disciplinary power that rests in their office. Perhaps that is one of the limitations on their abilities; perhaps (and especially among the Oriental) that is the only certain way. Who knows? Nevertheless, it is heartening to meet one who has no scruples against applying Christian principles."

From the feeling of the heat in his face, Cameron knew that he had reddened, and he was confused. Just what should he say after such tribute. *Hell*, he pondered, *all I was doing was to hand in some food to help out their good work. Damnation! I've been hungry for years; and if I can keep some other guy from starving, I guess I'll have to do it.* "You are very kind," he finally stammered. "I must be getting along."

"You have told me nothing about yourself," the mother superior said as they walked toward the door. "Do you have a wife and children?"

"Indeed, yes. She is a very lovely woman, just like yourself, always wearing herself out doing things for those less fortunate. And the three little scamps, who I haven't seen for five years, will be just like her. They are getting that sort of training."

Will you lunch with us, say, day after tomorrow? I would like to ask a few people in who you would like to meet."

"Why, yes, it would be a great pleasure. Only ..."

"The food?" The other laughed. "Fear not! My guests will bring their own. They would keep us supplied here also, if I would permit it. They have ample, but not an abundance. On this very special occasion, permit them to give to the Church's need." Her laugh was infectious. Cameron had to join with her.

"Adieu!" called Cameron as he left, referring to the French relationship the nun had assumed for the protection of her convent.

"And you, too, I commend to God! May the Mother of God watch over you."

"Straight ahead, driver," Cameron directed as soon as he was again seated in his car. *Wonderful people,* he meditated. *Too damn good for the appreciation they get. I'm sort of all mixed up on this kindliness and helpfulness to others. It's a swell thing and you get a great bang out of it. Only the more you do for others, the more they expect. And I wonder sometimes if they don't just think people who give them everything aren't suckers. But won't that gang back in the barracks raise hell if they know that some of their precious food is being given away to strangers and nothing to be received in return? What a joke! And they are lying around all day stuffing themselves like they were at a Roman banquet. Well, they'll never know. I'll take care of that little detail.*

Another body lay sprawled on the sidewalk. This time it was a Nipponese soldier. Cameron felt squeamish. For some reason that he could not understand, he had the same sympathy for that man with a shaved head lying there in an enemy uniform as he had had earlier when he had seen innocent Chinese dead along the thoroughfare. What had happened? One of those detestable yellow bastards lying stretched out, lifeless, should have been cause for rejoicing. But there was nothing but remorse in Cameron.

His attention was suddenly awakened by the interpreter at his side, who nudged him and said, "Look at the mob down the street! What do you make of that?"

Cameron leaned forward and squinted through the windshield. "They are cleaning out that building, I'd say. Just good old-fashioned looting."

Like a column of bushy ants coming and going, a steady stream of natives, men, women, and children, marched in orderly fashion into the building empty-handed and retreated through an adjacent door with their arms laden. Out came boxes, packages, furniture, scales, and boards from the counter. Nothing was unimportant to these people, who could now get something for nothing. Every scrap could be put to some use. No wonder protection was needed. The Russians either knew nothing of that episode or cared not the snap of a finger.

"There!" called Cameron to the driver, leaning forward in the rear seat and pointing ahead. "Straight ahead and then make the circle to the right. The hotel there, the Yamato."

At the center of the circular turn, up on an incline, the car stopped, and Cameron and his interpreter alighted. They looked around at the desolation and slowly climbed up the many steps to the lobby. Occasionally, a Russian officer rushed past. One Chinese civilian was busy behind the desk. Otherwise, the expanse of the ornate lobby quietly absorbed in distant recesses the sound of Cameron's tread.

"Well, let's get busy," Cameron declared to his interpreter. "We have to find the top men around here and see what help they will give us. We need food, blankets, motorcars, cash, and most important to us is transportation to get us out of here and home."

"That last could be the most difficult. No trains are running now that the Nips have fled, and every bridge between here and Darien has been blown out."

"Something will have to be worked out. Damn if I want to stay here indefinitely. And they'll never get us all out by air with only two planes flying back and forth to China headquarters. Suppose we start on this clerk and get the lay of the land."

From innumerable questions and prodigious efforts, the two Americans gradually discovered which officials could make decisions and where those officers could be located. Commanding generals, commandants, and chiefs of section, one after another, were sought out in hotel rooms, municipal buildings, banks, and elsewhere.

The unusual courtesy extended to Cameron on every occasion by busy officials involved in setting up an occupation administration made his task lighter. At anytime of the day or night, he was welcomed by merely knocking on a door. At first he had to convince the many armed guards on duty everywhere, but soon he was equipped with passes that gave him instant entrée to the highest commanders.

Going about the street from one building to another, he met with the same unusual friendliness. Russian soldiers by the dozens would rush up to him, toying with their tommy guns carelessly—every soldier carried such a weapon—and coy, "Americano?" Upon Cameron's nod and grin, the response would be a hearty slap on the back and the acknowledgment, "Good! Good!"

"What do you make of all this brotherly love?" the interpreter inquired.

"It seems so universal," Cameron replied, squinting his forehead, "that I'm inclined to believe that an order has been passed down from the top. Of course, your talking to them in their own languages helps a lot."

"Wait until we ran across some drunks. We may find it more troublesome, especially with those damn tommy guns everyone carries and fingers nervously."

"They seem so young, don't they? Some of these kids can't be more than fourteen years old."

Food was obtained; trucks were procured. Too often, before those vehicles could reach the camp north of town, a squad of soldiers would confiscate them. Then the whole process had to be started over.

It was late each night before Cameron could leave his duties and wearily start homeward. No restaurants were open. Finding food for himself was a problem. The interpreter came to the rescue by going to the hotel kitchen and striking up conversation with the military cooks. Usually he could influence them to give a little food from off the generals' menu.

The first night, he arrived back at camp so utterly worn out and exhausted from having overextended himself that he wanted to flop down on his pallet and sleep for a week. The hour was long after midnight. Some few of his colleagues were still awake and enjoying themselves. Cameron dropped on his blanket, and something under him crinkled like a bit of paper. He reached under his body and clutched it.

A note! A message from home! The radio had been receiving telegrams all day long for the former prisoners. Word had been relayed back to the States. Names and campsites were identified. "My darling," he read. "God has filled my heart with gladness and thanksgiving to learn, after all these years, you are alive and well. Come as fast as you can. The children and I count the hours. My devotion, always!"

A contraction of muscles started down deep in Cameron's stomach and spread upward until he almost choked from emotion. When he had read and reread his note and had visualized the courage his family had shown for such a long time of uncertainty and not knowing, he took hold off himself. *Christ!* he cried within himself. *And you think you are tired and want to quit. Why, there are two thousand more families just like that back home with their loved ones here in camp. Never mind what you may think about a lot of these people. They have a right to get home as soon a possible, just as much as you have. You, you big lug, are the one that has to do the job. Get them home! Never mind your ailments and that burning body of yours. You'll have plenty of time to rest and get medical care when this job is done. Hang on!*

The luncheon at the convent proved to be austere but enlightening. One of their guests was a Japanese leader of the community, through whom the sisters carried on much of their social service work with the poorer Nipponese.

"I am sure you would not mind meeting me, here," he said to Cameron. His English, like his demeanor, was excellent.

"Why, why," Cameron stuttered. He had not expected this. The first impulse he had was to object violently, but he quickly recalled the atmosphere that prevailed in this house, where a man was measured not by his political affiliation but by his worthiness. Cameron saw the mother superior standing near, looking at him through her spectacles. Her arms were folded, and her eyes twinkled. On her face slowly appeared that sort of commanding smile that Paul had given Cameron on so many occasions. *There is something here that far transcends my puny little position in life*, Cameron contemplated. He nodded acquiescence.

"Any day, any hour now," his Nipponese acquaintance said, "I expect the call. It may mean deportation to Siberia, at least incarceration such as you have suffered and suffered nobly. Believe me, we would not have had it that way if we could have had a voice."

Cameron noted the number of chairs at the table, which corresponded with the number of guests. They took seats when directed, but Cameron remained standing. He was in a quandary. "Won't you have this chair?" he finally with politeness asked the mother superior who was hovering nearby.

"Thank you, no," she graciously responded. "Do be seated. It is against the rules of our order to sit at the table with others like this."

Sometime later, when the other guests were departing, she spoke to Cameron in private. "The food you promised us came promptly. And in such generous quantities. We will be ever grateful to you."

"It was such a little thing, Sister. Anybody would have one the same."

"I must disagree with you," she replied with a warm smile. "It is only on occasion one will go out of his way to help others, especially when he is as tired and ill as you look to be."

Cameron thought he blushed, but he could not be sure. His head was throbbing, and the heat of his body might be something else. "I hope what we could send you served a worthy purpose," he stammered.

"It shall. Now, I have a little something for that sweet wife of yours, something to take back to her from me and all of us here in the convent." She picked up a small package from a table and presented it to Cameron. "Have a look at it and tell me if it might be appropriate."

He clumsily undid the wrapper, muttering his thanks for her thoughtfulness at the same time. A gorgeous green silk kimono, beautifully embroidered with gold dragons, fell to the floor as he held it up by the neckpiece. Mechanically, he glanced at the label inside. The sister saw him and laughed aloud.

"No, it is not Japanese," she said humorously, relieving his chagrin. "It is a fine piece of Chinese work. There is much of that here, but it is kept hidden, out of sight. Our Chinese friends brought it to us."

Sometime during a life of discouragement and disillusionment there will appear a diversion, a moment of passing interest if not enjoyment that breaks into the monotony and dispels the prevailing gloom and melancholy. Stimulation and refreshment for the weary mind should result from an encounter with that rarity.

Soon after Cameron's entry upon his Mukden task, the goodwill toward Americans, which was so apparent in the actions of all the soldiers in the conquering military force, manifested itself officially. The local commander, with his staff, invited Cameron and a few of the senior officers from the camp to the Yamato Hotel for a luncheon. There was importance attached to that invitation for a number of reasons. The turn that Russian hospitality might be expected to take could be forecast by an American officer, based upon many reports, exaggerated or not, as had come to his notice during the years of his career. There existed, further, the condition of international amity, comity between allies and brother officers who together had battled dastardly dictatorships to a bitter but deserved termination. Not the least in importance was the willingness of most of the invited guests to get away from a humdrum existence for a few short hours. There would be food, to be sure. But the thrill in that thought rested in a holdover of the view that had prevailed during the years of scarcity and, further, in the belief that the menu would be different from what the former prisoners now had available. It was not assumed for one minute that a Russian expeditionary force, recently arrived, could have much more than austere military rations, with perhaps the addition of a few choice morsels that could be obtained from hidden local providers. These matters were discussed at length prior to the day of the luncheon. All angles were explored, and all assisted in raising the enthusiasm of those invited.

But through that mantle of excitement, which had been tossed over the select few, there was woven a discordant stripe. Liquor! Not that hardened old troopers were squeamish or had any scruples against tossing off a drink or two; that was not the disturbing thought. But for emaciated bodies to undergo the punishment of competing with sound and healthy ones would likely end in disaster.

Graciousness of great degree prevailed that noon. A field marshal and three- and four-star generals in abundance—the Mukden occupation area appeared well endowed with high rank—greeted their guests affably in the drawing room of the finest appointed suite in the hotel. Each host punctiliously sought out each guest, made himself known, and extended a personal welcome.

Amazing things appeared before the eyes of the redeemed prisoners. Those men had been completely divorced from the world for so long that everyday matters loomed large to them. The courtesy and warmth of the greeting they received served as a vivid contrast between gentlemanly conduct and social intercourse as normally conducted and the mean, selfish, and disagreeable attitudes that were accepted as standard in a prisoner of war camp. The sprinkling of uniformed women quietly moving about as interpreters and waitresses—imagine an army having females attached; how silly—added an incongruous touch. How could these officers be so immaculately uniformed under combat conditions, wearing glistening black riding boots, azure blue breeches with wide gold stripes, and smartly turned out tunics bejeweled with expensive decorations? There was personal attention by the Russian commander himself to the final touches being put on the luncheon table. He strode many times through the reception room carrying silver and vases to the adjacent room beyond a door that was kept closed except for his passage through. His raised voice issuing last-minute instructions floated toward the guests.

Now came the time! At a silent signal, two generals took the arms of each guest and, with grave courtesy, escorted him to a chair at the table in the adjoining room. The first sight of the luncheon arrayed on a long beautifully set table brought forth gasps of astonishment from the ragged skeletons when they entered the banquet room.

The field marshal had performed a miracle under adverse conditions. His knowledge of social grace and perfection manifested itself. On white linen were arrayed in perfect alignment and assortment flat silver glimmering salvers and bowls, goblets, polished glasses, vases of garden flowers, and plates. There two were heaped-up piles of steaming steaks, chicken, fish, vegetables, bread, sweets, fruits, and nuts. And in every space not otherwise occupied stood bottles of whiskey and vodka and assorted wines and liqueurs. A Roman banquet!

Either an English-speaking host was seated next to each American or an interpreter stood behind his chair. There was to be no difficulty with conversation at this luncheon.

Highballs were poured as the first ceremony—who cared if the food cooled off while this amenity was being performed? All present stood up with raised glasses. Along with the others, Cameron held his glass to his mouth. Warily he quaffed a gentle sip, but polite "ahs" came in response from his hosts. The officer on his right, with a hand on his heart, smiled and graciously bowed. He made an indication for his guest to raise his drink again, and laying a finger on the bottom of Cameron's glass, he increased the pressure and forced Cameron to drink completely without pausing for breath.

"You must remember," Cameron stuttered politely, mopping the corners of his mouth with a napkin, that we have not tasted liquor for over three years."

"Ah-h-h!" Again the hand across the breast, a smile, and a bow.

When Cameron pulled up his chair to the table again, he saw that his attentive hosts had already refilled his glass.

This will never do, Cameron swore to himself. *None of these foreigners could drink me under the table if I were normal, and I'll be damned if they can do it now.* One stiff drink seemed to raise his fighting spirit, but his mind was far from befogged. He had met such situations before, successfully. "Ah-h-h!" It seemed the proper expression to use if one wanted to satisfy his desires. With that, Cameron placed a hand on his heart and made a little bow. Then he reached for a bowl off small fish floating in oil, one of the many entrees on the table. He did not delay in absorbing in a graceful manner all the oil he could take.

Up again with glasses raised! Cameron selected several crackers from a dish and munched them hurriedly. Meanwhile, he glanced toward his compatriots, trying to sign to them to follow his procedure. They did not understand, or their first highball had thrown them off balance. Try as he would, even calling across the table to them, Cameron achieved nothing.

There was an "Ah-h-h!" at his elbow, and he felt a nudge at the glass in his hand. Up it went, and down went the highball.

Let's take stock now, Cameron deliberated. *I've had two drinks already. The round of toasts has not even started yet. At the moment, my mind is by no means beclouded, but there is much guzzling ahead, I fear. In any event, that terrible leg pain has been toned down, and I feel less exhausted. Why don't my friends look this way and take a hint? If I am not mistaken, they are already weaving in their chairs. Uh-oh! This is going to be bad. One of us, at least, for the honor of the country must walk out of this international brawl on his own feet. It's a cinch my compatriots have given no thought to the matter. They're just babes in the woods!*

Glancing down to the task in front of him, Cameron observed his glass had again been made ready by one of his most attentive hosts. *More oil and food with discretion,* he mused. Ah, an idea! Reaching over for the dish of preserved young herring, he permitted his elbow to tip over his glass and spill the contents!

"Well, how careless," he spoke, and acting the part of a polite guest, he set the glass up on its bottom without ado.

Instantly a most courteous host refilled it with apologies to Cameron for the accident.

Everyone followed the cue of the field marshal when he began his luncheon, to the extent of each one's desires, that is. The Russians ate heartily and jovially, paying gracious attention to the guests. Cameron bluffed his way through the meal, pretending, sampling, and eating after discreet selections.

Toasts! The commander stood to propose the first one; the others at the table leaped up courteously. It was an act that repeated itself countless times before the party broke up. "To the president!" "To the

Generalissimo!" "To the Army of Occupation!" "To the American Camp!" "To the host!" "To the guests!" "To …!" To …!" To …!"

The hour was advanced. There was no one of importance who had not been saluted and honored. Cameron smiled when he realized he was still on his feet, though very unstable. Others, in whom he was interested, were not. *They'll have a really bad night*, he speculated. *Why are they so naive, so rustic?* The hour was late. The party had tapered off. Punctilious courtesy keeping a guest's glass filled had abated. During the progress of the afternoon, Cameron had taken advantage of the situation to do his own pouring from the constant stream of liquor bottles passed his way. One must drink to a proposed toast. Good manners required that, unless one was completely incapacitated. So he had performed his stint, with smiling graciousness but circumscribed consumption. And he belched, bloated with oil on which floated a deep layer of alcohol. Something must be done about that, and soon, he rationalized.

Adieus were made; pleasantries were exchanged. Cameron refused the proffered arms of his allies to steady him. He could walk alone, if the others could not! At the porte cochere, there were further farewells and expressions of everlasting friendship. The Americans slumped down in the upholstery of their shabby sedan. It was comforting to be enclosed while driving through a downpour in the darkness of early evening. To the camp, driver!

No conversation enlivened the trip back to camp. The driver was too busy avoiding holes in the pavement and straining his eyes to see through the rain and darkness. Cameron relaxed while the others slept. He lounged in the center of the rear seat, bobbing his head back and forth to avoid the glare of headlights from behind, which reflected in his eyes from the rearview mirror. *The only other car within sight*, he grumbled to himself, *that is out on a night like this, and it has to keep jammed up against us. Why doesn't he fall back or pass us?*

"Here we are," Cameron finally called to his friends, nudging them. "Home, sweet home! Let's pile out."

They stood at the side of the sedan and gasped in amazement at the sight behind them. The headlights that had followed them all the way through Mukden came from an army jeep, which pulled up and scraped its tires on the gravel as the driver sharply applied his brakes. From the open car leaped a laughing Russian field marshal, quickly followed by two grinning generals and a lieutenant general. Their once immaculate gold-braided uniforms, now waterlogged. drooped and sagged. The men rubbed the rain from their eyes, and one of them spoke.

"We wanted to be certain our guests arrived home safely," he said.

The day of departure, like the day of redemption, landmarked the wartime careers of each former prisoner. Yet the sensations felt and the emotions raised were different than on that earlier day of gladness. Then, there was relief from the fear of uncertainty and thanksgiving because of that change, which had affected the Americans most. Something had terminated. Joy was expressed over an ending. There was a backward remonstrance. Today, other considerations brought about a thrill, a tingling sensation that crept through the whole fiber of a man. This time, the thoughts of the future were uppermost. We are going home! Home, that place that meant peace and happiness and comfort; America, a life of luxury, where one could ride in a motor car or attend the cinema, enjoy a glass of beer or use a telephone, squat with pleasure on a commode or hear a symphony concert over the radio; the hearth, lighted by the fires of love glowing from the hearts of long unseen but not forgotten family, from which one was called to perform a duty, grave but worthy—those were the things that symbolized home!

Deep in his soul, Cameron felt and hoped, he had performed his last mission. He was tired, so very tired, and he wanted to cast aside all care and responsibility. If he could only fall off asleep, he meditated, not to awaken until that time when he could plant a foot firmly on his native soil. He longed to grasp that earth hungrily in his hands, to joyfully toss it in the air, and to have it sprinkle down over him in a shower. The moment was a complete letdown, a relaxation, a denouement of a sort.

During that coach ride to Dairen, Cameron curled up in a seat and lived unto himself. It was badly needed rest that forced him into that position of retirement, secluded in the far end of the car. But his thoughts and meditation refused to be still and kept him in a mental whirl. Four different trends kept hammering away in his thoughts. They played leapfrog with one another in a confusing way until Cameron finally classified them and considered them in sequence.

The thought of greatest interest was sentimental. It was of reunion with those whom he loved most and held dearest in his heart. Laboring in rice paddies or tossing at night on his pallet, he had constantly seen them before him. He had endured a terrible loss, the news of which reached him only long afterward. Both his parents had gone, within a short time of each other, brokenhearted. But he knew now his wife and children were safe. Recent news had assured him of their health. *Five years*, he told himself, *nearly five years since we parted. I hope she has not grown old and embittered because of fate that has kept us apart and forced upon her the worry of uncertainty, of not knowing. But not she, she who has more courage and spirit than anyone I know. She would never give up.*

The kids, I won't know them. They will have grown up in all this time. I wonder if they'll know this ragged old hulk when I get back?

Yes, of course! he answered himself. *My darling would have seen to that. Probably never a day passed without her impressing upon them everything about me. Oh, yes. They'll know me in spite of the years. I'll be there soon. There is nothing I can do now to hasten the moment. I must let them slip out of my thoughts for the time being. God bless them!*

His thoughts turned next to good old Uncle Sammy! *Am I still on his payroll? Has he forgotten us over here? Are we in ill grace with him because of our failure, for our part in the debacle of Bataan? God knows we did everything possible with the little he gave us. Or did we? Maybe I am not qualified to judge. Wonder if he is embarrassed for leaving us out on a limb. Well, the damn thing happened, unfortunately. If he raises hell with us because we flopped, he himself may become enmeshed in some of the reverberations from that calamity. Surely, he is wise enough to realize that. No doubt he will go easy on us. It would save his own skin. An emotional outburst of praise from him would cover up the chagrin of disaster, divert the embarrassment of defeat, and save face. That would safeguard his dignity and preserve us from condemnation. Ho hum! It's completely out of my control. Forget it!*

What strange traits these compatriots of mine have shown during imprisonment, ruminated Cameron. *They have exhibited an amazing degree of selfishness and self-interest. I can understand how our imprisonment under such hazardous circumstances produced constant irritations and how such intimate living with one another with no privacy would build up dislikes, even antagonisms. Yet, those matters are superficial, merely a lowering of gentlemanly and courteous standards,* he concluded. No serious harm was done, nothing a return to normal life couldn't redeem. It was the definite loss or tossing away of character that Cameron couldn't understand. How could a civilized human being whose entire life has been lived in some semblance of culture degrade himself to the point of snarling, fighting, and killing, just as a rabid dog might do? Were we humans no better than the animals of the wild when we were forced to live under conditions not far removed from theirs? Of what permanent value was this so-called civilization if it didn't stand up in an emergency? There might exist an occasional person in a group like ours who is short on moral stamina or is without substantial character, but to find so many of that kind was an indictment of what all had known as civilization.

That was the thinnest sort of a crust, Cameron had to confess, easily broken and peeled off if the possessor did not have something more substantial down in his soul to hang onto. Fear, that damned scourge of a POW's life, must have been instrumental in arousing the hatreds that were exhibited. Some close connections between those two emotions must exist. How could some of these former prisoners ever expect to hold up their heads when they went back after the way they had conducted themselves over here? No doubt, if they could stoop as low as they had, they were likely without shame and had consciences of stone.

But to be charitable, had their actions been different from the way man acts usually? Didn't the God-given ambition in the average man and that man's desire to gain and hold drive him on to live, enjoy comfort, and amass material things at the expense of anyone else? Would he stay that ambition merely because it conflicted with that of somebody else? His acts were less obvious and subtler than those of a POW because the less there was to be parceled out, the more gruesome were the actions of one who must fight for his share.

Now, what is the truth about the Nips? Cameron inquired of himself. *Do they think and conduct themselves differently than we do?*

Yes, decidedly so! he decided. *The oriental philosophy and way of life is contrary to ours in many instances. Why, they even read backward and then accuse us of the same thing. From our viewpoint, they have set up an anomalous life, where the men come in from their labors in the rice fields and drink tea and arrange flowers ceremoniously. Effeminate, we would call it. Yet, on another day, those same men will do battle with fanatical zeal and thrust their bodies bravely, though stupidly, into the maw of certain destruction. I believe much of the misunderstanding between East and West results from not appreciating those differences of tradition, culture, political views, and economic interests.*

Those matters, Cameron continued to contemplate, *are a fact of the individual Nip's life, which are impressed upon him from the time he is first stropped on his mother's back, papoose like.* It seemed to Cameron that all of a Nip's training—religious, military, and academic—pointed to the glorification of the empire and of the few members of the oligarchy at the expense of the individual, whose only raison d'être was for that purpose. This hatred they had toward the white man and which they had applied to the POWs was a part of the major plan for empire aggrandizement. It had been more fanatically exercised because of the war. With each victory, the Nips developed an increased arrogance, which was reflected in their feeling of greater freedom from retaliation in their treatment of prisoners. When they met with a military disaster, they sought means for revenge or face-saving. There was available to them only one place where that could be accomplished with assurance and delight. The POW camps!

From Cameron's inquiries among the prisoners who were assembled at Mukden from a dozen different camps, he had discovered that many "reign of terrors" happened on identical dates among the several camps. Such treatment must have resulted from a common directive from Tokyo. At least the Nip interpreter had so admitted to Cameron after the former captives had taken over. But of course he may have intentionally tried to save his own skin by placing that responsibility on an intangible head, Tokyo. *How would our own troops have treated*

Nip prisoners if their superiors had harangued them daily on the merits of brutality and ruthlessness, on the belief that their compatriots were being diabolically slain in the war zone, and on the notion that they were now far back out of the combat area and must use local conditions for a release of their craving and enthusiasm for combat? Cameron wondered. *It is true that our worst treatment came from those who had not been in action. Those Nips we encountered on a few occasions who had experienced combat were a different breed. No, they didn't let down any, but at least they looked for a violation of rules or regulations before they went on the warpath.*

Cameron feared that, in spite of his firm resolution to the contrary, he might be growing soft. *And I am afraid that time will heal some wounds that we have vowed to keep open. How will we who are privileged to return ever keep faith with those we are leaving back here to rest forever in the deep Pacific and on unrevealed oriental soil?*

Well, it was a dilemma! Should one uphold his vow, given during the heat of passion, for retribution; or should he forgive and forget in accordance with a principle, a belief, a faith? What answer would Paul have had? *There is probably a compromise, if one is strong enough to accept it—exact justice, a justice that should be determined by calm, deliberating minds and not by our biased ones.*

Lurching and jerking on the cars at that moment brought to an end Cameron's soliloquy and the train trip. Similarly, he terminated with a jolt a long and hazardous journey over a road whose lurking perils and pitfalls had been a challenge to a man's physical valor and moral courage. It was the conclusion of a period and the opening of a new phase. Cameron had traversed the valley of the shadow; the pleasant hills beyond beckoned him to lift up his eyes.

In his turn, Cameron sauntered out of the coach and stretched his cramped legs. Looking about, he saw he was in a railroad yard. His compatriots were milling about in the early darkness of evening, uncertain as to where to go. Cameron did not know any more than they did. But he had been responsible for getting them here. Perhaps he had better try to lead them by the hand, once more.

While in Mukden, he recalled, the foremost mission he had set for himself had been to get his people out of the Orient and home. That included himself, and in his soul, he claimed no special altruistic motive. So, early, he had sought out the official charged with transportation matters and discussed with him arrangements for quick evacuation if American ships showed up at Dairen. Probably the Russians were anxious for their allies to depart. At least Cameron did not hesitate in his conversations to infer that it would be easier to complete the occupation if they were not around.

No news came from China about wholesale evacuation. The sick were still being taken out by air, a few a day. It would require months at that slow rate to move all the former prisoners. Had they been forgotten? Were they to be left on their own resources after the first flurry of interest had been manifested in them by distant headquarters? Maybe it would require pressure and urgent demands from families back home to set the gears grinding, to stir the cold military machine out of its lethargy.

Then suddenly a rumor had reached Cameron. An officer told him that an official had come up from Dairen and that some American ships were in the harbor. At that, Cameron dropped everything. Without rest or time for meals, he scoured the city in an effort to find the official. Success eventually was achieved. The statement was not a rumor but a fact. Next to the airport! Would the commander carry an American officer to Dairen to investigate and make arrangements for evacuation, After all, it was in the interests of the occupying army to move out these former prisoners. They were an unnecessary burden when so much had to be done in disarming the enemy and pacifying natives. Why, yes! A plane will leave in the morning.

Consequently, as Cameron viewed the apparent helplessness of his compatriots in the railroad yard, he felt that someone should lead them to their destination. Carefully looking beyond the tracks, he saw in the early darkness a broad expanse of flatness. *Water*, reflected Cameron. *The harbor! It's as simple as that.*

"This way, men. Follow me!"

He took off, with the others close behind. Fifty yards beyond, dark forms came running forward. Gobs! Dressed in Navy blue! Some few carried stretchers. Most were empty-handed. They quickly grasped the luggage the former prisoners were carrying and lent strong arms to assist them in making their way onward.

The procession turned round the end of a warehouse. The sudden dazzle that flashed in Cameron's eyes momentarily blinded him! It was not merely a physical picture he saw. It was symbolic of the greatest interest in his life at that moment. America, in her most glorious display, stood there before him. Her arms were extended to enfold him to her breast, while a sweet smile welcomed him home.

Cameron stared hard, as he blinked his eyes and gave a silent prayer of gratitude. Arrayed before him, riding in the dock, was a white vessel, made more brilliant by many spotlights shining on her flanks and lighting up huge red crosses. Loud speakers pierced the air with American dance tunes. The ship's company stood on deck. On the prow black letters told a story—RELIEF!

A word of welcome came from the skipper as Cameron reached the top of the gangplank; cheers from those gathered on deck struck his ears; hospital attendants in starched white courteously directed him to a stateroom; a nurse took over.

"Hop on that bunk," she ordered. "Strip off those filthy rags. I'll have a man in here immediately to bathe you. Here are fresh pajamas. Probably the first clean sheets you've been between for a long time.

"You're lovely," he replied, meaning everything that she represented.

"I know it." She laughed back. "At least a thousand others have told me the same thing in the past two years. They were hauled in off the beaches—men with legs gone, gaping holes in their bodies. Well, you can eat your old head off from now on, soldier. Anything and everything you want."

"Any ice cream?"

"You bet! Ice cream."

"Good! Ice cream."

Japanese Vocabulary

Arigato - Thank you

Banzai - Battle cry

Benjo - Toilet

Bushido - Historical code of honor of Samurai

Ichi ban - Number one

Eso - Jail

Hai - Yes

Honcho - Leader, man in charge

Imo - Sweet potato, yam

Kang Kong - Leafy vegetable

Keirei - Formal, exaggerated form of bowing

Kempeitai - Military police of Japanese army

Kiotsuke - Warning, be careful!

Kura - Storehouse

Kuwa - Hoe-like garden tool

Maru - Circle, as in navigational "great circle," ship names

Miso - Vegetable paste, from soybean, barley. etc.

Mizu - Water

Nipponese - Derivative form of Nippon, the Japanese word for Japan/
non-derogatory

Nip/Jap - Derogatory abbreviations

Rescript - Official edict or announcement

Shima - Island

Tsuji - Proper name

Seiki - Proper name

Tenko - Formal roll call, muster

Wakamoto - Food supplement tablets of dubious dietary value

Yasumi - Holiday, day off

BIBLIOGRAPHY

General Wainwright's Story, 1945 - Robert Considine, ed.

The Life of a P.O.W. Under the Japanese: In Caricature, 1946 - Col. Malcolm Vaughn Fortier

The Hard Way Home, 1947- Col. William C. Braly

South to Bataan, North to Mukden, 1971 - Brigadier General W. E. Brougher

Hero of Bataan: The Story of General Jonathan M. Wainwright, 1981 - Duane Schultz

Prisoner of War (Artworks),1986 - Ben Steele

POWs of Japanese: RESCUED!, 2003 - Harold "Hal" Leith

Prisoner of the Rising Sun: Brig. Gen. Lewis Beebe, 2006 - John M. Beebe

To Bataan and Back, 2016 - Maj. Thomas Dooley

Col. "Nick" Galbraith receiving the Distinguished
Service Medal from Gen. Wainwright

APPENDICES

APPENDIX 1

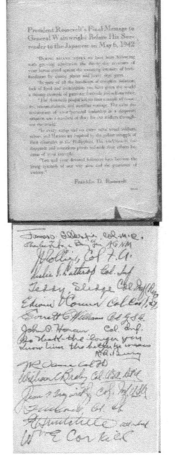

APPENDIX 2

Fort Sam Houston, Texas
19 March 1946

SUBJECT: Report on North Luzon Episode Following Corregidor
Surrender.

TO   : General Jonathan M. Wainwright.

Having been requested to consolidate and record the facts
of the North Luzon Episode for use by your Awards Board, I
am submitting that information below. It may also be considered as a more permanent type of report to you than the verbal report with notes that I submitted upon my return to
Tarlac in 1942.

All the facts involved have long since become common
knowledge. There is nothing new except the personal angle,
and a more intimate presentation has been made.

When conditions made it imperative to offer the surrender of the Fortified Islands on May 6, 1942, General Homma,
Japanese military commander in the Philippines, refused to
accept that offer unless all the units in the Philippines
were also surrendered. Failing that, he threatened to destroy
the unarmed garrison of the Fortified Islands. As part of
the necessary effort of General Wainwright to fulfill these
demands and avoid calamity, he dispatched G, as a staff officer to North Luzon, in custody of a Japanese detachment, to
locate, issue orders to, and obtain the signed acknowledgement of the commander of U.S. troops in the area west of the
Cagayan Valley. The location of this commander, Colonel John
P. Horan, Infantry, was unknown, it might have been anyplace
within the area Bontoc-Appari-Vigan-San Fernando. Haste was
imperative to assure the safety of General Wainwright, his
staff, and the garrison. However the mission assigned to G.
was accomplished, the procedure of which is unimportant here.
Colonel Horan was contacted, his personal surrender obtained,
and his signature to General Wainwright's orders procured.
Naturally, the imperative thought of G. was to expedite his
return to his commander and assure him of the circumstances,
so that the latter could present that fact to General Homma
and procure the release from a hostage status of himself and
colleagues. To dally a single day in bringing this vital information back might be fatal to 14,000 Fil-Americans.
During conversations with Colonel Horan prior to returning to Manila, G. discovered that a most unusual and unorthodox situation prevailed in the Command of Colonel Horan. Time
and conditions, since the receipt of authority to assume command and establish an organization, had not permitted him to

join together the many units fighting separately in that area.
Cohesion and entity did not exist. The only approach that had
been possible towards unifying these scattered groups was a
conference held at Bontoc some time earlier at which the senior
officers of areas, in which they operated independently by
mutual agreement, had met with Colonel Horan to set up a single
command. Some of these officers had to travel five days
on foot across the mountains to return to their own local
jurisdictions. During this period several columns of Japanese
troops had converged on Colonel Horan's headquarters, and it
was essential for the preservation of life for him and his
staff to flee to the mountains. Naturally, disintegration followed. No modern communications existed between elements, there
was no telephone or radio contact. The only means of transmit-
ting messages through that rugged country was over the foot-
trails by runners. Thousands of square miles of tropical, mountain terrain were involved. Independent units, to avoid jeopardy and Japanese pressure, would move from barrio to barrio.
Other units would be temporarily demobilized, to be called together for occasional ambush on Japanese columns. Military
action was sporadic and contingent. Of the few American officers, practically none had had any military training. They
had been, principally, mining engineers in North Luzon who
were commissioned through the efforts of Colonel Horan following the outbreak of war. Men of ingenuity, thoroughly familiar with the mountains and the natives, they could not be
expected to voluntarily surrender, even on the orders of
General Wainwright, whose legal authority after the surrender
was questionable.

It was quite obvious that Colonel Horan was in a most undesirable position. His task of collecting his troops and
surrendering them had elements of the impossible. Accordingly
it was more imperative than ever that G. return to Manila
with his recorded information on the surrender of Colonel
Horan, so that General Wainwright could have that data to
convince General Homma that surrender conditions had been fulfilled and to negotiate with him for transfer from hostage
to prisoner of war status. If the impossible condition in the
North became known to the Japanese, as it soon must, release
from hostage might never occur.

Nevertheless, balanced against this need for immediate
return to Manila was the obvious consideration that would
occur to any soldier, that departure would be in the nature of
deserting a comrade in peril. But, significant as that may be,
it was only a minor point compared to that far greater factor,
an assumed responsibility for the lives and destinies of the
Commanding General and 14,000 Fil-Americans. In consequence,
any action taken by G. must be consistent with that feeling
of responsibility. The question naturally arose, if he remained
here in North Luzon and expended all effort possible to assist
Colonel Horan in his insuperable task, would it convince General
Homma that the fullest good will and in-

tention were being exercised to comply with his demands?
This might be particularly effective in Homma's mind because G. was the personal representative and General Staff
officer on the ground of the American commander. Surely Homma
was not completely unreasonable and would give credit
for effort even though results were not obtained. Would G.
be violating General Wainwright's instructions? Even that
contingency had to be subordinated to the new conditions of
the moment. This unusual situation, was devoid of spectacular
military action were emotions too frequently control conduct,
and sensational factors were absent. The requirements of the
moment demanded cold analysis, contemplation, prayer, and
deliberate decision.

From the psychological aspect, that line of action that
would assure the most favorable response from Homma, it appeared that the weight of the analysis lay on the side of
remaining with Horan. But would G. be expected to take this
decisive step? Would he be reproved if he did not? To return to Manila, with the satisfaction of having completed
successfully his mission, and take advantage of the relative
security afforded by a prisoner of war camp was a tremendous
temptation. G's remaining in the mountains would at the best be
only a gesture, although a very vital one, of showing honesty
of purpose and good intention to Homma. It would involve obvious failure in any effort to obtain the surrender of any
material group of combatants, G's probable execution because
of that failure, possible destruction even though successful,
because of then having lost any future value or usefulness to
the enemy, necessity of crossing and recrossing battle lines
that could not be pre-determined because of the precarious
conditions of mountain fighting and sporadic action. Each side
would be hostile, the emeny obviously, and "friendly" troops
because of suspicion and fear and of the universally known
feeling on the part of the Filipinos that any Occidental not
actively engaged with them was a German spy and subject to
summary execution. G. would be a direct target for anyone with
a weapon, regardless of the side on which he was fighting.
Food would be difficult to procure. Malnutrition in G. had
already developed, following a severe and continuous campaign of considerable length on very restricted rations. Disease
might well be expected. The rigors of tramping rugged mountains, days on end, in G's physical condition, and at his age,
was not a pleasant thought. There was a professional distaste
in operating under an officer junior in rank. Should wife and
children be given any consideration? The chances of coming
through this episode alive and unbroken were exceedingly small.
Even though successful it would mean starting off a long
period of Oriental internment with physical and mental qualities at low ebb.

3

Every one of these arguments was joined by a common thread, and it was related to personal security. No real soldier at such a time could be thus influenced and hope to live in peace with his future conscience. Self-sacrifice was indicated, the decision was made, the die was cast.

Accordingly, with Colonel Horan a plan was developed whereby G. would stay on to assist him, and the mountain area would be roughly divided into halves, with each officer working within one of the portions. The plan was then laid before the Japanese, who, after obtaining its approval from their headquarters, put it into effect.

The points in the earlier analysis, being only too obvious at the time, materialized. Extreme military hazards did occur almost daily. Passage through a combat zone from side to side a score of times is a most unusual risk that has not been within the experiences of many soldiers. Kidnapping to preclude G's operations and prevent his issuing surrender orders was thwarted. The consummation of such an event would probably have had horrible repercussions. G's failure to return to enemy custody at the proper time would have sacrificed American honor and nullified the effort to show honesty of intention in fulfilling the surrender terms. A car on the road or a white man trudging in the mountains was subject to ambush by Filipinos or being fired upon by enemy patrols. Failure to obtain prompt results caused an unfavorable reaction from the enemy high command against the officer in charge of the detachment, which resulted in threats and intimidations against the person of G. by pointing of pistols and flailing of samurai swords. These uncertainties were countered and the failure to obtain results was mitigated by constantly impressing upon the Japanese commander that his prestige and destiny were bound up with G. To destroy the latter, even though justifiable to his superiors, would eliminate the chief source of aid to him in the pursuit of his task. If, however, he would daily impress and eventually convince his higher authorities that every conceivable effort was being honestly and conscientiously made to produce early results, both he and G. would retain their prestige and both would be materially benefited. Every move was spied upon by Filipinos, paid or coerced, and reported, with true Oriental ethics as their advantages dictated, to the Japanese. The uncertainty and worry because of this situation was a harrowing experience.

The tremendous results and achievement obtained justified any sacrifice and effort made by G. The eventual release of hostages and their reclassification as prisoners of war may be attributed in no small measure to that effort. That can be noted specifically by the fact that soon thereafter G's work in North Luzon was suddenly terminated by order of the enemy high command, he was commended by the Japanese for his strenuous endeavors to assist them in their effort to stop

4

further slaughter, and was returned to his own commander.

N.F.GALBRAITH
Colonel, G.S.C.

1 incl. (Surrender Order)

APPROVED

J.M.WAINWRIGHT
General U.S.A.

APPENDIX 3 –
GEN. WAINWRIGHT'S
SURRENDER BROADCAST

APPENDIX 4 –
GEN. WAINWRIGHT'S
SURRENDER ORDER

HEADQUARTERS
United States Forces in the Philippines

Fort Mills, P. I.,
7 May 1942.

Subject: Surrender.

To: Colonel J. P. Horan.

To put a stop to further useless sacrifice of human life on the Fortified Islands, yesterday I tendered to Lieutenant General Homma, the Commander-in-Chief of the Imperial Japanese Forces in the Philippines, the surrender of the four harbor forts of Manila Bay.

General Homma declined to accept my surrender unless it included the forces under your command. It became apparent that the garrisons of these forts would be eventually destroyed by aerial and artillery bombardment and by infantry supported tanks, which have overwhelmed Corregidor.

After leaving General Homma with no agreement between us I decided to accept in the name of humanity his proposal and tendered at midnight, night 6-7 May, 1942, to the senior Japanese officer on Corregidor, the formal surrender of all American and Philippine Army troops in the Philippines. You will therefore be guided accordingly, and will repeat will surrender all troops under your command to the proper Japanese officer. This decision on my part, you will realize, was forced upon me by means entirely beyond my control.

The Staff Officer who will deliver this to you is fully empowered to act for me. You are hereby ordered by me as the senior American Army officer in the Philippine Islands to scrupulously carry out the provisions of this letter, as well as such additional instructions as the Staff Officer may give you in my name.

J. M. WAINWRIGHT,
Lieutenant General, U. S. Army.

APPENDIX 5 – HORAN

—▸◆◂—

Headquarters United States Army Forces in the Mountain Province

Bontoc, Mt. Prov., P. I.
May 22, 1942

Subject : Surrender.

To   : All American officers and enlisted men.

      1. From Col. N. F. Galbraith, GSC, I have this date received an official order from Lt. Gen. Wainwright, Cmdg. Gen., USFIP, to surrender all officers, enlisted personnel, weapons, ammunition and equipment to the nearest Japanese Commander.

      2. You are therefore directed to collect all the American officers and enlisted men and Filipino soldiers possible in your area and report to the nearest Japanese Commander without delay.

      3. This is an official Order. Noncompliance will be considered as direct and willful disobedience of the orders of the CG. USFIP.

      4. Col. N. F. Galbraith, GSC, and Major G. C. Heinrich, Executive Officer, 121st. Infantry (PA), will arrive in your area soon. You may contact them for further instructions upon their arrival.

                                 John P. Horan,
                        Colonel, 121st Infantry (PA)

HEADQUARTERS UNITED STATES ARMY FORCES IN THE MOUN TAIN PROVINCE

Bontoc, M t. Prov., P.I.
May 23, 1942.

TO WHOM IT MAY CONCERN:

Major C.C.Heinrich, Executive Officer , 121st Infantry (whose signature appears below) has authori ty to act for me in my absence, and to issue orders in my n ame. His instructions and orders will be obeyed accordingly.

JOHN P. HORAN,
John P. Hor an,
Colonel, 121st Infantry (PA)
Commanding.

C.C.HEINRICH,
C.C.Heinrich,
Major, 121st Inf. (PA)

I certify that the above is a true copy of the original:

Lt Col P.C.
N F Galbraith
Col GSC
CCHeinrich
Major 121st. Inf (PA)
Jm Anderson
Supv. Teacher, Ifugao District

Fort Mills, P. I.,
7 May 1942.

Subject: Surrender.

To: Colonel J. P. Horan.

      To put a stop to further useless sacrifice of human life on the Fortified Islands, yesterday I tendered to Lieutenant General Homma, the Commander-in-Chief of the Imperial Japanese Forces in the Philippines, the surrender of the four harbor forts of Manila Bay.

      General Homma declined to accept my surrender unless it included the forces under your command. It became apparent that the garrisons of these forts would be eventually destroyed by aerial and artillery bombardment and by infantry supported/tanks, which have overwhelmed Corregidor.

      After leaving General Homma with no agreement between us I decided to accept in the name of humanity his proposal and tendered at midnight, night 6-7 May, 1942, to the senior Japanese officer on Corregidor, the formal surrender of all American and Philippine Army troops in the Philippines. You will therefore be guided accordingly, and **will** repeat **will** surrender all troops under your command to the proper Japanese officer. This decision on my part, you will realize, was forced upon me by means entirely beyond my control.

      The Staff Officer who will deliver this to you is fully empowered to act for me. You are hereby ordered by me as the senior American Army officer in the Philippine Islands to scrupulously carry out the provisions of this letter, as well as such additional instructions as the Staff Officer may give you in my name.

J. M. WAINWRIGHT,
Lieutenant General, U. S. Army.

Copy for Lt. Col. Wm Thorpe for compliance as respects detachment under his command J. M. Wainwright Lt. Gen. Comdg.

The following instructions were received by General Wainwright

The following instructions were received by General Wainwright
governing sonditions under which surrender of forces under his command would be accepted only if faithfully carried out:

To your troops operating in other parts of the Philippine Islands
the order shall be given to disarm voluntarily immediately and to
take the under-stipulated steps:
Those remaining in Northern Luzon to assemble at Bayongbon or
Bontoc and the commanding officer to present himself to Japanese
Army in Baguio and notify him of their surrender. Those remaining
on Panay Island to assemble northern environs of Iloilo City,
on Negros Island in the vicinity of Bacolod City, and the commanding
officers of both regions to present themselves to Japanese Army in
Iloilo City and notify of their surrender.
Those remaining in Bohol Island to assemble in the vicinity of
Roai and the commanding officers to present themselves to Japanese
Army in Cebu and notify of their surrender. Those remaining on Leyte
Island and on Samar Island to assemble in the vicinity of Tacloban
and Catbalogan respectively and the commanding officers to present
themselves to Japanese Army in Legaspi and notify of their surrender.
Those remaining in the district of Lanao and Zamboanga in Mindanao
Island to assemble in the vicinity of Iligan and those remaining
in the vicinity of district of Malaybay and Agsan Basin to assemble
in the vicinity of Malaybay or Butuan and their commanding officers
to notify of their surrender.
The order shall be carried out within four days.

It is strictly prohibited to to destroy, burn or desperse arms,
materials, vessels, and any establishments, either part or whole.

Portable and easily- movable weapons to be gathered all together
in the vicinity of the assemble area of the troops.
Heavy arms, materials and establishments to be remains intact
and the location thereof to be repoted with the sketch.
Vessels in the waters around Corregidor Island to the port of
Cagayan.
Defence measures, specially those areas wherein land mines or
sea mines were laid to be reported with the sketch, and the actual
spot to be distinctly indicated with some suitable means, if such
is ata all possible.
Japanese war prisoners, if any, to be handed over immediately.
Further order will be given if such is found necessary.

Candon, I.S.
7 June, 1942.

Captain ~~orden~~ Centeno:

It is absolutely imperative that I have an immediate contact with you in order to explain the Commanding General's military orders to you.

This situation rapidly is reaching a serious stage because of several small unit commanders refusing to obey General Wainwright's and Colonel Horan's orders on surrender. All units in the Philippine Island already have surrendered except some of those in the mountains of Northern Luzon. The honor of the U.S.Army is at stake as well as the security of yourself and the civilians in the area.

The Japanese authorities have assured me of safety and well treatment for you and all of your command if you surrender voluntarily. However this assurance cannot be expected to continue much longer because the general's orders are now a month old. Should it become necessary for the Japanese Forces to proceed against you, your status and that of the men under you will be that of outlaws and renegades, and in that event you cannot expect the protection of military prisoners. Furthermore the U.S.Army will have a claim on you for direct disobedience of military orders in war-time, in which case you will have no one to look to for defense and protection. Also the civilians who aid and abet you by supplying food, protection, etc. will meet the same fate.

You are directed by the Commanding General to surrender immediately, and if you desire further information to arrange for a contact and meeting with me, Major G.C.Heinrich, who has the same authority as I, is now in the mountains proceeding from S. Emelio to Conception to Andeki. I will be in Candon for several more days. All personnel as well as arms and ammunition must be surrendered to the nearest Japanese Forces.

It is unfortunate that the military situation has taken this turn, but the United States Government is responsible for the conduct of the war and no subordinate can take it upon himself to handle any phase according to his own way of thinking. I am giving you the law in the premises, and it is ridiculous to adhere to some of the rumors that I have heard circulating in the mountains.

Again let me repeat that your safety and good treatment is positively assured by the Japanese Forces for a voluntary surrender.

By direction of Lieut. General Wainwright,

N.F.Galbraith,
Colonel, General Staff Corps,
U.S.Army.

APPENDIX 6 –
JAPANESE SURRENDER ORDERS

The Imperial Japanese Forces earnestly wish the public peace and happiness of all the inhabitants of the Philippines. Therefore, they will severely punish those who will disturb the public peace and order, and who will threaten the happy lives of the law-abiding people.

The Japanese Forces strictly forbid the public to keep war arms for their ownselves, since these are the articles that threaten the public peace and order.

Those who have or can find arms are expected to return or report them to the Japanese Forces in the nearest Japanese Army Station, immediately. Those who hide arms or ammunitions, or have them with themselves secretly, shall be recognized by the Japanese Forces that they disturb the peace and order of the law-abiding citizens and shall be severely punished by the said Forces.

The Commander-in-Chief of the
Imperial Japanese Forces

大 日 本 軍 司 令 官

THE NIPPON IMPERIAL ARMY
AT CANDON

June 18, 1942

N. F. Galbraith
Colonel U.S. Army

<u>O R D E R</u>

Sir: You are ordered to report in person to
Captain Hitomi at Candon at once for conference
with Colonel Horan.

It is understood that those who accompanied
you shall abandon their work and return to C andon
with you.

J. Hitomi
Lieutenant
THE NIPPON IMPERIAL ARMY

PLEASE DELIVER TO COLONEL HORAN

Headquarters—United States Forces in the Philippines
Fort Mills, P.I.
May 7, 1942

Subject: Surrender
To: Colonel J. P. Horan

To put a stop to further useless sacrifice of human life on the Fortified Islands, yesterday I tendered to Lieutenant General Homma, the Commander-in-Chief of the Imperial Japanese Forces in the Philippines, the surrender of the four harbor forts of Manila Bay.

General Homma declined to accept my surrender unless it included the forces under your command. It became apparent that the garrisons of these forts would be eventually destroyed by aerial and artillery bombardment and by infantry, supported by thanks, which have overwhelmed Corregidor.

After leaving General Homma with no agreement between us I decided to accept in the name of humanity his proposal and tendered at midnight, 6-7, May, 1942, to the senior Japanese officer on Corregidor, the formal surrender all American and Philippine Army troops in the Philippines. You will therefore be guided accordingly surrender of all American and Phil. Army troops under your command to the proper Japanese officer. This decision on my part, you will realize, was forced upon me by means entirely beyond my control.

The staff officer who will deliver this to you is fully empowered to act for me. You are hereby ordered by me, as the senior American Army officer in the Philippine Islands, to scrupulously carry out the provisions of this letter, as well as such additional instructions as this Staff Officer may give you in my name.

J. M. Wainwright
Lieutenant General, U. S. Army

PLEASE DELIVER TO COLONEL HORAN

May 8, 1942

Col. Horan:

The undersigned, representative of General Wainwright, has reached Baguio this date enroute to Bontoc area to deliver the above instructions to you. The condition of the Baguio-Bontoc road makes it necessary to proceed many kilometers on foot, thereby losing considerable valuable time. Upon receipt of a copy of this mimeograph you will send an officer under a white flag of truce to meet the representative of the Japanese Army in Bontoc. Your staff officer will await my arrival for delivery to him of official orders covering the copy noted above.

Japanese forces in Bontoc are being notified of these arrangements.

N. F. Galbraith
Col. G.S.C.
U. S. Army

APPENDIX 7 – MARUS

鈴谷丸

Otari Maru (top) and Oryoku Maru (bottom)

APPENDIX 8 - POW CLOTHING

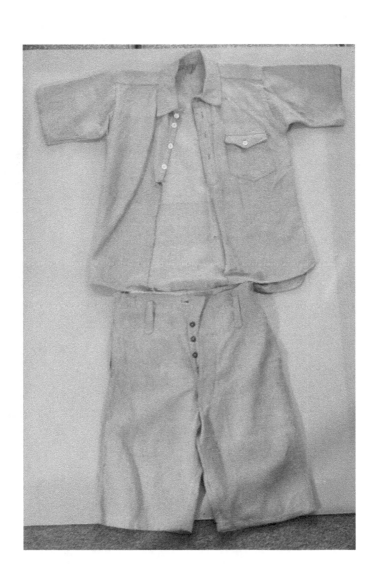

Nick Galbraith's identification patches

Mess Kit

Courtesy of the Colorado Springs Pioneers Museum

APPENDIX 9 – LABELS

Vitamin Pills

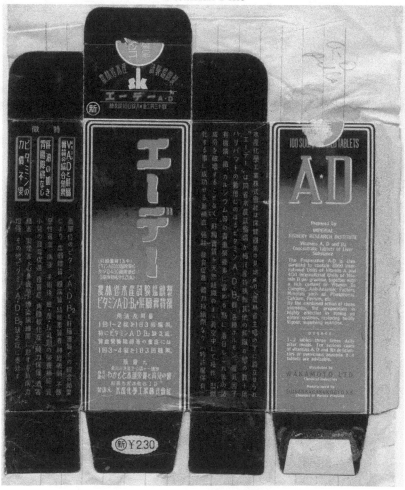

Vanilla, Playing Cards, Mail Envelopes

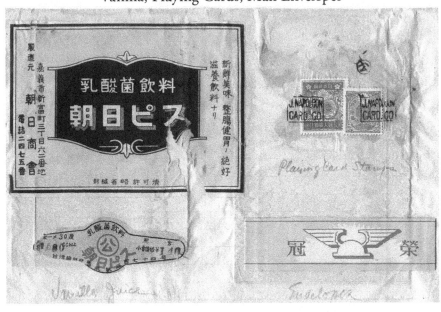

Work Suit, Tea, Salt, Nip Beer

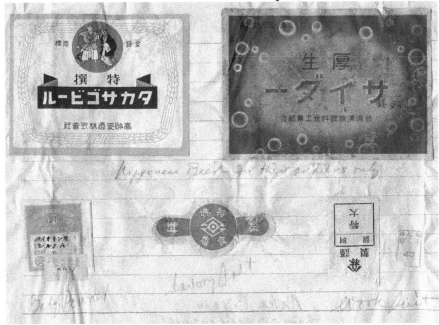

NEEDLER'S DESSERT CHOCOLATE

Needler's

SUPERFINE

Dessert Chocolate

QUARTER-POUND NET.

MADE FROM EMPIRE COCOA

FACTORIES: HULL, ENGLAND.

"Flit"

Cigars

Coolie Hat, Fish Flakes

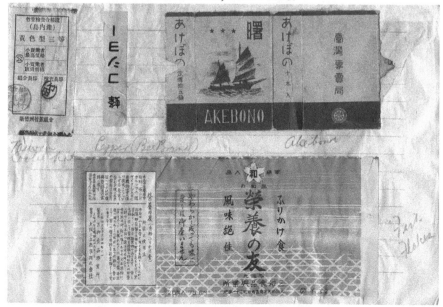

Curry Powder, Pepper, Lotion

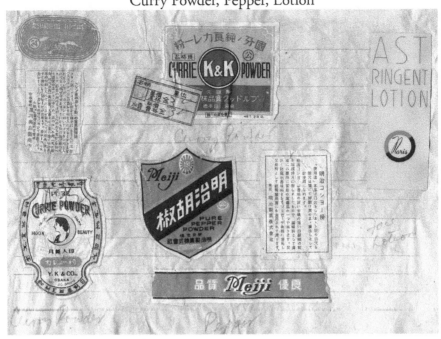

Ketsup, Saki

Old Golds, Soy Sauce

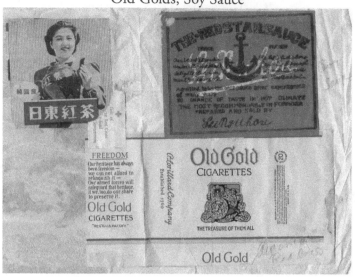

Tobacco, Face Cream

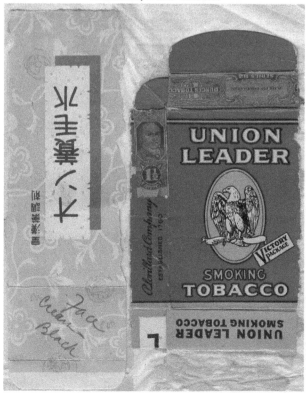

Soap, Playing cards

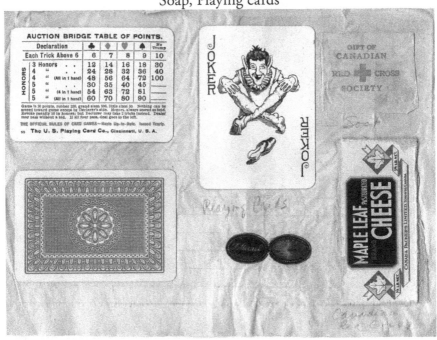

Toothbrush

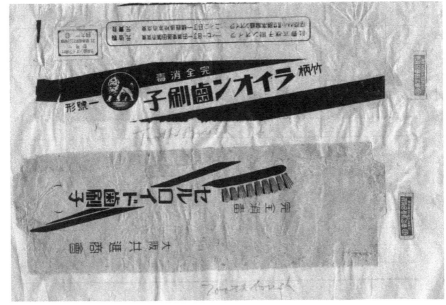

Toilet Paper

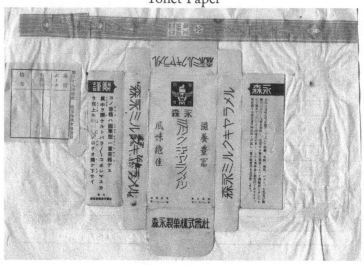

Tobacco, Face Cream

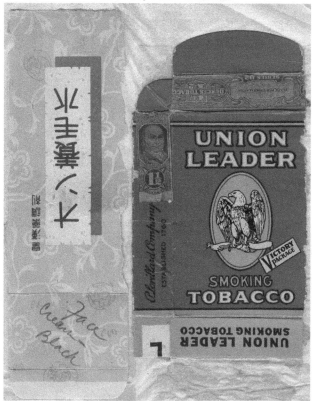

Worchester Sauce

七月 枝の庭

（愛）節 五大 下 山　　　（10）

Cigar, bullion,

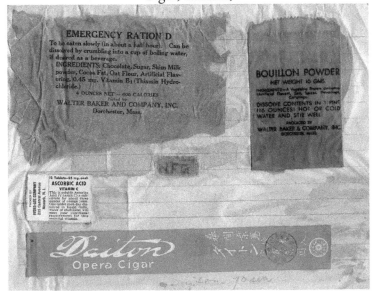

Cigarettes

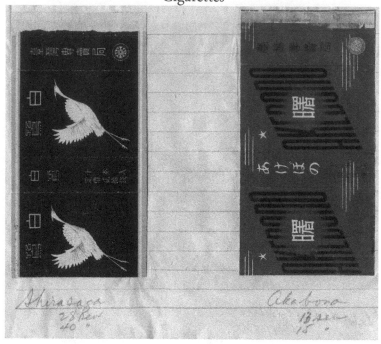

Shirasaga
28 sen
40 °

Akabono
13 sen
15 °

Cigars

TABACOS
PUROS
MONOPOLIO
DEL ESTADO
DE FORMOSA

Noko Cigar
from 27 sen originally
its 6 it sent to met tax

Fountain Pen, Paste, "Pee Card"

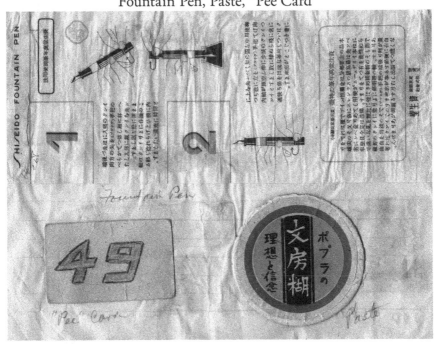

Papaya Jam, Lotion, Beer

Papaya Jam, Oyster Sauce

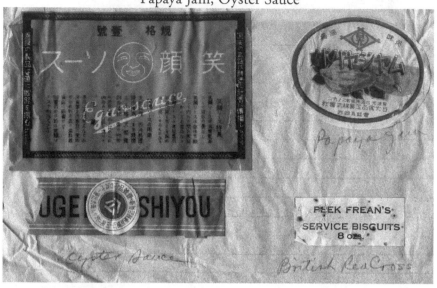

Strawberry Syrup, Cigars

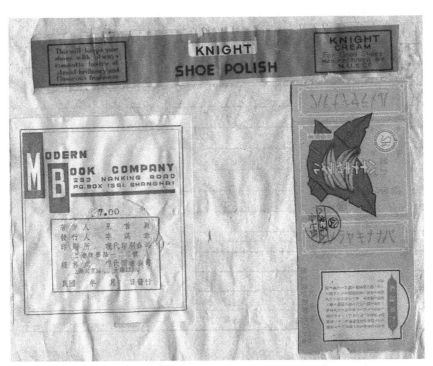

Silk Handkerchief, Pickles

Fish flakes

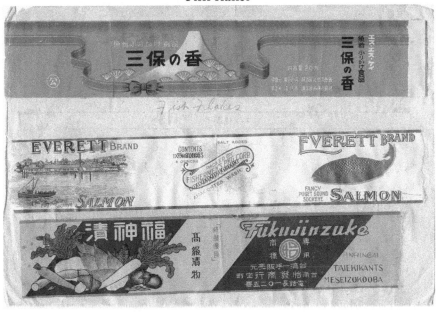

Cigarettes, Powdered Seaweed

Fish Flakes, Wakamotos

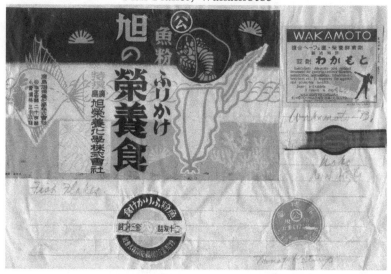

Japanese Occupation Bills

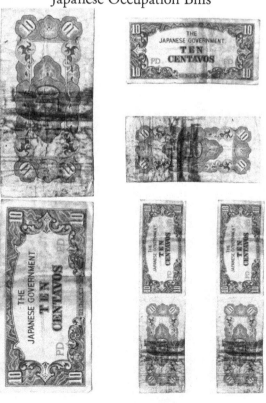

Vegetables, Ink, Menthol

British Red Cross Tomatoes

Potatoes

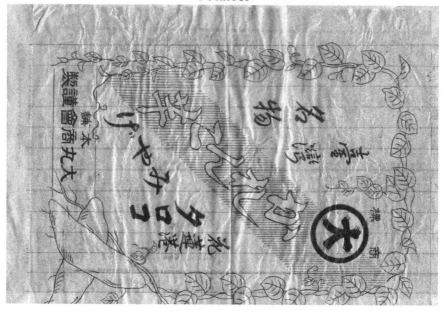

Razor Blades

Rice Krispies

Salt, Tooth Powder

Soy Sauce

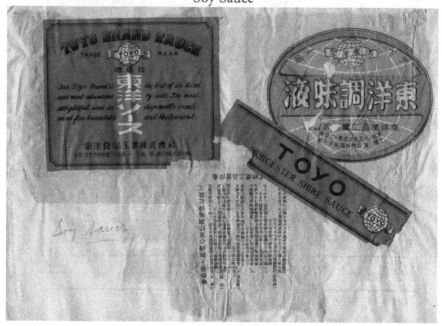

APPENDIX 10 – PHOTOS COURTESY OF THE LEITH FAMILY

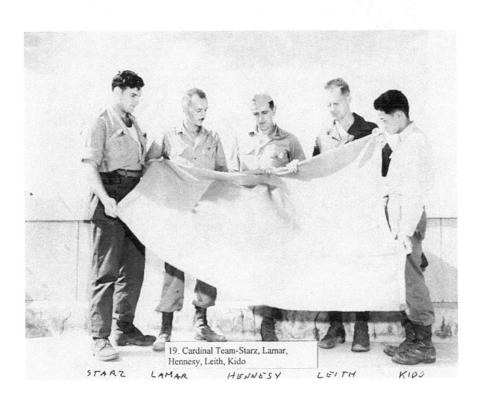

19. Cardinal Team-Starz, Lamar, Hennesy, Leith, Kido

STARZ   LAMAR   HENNESY   LEITH   KIDO

35 **Russians & Americans**

27. Hoten-Soviet liaison

46. Mukden-Russians

Americans with Camp Hoten Commander Matsuda

28. Hoten-Japanese officers (Matsuda)

MATSUDA   DR. OKI

Camp Hoten POW cemetery

APPENDIX 11 – EPILOGUE

The Line of Demarkation - August 17, 1945

I can now write as I choose without that eternal fear of some goddamn savage ramming a bayonet through my guts for some insignificant reason - I need no longer pick and choose my words or write in riddles or reverse expressions, but, am in a position to speak my mind and thoughts fully and in truth and honesty - my thoughts and feelings are merely representative of each and everyone who has had the grave misfortune of being in the control of fanatics during their period of ascendancy. The only thing they understand, the only power they recognize, the only influence in them is force - might. And they finally gained the position of superiority that forced them to squeal and cry for quarter. How vast a change from the dominating, egotistical attitude while they had the upper hand.

We have been following the news, so much of it was published in Nip and local papers, surreptitiously brought into the compound at great risk. Russia came in an the 8th and we had several days of the successes in the North. Our infallible contacts at the two factories gave us landings by U.S. in Korea - south movement of Outer Mongolian troops, and rumors of uncertain origin of landings in Kwantung peninsula and their junction with the Mongolian troops by air troops. A lot of "hell a beleu" re move from here, etc.

At about 11 a.m. 8/16, a B-24 circled around and a number of luggage parachutes dropped. Then six men baled out. Usual P.W.

comment and speculation. Balance of other camps came in during the afternoon.

About 5 P.M., Nip M.P.s escorted into compound six men with luggage and parachutes. Then speculation was rife. All kind of stories from eye-witnesses - no bayonet guards - white officers - went to hdqrs. - locked in guard house, etc., etc. As excitement died down some P. W.s slipped through main building and peeked into colonel's office. He sat there in a kimono. The parachutists were talking with him. They appeared to have upper hand. Nip soldiers came in and bowed to them - they appeared armed and pointed and shook their finger at the colonel as they spoke with him. Tea drinking in order. From this incident the braver optimists predicted that war was over and they had come in to lay the preparations for P.W. turnover. The "die-hards" proceeded to "bang their gums" almost in anger at the vivid imagination being displayed. The British insisted the new arrivals were Red Cross representatives. In any event everyone started smoking all over the compound. Many sat up most of the night playing poker and smoking. The occasional guard that came through asked for no "kanais," but, ignored the P.W.s. One passed out cigarettes to the harmony crowd in the "benjo." The prisoners were turned out of the "eso". This morning the story came out piece meal. A Nip soldier here and there told all. The war was over! Everything relaxed today (8/17). Smoking at will - no Nips in sight - the three seniors called for conference. Results were given by the head of each nationality; viz., armistice with all allies except Russian, who still fights on (Razzberry) - no disorder, etc. - Nips still control.

Surprising how many fall for this coverup - instead of honestly announcing that until allies took over we had to be protected and Nips were guaranteed protection. The parachutists and P.W.s get together as might he expected.

Later held a meeting with seniors and section leaders. Nine from Wedemeyer's Hq. had intended to drop explanatory leaflets earlier, but, it failed. Brought in some medical supplies, cigarettes, radio equipment, K-rations, rifles. Were to send forward members of P.W.s and immediate requirements and arrange for air field.

Were somewhat misused upon landing as Nips did not have word of surrender, but, by time they reached M.P. Hdqrs. blindfolded, the news was out and they were treated like kings. This morning mail that has reportedly been here for two years, plus recent additions, was turned loose in a flood, thousands upon thousands of letters. The area we occupy was labeled by Nips as airplane assembly plant - (they certainly wanted to forget us). Red Cross food rumored to be out this afternoon. The O.S.S. and their operations, Gen. Parker takes over command - discipline - sanitation - Articles of War, etc. etc. Nip cigarettes and matches issued. Nips hold "tenko" tonight and tomorrow morning, then our own calls, etc. Will set up radio and broadcast to Wedemeyer's Hq. at 6 pm tonight. Note on treatment of P.W.s in Germany - Some dozen or so patients to be flown out - balance probably by boat in a week or so - Russians expected in momentarily - The colonel told the C.O. of the paragroup that he would have to commit "hara-kari" tomorrow - The major replied to go ahead, that he didn't want to interfere in his politics. For some reason or other the Nips were to take roll call last night and this morning - although all Nips stayed out of the compound except an occasional one on business. So, now we have probably seen the last of the yellow bastards. Our rear porch was turned into a café last night - R/C food which was issued yesterday p.m. (2/3 box per), plus hot water from kitchen - cards and "bull-ing" - lot a lot of young blades out "hell-ing" - the were some there all night. The radio brought in was set up - first effort to contact China Hq. failed - but we are getting regular news front stateside broadcast - the first in 3 1/2 years . Buns were increased from 2 to 5 yesterday - larger soup - sugar in mush this a.m. - looks like the stuff is available, but, just denied to us in the past - I gave Ted Sledge a pair of G.I. shoes when I left the tunnel May 7, 1942. Yesterday he gave them back - had worn but little - better than the heavy Br. R/C ones I have.

Aug. 18 - The 14 aviators captured in recent months and confined outside of compound in seclusion were brought in this a.m. Yesterday one of the paras took train for senior generals camp and is expected to escort Gen. Wainwright and group in today. Nip towel and pair of socks issued today - also a few pairs of shoes for those in dire need.

Sketches: the P.W. who contracted to swap all his future R/C food issues for 90 buns. He recd. 30 - the situation cracked - 2/3 box of R/C issued - 5 buns (up from 2) and a large chunk of corn bread now daily ration - dilemma - The emotional greeting between man who lost an arm last Dec. U.S. bombing and the pilot of the B-29 - note the message on request of Nips that the former had sent: We lost some men and many injured, but, send over a thousand more - planes on same missions. The joyous welcome between some camp men and their fighting comrades already here. The Nip fence guard left today -

The hosp. cracked the Nip warehouse today and dragged out into light of day med. supplies rec'd. from R/C year and a half ago.

Note: no sick call if Nips orderly with key didn't feel like coming over to open door - my personal experience.

Aug . 20 - By Pres. Proclamation yesterday was day of Prayer and Thanksgiving. This first time we had any prompt news in 3 1/2 years - available because of the radio brought in by the "paras" - We had appropriate services here - octet sang - no "Kareis" - no begging of Nips for their graciousness to permit us to hold a religious service - no limiting the service to prayers only, the two chaplains were able to freely express themselves in fine sermons.

Being abreast of the world broadcast is wonderful stimulation - and any thoughtful person can readily distinguish the difference between freedom in thought, word, and deed and suppression thereof. The Govt. is making undue effort to get P.W.s out of this mess - volunteers contacting camps before end of hostilities by parachuting, hospital ships being dispatched from Eastern ports to pick us up, flying Gen. Wainwright to Chungking today or tomorrow, etc.- etc.

Effort was made for B-24 to come in yesterday with initial necessities and probably take out sick and mail - failure probably because of armistice pact between Nips & Russia - that foreign planes could not land until R. took over - or some similar technicality. Russians expected in this area momentarily - local soldiery being disarmed by their own M.P. and shipped south - Nip guard on outside fence - still responsible for our protection until formal transfer of P.W.s is made.

Disgusting, selfish characteristics still displayed - our newcomers being pursued for data on pay increases, donations by commercial firms, etc. They seem to have no gratitude for the tremendous gifts the Govt. has already bestowed on a group of failures. They do not seem to realize a large portion of this Bataan "hero" stuff is emotional cover up for the chagrin and disappointment of defeat - rather than acknowledge the latter, the "hero" tact forces itself forward. Of course there is the other side of the picture as well. The force was well out on a limb - not adequately supplied or prepared by its Govt. which was caught "short" - then the delaying action in P.I. forcing Nips to return troops from South for the final assault must have had a great delay on Nips effort at Australia.

But, in spite of the pros and cons I can't feel entitled to any preference because of Bataan - why not Guadalcanal - Sicily - Okinawa?

Have had a ragged cold for a week - high temp - earache - daily treatment - temperature again yesterday but in good shape today. Been troubled with what may be sciatica in my left leg - been keeping it quiet hoping it would disappear - raised hell with me yesterday and normally would have gone to doc to see if he could give any relief, but, with the prospects of a plane load sick leaving here in a few days I'll be damned if I'll put into myself into a position of looking for an early ride out of here. My conscience from the very beginning has been kept clear from the seeking of special treatment or obtaining any advantage over a colleague. I've been a sucker on many an occasions by standing aside or giving up to others -

It is very seldom appreciated but the internal happiness I possess because of such actions makes me want to shriek with joy sometimes - to think that I am big enough to overcome in part at least one of the basic disagreeable traits of humanity - of course only in a very small insignificant scale, but, even that madness has buoyed me up with a great feeling of joy. But, to be completely honest, two officers in the past week did let their hair down and tell me something or other about standing high in their estimation, etc. It isn't credit that one wants, but, an assurance that he is not being imposed upon or taken advantage of - that riles me up about as much as anything in life.

August 20 - 8:45 p.m. - Just in from the compound - one of the most stirring and emotional evenings ever - only a movie ending could compare with it - occasional planes, strangers, here and there at some distance - about supper time a heavy bomber flew low over the camp - pamphlets were dropped stating reps. from Am.-China Hq. would arrive at all P.W. and internee camps and coordinate with Nips for relief, etc. of all - responsibility still remained with Nips for compliance with provisions of surrender terms. Much dispute as to markings on plane - I saw black circles - no stars - others saw G.I. stars - etc. etc. - the choke in the voice and tears of joy in the eyes blurred vision and senses. The plane returned shortly and dropped more leaflets. Big feed tonight - must be lots of food someplace: boiled new potatoes, steamed millet, baked beans, gravy, plus R/C additions - Musical concert at 1:00 P.M. - started out by mass singing of Dutch national anthem. The throats were so constricted that it was difficult to make much of a sound. In the middle of the program all were called to the entrance gate and there on the hospital steps in sight of all were several Russian officers - our Deliverers! The general in command of the R. held up his hand for quiet and a great cheer answered. He removed his garrison cap and gave the Communist - his statements were short sentences and pithy - Sgt. Hurley - 31 Inf., a native Russian, interpreted each sentence - "by order of the commander of the Russian Red Army, I declare you from this moment F R E E!" Wild cheers of thanksgiving (7:23 p.m) - and chokes of emotion. "I congratulate the United States Forces on its successes. I congratulate the United States, Great Britain and allies on their defeat of Japan. We have marched 1000 miles over mountain and through valleys, without roads to free this country from the domination of Japan."

The Nip garrison was standing adjacent listening to all. More cheers, etc., and all back to concert for about five minutes. when we were told to return to barracks. As soon as we were in the Nips were marched out on the parade ground and all P.W.s immediately assembled along the sidelines.

These Russians work faster than any crowd I ever saw. The Nips laid down their arms and fell into formation. The R. commander called for the newly organized American guard to parade in front of him. He picked up the surrendered Nip arms and handed one each to each member of the guard with a comment, "I congratulate you." Formal presentation. The general picked up an officer's pistol and handed it to Gen. Parker in token of his assumption of command and a gesture of friendship. (By the way, Gen. Parker made a short speech in reply earlier and said he was grateful to and congratulated the Russian "Imperial" Army - maybe he was choked up too). Our guard then marched the Nip prisoners out of the compound and the R. general announced that they were now leaving this camp forever. Not a sound from the entire 1,700 P.W.s. No demonstration, no assaults, no bayonets thrust at helpless prisoners. God, what a contrast to the ruthlessness when the Nips took us over. It was growing quite dark as the ceremonies progressed and Sgt. Hurley in a fine sounding voice acted as announcer. Gen. Parker took over Col. Matsuda's office and the area is finally free of Nips. Soldiers were placed in the guard house and the officers in quarters next to the compound. Taps continued from 10 to midnite. In informal talks afterwards the R. general said he was 31 yours old, had been fighting 4 year as a general. The party made a great impression at first glance as fine-looking soldiers. O.D. uniforms, caps, Sam Browne belts.

Everything short and snappy and mighty business like without a lot of preliminary palaver - click - click - click - and all over. He also said let this be a lesson never to lose a war - bridges out and may take three weeks to move us by train - harbors not safe yet either - air move would be simplest. Will make every effort to expedite our departure.

Aug. 21- Still in compound - no Amer. flag hovers over us - there is complete quiet - no stimulation on the part of our leadership - the transition is far from complete - especially the emotional and physical sides - Our guard had the Nips out digging potatoes this a.m. - So what!

On my mission to the Mt. Provinces after the capitulation the Nips gave me a small printed American flag and a similar Nip one so I could pass freely from one line to the other by waving a white flag and the American one in going over to the U.S. lines and reversing the process coming into the Nip lines. I have preserved them and hidden them and risked execution for the possession of than for over 3 1/2 years - anticipating their historical value and awaiting this moment of freedom. So, in line with the latter last night I retrieved from its secret spot the Stars and Strips cheap little ten cent store product that it is (probably printed in Japan originally). I bring it over to my straw sack where everyone could see it and had a hope it might cause a swelling in some breasts as it did in mine. Some looked and said nothing; a few even looked and saluted, facetiously perhaps; one came up with a "hurrah" and unembarrassed kissed it. But, the trait that I'm trying to understated was exhibited by so many, walking up with note of an appearance of curiosity than anything else, fingering the flag and counting the stars. Then the expression, "Oh, but there are only 42 stars here." Sort of an attitude of brilliant achievement on their part to have discovered that it was not perfect in make. But, many other defects were present, the shape was nearly square, the 13th stripe was only a half one, etc., again but an interesting trait of human nature.

APPENDIX 12

Post rescue/release diary entries.

EXCERPTS FROM THE LETTERS OF COL. KENNETH F. GALBRAITH.

Camp Hoten, Mukden, Manchuria.

"August 15, 1945.----Full realization of what all these conditions before us really mean is slow in materializing. We are still in a fog, the emotions have not yet had opportunity for release; the transition period of thoughts from the one extreme of suppression to the other of freedom is much slower than I anticipated. That we need for a complete "bust" is the sight of an American flag with some G.I. troops marching into this compound.

For much over a year we have been held incommunicado, totally, with the outside world. No papers, no mail, no news of any sort, not even a slip of the tongue on the part of the Nips, so the risk was; and under certain conditions it worked effectively. But superior American intelligence can always overcome the stupidity of Nips by keeping a careful watch for an opportunity. For some time we have been introducing into our "jail" a daily hip paper by ingenious methods. Even the rigid search of the sentries was not able to detect it. In consequence we were able to keep from going completely crazy here by keeping abreast of most of the war news.

This morning a large unidentified plane passed in range of our vision. Later a number of paratroops dropped out, followed by six flyers. That caused all sorts of speculation-- most of which, as usual, was PW slip-shed talk. Paralleling events did point to a trend; the sudden change of plans to move the senior officers out of here to an unknown; and likely would have been a 'never known') destination; the hysterical movement of other PW's to this compound from other sub-camps; the hasty closing of the factories across the field where most of the PW's worked in the daytime.

About 5P.M. six flyers were brought into the compound by Nip M.P.'s. A truckload of luggage accompanied them. They were armed with their side-arms and went to the commandant's office. By morning the news was out. The six paratroopers were volunteers on a hazardous mission from China Headquarters to locate this camp and contact the Nips, find out the number of personal and immediate needs. Contact was arranged for by the radio equipment they flew in with them. It happened they knew only generally that a P.W. camp was located this side of Mukden, our particular compound being labeled and publicized by the Japs as an airplane assembly parts plant.

August 23.---- Unfortunately our letters did not get away as soon as planned; because the second B-24 met with a slight mishap. The Russian guard got tight and in a spirit of fun bayonetted the tires. This meant a 48 hour delay until new rubber ones could be flown in. Also the sick who were scheduled to depart were held up.

All of us are so completely burned up with this animal and convict life that we've been forced on us by these low barbarians that we are most impatient to be on our way. And the thrills I look forward to in seeing America again!   I am still 30 pounds underweight, weak and tired. We have had no animal proteins, fats or sugar in 3½ years. A couple of pounds of each would cover all in that time. They refused to give us Red Cross food which must have been shipped over by thousands of tons. Our ration has been a small teacup of boiled rice and a small bowl of vegetable water. I have had malaria , dengue, this is probably the only time I will ever mention it), edema, and a couple of other fevers which came and went without too much trouble. But by scrupulous care I have avoided dysentery which most here have had. I have eaten snails from the trash pile where they like to